250

CONDUCTING EXPERIENCES
IN ENGLISH

CONDUCTING
EXPERIENCES IN ENGLISH

A Report of a Committee of the National Council
of Teachers of English, Based on the Contributions
of 274 Coöperating Teachers of English

by

ANGELA M. BROENING
Chairman

ETHEL MABIE FALK

W. WILBUR HATFIELD

DORIS E. McENTYRE

MARGARET SOUTHWICK

A Publication of
The National Council of Teachers of English

APPLETON-CENTURY-CROFTS, INC.
NEW YORK

39-32971

PRINTED IN THE UNITED STATES OF AMERICA

PREFACE

Principals, supervisors, and teachers everywhere report that their courses in English are based upon the experiences of their pupils. Book selection committees assert that every salesman claims that his new book is in harmony with *An Experience Curriculum in English*. University students state that professors of the teaching of English are promulgating the philosophy of English as experience.

Can all these claims, and more, be true? Are teachers, supervisors, curriculum-makers, textbook-writers, test-makers, publishers, and salesmen working together to have boys and girls *experience* English? If so, why and how?

Why? . . . Something had to be done about the English curriculum: youth, society, and educational theory—all were changing faster than school practice. With the enforcement of compulsory attendance laws, all kinds of children were attending school and staying on to graduate. Scientific measurements were disclosing a wide range of differences among pupils previously considered alike. Educational theory was taking its color from the Dewey philosophy of education as experience. But even so, a one-sided battle was being waged between out-of-school life and in-school English. The recreational facilities of the photoplay and the radio were offering too successful competition with reading as a leisure-time activity. "Pulp" literature was providing a short-circuit to the lower emotions of students not adequately trained to read good literature with ease and enjoyment. As a consequence the "pulps" were winning the contest with the classics in the traditional curriculum. As a final complication in the English situation, unemployment was driving back to school more and more restless youths who, though they "experienced" little of what was being taught, enjoyed camaraderie during extracurricular activities—and the steam heat in the improved school buildings. Yes, something had to be done about the English curriculum.

In various places throughout the country there were elementary, secondary, college, and university teachers of English who were struggling to save the cultural heritage expressed in language and literature, and to produce a functional literacy among all the kinds of pupils attending school. Investigations of the life needs for English, learning difficulties in spelling, reading, and grammar, and of methods of teaching yielded significant data which stimulated revision of the English curriculum.

Between 1929 and 1935 a pattern for this urgently needed experience curriculum was evolved by the Curriculum Commission of the National Council of Teachers of English. This Commission was composed of representative leaders (1) in the movement to utilize the educative opportunities for communication and reading inherent in the in-school and out-of-school environment of pupils and (2) in the movement to teach diagnostically so that each individual may secure habit-forming practice at the specific point where his language falls below the level of acceptable colloquial English.

So well did their published study, *An Experience Curriculum,* articulate the philosophy of the best teachers of English throughout the country that this volume became the center of professional discussions in the conventions of the National Council and in local meetings everywhere.

Then, as interest widened, more and more teachers, not personally in touch with members of the Commission which produced the pattern curriculum, besieged the office of the chairman of the curriculum commission, both in his capacity as chairman, and in his double capacity as secretary of the National Council and editor of the *English Journal.* Their letters—in addition to informal discussions at conventions—not only gave evidence of the stimulating value of the monograph but also led to the realization that teachers and supervisors over the country wished to find out how the experience idea was working—what others were doing about it.

How? . . . In 1937, the National Council appointed a committee to answer these inquiries. The committee was composed of five persons scattered over the United States, and responsible individually for different administrative levels of the English curriculum. The illustrative materials were secured through a general invitation to Council members to contribute and through individual invitations to persons who were known to the committee to be doing outstanding teaching of English. To those contributions, the committee has added its interpretation of those aspects of *An Experience Curriculum in English* which were illustrated. Only where the necessary illustrative material was not submitted by persons outside of the committee, did the members utilize experience-centered research directed by them in their local school systems.

The topics in the contents of the present volume, *Conducting Experiences in English,* were evolved from a study of what thousands of persons have asked and what hundreds have attempted when considering for themselves the problem of translating the "experience philosophy" into classroom activities. This volume contains, therefore, materials of interest to teachers, supervisors, librarians, administrators, and curriculum workers.

The committee offers this volume, then, as a concrete account of the dynamic process of adjusting the English curriculum to a changing school population, a changing society, and a changing philosophy of education. Only a perusal of the report itself can give the answer to the question, *"How is the 'experience idea' functioning in the classroom and in local curriculum revision programs?"*

A. M. B.
E. M. F.
W. W. H.
D. E. McE.
M. S.

ACKNOWLEDGMENTS

The illustrative materials in this volume were secured through a general invitation to Council members to contribute and through individual invitations to 175 persons who were known to the committee to be doing outstanding teaching of English.

It is regrettable that unexpected handicaps, such as sickness, death, and added domestic or professional responsibilities, prevented some invited contributors from submitting promised manuscripts and that lack of space did not permit the use in full of much of the excellent material contributed.

It is a pleasure to acknowledge indebtedness for the coöperation of the Executive and Publications Committees of the National Council of Teachers of English and of the staff of D. Appleton-Century.

To the 274 contributors of narrative accounts, outlines, unit assignment sheets, notes on experience-centered curriculum studies, courses of study, and critical suggestions, the committee is especially grateful. As the lists on page ii and pages ix–xiv show, the contributors are *conducting experiences* in every section of the United States, and in both rural and city schools.

THE COMMITTEE

Angela M. Broening, Baltimore, Maryland
Ethel Mabie Falk, Madison, Wisconsin
W. W. Hatfield, Chicago, Illinois
Doris E. McEntyre, Oakland, California
Margaret Southwick, Gary, Indiana

——

Helen Ackermann, Davenport, Iowa
Myra J. Adams, New York, New York
Alleghany County Board of Education, Maryland
Marion R. Allen, Minneapolis, Minnesota
Lenore Lear Anders, Cleveland, Ohio
Nellie Appy, Seattle, Washington
Clara S. Bacon, Amsterdam, New York
Eula Bear, Ardmore, Pennsylvania

H. C. Baker, Stanford, California
Mary L. Baker, Syracuse, New York
Baltimore City Board of Superintendents, Maryland
Baltimore County Board of Education, Maryland
Ray A. Barnard, Newark, New Jersey
Ruth A. Barnes, Ypsilanti, Michigan
Walter Barnes, New York, New York
Hortense Barten, New York, New York
William F. Bauer, East Orange, New Jersey
Winifred Bevan, Logansport, Indiana
Emma J. Bender, Hammond, Indiana
Elsie L. Bender, Kalamazoo, Michigan
Adele Benson, Oshkosh, Wisconsin
Ada M. Bing, Indianapolis, Indiana
Merrill Bishop, San Antonio, Texas
H. H. Bixler, Atlanta, Georgia
William H. Blauvelt, New York, New York
Joseph Block, New York, New York
Albert Blohm, New York, New York
Clara S. Bodey, Cincinnati, Ohio
Miriam B. Booth, Erie, Pennsylvania
Margaret W. Boutelle, Gainesville, Florida
Florence B. Bowden, Bridgeton, New Jersey
Philip A. Boyer, Philadelphia, Pennsylvania
Rose Bring, New York, New York
Grace D. Broening, Baltimore, Maryland
Mary L. Broening, Baltimore, Maryland
Bertha D. Brown, New York, New York
Winifred E. Brownell, Syracuse, New York
Margaret C. Buchanan, San Antonio, Texas
Laura Cairnes, Baltimore, Maryland
Sophie C. Camenisch, Chicago, Illinois
Cleva J. Carson, Gainesville, Florida
Ruth R. Carver, Linden, New Jersey
Viola Cassidy, Kalamazoo, Michigan
Stella S. Center, New York, New York
C. C. Certain, Detroit, Michigan
Henry I. Christ, New York, New York
Louis Chutroo, New York, New York
William L. Connor, Allentown, Pennsylvania
Margaret Cook, Gary, Indiana
Anne L. Cosse, New York, New York
Amy C. Crewe, Baltimore County, Maryland
Adelaide L. Cunningham, Atlanta, Georgia
C. J. Dalthorp, Aberdeen, South Dakota
Hazel L. Davies, Scranton, Pennsylvania

Janet Dewhurst, Seattle, Washington
Belle L. Dickson, Arcata, California
Elizabeth Duane, Philadelphia, Pennsylvania
Wendell E. Dunn, Baltimore, Maryland
Mary Herold Easterbrook, New York, New York
Cora Ebert, Kalamazoo, Michigan
E. M. Egan, New York, New York
Stella Eliashaw, New York, New York
Nellie Fawcett, Portland, Oregon
Ella Flynn, New York, New York
E. C. Fontaine, Maryland State Department, Baltimore
Opal French, Gary, Indiana
Blanche Fuqua, Terre Haute, Indiana
Elizabeth D. Gelvin, Bowling Green, Ohio
L. Eunice Genthner, East Orange, New Jersey
Roland A. Gleisner, Ironwood, Michigan
Mabel Goddard, Indianapolis, Indiana
Ruth M. Goldstein, New York, New York
H. Gordon, Philadelphia, Pennsylvania
M. Annie Grace, Baltimore County, Maryland
Mary Green, Atlanta, Georgia
Lambert Greenawalt, York, Pennsylvania
Catherine Greenwald, Gary, Indiana
Florence Guild, Indianapolis, Indiana
Julia C. Harney, Jersey City, New Jersey
Edna M. Heilbronn, Mt. Pleasant, Michigan
Mary E. Herbert, Allentown, Pennsylvania
Max J. Herzberg, Newark, New Jersey
Mabel Higgie, Seattle, Washington
Vinna R. Hill, San Antonio, Texas
Evelyn Hine, Syracuse, New York
Ellen Hinton, Atlanta, Georgia
Dorothy Holland, Ardmore, Pennsylvania
Leon C. Hood, East Orange, New Jersey
Eliza Hoskins, Little Rock, Arkansas
Dorothy T. Houghton, Gary, Indiana
Snow Longley Housh, Los Angeles, California
Frances Hudson, Atlanta, Georgia
Alice Hughes, Ypsilanti, Michigan
Violet Hughes, Madison, Wisconsin
Mary Jane Hunter, Pittsburgh, Pennsylvania
Allegra J. Ingleright, South Bend, Indiana
Ida T. Jacobs, Des Moines, Iowa
Mildred Jacobs, Baltimore, Maryland
Irene Jaworski, New York, New York
Frances Jenkins, Cincinnati, Ohio

LaRue Jensen, Litchfield, Minnesota
Evelyn Jerdee, Hudson, Wisconsin
LaMar Jeter, Atlanta, Georgia
Betty Johnson, Ypsilanti, Michigan
Mary T. Johnson, Minneapolis, Minnesota
Ethel Kaump, Madison, Wisconsin
Margaret Kellenbach, Indianapolis, Indiana
Henry E. Kentopp, East Orange, New Jersey
Luella M. Kerwin, Jersey City, New Jersey
Martha King, Atlanta, Georgia
Maude L. Knowlton, Syracuse, New York
Merle L. Koch, Landsdowne, Pennsylvania
Charles L. Kopp, Alleghany County, Maryland
A. T. Krider, La Porte, Indiana
Lillian Krohn, Marinette, Wisconsin
Irene M. Lansing, Seattle, Washington
Alexandra B. Lewis, Newark, New Jersey
Elizabeth M. Lincoln, Leominster, Mass.
Dorothea Lindenau, Portage, Michigan
Florence M. Lynn, Seattle, Washington
Mary E. MacGarvey, New York, New York
Helen K. MacKintosh, Washington, D.C.
Helen F. McCadden, New York, New York
George H. McClellan, Frostburg, Maryland
Merle McKelvey, Seattle, Washington
Florence E. McLouth, Kalamazoo, Michigan
Dora Mabrito, San Antonio, Texas
Frank Mantinband, New York, New York
Sister Marion, C.S.J., St. Paul, Minnesota
Esther L. Marshall, DuBois, Pennsylvania
Maryland State Department of Education, Maryland
Johnowene Menger, San Antonio, Texas
Dudley Miles, New York, New York
Helen Rand Miller, Evanston, Illinois and California
Tom R. Miller, Syracuse, New York
John P. Milligan, Newark, New Jersey
Leon Mones, Newark, New Jersey
Frances Montague, Seattle, Washington
Mabel Mulock, Allentown, Pennsylvania
J. D. Myers, Philadelphia, Pennsylvania
Bess Seale Nash, San Antonio, Texas
Winifred H. Nash, Roxbury, Massachusetts
Cornelia M. Neal, Atlanta, Georgia
Elizabeth Neterer, Seattle, Washington
H. C. Newton, Syracuse, New York
Alberta R. Noble, Coleraine, Minnesota

ACKNOWLEDGMENTS xiii

Elsie North, Madison, Wisconsin
E. Louise Noyes, Santa Barbara, California
Maxwell Nurnberg, New York, New York
Emily Hanson Obear, New York, New York
Corinne Oertel, New York, New York
W. A. Olson, Moscow, Idaho
Helen C. Ormond, New York, New York
Mary Moore Parrish, Baltimore, Maryland
Charles S. Pendleton, Nashville, Tennessee
Gladys Penton, Watertown, South Dakota
Caroline Perksen, Chicago, Illinois
Anna J. Petersen, New Brunswick, New Jersey
William R. Phipps, Talbot County, Maryland
Irvin C. Poley, Germantown, Pennsylvania
Enoch Pratt Free Library Staff, Baltimore, Maryland
Carrie Rasmussen, Madison, Wisconsin
Anne Ray, Atlanta, Georgia
Anne Reidy, Kalamazoo, Michigan
Helen Reets, New York, New York
Edith Reilly, Cincinnati, Ohio
Carmelita C. Rettaliata, Philadelphia, Pennsylvania
Helen M. Reynolds, Seattle, Washington
Lucille Richardson, Ypsilanti, Michigan
Eleanor M. Ritter, Allentown, Pennsylvania
Ella P. Roberts, Portland, Oregon
Alice E. Rood, Madison, Wisconsin
Miriam Rosenthal, New York, New York
Augusta Rosenfield, New York, New York
Agnes Roycroft, Ardmore, Pennsylvania
Sylvia Russell, New York, New York
Elsie Satlow, New York, New York
Mabel P. Schmidt, New York, New York
Mildred C. Schmidt, Fairmont, Minnesota
Parke Schoch, Philadelphia, Pennsylvania
Edith G. Schraub, New York, New York
Lydia Schroeder, New York, New York
Florence Schwartz, New York, New York
Joseph J. Sexton, New York, New York
L. Grace Shatzen, Cumberland, Maryland
Lena Shaw, Detroit, Michigan
Jennie Silvey, San Antonio, Texas
I. Jewell Simpson, Maryland State Department, Maryland
M. Lucetta Sisk, Baltimore County, Maryland
Mary E. Slevin, New York, New York
Edith Mae Smith, Milwaukee, Wisconsin
Elizabeth G. T. Smith, Oklahoma City, Oklahoma

Florence M. Smith, East Orange, New Jersey
Virgil W. Smith, Seattle, Washington
Lucinda B. Snyder, Terre Haute, Indiana
James E. Spitznas, Maryland State Department, Maryland
Evelyn Sprado, New York, New York
Minnie C. Squire, Washington, D.C.
Ruth M. Stauffer, Washington, D.C.
John L. Stenquist, Baltimore, Maryland
Jane Strain, Indianapolis, Indiana
Edna L. Sterling, Seattle, Washington
Bess Stinson, Kalamazoo, Michigan
Marion A. Sturdevant, Wilkes-Barre, Pennsylvania
Flora L. Taylor, New York, New York
Margaret Tennis, Upper Darby, Pennsylvania
Muriel I. Thomas, Scranton, Pennsylvania
Helen Tipton, Indianapolis, Indiana
Helen Tompkins, Seattle, Washington
J. C. Tressler, New York, New York
Mabel A. Tuttle, Linden, New Jersey
Frances Uncapher, Gary, Indiana
Lillian Van Wormer, New York, New York
R. G. Vanderlip, Washington, D.C.
Jeannette Veatch, Kalamazoo, Michigan
Abby Wager, Norristown, Pennsylvania
Alma M. Ward, Seattle, Washington
Edith M. Ward, New York, New York
David E. Weglein, Baltimore, Maryland
Angie Weibling, San Antonio, Texas
Albert E. Weston, Glenside, Pennsylvania
Joseph L. Wheeler, Baltimore, Maryland
Elizabeth Wild, Shorewood, Milwaukee
Nellie S. Willison, Cumberland, Maryland
Clara L. Wilson, Seattle, Washington
Dorothy M. Wilson, Sauk Centre, Minnesota
Jessie Wolcott, Cleves, Ohio
Anne Workman, Commerce, Texas
Alice C. Wright, Brooklyn, New York
W. Finley Wright, Indianapolis, Indiana
Bess Wright, Indianapolis, Indiana
Sybil Yates, Albert Lea, Minnesota
Caroline L. Ziegler, Baltimore, Maryland

CONTENTS

PART THREE

SOLVING TEACHING-SUPERVISORY PROBLEMS

page 259

INTRODUCTION

English as Experience

ENGLISH AS EXPERIENCE

When people are creating anything, when they are spending their time, their energy, their money on this, they take the trouble to think, and the levels of life are raised.[1]

ENGLISH should be a creative experience for teachers as well as for pupils. The ability to think creatively has always been the distinguishing characteristic of great teachers and responsive students. Now that teachers everywhere are being guided by the dynamic philosophy of English as experience, the quality of life of more and more students is being raised despite the negative influence of the pulp literature and the coarse entertainment which are bidding for the attention of youth.

Although the movies and the radio may be the eyes and the ears of modern youth, it is, now as always, in great literature (where the subtlest and best use of language is preserved) that boys and girls are discovering their spiritual tradition—the *"picked experience of the ages."* Since literature is the "lasting expression in words of the meaning of life," teaching literature implies bringing to the attention of the reader the factors in his experience essential to re-creating the experience communicated by the writer.

Eastman [2] tells us that persons who are capable of literary appreciation are interested in "receiving experiences," are lovers of the qualities of things, are not engaged in becoming adjusted to their environment but in becoming acquainted with it. "The secret of appreciation," according to Woodberry [3] "is to share the passion for life that literature itself exemplifies and contains. Out of real experience, the best that one can have, to possess oneself of the imaginary experience which is the stuff of the larger

[1] A. E., *The Living Torch* (Macmillan, 1938), p. 381.
[2] Max Eastman, *The Enjoyment of Poetry* (Scribners, 1921, p. 196).
[3] George Woodberry, *The Appreciation of Literature* (Harcourt, Brace, 1922), p. 26.

3

life the gateway to which is primarily literature." According to Tracy,[4] the way to appreciation is "to read literature with the heart, hear it with the ear, say it with the voice. 'To read with the heart' is no soft sop of sentiment but a mood which the lines evoke." Bennett [5] asserts: "All literature is the expression of feeling, of passion, of emotion, caused by the sensation of the interestingness of life. . . . He who has not been presented to the freedom of literature has not wakened out of his parental sleep. He can't see, he can't hear, he can't feel, in any full sense. He can only eat his dinner."

In the modern classroom in which literature is read as human experience, in which pupils are allowed to choose books within their emotional and intellectual maturity, and are encouraged to explore books—for self-revelation, self-expression, self-improvement, and self-realization—in this sort of classroom, teaching literature is directed toward developing the perfect readers whom Christopher Morley [6] describes: "O the Perfect Reader! His clear, keen, outreaching mind is intent only to be one in spirit with the invisible author. As long as there are perfect readers who read with passion, with glory, and then speed to tell their friends, there will always be a perfect writer."

The reader's own experience is the key to literary appreciation. He takes as much of a book as he can, rewriting it, as it were, in the imagery of his own experience. Conversations and panel discussions centered upon main events and impressions, upon the larger aspects of character, and upon the theme; brief comment accompanied by citation or oral reading; comparison of the photoplay version with the book; the radio presentation with the poem or play as read silently; these are popular activities with modern youth because they are satisfying treatments of such esthetic elements as plot consistency, character consistency, truth to human experience, a sound basis for genuine emotion, verbal magic, and metrical form.

Paralleling this change in the philosophy of teaching literature, testing turned objective and diagnostic. Then was revealed the

[4] Henry Chester Tracy, *English as Experience* (Dutton, 1928), p. 212.

[5] Arnold Bennett, *Literary Taste and How to Form It* (Doran, 1918), p. 29; p. 7.

[6] Christopher Morley, "The Perfect Reader" in *44 Essays* (Harcourt, Brace, 1925), p. 25.

most significant cause of some pupils' revulsion to the classics and absorption in the pulps. *Thousands of boys and girls could not read with enough comprehension and speed to experience great literature.* A chasm had grown between the teachers who read creatively and the pupils who, through no fault of their own, could not read with alertness and satisfaction the few required classics that were stretched out to fill the school year. The results of silent reading tests, however, showed these teachers where to begin so that the boys and girls could get quickly into communication with an author who had written something vital to them.

Teachers of other subjects than English also began to stack up evidence that high-school (and, of course, elementary-school) pupils could not read well enough to understand textbooks and collateral readings. Something had to be done because school administrators were unwilling to allow repeated failure, and business and industry, unable to employ all graduates, had no interest in those pupils who left school because of failure.

Teaching boys and girls to read involves training [7] in discovering the central idea, answering specific questions, skimming to locate information, reading rapidly to get the gist of a selection, remembering what is read (by outlining, making a précis, recognizing sense-appealing words and apt comparisons, and building a meaningful vocabulary through contextual clues), finding appropriate reading materials (through using a card catalog; the title page, contents, preface, and index of a book; unabridged dictionary; atlas; magazine indexes; encyclopedias; dictionaries of biographies and of history; anthologies and books of quotations), and discriminating as to which method of reading is appropriate to the intended purpose of a reader.

To build reading skills to a point of effective use in the pupils' in-school and out-of-school reading, it is essential that they *experience* these reading methods with serious and humorous articles, fiction and poetry, and selections from every subject-matter

[7] In the cases of serious eye difficulties, clinical procedures are needed before the psychological approach to reading described above can be effectively used. The ophthalm-o-graph and metron-o-scope are useful for testing and teaching pupils with such difficulties. In more severe cases of defects of vision and fundamental language confusions, the telebinocular tests devised by Betts may lead, on the one hand, to suitable medical attention, and, on the other, to appropriate reading exercises to overcome physical handicaps to reading.

field—this, to give information, challenge thinking, arouse new interests, and encourage worth-while reading at the same time that the pupils are reading to improve their skill.

During the literature units, and after specific training with material graded as to reading difficulty and appropriate to the reader's purpose and the skill being developed (that is, only content with a central idea is used in developing techniques for discovering the central idea), practice is afforded through the questions which the teacher asks in order to stimulate a natural, vital discussion of the experience shared by the author. Such questions focus pupils' attention first upon the total meaning of the selection and later upon the concrete imagery that captures the heart and the mind of the reader and thereby helps him to remember the significant experience communicated through the written symbols.

Students of all grades including high school enjoy extemporaneous writing when their literary experience has such high emotional tone that they *have* to express themselves. This kind of writing, however, is very different in origin and in outcome from the painful, analytical book report formerly required as evidence that a pupil had read every word of a book and had not discussed it with anyone else who had read it.

Experiences—vicarious or real—are the stuff of communication. Whenever an individual is emotionally identified with an experience, he has something to communicate. When he has a motive—a need to share his experience—he finds words in which to convey his ideas and feelings. His purposive attitude is a safeguard to the organization of his ideas. Knowing what he wishes to share helps him to reject irrelevant ideas and to arrange details clearly and forcefully. If, in addition to his having a motive for reaching other minds, the emotional tone of the situation is sufficient to cause him to lose himself in his purpose, he writes or speaks with the force and unity that come only from emotional intensity.

Experience furnishes not only motivation and emotional tone but also the opportunity to develop (1) keenness of perception, (2) readiness of ideas, (3) adequacy of vocabulary, (4) language skills necessary for free expression, (5) intelligent methods of note-taking and of outlining, (6) appreciation of excellence in performance, (7) tentativeness of attitude toward what has been written, (8) social maturity, and (9) continuity of time in producing a piece of writing—the other nine factors [8] which determine the success of a piece of writing.

The vital, fully socialized units in the experience-centered courses in English are intimately built on pupils' everyday needs and dynamic interests. These units teach in terms of life, draw from the past and present experiences of the pupils, and lead to the habit of seeking valuable, new first-hand and vicarious experiences. Out of these units pupils realize the significance of their own experiences and those of others. Techniques of language—sentence structure, proper subordination of ideas, punctuation and capitalization as aids to clearness, and established spelling—become instruments, "accessories to the life experienced." [9] No phase of grammar or of rhetoric is neglected if it functions in helping the pupils to grow in power to use language to span time, space, and even conflicting emotions in the listener or in the reader.

Thus learning to reach other minds is in the modern school a dynamic experience directed toward forming these life-habits: (1) recognizing a purpose in writing or in speaking, (2) selecting relevant ideas, (3) organizing ideas, (4) expressing ideas, (5) re-reading for errors and ineffective words (if written), (6) maintaining clear and pleasant tone of voice (if oral), and (7) using devices for holding or reclaiming the attention of the audience (if oral).

Not only teaching but also testing has changed with the spread of the philosophy of English as experience. The content and techniques used in the best available tests have taken flavor from genuine life experiences. Tests now measure as nearly as possible not only a skill required in actual life but also in the kind of situation in which the skill is needed. The stilted artificiality of the early objective tests is seldom found any more. The content of reading tests has intrinsic value to the reader being tested. Specimens of pupils' actual writing are utilized in usage tests.

[8] Cf. Angela M. Broening, "Factors Influencing Success in Written English," *Practical Values of Educational Research,* Official Report of 1938 meeting of the American Educational Research Association, a department of the National Education Association, pp. 51–53.

[9] W. Wilbur Hatfield and others, *An Experience Curriculum in English* (Appleton-Century, 1935), p. 6.

Various phases in the compositional act have been analyzed and set up in a way that makes possible an accurate diagnosis of pupil difficulties.

Textbooks in all phases of English have been truly made anew. Content, style, format, study-aids, exercises, and creative activities make a direct appeal to the learner at his level of experience, leading him to the cumulative goals set up in *An Experience Curriculum in English.*

Because the zest of life is at the growing edge for teachers (and supervisors) as well as for pupils, the philosophy of English as experience has captivated the imagination of teachers and released the dynamic teaching recorded in this volume.

PART ONE

Directing Experiences Through Literature

DIRECTING EXPERIENCES THROUGH LITERATURE

L ITERARY critics and great teachers of literature have long been agreed that literature is the embodiment of experience and that the function of reading literature is to broaden the reader's experience.[1] The inescapable implication is that good reading of a piece of literature is reliving whatever experience its author put into it. Such reliving is what *An Experience Curriculum in English* calls "experience through literature." It may often—very profitably—be followed by reflection upon that experience, connecting and comparing it with other experiences both direct and vicarious, interpreting it, evaluating it.

Our older teaching of literature became so intent upon this reflection that it either neglected adequate reliving of the experience upon which the reflection was to be based, or so prolonged the reflection by the inclusion of unimportant detail and of all the techniques by which the author conveyed his experience, that youngsters were bored and repelled. We asked the novice readers to get at once all that we—who are especially sensitive to literature, who have more direct experience by which to interpret the one that the author is trying to give us vicariously, and who have years of practice in reading literature—get at the fifth, or perhaps the twenty-fifth reading. It is no wonder that they could not perform such a miracle, nor that they soon resented our demands upon them.

For some years now, a reaction has been in progress. Many "reformers" retain a moderate amount of rather intensive study of literature in order to teach students how to read and to "linger with energy" on "the lasting expression in words of the meaning of life." They supplement, however, this intensive reading with opportunities to read extensively both in school and out. This is today probably the commonest pattern of literature teaching in schools which think themselves liberal. Some break further away from the

[1] For an effective massing of such opinions see Chapter I of Dr. James F. Hosic's, *Empirical Studies in School Reading* (New York, Teachers College, Columbia University, 1921).

11

old procedure by having only extensive (frequently individual) reading centering about a topic or types chosen by or assigned to the whole class. A few radical schools have absolutely "free" reading programs in which each student reads what he pleases and— they hope—grows through his reading and through occasional conferences with the instructor and with his classmates into a more perceptive and more discriminating reader. These enthusiasts for freedom without responsibility say that we adults read what we please when we please and that any compulsion is foreign to the *leisure* habit which we wish to establish; they make little or no attempt to give the benefit of their own reading mistakes and successes to their students. They minimize the enjoyment and educative values of discussing with peers and adults a book or selection which all have "experienced."

The best "free reading" programs, however, aim to improve taste in addition to allowing pupils to read books and magazines on the pupils' present level of taste and comprehension. That this policy —respecting the individual's needs and interests—also guides teachers who are using the intensive-extensive method of teaching literature points to the obvious conclusion that *how* literature is presented and *what* follows the presentation influence pupils' immediate enjoyment and future habits of reading.

I

INTENSIVE AND EXTENSIVE READING

WHEN a child's observation is sharpened by a sudden and shocking or satisfying experience, words are needed to convey to another what he has experienced. A blizzard had just been experienced by a group of eighth-graders. They were trying to tell what they had seen and felt. Their alert and well-read teacher grasped this opportunity to share with them poetic descriptions of snow-storms like those they were experiencing. When they began to read silently as the teacher read aloud, they were in the author's mood and had near the threshold of consciousness the direct experience for which the poet's imagery gave expression. Seeing literature as life and seeing life as literature gave them the dual experience of "lingering with energy" [1] on "the lasting expression in words of the meaning of life" and of finding words adequate for communicating their own emotional response to a personal experience.

WINTER LYRICS [2]

It is the day following a near blizzard such as occurs about once a winter. The children (eighth grade) arrive puffing, blowing, and rosy-cheeked. From the locker rooms come much stamping of feet and excited laughing, followed by a stampede of the classroom. They talk of nothing, think of nothing, but the storm. This is just the time for which the teacher has been waiting to teach a unit of winter poems.

After informal discussion of what they saw and felt in the storm, the teacher reads Emerson's "The Snowstorm."

From re-reading in response to questions focused on the poet's experience and the words which give vivid pictures, the children memorize naturally and pleasantly many lines from the poem.

A second poem, "Velvet Shoes" by Elinor Wylie, offering a contrast to the first, is next read. Again it is snowing, but there is no wind. We are invited for a walk, to get the feel of the new-fallen

[1] Max Eastman, op. cit., p. 175.
[2] Reported by Ruth R. Carver, teacher, Junior High School and Mabel A. Tuttle, Supervisor of English, Linden, N. J.

snow beneath our feet. Children and teacher pick up imagery for which they have had a real experience.

Following this intensive treatment of two poems, the children are invited to read other winter poems, and to bring to class for reading and discussion the ones enjoyed most.

To facilitate the handling of so many poems brought in by the pupils, the class is separated into groups of seven or eight. After each child reads his poem to the group, the best one is next selected to be shared with the entire class. The group is prepared to discuss the poem, and the chosen reader practices reading it aloud to his group so as to present it effectively to the class.

When the groups come together, each child is given a copy of the poem, or if this is not practical, it is written upon the board. After the oral reading there is discussion by the group responsible, while others in the audience connect the poem with life experiences.

It has happened that a child wishes to read an original poem. It is one function of the literature teacher to encourage the children to make observations of their own, to use figurative and vivid language, and to write experiences they wish to share.

Some children not able to write original verse collect favorite lines from poetry and make booklets. The sources of the lines are always recorded.

How to use the cultural backgrounds of the boys and girls in a class is excellently illustrated in Frances Uncapher's account of her experience in Gary.

Experiencing Poetry of Fourteen Nationalities [3]

A ninth-grade class in a foreign district was reading narrative poetry. The pupils noted that *The Pied Piper* is an old German story. A member of the class contributed the information that her parents had told her many stories in the verse of another country. Most of the pupils, it appeared, themselves knew poems which they wished to recite or to sing. "But what do the poems say?" asked the teacher. A little Czechoslovakian boy translated his song: "A child has returned home after visiting a neighbor cousin. 'What did you do at your cousin's?' asks Mother. 'I had a glass of wine and now my heart hurts.' " A Greek boy concluded his translation:

> How long, my followers,
> Will we be living in the mountains

[3] Reported by Frances Uncapher, Froebel School, Gary, Ind.

Alone just like lions,
In the caves of the mountains?
It is better to have one hour
Of free and happy life,
Than to have forty years
Of slavery and imprisonment.

After a number of recitations had been given, the teacher called attention to the fact that although few in the class (there were fourteen nationalities present) could understand the poems, all found the poems pleasant to listen to. It was obvious even if the words were foreign that poetry has rhythm, melody, emotion.

To make a collection of well-known poems in other languages and to translate them for the benefit of their classmates now appeared to be the wish of the class. In this they needed the help of their parents. So for the next few days parents and friends in the community were kept busy reciting and writing out and helping translate the poems that they learned when they were in school in the old country. Interesting comments were brought in. A Roumanian mother said, "When I was in school I learned all the great poems of my country. Boys and girls in American schools do not learn enough poetry." Pupils checked this statement at home with their parents and came back reporting general agreement with it. Most of their parents knew more poetry than they did. "My dad knows a lot of patriotic poems like this one. Are there any patriotic poems in America?" asked Greek Harry Thanos.

Meanwhile the reading of narrative poems went ahead in class: "Incident of the French Camp," "Herve Riel," "Sohrab and Rustum," "The Highwayman," and all the old favorites.

The little excursion into the literature of other lands helped develop an understanding of and an appreciation for the riches that come to us in America with our foreign citizens. It gave parents and children, who in a new world environment are too often at odds, a chance to bend heads over the same paper in happy collaboration. It gave opportunity for interviewing, translating, and oral reading in the best sort of audience situation. As for poetry, it made clear the fact that rhythm, emotion, and imagination are common to poetry of all nations.

In reading Mrs. Snow Longley Housh's account of her elective poetry course in Los Angeles High School bear in mind that she was trying to show how this course differs from other courses in poetry. Only incidentally does she reveal that in spite of the attention to poetic form the chief emphasis still remains upon what the author is trying to communicate. The course is generally regarded by outsiders as devoted to creative expression.

A Laboratory for Experiencing Poetry [4]

This report grows out of thirteen years of teaching modern poetry with the added suggestion from the head of department, "Give the young people a chance to try their hand at writing verse." The course is an upper-grade elective in a senior high school. Numbers have ranged from a minimum of eighteen to a maximum of forty-three. Members of the class cover a rather wide range in "I Q's" and cultural background though the community drawn on has an above-average standing. An appreciable number of maladjusted young people drift into the class or are sent in by other teachers for a last-aid poetry cure.

The primary objective of the course was originally to acquaint its members with the poetry written today, but with increased emphasis on creative writing the horizon has widened. Recent poetry is still the basis of reading since it avoids the hurdle of the unfamiliar in style and subject-matter, but stress is placed upon the study of poetry as poetry rather than upon separate poems or poets. Certain definite principles that have grown out of the teacher's experience will be stated briefly as a clue to the description that follows.

Writing poetry is translating experience into words.
Reading poetry is translating words into experience.
Writing poetry is creation.
Reading poetry is re-creation.

The method for any teacher will vary with the class before her, her own range of experience, even her mood. Method must be creative rather than stereotyped. This truism is peculiarly true of a class in creative writing, where a spirit of happiness and free expression must prevail. Perhaps the one principle of teaching creative writing is: *Enjoy yourself.*

With such a "credo," experimentally developed, this particular teacher uses a flexible method something like the following:

The unit begins with definitions of poetry, individually composed or dictionary-made at will. On the board are a few definitions by the poets, surely including one by Marguerite Wilkinson: "Poetry is the

[4] Reported by Snow Longley Housh, Los Angeles High School, Los Angeles, Cal.

sharing of life in patterns of musical words." Class definitions are read, and the ones the students wish to keep are also written upon the board. This is the basis for individual note-books, not show books but work books where the students keep what will be of value to them during the course. A little guided discussion based on these definitions and supplemented with individually selected illustrations from an anthology text establishes the two basic principles of poetry: emotion and imagination. These principles are carried over to the other fine arts, and it is discovered that poetry is closely related to the sister arts of music and painting. Out of these relationships are developed the four elements of poetry:

Movement (rhythm)
Melody (tone color)
Pictures (imagery)
Structure (patterns or blue-prints for standard poetic forms)

A variable number of weeks is spent in developing these elements: (1) Rhythm, first as shall be found in life, in dancing, in sports, in our heart beats, in day and night, and the procession of the seasons, in life and death; second in poetry, the dancing rhythms, the riding rhythms, the more staid walking rhythms, all with generous illustration, their own choices first, with an occasional opportunity for the teacher to share her favorites; finally names as handles, the Greek names with apology for their remoteness, rising and falling rhythms in two part, three part, and four part for everyday use (though the students usually prefer the high-sounding names). (2) Tone color, because melody suggests the more familiar art of music; its basis in the love of repetition and the instinct for imitation; the joy of repetition in refrain (corresponding to the chorus in music) in rhyme and its inverse effect in alliteration; imitation in the onomatopœtic beginnings of spoken language, of "baby talk," its survival in current speech, even the values of the more obvious consonant sounds, the soft hushing sound, the lulling "liquids," the hissing of the *s* so often associated with the sea, the *w* of the wind, the humming of the *m*'s and *n*'s—all these help the students to discover that poetry is woven of the very stuff of daily speech. (3) Pictures—first, the obvious pictures in almost every poem, landscapes, portraits, color effects; the need for imagination ("that inward eye which is the bliss of solitude" in the poet's definition) to see a poem; then the process of the poet's imagination, how the seeing of one object awakens a flock of twittering images, climaxing in the flight of Shelley's transcendent fancy in "To a Skylark"; then the figures of speech not as labels, but as degrees and phases of "imaginative realization"; the simile from the trite phrases like "brown as a berry," to the fresh vision of the poet; the delicious metaphors of slang and the profound metaphors of the philosophic passion; perhaps the less used personification with its beginnings in childlike animism and its lovely fancy in the symbols of the primitive Greek religion; that principle of symbolism which leads the sensuous human mind to clothe its dearest associations in tangible form, the flag for the country, the cross for the Christian religion, even its more amusing illustrations in John Bull and Uncle Sam, the familiar donkey and the elephant. Perhaps there will be time to suggest symbolism in narrative, the prose fables of Æsop with their appended morals, the poetic suggestion of the parables of Jesus, the dignified sweep of the allegory which is ultimately found to underlie all great narrative. (4) Structure or patterns for poems, with the possible relation to the fine art of architecture; the sonnet, blank verse, and the ballad for their enduring significance in English poetry; other less famous patterns, including the French forms, for reference and individual experiment at will; later experimentation in free verse and cadence, especially in relation to radical departures in painting and music—all these based on an understanding of the subtle relation of form to thought.

The preceding summary is not particularly striking. It is based on facts known to every trained teacher of English. But most teachers have learned their prosody intellectually, and only experience emotionally apprehended can function in either appreciation or creation. Rhythm is not an abstract name, but a creative experience of reading for verse pattern in the childish sing-song dear to our youth but anathema to teachers. It is soon discovered that the usual reading of a poem is a blend of the deep harmonies of the verse rhythm with the melodies of the speech pattern. Onomatopœtic words are to be rolled on the tongue to get their peculiar flavor. Figures of speech are not for classification, but for the imagination to play with, following the footsteps of the poet. Studying a poem is not getting its thought as factual material but sharing the experience of the poet until we can in our small degree share his feeling.

While the class is experiencing poetry as poetry, creative writing is not forgotten. Generally by the end of the second week, there is anxious inquiry as to "When are we going to write?" Then the teacher sets a day for a talk on writing poetry. She develops the four slogans enumerated earlier in this article, with special emphasis on the fact that all our lives we translate experience into words, while getting experience from the printed page is a much slower and more difficult

process than learning to speak. She suggests to them the lyric process of impression, reflection, expression which underlies creation. She
reads with them Wordsworth's poem "Daffodils," which tells with
utter simplicity how he came to write it. She usually reads to them
Edwin Markham's account of how he wrote his "Lincoln, the Man of
the People," from a copy of *The Dearborn Independent* published in
February, 1926. There is no definite assignment. A near day is set
when poems are to be read. Some already have "something"; others
are admonished to give some time to quiet thought in a garden, at
the seashore, or in the mountains, letting nature speak to them. No
pressure for results is put on any member of the class, and a prose
essay, provided it is descriptive or imaginative, is as welcome as verse.
Ultimately certain requirements of the department for written work
serve as a stimulus for laggards, but most members of the class keep
far ahead of the minimum quota. Creative writing is a free will offering, a self-expression in which the writer is left absolutely free as to
form, theme, and thought. As wider reading and further study gradually establish standards, self-expression comes nearer to an art product. At least one day a week is spent in reading aloud what comes to
hand. This is a breathless day. Some students elect to read their own
offerings, but in most cases the teacher is the reader. Criticism develops slowly, but a silent gasp of appreciation can be supplemented
as needed, and some point of artistry can usually be found in the
poorest material.

Creative writing never takes the place of the reading of poetry.
After a working knowledge of the craft of poetry has been developed
as a basis for either creation or re-creation, the class plunges into reading along varied lines. For the most famous poets there is class recitation with informal discussion. There are reports by students on chosen
poets. Always informal methods are stressed. The "study period" becomes an opportunity for reading aloud in groups that gradually form
from common interests or fluctuate at will. Such activities give time
to the teacher for individual conferences. Brief weekly reports on
home reading of poetry give another personal touch. Every effort is
made to give to the young people freedom of choice and to break up
the lock-step of assignment, recitation, study, grade. Only out of an
atmosphere of happy spontaneous activity can real creative writing
issue. Such writing is as natural as speech and affords the same emotional release. Results of such emotional release in particular are beyond the scope of this report. They can be duplicated in the experience
of any teacher who gives opportunity for any form of creative ex-

pression. Such results are not limited fortunately to an elective class. Any course in composition or literature gives time for a unit in poetry, its artistry taught in connection with reading, the time allotted to composition an opportunity for free poetic expression. With such a background, a poetry elective would truly become a place for the training of artists.

A great educator and religious teacher (Felix Adler, for many years head of the Ethical Culture Society) once said, "I do not believe in God. I have experienced God." May we without irreverence apply this conception to the teaching of poetry? We do not want our boys and girls merely to read poetry, to grasp its technique, or even to write it according to a formula. To the fullest of their individual powers of impression, reflection, and expression, we want them to experience poetry.

When a method of teaching succeeds in developing pupils' appreciation, few teachers have time to study whether any other method would produce greater appreciation. Because Miss Carrie Rasmussen made such a study, an abstract is given of her experimental research with eighty-eight fifth-grade children. Her conclusion scores a point for literature as experience.

A COMPARISON OF THREE METHODS OF TEACHING POETRY [5]

Problem. To compare in an experimentally controlled situation results of (1) casual reading of poetry by pupils and teacher, (2) much reading of poetry by pupils and teacher, and (3) living around and with poetry, as well as reading and having it read.

Limitations of study. (1) Validity of test is not established. (2) Only eighty-eight children were tested.

Procedure. An appreciation test was constructed. This test was given to three classes of fifth-graders, with quite similar I Q's, before and after the teaching of a poetry unit lasting four weeks.

The teaching of the three groups proceeded as follows:

In group 1, poetry was studied as it would be in any regular classroom. Teacher and pupils did not know that the tests were being evaluated.

In group 2, children read poetry. The teacher read poetry to class, calling attention to pictures, rhyme, rhythm, stories, beauty.

In group 3, children read poetry, dramatized it, correlated it with

[5] Reported by Carrie Rasmussen, "A Comparison of Three Methods of Teaching Poetry to Fifth-Grade Children," Independent study, Public School, Madison, Wis., 1938 (unpublished).

art, music, social studies, did choral reading, used slides, and composed poetry.

Conclusions. Group 1 showed little significant change in their attitude toward poetry, after the four weeks of special poetry study. There is evidence that the modern teacher teaches poetry in an interesting way, for all the children said they liked poetry both before and after the unit was taught.

Group 2 showed some change in attitude. The children said more things about liking poetry after the unit had been taught. The two definite things they seemed to learn from the study were that there is rhythm in poetry and that all poetry does not rhyme. All children said they liked poetry.

Group 3 showed a marked change in attitude. Fun, rhythm, rhyme were what they said they got from poetry. They all said they liked poetry so well that they did not want to change to another unit.

Finding the elements of romanticism in English poetry is an experience to Winifred Bevan's [6] pupils. She encourages them to compare poems, to discover the effectiveness of the poet's expression, and to linger with energy upon imagery which captivates their imagination. Love of nature, emphasis on the ego, the spirit of democracy, interest in lower animals, sympathy with the downtrodden and oppressed, subject-matter of the far away and the long ago—these characteristics of romanticism are so intrinsically connected with the essence of experience shared by the poet that Miss Bevan's students experience poetry as they add some literary history to their store of knowledge.

"The Relationship of Ideals and Habits to the Stability of a Social Group" is the title of a unit in which W. Finley Wright [7] directed his pupils' reading of Tennyson's *Idylls of the King.* The activities set up in the unit help pupils to sense the conflict between individual desire and social sanctions and lead, without painful moralizing, to a sound philosophy of life.

An examination of the courses of study listed in Appendix A will reveal striking variation in the treatment of the *Idylls of the King.* Erie, Pennsylvania, for example, presents these stories as "Folk Literature Retold," whereas the Baltimore, Maryland, unit "Changing Styles of Heroes and Heroines," introduces the *Idylls* as a series

[6] Winifred Bevan, Logansport Senior High School, Logansport, Ind.
[7] For details write to W. Finley Wright, Manual Training High School, Indianapolis, Ind.

of romances emphasizing some heroic qualities that are lasting and others that reflect the specific times in which the hero or heroine lived.

A somewhat modern parallel to the Guinevere-Launcelot-Arthur situation occurring three years ago in England gave a special edge to the story. Gareth's wishing to leave home to make a name for himself, Geraint's "taking true for false or false for true"—are but two other examples of the contemporary quality of the emotional situations in which the knights found themselves.

Miss Rose Bring's unit which follows may be thought of as a study of a type—myths—though the students thought of it as the study of individual stories of the past in relation to contemporary life.

MYTHOLOGY IN THE TWENTIETH CENTURY [8]

Experience in literature was supplied through the medium of the study of Greek and Roman mythology. Before my classes were to study a collection of poetry and another of interpretative essays concerning poets and their poetry, I used an extensive study of mythology to develop the imaginative mood.

I furnished such guides to reading the myths as would encourage the students to become acquainted with (1) the chief gods and goddesses; (2) their special significance; (3) their outstanding characteristics; and (4) an acquaintance with a reasonable number of myths.

With this as a basic thought, my next step was to ascertain from the students if there was anything in the life about them, or in the range of their experiences, which in any way linked up with mythology. This discussion led to a desire on their parts to engage in two separate and distinct activities. First, they wished to investigate, and second, they desired to do some original writing.

As a result, the following plan was formulated. The entire class was divided into research groups. Each group worked on one of the following topics: mythology in relation to art, literature, language, music, science, and advertising.

At an appointed time, each member presented a brief talk on her special phase; this was subsequently made a part of a joint group effort expressed in one paper—for each topic. Naturally the research was not limited to reading. Whenever, and wherever, the topic permitted, excursions to various parts of New York City were under-

[8] Reported by Rose Bring, Walton High School, New York City.

taken. Thus, for instance, the façade of the New York Stock Exchange Building was discovered to resemble that of the Parthenon in Athens; and the group on top of the Grand Central Station definitely showed Mercury, Vulcan, and Minerva representing, respectively, speed, industry, and invention. Even an ash tray found in a dime store was decorated with a statuette of Mercury.

For the literature research, we were literally embarrassed by a wealth of material, so much so, that the topics were classified under such captions as love, faith, dreams, immortality, simplicity, and ideals. Each topic was adequately illustrated with exact allusions. The range of authors was varied indeed. Among them were Shakespeare, Milton, Scott, Shelley, Keats, Byron, Morris, Wilde, Longfellow, Bridges, Sitwell, Erskine, and O'Neill.

Needless to say, language offered a fruitful field. Words in everyday use assumed a new interest. *Phosphorus, fatal, lunatic, cereal, siren, ocean, floral,* and *zephyr* became veritable toys.

As for music, great enthusiasm was displayed in finding the source material of works by Bach, Gluck, and Weber.

The science group was eager to tell us all about Mercury, and not a little about Orion and Calliope.

But the field arousing the most whole-hearted response was that dealing with advertising. We were literally flooded with material culled from innumerable sources. How proud they were to learn about *Atlas* Cement, *Vulcan* Toasters, *Hercules* Hooks, *Ajax* Tires, *Prometheus* Plate Warmers, *Nectar* Tea, *Venus* Pencils, and *Midas* Metal Polisher.

So much for the research! For the creative phase of the work, each girl worked independently. The fundamental idea of these *Modern Myths* was that they were to be fantastic explanations of the origin of subways, airplanes, electric lights, automobiles, and "big business." The approach, stylistically, was completely free. A student, if she so wished, might be satiric, poetic, imaginative, or very matter of fact.

Some of the results obtained may be deduced from listing of a few of the titles:

The Prosperity Myth—deals with the depression.
The Lights—why lights appear in Park Centralia.
The Airplane—Pilot Bellerephon rides Pegasus to Los Angeles.
Why the Signals Blink—explains the red and green lights of our traffic
    system.
Incendargus—the story of how electric lights came to be.
The Subway—how the Dragon who swallowed millions was turned into
    iron.

The Refrigerator—how Frostus battled Avidus and Cupidus, and finally how Electra intervened.

Mr. Prometheus—how the robot was created and new light was brought to mankind.

The Modern Phaeton—the story of the development of the motor car.

Thus through the two specific devices, mythology as such became an actuality in the lives of the students. Moreover, it seems to me, that through this work, there was an enrichment which the students could bring to the study of poetry.

Children in the elementary grades are also interested in the answers myths give to thousands of why's which come into their minds. The following unit shows an appropriate approach, simpler than with high-school pupils, made by sixth-grade boys and girls.

NATURE MYTHS [9]

In connection with their study of Greece, the 6A classes took up the reading of Greek myths and hero tales. They discovered that the myths were in many cases artistic and imaginative explanations of puzzling natural phenomena. The style of the myths was carefully studied. The brevity, the picturesque quality, and the element of surprise frequently found at the end were especially noted.

Stories were read to the classes by individual pupils. Long stories were sometimes told. After a number of myths and tales were read, several books were brought in from the library for further reading. Qualities admired by the Greeks were brought out in connection with this reading. The children enjoyed "Greek Tales for Tiny Tots," after reading the stories in their original form.

Preparation for writing. About a hundred questions concerning nature were submitted by the pupils as subjects for original myths. The following titles are typical:

What makes people sleep?
What makes the wind blow?
Why does the sun rise and set?

The pupils were expected to investigate and write either a true explanation or an imaginative explanation of the questions they selected.

[9] Reported from Randall School, Madison, Wis. (Principal, Mrs. Alice E. Rood).

Writing. All but two pupils preferred to write whimsical, imaginative myths rather than scientific explanations of the phenomena.

The stories were read to the class for criticism and then revised and corrected by the authors. Illustrations were sketched to be used as a design around the page.

A cover design was made and the stories were dittoed to make a book of "Nature Facts and Fancies."

EXPERIENCING *HAMLET* [10]

PRIMARY OBJECTIVE. To read *Hamlet* for its revelation of character

ENABLING OBJECTIVE. To learn how to read drama imaginatively so as to visualize the scene and to interpret the emotions of the character; to understand such terms as *theme, dramatic conflict, inner struggle, soliloquy, dialogue, irony, forecast, climax, scenery, stage business, comic relief, poetic diction* as they are used in discussing the play

TEACHER ACTIVITY

1. Help pupils to sense the dramatic situation of the opening lines; help them to imagine the scene, to hear the tones of voice, to visualize the make-up and costuming of the Ghost and of the others. Let them dramatize it. Then follow with rapid reading yourself, getting them to note points in the "exposition" in Scene 1. Help them to perceive at once the directness of Horatio's character. Get them to the point of wondering what is to happen next, of looking forward to the first appearance of Hamlet.

2. Help them to *visualize* Scene 2, Act I.

3. Read to them lines and speeches in Scene 2 that reveal the characters of Claudius, of Gertrude, of Polonius, of Hamlet; of Ophelia, of Laertes in Scene 3; and help them to see how Shakespeare accomplishes this.

4. At first, substitute, as you go along, modern equivalents of unusual words, phrases, etc. so that their meanings will be communicated to the pupils.

5. Assign reading at home, but precede each assignment with a general brief statement of what it is about. Follow by class discussion and reading. (Pupils find Shakespeare very difficult to read by themselves. When the teacher reads the lines aloud, the passages which perplexed the students are suddenly illuminated: proof that Shakespeare depended on the actor's interpretation to get the play over to the audience.)

[10] Reported by Ruth M. Stauffer, McKinley High School. Washington, D. C.

PUPIL ACTIVITIES

1. Reading of the play
2. Visualization of dramatic scenes: setting, costume, stage business, stage presence, acting
3. Interpretation of character: proving points from lines in the play
4. Learning to read blank verse, and Shakespeare's prose
5. Dramatizing some of the scenes (Prepare beforehand and read in class. Avoid "elocution" in reading.)
6. Discussion of questions arising from the play, such as: Was Hamlet mad? Did Gertrude know of the murder of the King? How did Ophelia fail Hamlet? What kind of person is Hamlet? Contrast the types of young men presented in the play. Contrast Hamlet and Macbeth as tragic figures. Discuss the comic relief. Discuss the essential tragedy in the play. Why is not this play mere melodrama? Why does this drama play to packed houses even today?
7. Interpretation of some of the famous soliloquies
8. Becoming familiar with some of the famous lines
9. Discussion by those pupils who have time and inclination to investigate further any of these topics:
    a. Analysis of Hamlet's character by famous critics
    b. Famous actors of the part of Hamlet
    c. *Hamlet* as a reflection of Elizabethan taste in the theater
    d. Shakespeare's Theater
    e. The Mermaid Tavern
    f. Modern Stage Settings

EVALUATION OF RESULTS

1. Pupil satisfaction at increase in power to evaluate character, to appreciate great tragedy, to understand and remember the play
2. Desire to carry over this satisfaction into seeing *Hamlet* on the stage
3. Reading of at least one other tragedy by Shakespeare or by a modern author (For example, *Romeo and Juliet, Othello, King Lear, Anthony and Cleopatra; Cyrano de Bergerac, Elizabeth the Queen; Abraham Lincoln; Journey's End; The Emperor Jones; The Silver Box; Antigone, The Trojan Women, Œdipus the King*)
4. Written discussion of some subject drawn from the study of the play, showing power to organize and think through a fairly long

discussion, with adequate vocabulary and originality of expression

5. An original character analysis, using quotations to prove points (learning how to introduce quotations within composition; understanding how character is revealed in real life)
6. Appraisal of reviews of current plays and motion pictures by the best reviewers in newspapers and weekly magazines

Although Miss Mary S. MacGarvey's unit, "Understanding America," taught in the Newtown High School, Elmhurst, New York City, takes all its materials from a book of essays, it is primarily a topical rather than a type study. Again the teacher must read the outline notes with imagination, thinking constantly of the pupils' reactions—emotional as well as intellectual reactions.

Miss Helen Tipton's unit based upon a text which corresponds to "popular non-fiction" for adults is included to show that reliving what the author put into the book is the ideal in leisure reading of factual material as well as of imaginative writing.

Miss Margaret Kellenbach of Indianapolis, Indiana, in a brief outline lists questions which served as keys to the intensive reading of biography.

Understanding America [11]

1. *Students read.* "Plunder of a City" by Walter Liggett, "The Fourth Estate" by Peter Odegaard, "Radio—A Brief for the Defense" by Deems Taylor, "American Music" by Pitts Sanborn, "The Need for Housing" by Editors of *Fortune,* and others dealing with present-day America
2. *Class discussion.* In case of "Plunder of a City," the Queens sewer scandal was brought up by students, the blame placed ultimately on the indifference of taxpayers. Similar local situations were reviewed, such as, condemnation awards for schools, fairgrounds, etc. In case of "Fourth Estate" work on propaganda pursued during the first part of the term was recalled as having direct bearing on this essay. Same procedure was followed in all essays; that is, discussion, questioning, objecting, etc.
3. *Home reading.* Any other essay in the book to answer the editor's questions on that essay. The students also wrote a brief answer to

[11] Reported by Mary S. MacGarvey, Newton High School, Elmhurst, New York City.

this question: These essays are supposed to "Sting you into an awareness of contemporary civilization . . . to make you acquainted with many aspects of American civilization, help you to assess significant currents of thought, to envisage a few of the salient problems which we must solve if we are to make any appreciable progress toward the development of a truly satisfactory human society." How has the above statement proved true in respect to your essay?

4. *Class trips*
   (a) Municipal housing development in Williamsburg under guidance of City Housing Authority
   (b) Slum dwellings under guidance of Henry Street Settlement
   (c) Individual trips to *Daily News, Times*
   (d) World's Fair Grounds, North Beach Airport (these last for "Plunder of a City")

5. *Discussions as outgrowth of reading*
   A. Written—The Family and the Home
      1. What Makes a Successful Marriage?
      2. Marriage à la Tabloid
      3. Does Radio Make a Difference in the Family?
      4. What Makes a House an Artistic Success?
      5. What Has Housing to Do with Crime?
      6. Some Things That the City Should Do To Make My Family Healthier or Happier
      7. Report on a Trip
      8. Romance and Realism in the Movies
      9. Houses in California
         (And a dozen other topics)
   B. Oral—Housing
      1. Reports on trips
      2. Playgrounds and Crime in Queens
      3. Accidents in Queens and the Playground Situation
      4. Slum Clearance in New York
   C. Review of additional books read (titles such as the following were included: *The Slum and Crime* by Halpern, *Bury the Dead* by Irwin Shaw, *Waiting for Lefty* by Clifford Odets, *Fontamara* by Silone, *New Deal* by Stuart Chase, "Vienna Houses Its Workers" in *New Republic, Modern Art* by Thomas Craven, *Tin-Pan Alley* by I. Goldberg, *I Found No Peace* by Webb Miller, "Movies Commit Suicide" by Gilbert Seldes in *Harper's*, "Funneling the European News" by John Gunther in *Harper's*)

D. Vocabulary lists: The teacher doubted the practical value of this, but allowed it, since it was a spontaneous activity.

THIS NEW AGE [12]

This 9A exploratory reading unit is planned for three weeks. As not all the selections could be included in this time period, the members of the class chose those industries and topics about which they were eager to read. The class was divided into two groups. Each pupil was given an opportunity to act as chairman for his group. At the beginning of the class period, the chairman distributed topics for individual reports on the chapter material, and supplemented this procedure by questioning members of the group and by leading the discussion.

Using "A Reference List of Free and Inexpensive Materials," issued by the Education Division, Federal Emergency Relief Administration, Washington, D.C., a committee selected names and addresses of industries and organizations from which students could order interesting booklets, pamphlets, and illustrative material. Each pupil then had the opportunity of writing one or more business letters and of reporting to the class the information he had received.

After visiting Eli Lilly Pharmaceutical Products Company, Polk's Sanitary Milk Company, Polar Ice and Fuel Company, and West Baking Company, the class members wrote detailed accounts of their observations and compiled an illustrated book for display.

THE ACHIEVEMENT OF OTHERS [13]

Objective. To consider thoughtfully the principles underlying success; to develop desirable attitudes towards the making of a life as well as the making of a living

Activities

I. Raising for discussion such questions as these:
1. What is success?
2. Can you measure success by money?
3. How can you measure success?
4. What personal qualities did these men possess which contributed to their success?
5. Does luck ever play a part in a person's success?
6. What is the relation between fame and greatness?

[12] Reported by Helen Tipton, Manual Training High School, Indianapolis, Ind.

[13] Reported by Margaret Kellenbach, Manual Training High School, Indianapolis, Ind.

7. What is the relation between reputation and character?
8. It has been said that we must make a life as well as a living—what does this mean?
9. Have you gained any information which relates to the occupation in which you are interested?
10. Can you name a woman noted for her achievements in science?

II. Encouraging each pupil to select a hero and to be responsible for informing the class on that hero's life. Two or three days may be allowed to prepare this talk, guided by these suggestions:
1. Look up all possible information on the topic assigned.
2. Organize materials, having a forceful beginning and satisfactory conclusion.
3. Put in any personal reactions which you may have.
4. Bring interesting illustrations or demonstrations or pictures to enliven topic.

III. Clinching the discoveries made through reading by discussing the truth or falsity of these statements: "The reward of a thing well done is to have done it." "Nothing great was ever achieved without enthusiasm." "History is the biography of great men."

The folk-tale unit conducted by Nellie Appy, Broadway High School, Seattle, was launched by taking advantage of an apparently accidental circumstance, but such circumstances are surprisingly numerous in the classroom of teachers who have learned to see them. There was no formal study of literary values, but some gain in discrimination through the inevitable comparing of tale with tale. The sensitivity that preserved the narrator's original language not only re-created vividly folk literature but also functioned in the student's use of language to communicate his own real experiences.

PRIMEVAL FORESTS [14]

A Western Lumbering Community Enriches a School's Contemporary Study of Folk Literature

Pine, hemlock, cedar, spruce stretching tall trunks upward toward a leaden sky. Beautiful giants of the forest they are, long the material around which the Quinaielt Indians built their stories and legends.

The Indians still inhabit the reservation but their songs of the forest are fewer. Money and leisure have eaten into their lives. And the

[14] Reported by Nellie Appy, Broadway High School, Seattle, Wash.

evergreens are there, fewer in numbers also for they have been translated from song into money and work for loggers.

Through all parts of the Washington forest today go the Finns,
the Swedes, the Poles, the Norwegians, the Croatians, big men tack-
ling a big job. It is these hardy nationalities who have become the
lumberjacks of our Northwest, followers of the mighty Paul Bunyan.
And they'll tell you, every one of them, that Lake Quinaielt itself
wouldn't be there if Paul's Blue Ox hadn't missed his footing one
day along a forested slope of the Olympics and planted a forefoot
deep in a ravine. In no time at all the steady downpour of the Puget
Sound rains filled the hoof print with water and made the lake.

In the coast schools are the children of these lumberjacks, proud
you might think of the mellow tapestry of their European heritage.
But they are not. They are new Americans, somewhat ashamed that
they speak a foreign tongue at home or go to night school to learn the
language of their fathers.

Several years ago, after I had been teaching for some time in a
western lumbering town, I became intensely interested in the un-
utilized foreign material in the backgrounds of the students in my
classes. Here lay a whole section of their out-of-school life which had
no recognized part in the in-school life of any one of them. Foreign
ancestry showed itself plainly enough in the lines of the husky bodies
that went into the football teams, in the ranginess of basket-ball and
track men, in the manifold forms of musical talents, in art work and
handcraft, in writing ability, in the brains of many honor-society
members, but not as a consciously acknowledged source from which
much of the richness of our school life came. And like our timber,
this natural resource of another sort had grown among us so long that
we had taken it entirely for granted and failed to see its significance
and place in the work we were doing.

Part of our basic American literature is, we know, folk literature,
building itself far less from contributions of the American Indian
than from the stories of the Negro and the occupational environ-
ments of many foreign-born. The day's job over, the boats of the
trollers in from the sea, the bunk houses filled with steaming men,
the fields hoed clean, the quiet cattle settled for the night, there in
a group of relaxed listeners many an American folktale is born.

Our study of folk literature came about in a circuitous fashion,
one day in a world-literature class during a discussion of the old
English ballad, "The Twa Corbies."

The community was besieged for tales. Many puzzled grown-ups
asked to have the meaning of folk literature carefully explained be-

fore they would contribute. One girl began her story: "Because my great-grandparents, the Thorps, were the first white settlers in Yakima County, I thought perhaps my grandmother could tell me an interesting early-day folk story. When I asked her, though, she was somewhat puzzled by the expression, *folk story*. After explaining what I meant, she told me a stirring narrative of her early girlhood."

Other community story-tellers could not be approached directly and had to be led skilfully into a discussion of their early lives. Some foreign parents seemed particularly reluctant to tell anecdotes or reminiscences of their early days.

Some told stories, but at first refused to allow them to be publicized. In many instances, however, adults enjoy being consulted.

Illustrations abound in the tales and hundreds of comparisons to modern life—studies such as one a boy made on transportation contrasting his grandmother's ride in one of the earliest trains with his in a recent trip by plane from Boeing Field; or another, a chap who, having spent years working for a certain newspaper, told of the earliest edition of that paper, in all its technically primitive state.

The stories gave insight into the customs in other countries or families; tragedies of all sorts; early occupations—fishing, lumbering, blacksmithing, farming, mining, cattle-raising, hunting; heroic deeds; all the chief American wars; immigrant tales; a Negro hanging; local bad men; fairy stories.

Written copies of the stories told then and subsequently have been kept over a period of several years, and in speaking of them from now on I refer to the total collection. They reveal many facts. Out of over three hundred narratives only ten are in poetic form. They were modeled on the ballad and had for themes such subjects as the modern gangster, mountaineer feuds, Amundsen and Byrd at the Poles, a Westport sea tragedy, the kidnaping of local boys.

Although these stories were later written out, they were originally presented in class in folk manner, in oral form. One boy, for example, had disliked English and had come into the class at mid-year in the forlorn hope that a change of teacher atmosphere might help him through, at least to the extent of getting necessary credit for the course. When called upon to suggest plans for a piece of work for himself, he had been so conditioned that he refused to show any signs of interest in anything any one could suggest. One day it was discovered that his mother had come from Germany as a young girl, and it was evident that the boy was very fond of her. He readily agreed to interview her on her school life, her voyage to America, and anything else she might care to tell. He planned the interview carefully and was well rewarded for his effort. The result was a series of talks, at first reluctantly, then eagerly given to the class, on his findings both from his mother and from comparative readings the boy had made on modern Germany. The class was heartily pleased to see him develop for they liked him and were truly concerned that he start to produce and become an active member of the group.

A fair idea of Helen Tipton's teaching of "American Life of the Middle West" through the novel may be gained from the abridged report that follows. The work was done in Emmerich Manual Training High School, Indianapolis.

AMERICAN LIFE OF THE MIDDLE WEST [15]

The unit includes four weeks of extensive reading, each eleventh-year pupil reading one novel per week and using three days of classroom time for reading, answering guide-sheet questions, and carrying out projects, with two days for class discussion. The class may be divided, one half reading one novel of certain era and the other half another, or all members may read the same weekly novel. The major objective guiding the unit is to develop an appreciation of American ideals and institutions as revealed in novels of the Middle West.

Materials
Sub-Unit I: *The Westward Movement*
   The Covered Wagon, Hough
   Cimarron, Ferber
Sub-Unit II: *The Homesteader*
   A Lantern in Her Hand, Aldrich
   My Antonia, Cather
Sub-Unit III: *Political Crisis of the Civil War*
   The Crisis, Churchill
   So Red the Rose, Young
Sub-Unit IV: *Modern Urban Life*
   So Big, Ferber
   Alice Adams, Tarkington

Activities
Select a novel suitable to the period, such as *The Covered Wagon* by Hough. After silent reading, let the group follow any of these activities which grow naturally out of their reading:
1. Discuss four reasons for the westward movement.
2. Discuss necessary preparations for the journey.

[15] Reported by Helen Tipton, Emmerich Manual Training School, Indianapolis, Ind.

3. What characteristics are necessary for successful leadership? Illustrate from a book read.

4. Explain reference to the five institutions that the pioneers were taking with them across the country.

5. The Indians made friends with such men as Bridger, but hated the pioneer wagon trains and plows. Explain the reason for such antagonism.

6. Discuss causes for disintegration of the group. Compare these with causes for lack of community solidarity today.

7. What knowledge and skills were vitally important for all pioneer women, but not for the majority of women today?

8. What qualities needed then, are still important for democracy? Illustrate.

Individual Projects

1. Make a chart of the barricade of the plains showing the means of protection during an Indian attack.

2. Make a chart of the route of the wagon train comparing with railroad routes today.

3. Prepare questions for a panel discussion of books read.

The three other sub-units, *The Homesteader, Political Crisis of the Civil War,* and *Modern Urban Life,* were similarly treated.

FINDING OUT ABOUT REAL PEOPLE [16]

Primary Objective. To have the literary experience of understanding people—their motives, personality, conflicts, consequent success or failure

Enabling Objectives. To develop reading and library skills necessary to understanding of biography

Materials. Collections of biographical sketches and a few booklength biographies within the reading and maturity levels of the pupils

Activities

1. By group discussion deciding upon interpretation of "success"

2. Presenting through group work a workable vocabulary to use in discussing biographies

3. Using for discussion material in the introduction of the collection of biography

[16] Reported by Catharine Greenwald, Department of Education, Gary, Ind.

4. Reading assigned excerpts, considering particularly the traits of the individuals, the environment, and the contributions to the time or the community of the subject
5. Using radio and motion picture experience to supplement reading (*The White Angel, The Life of Pasteur, Émile Zola,* etc.)
6. Sharing activities 4 and 5 with group
7. Reading lives of men and women of special interest
8. Reading as many biographical sketches as possible
9. Presenting orally to class pupil's choice or choices of outstanding men and women known through this reading (five minutes)
10. Preparing a bibliography of biography (This should be a list of material that the pupil obtained a knowledge of during this unit, not material that the teacher read. It should be a guide to future reading.)
11. Interviewing parents and relatives to prepare an autobiography or a biography of some close relative
12. Writing the biography or autobiography

Appraisals
1. Did the student show in his oral report an appreciation of the qualities found in these lives?
2. Has he increased his knowledge of people?
3. What has been the quality and quantity of reading of biography?
4. Has the student gained an appreciation of the fundamental qualities necessary to achievement?
5. Can or does he use this knowledge in understanding himself and adjusting himself to his world?

Other examples of the intensive–extensive treatment of literature are found everywhere that English is experienced. Such a reading unit for the eleventh grade was developed by Mary Jane Hunter [17] around the theme of Shakespeare's *Macbeth*. Though the class as a whole experienced *Macbeth,* students in committees explored a wealth of dramatic literature revealing the human conflicts and the tragic disintegration of the character of Macbeth.

Loyalty is the theme of an excellent literature unit developed by Belle L. Dickson, Arcata, California. This theme took her junior high pupils into narrative and lyric poetry, biography, history, fic-

[17] For further details consult Mary Jane Hunter, University of Pittsburgh, Pittsburgh, Pa.

tion, and drama—enough for them to experience the value of this quality and the conflicting human feelings that make it difficult at times to remain loyal.

In Atlanta, Georgia, Adelaide Cunningham developed a year course in English literature. Even though she uses an historical approach, she directs her pupils' reading along the line of their interests. The use of pictures, victrola records, dramatization, discussion, and creative writing assists the pupils in having a literary experience.

Ella Hinton and Martha King, also of Atlanta, Georgia, developed experience-centered units in American literature.

II

EXTENSIVE READING

IN MANY UNITS in all modern courses of study, pupils read both classic and contemporary literature extensively. Several illustrative units are included here to show a variety of approaches and organizations of such units. (See also pages 51–76.)

Ella Flynn, of Walton High School, New York City, solved the motivation problem by exploring the interests of her students and planning with them a unit to meet their needs.

EXPERIENCING THE ARTS [1]

Motivation. A discussion of the interests and hobbies of my English class revealed a keen interest in the arts and a desire to know a great deal more about them. Two members of the class of thirty-five were planning to become architects, one had been a member of a summer theater group, and three showed a decided talent in art. All were interested in the theater and the dance, and all were intelligent readers with a real appreciation of good literature. They concluded that a term's work based on the arts would be most helpful and enjoyable.

Procedure. The class fell naturally into groups, each girl joining the one in which she was most interested. Music, literature, painting, sculpture, architecture, the dance, and photography were the main topics; these in turn were subdivided: music, for example, into operas and symphonies, and the dance into ballets and modern dance forms. A chairman chosen in each group assigned the days for reports and assembled the material for the class book on *The Arts.*

Materials. Suggested reading lists were formulated by the class and teacher, both work-type and recreational reading being included. The music list contained such works as:

History of Opera, Elson
Music and Musicians, Lavignac

[1] Reported by Ella Flynn, Walton High School, New York City.

37

The Arts, Van Loon
Jean-Christophe, Rolland
Song of the Lark, Cather
The Story of Music, Bekker
Lucy Gayheart, Cather
Beloved Friend, Von Meck
Stories of the Opera
The King's Henchman, Millay
How Music Grew, Peiper
Music through the Ages, Bauer

Biographies of Nijinsky, George Arliss, Eva Le Gallienne, Noel Coward, Otis Skinner, Marie Dressler; of Van Gogh, Rembrandt, and Whistler; of all the great writers; and the articles and books by Wright, the architect, were read and reported on both orally and in writing. Those interested in the technique of the short story read Poe, Hawthorne, Chekhov, de Maupassant, Cather, and others.

Individuals and groups attended dance recitals, concerts, the opera, and the theater. They read newspaper and magazine articles and compared notes in class. In addition to the individual and group activities, the entire class attended performances of the Russian ballet; of the Indian dancer, Shav-Kar; of *Richard III;* of *Romeo and Juliet;* of the opera; they also visited the Metropolitan Museum of Art. The Whitney Museum, the American wing of the Museum of Natural History, and the Cloisters gave groups of students many happy hours which they shared with the rest of the class in oral reports.

Operatic selections on the victrola followed the stories of the operas.

Outcome. Each girl in the class kept a written record of her reading and of her activities. The artists in the group illustrated the text of the class book, *The Arts,* which represented the term's work in English. Both students and teacher found the work valuable and enjoyable.

The next two reports show how extensive reading may arise as a part—in these cases the major part—of a student project. The search for material to dramatize in a Book Week assembly occurred in a class taught by Lambert Greenawalt in the William Penn High School, York, Pennsylvania. The bibliography of readings bearing on vocations was constructed by juniors in Walton High School, New York City, under the guidance of Lydia Schroeder.

BOOK WEEK PROGRAM [2]

Planning an assembly program for Book Week opened wide vistas for one class; an effective program of extensive reading was developed as a result of preparing for the occasion. The project follows in outline:

Objectives. To interest all students in reading, and to raise their reading standards

Procedure
1. Informal class discussion of the real purpose of such a program
2. Volunteer student committees to coöperate in the selection of the type of material and of the presentation to be used (They selected dramatic scenes from modern books to be presented in an original setting.)
3. Extensive reading by all members of the class and final selections of titles and scenes best suited for purpose
4. Creative writing of original sketch into which dramatic scenes are to be fitted (The setting: a modern book shop equipped with stage for dramatic "advertising" by students.)
5. Try-outs conducted by student critics for students best fitted to impersonate the characters of selected scenes
6. Training of students for program also under student direction and supervision
7. Posters, placards, and stage properties assigned to committees

Outcomes
1. Demand by pupils for worth-while contemporary books to be added to the library
2. Approach toward critical evaluation of books and writers by members of class participating (This approach toward criticism was, of course, purely elemental and was built upon the simple reaction of the average young reader expressed in the words, "I like that book," or, "I don't like that book." With these statements as starting points, the teacher and an individual student engaged in conversations concerning the pupil's reasons for liking or disliking a book.)
3. Indexed card system to serve as a permanent record of reading done by class and also as a guide to a reader looking for a new

[2] Reported by Lambert Greenawalt, William Penn Senior High School, York, Pa.

book (Card contains personal comments, besides suggestions as to type of book. In the above activity, the group directly or indirectly involved reactions to individual life experiences. But even the reading experiences were directed more by the students than by the teacher, because the beginnings of the list sprang from suggestions from individuals, one title reminding someone of another, and so on.)

4. No need was felt for arranging books according to reading difficulty and theme. The various student opinions conflicted too much to permit an accurate appraisal according to difficulty, and it was deemed advisable to encourage students to read through the "catalogue" in their quest for a good book, so that, in the end, they would become familiar with all titles.

5. The Book Week program activity resulted in a permanent system for individual free reading. The card catalogue, set up as a record of the books investigated in order to choose the titles most adaptable for the program, served as an automatic stimulus. Academic and prohibitive standards had been removed from the program, and students enjoyed freedom in selecting books. New life and meaning were given to reading. A purely informal atmosphere was created.

Dr. Phelps' reading list of the best books of the year, selected lists to follow the completion of class studies, and timely lists suggested by current photoplays or special community events were posted in conspicuous places. Every student in the class reported his readings at regular intervals on a cumulative record card. A representative pupil's list for one semester follows: *Middlemarch* (Eliot) ; *The Old Inns of England* (Richardson) ; *Little Orvie* (Tarkington) ; *Pickwick Papers* (Dickens) ; *The Nine Old Men* (Pearson and Allen) ; *Victoria Regina* (Housman) ; *Innocents Abroad* (Mark Twain) ; *The Return of the Native* (Hardy) ; *Show Boat* (Ferber) ; *No Hero—This* (Deeping) ; *Mistress Pat* (Montgomery). The cumulative record also devoted space to magazines read regularly, and photoplays which had been made from recognized writings. Weekly student-planned and conducted programs gave frequent opportunities for oral discussion of books and writers. In this manner, the individual as well as the group reacted definitely to a free reading program.

EXPERIENCE IN READING FICTION [3]

Aim. To stimulate interest in reading for pleasure and to improve the taste of girls who found their chief interest in reading in tabloids or mystery stories.

Motivation. The girls were told of the need for an adequate bibliography of such books as girls might read in order to learn something about the profession they hoped to follow. (The published lists are for the most part inadequate. They include books now out of print and many not found in the ordinary public library.) The opportunity to be helpful and to have some concrete result of their work appealed to the girls. They decided to compile a bibliography that would be of interest and assistance to all Walton girls. This list was to include only the titles of such books as had been read by members of the class and found to be interesting and helpful.

Procedure. With a brief list of titles as a starting point, they began to work at the twofold problem of reading books and of recording information about them. They decided that each girl was to read books about the profession or vocation she hoped to select as her life work or one about which she had considerable curiosity.

Their first step, of course, was to declare a choice of profession or vocation. Their choices reflected the usual feminine interests, although one girl chose the career of veterinary surgeon, several the law, one medicine, and two aviation. The usual prerogative of woman to change her mind was allowed; a girl might even contribute to several different groups if she chose. Once every two weeks the girls reported orally on their reading, and if a book had been endorsed by at least two readers, the title was selected for inclusion in their bibliography.

As their interest grew, the girls decided to write brief reviews of the books they had enjoyed with a view to the preparation of a booklet (to be called "Vocations in Fiction") for the school library, where it might furnish guidance to the girls of other classes. Each set to work to put down briefly such comments as might be quickly read by others who sought a good book. This was no small problem, for they wished in most cases to write too much—often a résumé of the whole book.

It was found best to give definite directions: first, one or two sentences must give the theme of the book or enough of the plot to stimulate a reader; second, one sentence must give the reader's own reaction to the book. Each girl was asked to put herself in the place

[3] Reported by Lydia Schroeder, Walton High School, New York City.

of a girl in search of a good book and ask about her own report, "Would I have time to read this report? Would it persuade me to take the book out and read it?"

The following is a representative review:

Mary Roberts Rinehart: *The Girl from Scotland Yard*

This story is about a girl detective who is also a nurse. She solves a mystery that baffles the greatest detectives.

It is the best story I have read concerning my vocation, and I think it would be the first book any one whose ambition is to become a detective should read.

The reviews were given to the teacher first for necessary correction in English. Changes were sometimes made after conferences with the writer, for the opportunity to give help in written expression was a valuable one. The finished product was then turned over to a committee who selected the best of the duplicates (fifteen girls read *Little Citizens*). These were then given to a group who typed them.

The girls decided that it might be helpful to other students in Walton to post a number of these reports on a large bulletin board in a hallway near the library. For this purpose simplicity, brevity, and neatness were essential, and many lessons were learned before these qualities were achieved.

The young artists prepared the captions to attract the attention of those hurrying by. Above the board appeared this one:

GOOD BOOKS: WE KNOW FOR WE HAVE READ THEM

(Below were smaller ones.)

> *Interested in Art?*
>
> *Thrilling Books for the Detective*
>
> *Avez-vous Besoin D'Une Interprète?*
>
> *For the Next Amelia Earhart*
>
> *Do You Feel the Lure of the Footlights?*

And others similar.

Each review, typed on a separate sheet of paper, was put below the appropriate caption. The girls arranged the board to their own satisfaction and watched with interest to see some one jot down a title or two. The response gave them ample reward for their effort.

A competition was then held for the design for a suitable cover of the booklet for the library. The librarian was the judge and chose three instead of one. The girls thereupon decided to make duplicates, two books for the library and one to be given to May Lamberton Becker who had given them valuable advice and to whom they dedicated their efforts.

Elizabeth D. Gelvin (Board of Education, Bowling Green, Ohio) reports success similar to Miss Schroeder's. Miss Gelvin's pupils, under the guidance of student and critic teachers, prepare bulletin board displays. They use spacing, color, and lettering to "sell" books to other boys and girls. Book jackets, pupil-written book reviews, pupil-selected movie and radio reviews, and creative writing stimulated by reading good books are effectively arranged to attract attention and to guide free reading.

"The Influence of Leisure Time upon People of the Past and the Present" is the unifying idea of an experience-centered unit prepared by Frances Hudson.[4] Through newspapers, fiction, nonfiction, poetry, and drama, curricular and extracurricular activities in high school, the pupils come to an understanding of how leisure may be made re-creative.

"Our Temple of Fame" is the title of a unit in which Lillian Krohn [5] directs her pupils' reading of biographies and the literature of service.

"Intellectual Frontiersmen" is the key idea around which Sister Marion [6] developed a unit dealing with the lives of American scientists, naturalists, inventors, and explorers. Reading and discussions enabled her pupils to appreciate the scientist's devotion to truth, the personal sacrifices individuals have made to achieve scientific discoveries and inventions, and the significance to the present high-school generation of the accumulated knowledge of science.

Alma M. Ward [7] and her high-school students arranged for panel discussions of individual readings on the theme: "How

[4] For details write to Frances Hudson, Hoke Smith Junior High School, Atlanta, Ga.

[5] For bibliography and outline of activities write to Lillian Krohn, 1114 Pierce Ave., Marinette, Wis.

[6] For details write to Sister Marion, C. S. J., St. Joseph's Academy, St. Paul, Minn.

[7] For details write to Alma M. Ward, Roosevelt High School, Seattle, Wash.

Americans Live Together." The sub-ideas included the immigrant, home life, making a living, adventures in the outdoors. The quality of the pupils' reading was reflected in the keenness of their thinking and in the soundness of their conclusions about the major questions in contemporary society.

"The Growing Life" is the intriguing title given by Mabel Pearson Schmidt [8] to a unit in which the pupils read about and discuss ethical problems. Literature selected by her and her high-school students is used to focus attention on ideals and patterns of behavior that have brought about personal happiness and social service.

A list of the literary selections used as a basis for discussion in two of the twelve conferences will show the quality of thought and emotion stimulated by this unit.

SUBMISSION TO THE LAW

Echoes of the Over-Soul . . . . . . An unknown minstrel
  "A Caravan Crosses the Desert"
  "The Wheel of the Law"
"Freedom through Obedience to Duty" . . . . Thomas Carlyle
"Each in His Own Tongue" . . . . Herbert William Carruth
"Rest" . . . . Goethe (Translated by John Sullivan Dwight)
"The Kings" . . . . Louise Imogen Guiney
"If" . . . . Rudyard Kipling
Selection from Address at Springfield Lyceum . . . Abraham Lincoln
"The Lord Is My Shepherd" . . . . Psalm 23
"Work" . . . . Henry van Dyke
"All's Well" . . . . John Greenleaf Whittier
"Conduct from the Mahabarata" . . . . John Greenleaf Whittier
"Ode to Duty" . . . . William Wordsworth

THE CALL TO COUNTRY AND FLAG

Selection from *Epic of America* . . . . . James Truslow Adams
"America the Beautiful" . . . . . . Katherine Lee Bates
"The Soldier" . . . . Rupert Brooke
"The American Flag" . . . . Joseph Rodman Drake
"Concord Hymn" . . . . Ralph Waldo Emerson
"The Blue and the Gray" . . . . . Francis Miles Finch
"The Battle Hymn of the Republic" . . . . Julia Ward Howe
"Recessional" . . . . Rudyard Kipling
"The Spires of Oxford" . . . . Winifred M. Letts

[8] For details write to Mabel Pearson Schmidt, Morris High School, New York City.

III

DEVICES TO ASSIST PUPILS TO EXPERIENCE LITERATURE

BEFORE BEGINNING the reading of *A Son of the Middle Border,* Corinne Oertel, Richmond Hill High School, New York City, asked each pupil to interview an older member of his family and report any interesting experiences of that person's childhood in the exact words of the speaker. This accomplished several things at once—gave the pupils practice in forming appropriate questions and reporting the answers accurately, reviewed the rules for the punctuation of direct quotations, and awakened the interest of the pupils in the childhood adventures of others. Not many of the parents or grandparents had come from the Middle West, but students and teacher were amused by some incidents of life in "Little Old New York," and learned from several accounts of life in the Old World that "Truth is stranger than fiction."

J. C. Tressler, Richmond Hill, New York City, used three class meetings of the term—two after the study of *Modern Poetry* and one after the *Golden Treasury* and *Idylls of the King*—for poetry recitals. While the class was studying a book of poetry, each pupil was preparing for participation in the recital. He was free to select anything from the book studied. No minimum quantity was prescribed, but each pupil handed in a list of poems or selections memorized. The recital provides an incentive for memorizing poetry and interpreting its thoughts and feelings, and gives experience in reciting poetry and listening to it.

In teaching the *Odyssey,* Henry I. Christ, Richmond Hill High School, New York City, used three devices for enlivening recitations. The first of these was a mimeographed map, copied from the old chart of the *Odyssey,* with sea monsters, the North Wind puffing his cheeks, and the Mediterranean marked "The Great Gulf of the Sea." Four days were devoted, one chapter each day, to the adventurings of Odysseus in Books IX–XII. The maps were filled in; the wanderings were traced; and a clearer picture of the voyages was obtained.

The second device was intended to help the pupils through the initial difficulty of the names in the *Odyssey*. To help in understanding the alignment of unfamiliar gods, demigods, and heroes, the class formed imaginary football teams, comprising the important characters who were arranged on one side or the other in the toils of Odysseus. Zeus was the referee and umpire combined. Odysseus was captain and quarterback of "Odysseus' Wildcats." Poseidon held the same position on "Poseidon's Tigers," with Athene, Hera, and Apollo in the backfield for Odysseus' team. The students were never at a loss in the tangle of events, but knew at all times who was helping or opposing Odysseus.

The third device consisted of choosing actors and actresses to fit the parts of the leading characters.

After conducting a discussion of courage with her sixth-graders in Tolleston School, Gary, Indiana, Opal French divided her class into groups of five according to reading ability. When tales of heroic action were assigned to be read by a group who prepared for a sort of panel discussion before the class, classmates asked further questions about the content or technique of the story. Imitators must be careful not to put too much emphasis upon the preparation for reports and thus turn a leisure activity into a chore.

Students working under the direction of Minnie V. Squire, Western High School, Washington, D.C., discussed the purpose of education, the part that literature should play in it, and the goals of their literature work. They even participated so far as their knowledge of literature would permit in compiling the list of books and selections to be read. The readings were not arranged in topical units, but the students were at all times looking in their reading for nine types of experience, sometimes several of these in one selection. If the same list of things to look for had been furnished by the teacher, it would not have held the attention of the students. Supposedly their alertness to so many kinds of experience prevented the students from wresting a work from its author's intention to fit their purpose of the moment.

When her students have finished reading a novel or romance and have discussed the characters in it, Mabel Goddard, Arsenal Technical High School, Indianapolis, Indiana, uses one or several of these devices to make them more aware of types and personalities:

1. Pupils make lists of vivid people met in all their reading: villains, heroes, Westerners and outdoor men, children, old people.
2. Pupils discuss book characters they have seen growing, changing, developing.
3. Pupils discuss book people they have met who are artificial and unreal.
4. Pupils select motion-picture characters who would interpret the book personalities well.
5. Pupils write short character sketches of favorite book characters.
6. Pupils give talks picturing characters, concealing identities, while others try to guess who is being described.

Somewhat similarly, Sylvia Russell, Richmond Hill High School, New York City, stimulated second-semester high-school students to publish a class paper called *Sherwood Gazette,* presenting some of the sensational news items in *Ivanhoe.*

In the same school Mary E. Slevin's class, which had been studying a book of mythology, presented a pageant.

Each pupil represented a character in the book and in a brief speech introduced himself to the audience. On a placard was printed the name of the character. This the pupil held as he talked. A crude attempt at properties was made. Every one enjoyed the period and is likely to remember the myths which were enacted.

A Tale of Two Cities and *A Son of the Middle Border* illustrate the importance of adapting one's self to changing conditions and of developing a social personality. After a class discussion bringing out such a truth Helen Reets, also of Richmond Hill, has her students write themes upon specific applications of these general ideas. That these are something other and more than time-serving themes aimed to please the teacher is to be credited to the atmosphere of the classroom—and ultimately to the teacher's genuine respect for the thoughts and wills of the students.

In Walton High School, New York City, the girls in Emily Hanson Obear's classes made a Christmas Play for the school of Dickens' *Christmas Carol.*

In the Wadsworth School, Chicago, the seventh-grade pupils of Caroline Perksen discovered in the books they had read almost all the material needed for an imaginary trip around the world. They found books to fill in the gaps and prepared a sort of pageant-exhibit in the library, through which guides took groups of fifteen pupils from other upper-grade classes.

The teacher's purpose in all these newspapers, plays, and pageants is, in addition to the encouragement of self-expression, to bring about the vivid living of the literature necessary in the preparation of the publication and entertainments. These projects usually involve much rereading of an intensive sort.

"A Shakespearean banquet, given in honor of Queen Elizabeth at Penshurst," was used by Ida T. Jacobs to stimulate creative reading of the Elizabethan drama. The guests were to be drawn from two sources—Shakespeare's contemporaries and the characters of his plays; the setting was to be a verisimilitude of the period; and the entertainment appropriate to the occasion.

The students selected the Christmas season because its festivities afforded colorful notes. They decided on the following committees: drama, music, the dance, decorations, costume, etiquette, menu, service, and a general one having supervision over all. Each student selected the committee on which he wished to serve. Several weeks were given for individual research, while the regular class work (including a study of the period, the Shakespeare theater, and several of his plays) proceeded. Though each member sought material for the committee on which he served, whatever he found of interest to another committee he brought to the attention of its members. Then each committee through its chairman reported to the class.

The drama committee chose scenes from Shakespeare's plays which it wished to present, selected and directed the actors, produced an original interlude, and wrote a Shakespearean sonnet. The music committee selected Elizabethan songs and carols for the group singing, and arranged an orchestra. The costume committee painted designs for costumes of both the upper and lower classes and helped those who called upon them for suggestions. The committee on decorations planned the banquet hall and tables. The committee on manners told them what to do and what not to do according to Elizabethan etiquette. The menu committee planned the food and arranged for serving it, from the duty of the food taster to that of the carver.

The banquet was held in an Elizabethan setting, its guests appropriately costumed, eating food they might have had, in the manner of the day, disporting themselves in ways of Elizabethan England, bringing in the Yule log, singing the songs, dancing the dances, playing original interludes as well as scenes from Shakespeare's plays, and passing the wassail bowl with great gusto and exuberance. For that night Shakespeare's contemporaries mingled with the creations of his imagination, while the jester played his pranks among them, not even at times respecting the royal person of Elizabeth and her favorite Essex.

IV

FREE READING

THE LOGIC of our theories is driving us relentlessly toward *free reading as a part of the literature curriculum*. Out-of-school experience with literature includes the choice of what to read and when —and even whether to read at all. Adequate preparation for such activities must include similarly free choice now—but the pupils must not choose not to read and their choices of what to read must be progressively better. Our dilemma is that we must leave the child free and at the same time we must see that he takes the right road! Each *must* is as inexorable as the other.

Fortunately the dilemma is usually resolved by the provision of a favorable environment and the application of the teacher's friendly but strong personality. Children are suggestible, and reading is fun when the youngster gets a real taste of it. To entice a book-hater to read his first book or to lead the devotee of "confession" or "Western" stories to try more nourishing fare requires patience, understanding of children, and broad, intimate knowledge of the books that are within the reader's capacity. The task is largely one of individual guidance, though class discussions and other activities may set the stage.

Such work is reported by Alberta R. Noble, Greenway Junior High School, Coleraine, Minnesota. Note how she gained the confidence of her pupils and how she led them gently out of the swamps of trash up the hills of literature. Her use of class discussion is skilful, too, especially the final consideration of their own changed tastes.

INDIVIDUAL EXPERIENCES IN READING [1]

It was in my ninth-grade English classes of eighty-one pupils that I made my most serious efforts. Here was the girl with a reading abil-

---

[1] Reported by Alberta R̦. Noble, Greenway Junior High School, Coleraine, Minn.

ity far superior to the rest of her class (as discovered in informal reading tests) who was subsisting on Larrimore, Lutz, and worse. Here was the adorable little Irishman and his chum, Dood, who claimed they had never read a book and were never going to read any! Here were the boys and girls who didn't know what English was all about and didn't care one bit to find out.

We began with a reading diary, kept for a week at a time for a period of three weeks. Entries were made each morning in regular diary form. The contents of these diaries were amusing and revealing. Everything was reported—comic strips, sports-page articles, *True Story,* Bailey, Raine, Sara Teasdale's poems, among a wealth of other things.

These diaries had a twofold use. From them I had an intimate little picture of each boy's and girl's reading interests and habits. More, the daily entries brought to each boy and girl a realization that the work of an English class went beyond the four walls of a classroom into his daily living.

Some of the diaries I read aloud, omitting names, choosing representative ones with varying ranges of interests and varying degrees of worth-while materials recorded. My purpose in this was (1) to encourage those who were not recording freely and completely what they were reading, and (2) to make each pupil aware of his classmates' reading interests and habits as well as his own. At no time did I comment on or criticize what I found in the diaries. The boys and girls themselves made such comments voluntarily, whereupon I now and then added my own opinion to the discussions.

While we were still keeping our diaries, I suggested that we have a book, story, and author day. Each pupil might tell which author he *liked* and why; he might tell us a story he enjoyed that we might enjoy, too; he might tell us about a book he liked very much. The results were appalling. Out of eighty-one students who participated in these discussions a majority reported on Bailey, Grey, and Raine —on a book by these authors. Others told stories from *Liberty, True Story,* and western and detective thrillers. I concealed my horror carefully and was as well informed as they, mentioning books they had forgotten, telling about the real thriller I once read in a horror magazine and had never forgotten.

A little later we had a library reading day. On that day each boy and girl was to bring something to read to class. Everything appeared —comic-strip magazines, horror magazines, Raine, and the rest. As on our book-discussion day, the boys and girls were not sure I had meant what I said so the magazines and books were carefully concealed in their desks until all took heart when one bold adventurer engrossed himself in his horror magazines without any unfavorable reaction on the part of his English teacher. Some had nothing to read. For them the English teacher provided books and magazines from the school library, carefully selected to meet pupil interests.

I am not quite sure what happened next. We went on with our book-discussion days, completed our diaries, kept library reading days—and began to be acquainted. Boys and girls started to come to me in class and after school. "What book would you suggest?" they asked. I'd make suggestions that were sometimes followed and some-times not. They knew I wanted them to read—anything. I liked to read. I was the teacher. I must know things they'd like to read. I'd read things they'd read; they had confidence in my judgment.

Then I introduced my first more or less required reading units— the newspaper unit first, the magazine next, historical novels a little later.

All magazines read by the girls and boys were listed on a syste-matic form—including *Modern Romances* and the like. The require-ment was five magazines to be examined from a list of the best available magazines.

At first the outline was irksome. It was more fun to tell orally than in writing about magazine articles and stories, to make poem collections including magazine verse, to make original sketches for stories or articles. Later, however, the outline proved itself a valu-able source from which to draw up a list of magazines that the boy or girl could afford in his home. Actual subscription letters were writ-ten and sent by a few fortunate boys and girls; others began to make Christmas plans for their favorites to arrive.

In the unit on the historical novel, *Ivanhoe* was *not* selected. Neither were the five novels recommended in its place by the local course of study. Instead each boy and girl went to the card cata-logue, looked up the historical fiction listed under a period of history in which he was interested, examined the novel itself to see whether it appeared interesting, read it if he thought he would enjoy it, went to the encyclopedia and biography shelves to discover whether the characters in his novel were real or fictional characters, read pages, chapters, and even books on the period of history covered in his novel; then wrote a book review.

The review included a comparison of the novel with the history book as to the events and background of the period, a comparison of biography and encyclopedia references on real people in the novels with the characters as they appeared in the novel, a personal reaction to the story as a story, to people in the story as people, to adventure in the story as adventure. Before writing the reviews *Scholastic, Atlantic Monthly*, newspapers, *Time, Books* (New York *Herald-Tribune* book-review section), and other sources were consulted for reviews. The reviews once written were grouped according to periods or countries, and a series of programs was given, one of the better reviews being given on each program.

When the unit was over, we held a long delayed book-discussion day. Very little of Raine or Lutz was included. One boy spoke on Raine; he had nothing else to contribute and hesitated to give his report. Finally, however, he got up the necessary courage and told the story. No one seemed very much interested. Every one knew Raine a little too well. Something new was better—something like *The Unwilling Vestal* or *The Pirate of Barataria* (not included in both review programs in all classes).

Other units followed—poetry, biography, books of animals and nature. Toward the close of the year we had a summing up unit called "Why We Read." In this we tried to go back over what we had been doing in order to see its relation to all of our reading. For book-discussion days we brought back Raine and others. Why had we dropped that?—because we knew them too well; because there were too many required reading lists which did not include them? No, the pupils decided that they weren't so very interesting after all. Why not? That was a little hard to answer at first, but not for long. We had dropped them because one story was like all the rest, because the persons in the stories were not like us nor were they the kind of people we found interesting or admirable, because the West or the North wasn't the way they described it. That is what they said. I agreed with them, a little doubtingly at first. I had to be thoroughly convinced, and after many examples, I finally was. More, I encouraged them to believe that they were right with many examples and comparisons of my own—comparisons of *Les Miserables* and Gene Stratton Porter, or *True Story* and real adventures in living of common-place people I had known.

I kept no careful record of the reading we were doing. For me, the record lies in innumerable little incidents happening from day to day.

The story of free reading by low-ability pupils in Lincoln High School, Cleveland, Ohio, is told by Lenore Anders. It is concerned chiefly with stimulating the pupils to read, but includes also vocabulary work and other technical features.

A Free-reading Program with Low-ability Groups [2]

Many of the pupils evidently disliked material which they were assigned to read in the ninth-grade classes. This was especially noticeable in the low-ability groups, although many cases of maladjustment in English were to be found in other classes, particularly among boys. The pupils' one plea was for better books to read, and their reasons for this plea were very definite. One boy said he had had all the history he wanted in his history classes; another said he wanted to read stories about animals, not stories about wars. Girls asked repeatedly for books about girls, as all the books assigned in the regular course were, they said, for boys. Both boys and girls said that they did not understand such books as *The Black Arrow, The White Company,* and *Captains Courageous.*

This statement was not exaggerated. Recently three so-called average ninth-grade classes studying *The White Company* were divided into committees for the purpose of forming a vocabulary list from the book. These committees, working carefully with the aid of the teacher, compiled a list of from forty to fifty unfamiliar words from each chapter. Probably the foreign background of these pupils accounts in part for the large number of unfamiliar words, as they have little opportunity to hear colloquial English. No reader, however, can be expected to look up so many words and still enjoy the story.

In the Cleveland Public Schools all pupils are at stated intervals given group tests such as the National, Otis, Philadelphia, or Cleveland in order to determine the pupils' P. L. R. (Probable Learning Rate). Each teacher receives the pupil's P. L. R. with the pupil. To determine the reading grades of the pupils, the teacher gives at the beginning of the semester some good reading test.

Since low-ability pupils are generally poor readers and are not interested in reading, the first objective is to convince them that they will not be forced to read books which they do not like.

As a first step in this program back numbers of such magazines as *The Open Road for Boys, Boys' Life, Young America,* and *Good Housekeeping* are given to the classes to read during the class period. Magazines are chosen because low-ability pupils generally prefer magazine stories to books. In order to make the pupils conscious of books there are placed upon bulletin boards in the room many bright-colored book covers, which have been obtained from the school

[2] Reported by Lenore Lear Anders, Lincoln High School, Cleveland, Ohio.

librarian. These are changed from time to time, so that by the end of the semester about five hundred different covers have been displayed. These gay book covers help not only to make an attractive room, but also to arouse the interest of the pupils. As a result many times they decide that they wish to read some books after all.

The next step is to plan with the school librarian for a book day, and as there is a branch of the public library in this school, this is very easily done. Training young people to read good wholesome books may best be accomplished when the English teacher and the librarian work together. On book day the librarian places upon tables in the library, books of fiction which have been found suitable for pupils with low-reading ability. This is determined partly by records which have been kept over a period of time of the books which poor readers prefer. The pupils are now taken during the class period to the library where they are allowed to choose any book on the tables or on the shelves. Usually they find without difficulty some book which they think will interest them. No effort is made to influence any one to take a certain book, but if information is desired about any book, it is gladly given. The only restriction placed upon the pupils' reading is that all books must come from the young people's room or from the high-school room of the public library, unless special permission is given to take a book from the adult library. After the books have been chosen, a few class periods are devoted to reading them, and any one who has made an unhappy selection of a book is urged to make a change. Some pupils make several changes before a suitable book is selected. The pupils are requested after reading a book to make a short written report on it and to look up and to use correctly in sentences ten or more unfamiliar words. Sometimes a good book report is read to the class; at other times pupils are asked to tell the class about some interesting books which they have read.

When new books are received in the library, the librarian sends them to the teacher, and as soon as possible, the teacher discusses briefly with the pupils all suitable books. During the past semester such books have been presented as *Smoke Blows West* by Fernald, *Riding West on the Pony Express* by Skelton, *Susan of the Green Mountain* by Fox, *Jasmine* by Ratzesberger, *On Jungle Trails* by Frank Buck, and *Swift Walker* by Winifred Wise. Any opportunity which may present itself is used to call the pupils' attention to good stories in magazines. *The Voice of Bugle Ann* by Kantor appeared first in the *Atlantic Monthly*. *The Hurricane* by Nordhoff and Hall was published in the *Saturday Evening Post*, and a new serial by the same authors has recently been presented in this magazine.

Frequently authors lecture in Cleveland on their books. Their appearance here presents an opportunity for introducing the books of these authors to the class. Such was true of *The Flying Carpet* by Richard Halliburton. The filming of any book which may be of interest to high-school pupils opens up an excellent opportunity for presenting this book to a class. The filming of *Tom Sawyer* and its presentation in Cleveland aroused so much interest that the pupils were eager to review this book although for many pupils this meant re-reading. To add to the interest, pupils have helped the teacher make a collection of pictures from the various scenes. However, such books as *Tom Sawyer* and *Treasure Island* are so universally read that it is seldom necessary to urge pupils to read them.

As another method of stimulating interest, several hundred bright-colored posters have been made on which have been pasted clippings and comments about books. Gay pictures taken from newspapers and magazines are used to illustrate characters and scenes from the books, and several times during the semester are displayed about the rooms. Pupils are asked to look at these posters, to discuss them with the teacher, and to copy the titles of any books which promise to hold their interest. These posters, classified as to fiction and non-fiction, are divided into three groups: (1) for boys, (2) for girls, and (3) for both.

After the majority of pupils have become interested in reading, the teacher makes a very definite effort to teach them how to choose books of quality. As almost all pupils have a pronounced dislike for non-fiction, the teacher spends several days in acquainting them with non-fiction books in order to overcome this prejudice. Especially interesting books and authors are discussed; non-fiction posters are displayed; and a special trip is made to the library for the pupils to select their books. As an incentive for reading good non-fiction books, extra credit is given for each report. This same method may be used to introduce books on vocations, pioneer stories, short modern plays, or any group of books that might be of interest to the pupils after they begin to read such types.

Pupils are told that another reading test will be given at the end of the semester, and that their final grade will depend partly upon the improvement they have made during the semester. Special conferences are held with each individual at which times his reading grades, his choice of books, and other things that will aid the pupil are discussed. Charts are kept on which are recorded all the books each pupil reads. Colored squares are filled in after the name of each book indicating the amount of work which has been completed. Stars are awarded for satisfactory reports, and at the close of each grading period a gold star is given to every one who has reported well upon a reasonable amount of reading. This may sound like a kindergarten method, but the great interest shown in the chart, which is kept posted on the bulletin board, indicates that it is really of much value in giving pupils an incentive to work. Almost anything that will be an aid in persuading young people to read good books should be used, for in addition to being accomplished in the actual mechanics of reading, a pupil should be introduced to good literature if he is to develop a desirable reading taste.

Besides endeavoring to develop reading habits, the teacher should use devices to aid the pupil in becoming a proficient reader. Mastering the simple mechanics of reading for some pupils is apparently a rather complicated task, and so in order to make reading easier certain objectives must be reached. If pupils do not know the meaning of words, they cannot read with much understanding, and experience has shown that ninth-grade pupils are woefully lacking in vocabulary skill. During the semester several hundred words, which are drawn from the Inglis word test for high-school pupils and from the books which the pupils read, are studied. Every effort is made to make pupils conscious of words, and almost without exception pupils state that the vocabulary drills aid them in becoming better readers. Besides having vocabulary work, pupils are taught how to read with more comprehension and with greater speed. For the very low P. L. R. classes, selections chosen from sets of magazines are used for making out comprehension questions. In the better classes, however, regular books for the development of skills in reading are used. This work is supplemented by the remedial English classes where the poorest readers go twice a week for instruction. Before the end of the semester almost all pupils show a marked improvement in comprehension and in the speed with which they read.

A careful study has been made in Lincoln High School of the boys who were maladjusted in their English classes. It is definitely known that most of those boys were problems because of their dislike of reading and because of their inability to read the assigned work with understanding. Now, ninth- and tenth-grade boys not in a free reading class who have difficulty with English because of reading and who do not intend to graduate are placed in a boys' class where a modified plan of work similar to that of the regular free reading classes is used. From our experience with these classes we feel that these boys learn far more by being permitted to read books of their own choosing than by being forced to read books which others have selected, and beyond a doubt the boys are happier. One may well stop to consider here how much any pupil will learn if he is unhappy. One semester, records were kept of the work accomplished in one boys' class. Most of the work in this class was done during the class period. At the beginning of the semester it was impossible for the pupils to find in one period the answers to more than ten questions on a given piece of work. By the end of the semester the pupils could read a selection and answer twenty questions in one period. In this class an average of eight books was read besides six complete issues of *The Open Road for Boys* and seventeen issues of *Young America*. Records of standard reading tests given this semester showed a gain in reading grade from 6.1 to 7.4.

The work of the free reading classes as compared to the work of classes following the regular course of study has been subjected to a careful statistical analysis under the supervision of the research department of the Cleveland Public Schools. For this study two groups of 9A students and two groups of 9B students were formed. As a control group for the 9A experimental free reading class, one of the teacher's own 9A classes was used, and for the 9B experimental class a 9B group was formed of pupils selected from all the other 9B English classes. As nearly as possible an equal number of boys and girls with the same P. L. R.'s as the experimental group were chosen. At the beginning of the semester, all the classes were given a Thorndike-McCall Reading Test, Form 9, and in ten weeks' time a second Thorndike-McCall Test, Form 5, was given. During this semester the 9A control group followed the regular course of study both in reading and in composition and grammar. The 9B control pupils all remained in their individual classes, where the regular course of study was followed. The free reading classes followed the regular course of study only in composition and in grammar. Besides the free reading which the pupils in the experimental class did, thirteen selections of prose and poetry from books were chosen for drill work. The pupils were given both comprehension and memory questions on these selections and were timed for speed in reading. Regular vocabulary work was given during this semester. No pupil, however, took any remedial work outside of the class. Tables I and II on page 60 show the results of the semester's study.

The results of that semester's careful study show beyond any doubt that the program followed in the free reading classes produced

TABLE I

GRADE 9B EXPERIMENTAL AND CONTROL CLASSES

Tests	Median Reading Grade		Median Reading Age	
	Experimental	Control	Experimental	Control
Thorndike-McCall Form IX	6.3	6.1	12.5	12.3
Thorndike-McCall Form V	9.2	7.0	15.1	13.4
Gain............	2.9	0.9	2.6	1.1

TABLE II

GRADE 9A EXPERIMENTAL AND CONTROL CLASSES

Tests	Median Reading Grade		Median Reading Age	
	Experimental	Control	Experimental	Control
Thorndike-McCall Form IX	7.0	7.0	13.4	13.4
Thorndike-McCall Form V	11.2	7.4	15.8	13.9
Gain............	4.2	0.4	2.4	0.5

better results than were obtained from the classes following the prescribed reading. These results have been verified by tests given in other free reading classes in succeeding semesters.

The question may be raised as to whether the same results can not be obtained by giving comprehension drills to classes which are following the regular course of study. Approximately the same gains have been made by some such classes in this school. However, the teacher's firm belief is that the ability to read well will not in itself produce the ideal reader. From questionnaires filled out by both high P. L. R. and low P. L. R. classes, from conversation with classes and with individual pupils, and from actual observation, the conclusions reached are that large numbers of pupils read trashy books and magazines, that many pupils obtain the greater share of their books from the adult library, and that the present method of handling required reading of standard classics is not fostering in pupils a desire to read good books.

Records kept over a period of time indicate that the free reading classes read more books than the regular classes. A representative list of books read by pupils who have P. L. R.'s between 70 and 88 includes such books as:

Girls	Boys
Log Cabin Lady, Anonymous	*The Great Adventure*, Parsons
Mountain Girl Comes Home, Fox	*The Will to Win*, Meader
College on Horseback, Hall	*Trap Lines North*, Meader
College in Crinoline, Medary	*With the Indians in the Rockies*, Schultz
Bright Island, Robinson	
Uncharted Ways, Snedeker	*Adventure*, Wells
Phebe Fairchild, Lenski	*Kari, the Elephant*, Mukerji
Nurses on Horseback, Poole	*The Cruise of the Dazzler*, London
Wild Folk, Scoville	*Mounted Justice*, Mayo
Secret of the Blue Macaw, Forrester	*Typhoon Gold*, Strong
	Under the Big Top, Cooper
Let the Hurricane Roar, Lane	*Swords and Statues*, Stratten

This list is formed from records kept over a period of semesters. No pupil had had more than one semester of free reading, which is, of course, too short a time in which to make the greatest possible improvement in reading tastes.

Free reading proved a "new broom" in the Bridgeton and Port Norris experiment reported by Florence Bowden, Supervisor of English, Bridgeton, New Jersey.

THE CLASSROOM LIBRARY [3]

Believing that a reading plan might be evolved to provide more satisfying experiences for the slow reader and the non-reader and to provide richer experiences for those pupils who enjoy reading and who read with understanding, a committee of Cumberland County teachers, consisting of Mrs. Frances Stintsman and Mr. Don Hitchner of Bridgeton, and Mr. Nelson Bateman of Port Norris began the development of such a plan in the fall of 1935.

The committee considered enjoyment of reading to be the first requisite of the plan. It was assumed that pupils would read with understanding and enjoyment when they were given books which they could understand and which contained meaningful experiences touching their everyday life.

It was decided that, for the first year, the reading plan in the

---

[3] Reported by Florence B. Bowden, Supervisor of English, Bridgeton Public Schools, Bridgeton, N. J.

Bridgeton High School should be introduced into two classes of slow readers and non-readers. In the Port Norris High School, a class of pupils was chosen whose abilities, interests, and tastes in reading varied greatly. Each of the three teachers on the committee was provided with a class library of fifty books to take the place of the five or six classics usually studied intensively by the entire class. The books chosen for the libraries were books written in language that these pupils could read with understanding and, at the same time, were books which contained experiences interesting to pupils of their chronological age.

Selecting books for the library. The selection of books for this type of class library required careful thought and planning. Before any mention of the proposed reading program was made to the pupils, the teachers first made the acquaintance of the individuals within their classes. They learned as much as possible of the home life of the pupils, their companions, their interests, and their success or failure in their school life. Since the teachers were primarily interested in the previous reading experiences of their pupils, they questioned them to discover what books, if any, they had read, what kinds of stories they enjoyed, and what books and magazines the home provided. This questioning was done informally and sympathetically so that the getting-acquainted periods created a closer bond between the teachers and the pupils.

With sufficient information concerning their pupils to help them in understanding the pupils' reactions, the teachers solicited the pupils' aid in choosing the books for the library. The teachers told the pupils frankly that they were to have an opportunity to select a class library consisting of books which they would enjoy reading. The pupils were encouraged to suggest types of books or to give actual titles. This plan of approach in selecting the books for the library was invaluable because it caught the attention of the pupils.

In the organization of the library, the teachers were careful not to make the pupils feel that they were different from other pupils or that they were objects of experimentation. Rather, the pupils were made to understand that the plan was a natural approach to reading and that they were fortunate to have an opportunity to determine its value. The members of the committee also held several conferences to discuss possible books and to make notes from various book lists. Each teacher then made a tentative list of books which he thought might be desirable for his class.

Purchasing books for the library. After devoting considerable time and thought in planning this tentative list of books, the teachers spent an afternoon at a book store, checking the tentative lists and browsing among other books for possible choices.

Introducing the books to the class. The class period for introducing the new books was a most informal one. The teachers allowed the pupils to unpack the box of new books and place them where they could be easily inspected. Two or more class periods were devoted to the pupils' browsing among the books and exchanging comments with one another. The teachers were inspiring agents in the introduction periods. They read orally exciting incidents, some mysterious or humorous situations. They spoke very informally to their pupils concerning books which they thought certain individuals might enjoy. The natural result was that some pupils immediately discovered an interesting book and began to read. The teachers, sensitive to this situation, turned the class into a reading period so that the pupils could begin to read while in the mood.

Procedures for the reading periods. The number of class periods utilized for reading depended upon the interest span of the pupils. The teachers were on their guard lest they and the pupils become so absorbed in the reading that they neglect the other phases of English work—spelling, vocabulary, sentence structure, and good usage. However, when the class time was devoted to the more formal work, the pupils were still allowed to take the library books for reading outside the class period.

The teachers varied the procedure for the reading periods. It seemed unwise for them to walk about the room because of annoying those who were trying to enjoy their reading. Occasionally, they sat at their desks and watched the reactions of the pupils as they read. Frequently, the teachers used the period for informal conferences with individual pupils. These conferences gave the teachers and pupils an opportunity for sharing experiences concerning the reading. Informal questioning and an evidence of interest in the pupils' reading were usually sufficient means to learn what each pupil was gaining from his reading. For this type of conference, teachers themselves must be lovers of books and must be aware of the possibilities which different books offer—humor, pathos, character, mystery, excitement, and the beauty of description. They must also be alert to the moods of the pupils and, above all, must gain the confidence of their pupils.

Procedures for checking. An important problem with which the committee had to concern itself was the devising of methods to check whether the pupils really were reading and with what degree of understanding and appreciation. Since a vital part of the plan is for the pupils to experience the joy of reading because of the pleasure which reading brings to them, it was necessary to devise checking procedures that would not detract from the naturalness of the situation which it had been the aim of the plan to create. It seemed wise not to use the checking procedures which had been employed in the teaching of the classics. The lengthy book report was avoided because the committee members had already discovered from their experiences with supplementary reading that, even though many pupils liked to read, they heartily disliked writing the formal book report.

The individual conference with the pupils was an excellent way for the teacher to discover what the pupils were gaining from their reading. Frequently, informal class discussion gave the teachers an opportunity to learn what books the pupil had read and his reactions to those particular books. In many cases, the teachers observed from the attitude of a pupil during the reading periods whether the pupil was interested in his book and whether he was getting some satisfaction from the reading of it. Following the introduction of the books, the teachers devised a kind of record that would give them the titles of the books which the pupils had read. This type of record was not used in the preliminary stages of the plan for fear that the pupils would confuse this record with the old type of book report. When the teachers felt that they had gained the coöperation of the pupils, teachers worked with pupils in making a record of what would help readers to select books.

Both teacher's observation of pupil growth and a formal survey after the plan had been in operation more than a year and a half showed that the pupils were reading more than before and that they felt they were getting more benefit from their English work.[4]

The Wilkes-Barre, Pennsylvania, High School, according to a report by Marion A. Sturdevant, dropped its requirement that seniors read and report on at least three books each semester to receive a grade of A. Next the comparatively narrow list from which home-reading books might be chosen was abolished, and the school board persuaded to make a liberal appropriation for new books. The students were enlisted in preparing the list of books to be purchased. "A" students were permitted to go to the library during one English period per week; later this library leave was

---

[4] For a detailed analysis of the results including book lists, please write directly to Florence B. Bowden, Supervisor of English, Bridgeton, N. J.

increased to two periods, and high "B" students were permitted to go for one period. The net result seems to be better work throughout, as well as much more individual reading.

In the Ardmore, Pennsylvania, High School, Agnes Roycroft kept her own personal lending library in her classroom and stimulated reading by informal and incidental comment upon the individual books. Every year her books have been supplemented by others brought from home by students. Finally an eleventh-grade class brought a large number of books and organized them into a circulating library. Other classes followed the example. Miss Roycroft appends to her report some devices, which she says are not new, for use in a year-round campaign to extend good reading.

DEVICES FOR A GOOD READING CAMPAIGN [5]

1. Naturally first discuss how to choose books: the relative value of selecting by color; conversation; title; standing of author; opinion of family, friend, teacher, librarian; book review; advertising; appearance on radio, stage, or in movie. Set up flexible standards for first class, second class, third class, and the rod riders. Stress the superficiality of the Halliburtons, the Guests, and the VanDines. I have found this to be a safe and inoffensive policy, "Read what you want but in class discuss the best only. Otherwise the weeds will crowd out the flowers. There are attractive weeds, to be sure, and there are misleading weeds. If you can't decide what you are cultivating, bring your problem to class."

2. Encourage "must" lists or "What I should read before I receive my diploma" lists.

3. Make the most of Book Week since it comes in the fall: favorite author contests, posters, book exhibits and reviews, dramatizations.

4. Subscribe through any book store to the New York *Times* and *Herald-Tribune* literary magazines (a quarter each, yearly to cover postage) or have two students bring their weekly issues in on Monday morning. Keep the previous year's supply until September for class textbook use. Before they are finally thrown away, have all prominent authors' pictures clipped. When you have at least one good-sized picture of most great writers, make a Book Week project of the mounting of them on colored paper with suitable printing about dates, types, and major works. These may then be used collectively as a pictorial survey of literature, or individually as the need arises.

[5] Reported by Agnes Roycroft, Ardmore High School, Ardmore, Pa.

5. Be on the mailing list for the monthly book list of any book store. Post on the bulletin board along with such book-club notes as will be brought from home.

6. Use a blackboard border of book covers brought from home. Prune the collection to the best only, and it will be a popular consulting list as well as a quick reminder of title or authors.

7. Have an author bulletin board: "Authors in the News." When ten students bring in the same set of pictures of the Pulitzer Prize winners, post the first and suggest that the others add to their clipping note-books. This encourages proper reading of the newspaper and magazine.

8. Have one class responsible for annotating for the benefit of all a "Radio Program for the Week," another "Drama," a third "Movies," always with the emphasis on dramatization of good literature and deliberate not accidental attendance. Occasionally give movie assignments, George Arliss in *Disraeli*, for instance.

9. Have students collect literary allusions and quotations. In two recent cases, the accused has been called by the judge a modern Jean Valjean. Some penny scales have the inscription "O, that this too, too solid flesh would melt." Eventually there is material for a Professor Quiz program.

10. Constantly make strong recommendations of good authors and specific titles so that the pupil will have them in mind when he goes to the library without a list.

11. Encourage the bringing of books to class. Be enthusiastic about the good ones; have them exchanged. Read a sample here and there: the violin lesson from the Day essays, the "Barkis is willin' " passage from Dickens, "Grass" from Sandburg's poems. Soon there will be too many stopping at the desk before class to tell you how much they like their latest book. Turn these into extemporaneous before-the-class recommendations. Timid pupils sometimes overcome their shyness this way.

12. Allow books to be discussed in small groups with one class report from each group.

13. Sponsor the club feeling with books. Suggest that John let Henry know when the book goes back to the library. "Who knows where Jane can get a copy of ——— ?" Borrow a book from a student occasionally. If the right spirit is created, no pupil will claim to have read or finished a book when he has not.

14. Air the "I don't likes." Encourage frankness but frankness backed by specific detail. This year one girl freely professed a dis-

like for *The House of the Seven Gables,* but her discussion persuaded four members of her class to start reading it at once.

15. Suggest the re-reading of some books for better understanding, the noticing of details, comparison of reaction between junior high reading and senior. Illustrate by a class exercise in re-reading a play, perhaps.

16. Encourage some intensive unit reading: several books by one author, several books on one subject, books by and about an author.

In the Hammond, Indiana, High School, a similar problem was met in a similar fashion, Emma Jane Bender reports. Her ninth-grade group was largely composed of boys, and so an animal-story unit was presented. Assigned work-corrective drills and class discussion of articles on animals occupied four days of every week; the fifth was devoted to free reading of materials, within the pupils' ability, available on the shelves. After the animal unit, more attention was given to developing specific reading skills but some part of each day was free for individual reading. The results were satisfactory.

The free reading program of the Sudlow Intermediate School, Davenport, Iowa, reported by Helen Ackermann, is particularly rich in devices for getting poor readers to try to read.

An Individual Free Reading Program [6]

I. *Introduction of the Plan*

The charts on the next pages formed the basis for the following informal class discussion:

"In a previous discussion we have set up the various types of English activities that everybody must use in his everyday living. What were these three activities?" (Reading, speaking, writing.) "When we discussed reading we noticed that we use two different types." (Recreational reading and work-type reading.)

"The charts on the bulletin board illustrate the pleasure type of reading which is after all the type that is most used in our daily living. Step I on the magazine chart illustrates the names of the magazines that are not of the best type to read; Step II indicates those that are good to read, the starred ones being especially interesting for people of your own age and grade; and Step III indicates those

[6] Reported by Helen Ackermann, Sudlow Intermediate School, Davenport, Iowa.

that are quite hard reading." (Call attention here to a goal to be achieved as their reading appreciation develops. Explain the book chart in similar manner.)

After the above explanation has been given about the charts, call attention to the magazines and books listed in each step. Discuss the problem informally, giving pupils the chance to ask questions about other magazines and books that are not on the charts. Teachers will undoubtedly be confronted with evident dissatisfaction because some of the magazines and books the pupils like best rank in the lowest step. In dealing with this problem I have found it very successful to tell them that those books and magazines are too easy reading and beneath the dignity of people of junior high-school age. Call attention to the cheap make-up of the poorer magazines and books, the cheaper advertising, and the untruthfulness of much of the material given. To do this successfully it will, of course, be necessary to have ready some of the poorer magazines and books that are definite proof of the points you wish to make. Read passages from both (for further illustration). Be one jump ahead of the pupils by having a good book or magazine within range of their reading ability to take the place of the poorer ones. For example, to a boy who enjoys *Flying Aces* suggest *Popular Aviation* for a substitute. Suggest Siple's *A Boy Scout with Byrd* and similar books to take the place of the Tom Swift books. For those who like the Tarzan books, be ready to suggest such books as Mukerji's *Hari, the Jungle Lad* or Du Chaillu's *Lost in the Jungle*. Girls who enjoy *The Bobbsey Twins* series might be given such books as Alcott's *Little Women* or Wiggin's *Rebecca of Sunnybrook Farm*. A list of such books as substitutes made out before the discussion takes place will be very helpful. A good follow-up for this discussion might be the making of programs of reading interests by the pupils themselves. (See A under II for detailed explanation.)

II. *Special Projects Used to Guide Pupils in the Selection of Books*

  A. Making programs of reading interests
    Pupils will take a keener interest and have a more wholesome attitude toward reading better books if they have an active part in making up reading lists. We began this project with an informal discussion of the various types of books they had read, listing titles on the blackboard as they were suggested. After the discussion, the following mimeographed information blank was given to the pupils to fill out. Later these are filed for future reference in directing reading.

READING INTEREST INFORMATION BLANK

NAME:———

GRADE:———

I.
Directions: Below are listed various types of books that people like to read. Place a (1) by your favorite, a (2) by those you read occasionally, and a (0) by those you never read.

( ) Humorous

( ) Mystery

( ) Travel

( ) Pioneer and frontier

( ) War

( ) Aviation

( ) Dog

( ) Horses

( ) Jungle

( ) Discovery and exploration

( ) Detective

( ) Western

( ) Adventure (girls)

( ) Adventure (boys)

( ) Sea

( ) Indians

( ) Books on mechanics

( ) Sports

( ) Legends and myths

( ) Nature

( ) Biography

On the back of this blank form, the following additional information was requested:

II. List the names of any magazines that you enjoy reading.
III. What do you like to do in your leisure time?
   What are your hobbies?

CHART I—WHAT MAGAZINES DO YOU READ?

Step III

Harper's	*Travel*
Atlantic Monthly	*Étude*
Time	*National Geographic*
Review of Reviews	*Reader's Digest*
Scientific American	*Nature*

Step II

Colliers	* *Open Road for Boys*
Liberty	* *Young America*
Saturday Evening Post	* *American Boy*
Radio Guide	* *American Girl*
Pathfinder	* *Forest and Stream*
Life	* *School Musician*
Woman's Home Companion	* *St. Nicholas*
Good Housekeeping	* *Sports Afield*
Cosmopolitan	* *Fact Digest*
McCalls	* *Scholastic*
Popular Mechanics	* *Child Life*
Woman's World	* *Boys' Life*
Better Homes and Gardens	* *Popular Aviation*
Pictorial Review	*American*

* Magazines that junior high-school students will find especially interesting and entertaining.

Step I

True Confessions	*Fighting Wings of the Aces*
Flying Aces	*Screen Romances*
True Story	*Modern Screen*
Love and Romance	*Star Detective*
Daring Detective	*Western*
American Detective	*Ranch Romances*
Western Trails	*Texas Ranger*

Chart II—Can You Get To The Top?

Step IV

Stevenson, Robert L.	—*Treasure Island—Kidnapped*
Scott, Sir Walter	—*Ivanhoe*
Wister, Owen	—*The Virginian*
Masefield, John	—*Jim Davis*
Parkman, Francis	—*Oregon Trail*
Kelly, E. P.	—*Trumpeter of Krakow*
Verne, Jules	—*Michael Strogoff*
Verne, Jules	—*Twenty Thousand Leagues Under the Sea*
Blackmore, Richard	—*Lorna Doone*
Boyd, James	—*Drums*
Cooper, James F.	—*The Last of the Mohicans*
Hough, Emerson	—*The Covered Wagon*

Step III

French, W. F.	—*The Lance of Kanana*
Lewis, E. F.	—*Young Fu of the Upper Yangtze*
Grey, Katherine	—*Rolling Wheels*
London, Jack	—*Call of the Wild*
Custer, Elizabeth	—*Boots and Saddles*
White, Steward E.	—*Daniel Boone, Wilderness Scout*
Meigs, Cornelia	—*Swift Rivers*
Twain, Mark	—*Tom Sawyer*
Twain, Mark	—*The Prince and the Pauper*
Sawyer, Ruth	—*Roller Skates*
Kipling, Rudyard	—*Jungle Books*
Kipling, Rudyard	—*Captains Courageous*

Step II

Altsheler, Joseph	—*Horsemen of the Plains*
Adams, Mrs. J.	—*Mountains Are Free*
Adams, Katherine	—*Red Caps and Lilies*
James, Will	—*Smoky—Sun-Up*
Mukerji, Dhan G.	—*Hari, the Jungle Lad*
Grey, Zane	—*Riders of the Purple Sage*
Baker, Olaf	—*Shasta of the Wolves*
Pyle, Howard	—*Otto of the Silver Hand*
Salten, Felix	—*Bambi*
Meader, Stephen	—*Lumberjack*

Step I

Alger, Horatio	—Series
Appleton, Victor	—Series, *Tom Swift and His Air Glider*
Burroughs, E. R.	—Tarzan Books
Hope, L. L.	—Bobbsey Twin Series
	—Mystery Stories
Baum, Frank L.	—Wizard of Oz Stories
Edwards, Leo	—Jerry Todd Series
Carter, R. G.	—Boy Scout Series
Finley, Martin	—Elsie Dinsmore Series
Johnson, Mrs. O. F.	—Little Colonel Series

After all this information had been gathered, the pupils were divided into various groups according to their reading interests. For example, those who indicated an interest in aviation were divided into one group, those interested in war stories another group, etc. Each group was then asked to be responsible for making out a reading list made up of books available in the school libraries. This was done by consulting book lists and library card files, as well as from their own reading experiences. The following list was suggested by a group working on aviation (lists were typed and posted in the English room and in the library):

AVIATION

Committee Members: Harry Smith
John Demer
Ralph Peterson
Richard Barnes

BOOKS:

1.	Adams, Eustace	—*Fifteen Days in the Air*
2.	Allen, C. B. and Lyman, L. O.	—*The Wonder Book of the Air*
3.	Buck, Robert	—*Battling the Elements*
4.	Burtes	—*Haunted Airways*
5.	Byrd, Richard	—*Skyward*
6.	Charnley, M.	—*Boys' Life of the Wright Brothers*
7.	Crump, Irving	—*Boys' Book of Airmen*
8.	Dixon, Frank	—*Over the Ocean to Paris*
	Dixon, Frank	—*Flying Against Time*
	Dixon, Frank	—*Through the Air to Alaska*
9.	Fraser, Chelsea	—*Heroes of the Air*
	Fraser, Chelsea	—*Model Aircraft Builder*
10.	Gould, Bruce	—*Sky Larking*
11.	Green, Fitzhugh	—*Dick Byrd, Air Explorer*
12.	Guggenheim, Harry F.	—*Seven Skies*
13.	Halliburton, Richard	—*The Flying Carpet*
14.	Hawks, Frank	—*Once to Every Pilot*
15.	Lindbergh, Anne M.	—*North to the Orient*
16.	Lindbergh, Charles A.	—*We*
17.	Tomlinson, D. W.	—*Sky's the Limit*
18.	Verrill, A. Hyatt	—*Harper's Aircraft Yearbook*

MAGAZINES:

Popular Aviation

B. Book-review card file

The book-review card file such as the example was really used with the idea of a follow-up activity, but it also proved to be a decided help to pupils in the selection of books. Pupils took considerable pride in writing these cards for the files to be read and used by other English students. It proved to be a very effective means to teach the art of summary writing.

MUELLER, Peggy   11/15/37   *Rating:* excellent

Hess, Fjeril
Saddle and Bridle

    Brenda Coleman, a girl from New York, visits her grandfather at his ranch in Sugar Loaf, Butte, Wyoming. She and Patricia Hardcastle have several exciting adventures shooting mountain lions and black hats under which there are men's heads.

III. *Follow-up Activities*

  A. Book-review card files (See *B* under II for complete explanation.)

  B. Group discussions. Pupils were divided into groups according to the types of books they had been reading. During a regular class period these groups met to discuss the books each had read. Each group appointed a chairman to see that the discussion was carried on according to the standards for group discussions as set up by the class. Sometimes a certain group had the discussion in front of the entire class instead of having all the groups in session at one time. This proved to be an effective means of broadening reading interests as well as of stimulating more interest in group discussion technique.

  C. Informal class discussions

    1. Pupil reports. Strange as it may seem to some, pupils did enjoy getting up in front of the class to tell about a book they had read.

    2. Class discussions led by a chairman. The day before the discussion each pupil listed two books that he had read and could summarize briefly. The chairman made a list of these books, dividing them with the help of the teacher into such specific groups as dog stories, humorous stories, etc. The following day the chairman led the discussion calling on various pupils to report on specific books. (For a slower class the teacher may find it necessary to act as chairman for a few times in the beginning.)

PERMANENT READING RECORD

Date Finished Reading	Author (Last name first)	Book	No. of Pages	Assigned	Suggested	Choice	Rating of Book
9/20/37	Wert, James	Lone Scout of the Sky	297		✓		Excellent
9/29/37	Borup, George	Tenderfoot with Peary	298			✓	Good
10/ 6/37	Eastman, C. A.	My Indian Boyhood	275			✓	Good
10/12/37	Seton, Ernest	Biography of a Grizzly	278			✓	Excellent
10/19/37	Wheeler, Robert	Boy with the U. S. Census	265			✓	Excellent
11/28/37	Lindbergh, Charles	We	318			✓	Good
12/ 5/37	Looker, Earl	The White House Gang	244			✓	Good
12/10/37	Stevenson, Robert	Treasure Island	306			✓	Good
12/24/37	Keyhoe, Donald	Flying with Lindbergh	299			✓	Excellent
1/21/38	Ricker, Elizabeth	Seppala, Alaskan Dog Driver	295			✓	Good
2/10/38	Green, Fitzhugh	Dick Byrd, Air Explorer	282			✓	Good
2/18/38	Nicolay, Helen	American Wars	468			✓	Good
2/25/38	O'Brien, P. J.	Will Rogers	288			✓	Excellent
3/ 2/38	Collins, Frances	Sentinels Along Our Coast	272			✓	Good
3/11/38	Crump, Irving	Boys' Book of Forest Rangers	253			✓	Excellent
3/24/38	Parkman, Francis	The Oregon Trail	364			✓	Excellent
4/ 1/38	Nida, William	Man Conquers the World with Science	256			✓	Good
4/15/38	Ellsberg, Edward	On the Bottom	324			✓	Excellent
4/29/38	Crump, Irving	Boys' Book of Mounted Police	297			✓	Excellent
5/16/38	Fraser, Chelsea	Heroes of the Air	582			✓	Excellent
5/23/38	Tomlinson, Everett	Search for Andrew Field	313			✓	Good
6/ 1/38	Hall, James	High Adventure	240			✓	Excellent

REPRESENTATIVE PERMANENT READING RECORD FOR A SEVENTH-GRADE BOY FROM THE STANDPOINT OF THE AVERAGE NUMBER OF BOOKS READ AS WELL AS OF THE VARIETY OF TYPES READ.

D. Making posters and book covers to advertise books they had read.

E. Writing verses on books. Pupils especially interested in writing poetry took delight in advertising books by suitable verses they had written. These verses were often published in the school newspaper or were placed on the bulletin board in the library or in the English classroom. Examples:

   1. Tarkington, Booth, *Penrod and Sam*

      You'll squirm and you'll wriggle,
      In scrape and in jam;
      You'll live and love life
      With Penrod and Sam.

   2. Sidney, Margaret, *The Five Little Peppers*

      The Five Little Peppers and How They Grew
      Is a wonderful story all the way through.
      You'll laugh till you ache
      When you see how they bake
      Their cookies and cakes and gingerbread too.

F. Permanent reading record card. The school furnished the printed record cards upon which the pupil listed all the books he had read in or out of school. By doing this, teachers could discover the type of books read outside the English classroom. These records had nothing whatsoever to do with school grades; consequently pupils were not hesitant to include both the good and poor books they had been reading. The figure on page 74 shows a representative card.

G. Making a book ladder. Pupils found it interesting to take the books they had listed on their Permanent Reading Record Card and make an Adventure Ladder of their own. It proved to be an excellent means in the improvement of literary tastes.

H. Making annotated book lists. The English work in this system was divided into units based upon science, history, travel, radio, etc.; after a unit had been completed, pupils consulted the card files for the books read pertaining to that unit. These were mimeographed, making attractive book lists for use in the library and in the classroom.

IV. *Guidance in the Program*

A. By the teacher
   1. Individual conferences during free reading periods. Good use was made of each pupil's Permanent Reading Record

Card and his Reading Interest Information Blank in the matter of guidance. One day was set aside each week for free reading. During this period individual conferences were held to suggest new books to read, etc.

2. Making suggested lists of books for those having special difficulties. For those pupils who apparently had no interest whatsoever in reading, special lists of books were made out after consulting their information cards and after personal conferences to find out what their hobbies were. Books were brought into the room on free reading days for them to read, hoping that they might possibly find one to their liking. Annotated lists were supplied to these youngsters as their outside interests were discovered.

B. By the librarian
 1. Individual conferences
 2. Posting reading lists that were made in the English classroom

V

READING AND OUT-OF-SCHOOL SOURCES

In adjusting the English curriculum to a changing world and to a changing school population, teachers all over the country are finding it necessary and worth-while to use newspapers, magazines, photoplays and other visual aids, and public libraries. The units which follow are indicative of the movement to bring out-of-school and in-school English together so that pupils may experience it as a living language with a glorious past.

NEWSPAPERS AND MAGAZINES

Teachers all over the country are discovering the necessity of training boys and girls to read, with discrimination, periodical literature. Several reports are presented to show how reading periodicals can be handled as experience in the English classroom.

The following rather complete outline of student activities in the study of the newspaper is offered by Helen Rand Miller. Most of these questions if asked engagingly would arouse student interest; the resulting explorations and discussions would certainly lead to thorough knowledge of the newspaper and, if democratically conducted, should produce the attitude of interest tempered by skepticism which we ourselves take toward the dailies.

Adventure on the News-stands [1]

I. Discovery

A. *A Hastily Sketched Field Map*

1. What's in a newspaper?

2. Can the variety of things in a newspaper be grouped into a few classifications? How many different ways may we classify them?

3. In what proportion does each classification appear in a single issue?

[1] Reported by Helen Rand Miller, formerly of Evanston, Ill., now at Mills College, Cal., as an outline for a unit or a course in reading newspapers.

4. From this survey, can we determine the function of the newspaper? Let's not hurry the answer, but let us ask the question early and often.

B. *The Province of News Without Boundaries*

1. What is a news story? What kind of subjects are used for news stories?

2. Are news stories different from short stories, essays, poetry, plays? Why, or why not?

3. Where do newspapers find news? Why does one issue of a paper describe events around the corner from the school, in the near-by town, in the state capitol, in Utah and in North Carolina, in Spain and in New Zealand, in Washington and in Libya, in Finland and in Guatemala?

4. What general classifications of news stories can you discover? (Crime, government affairs, disasters, etc.) What percentage of each in inches, columns, or pages appears in different papers of the same day, or in different issues of the same paper?

5. Can we now hazard a tentative definition of news?

C. *Into the Land of Controversy*

1. How many of the class have ever read editorials in daily papers? In the school paper? Why are editorials popular, or are they popular? Why?

2. About what kind of subjects are editorials written? Are they all concerned with immediate happenings? Can you trace the origin of all the editorials in one issue of a newspaper?

3. Does the newspaper have a platform of stated policies in which it believes and for which it campaigns? During a week's time, how many editorials are expressions of this platform?

4. Why, or how, is an editorial different from a news story? Are the editorials more, equally, or less important than the news stories?

D. *The Great Market-place*

1. How many pages of the newspaper are given over to display ads? How many have classified ads? What proportion of a newspaper issue is given over to advertising? Why are classified ads grouped in harder-to-read, solid-type pages, whereas display ads are usually arranged so that they adjoin news matter?

2. Do you find any general types or kinds of display ads? (Retail stores, retail items advertised by manufacturers, intangibles like insurance, travel, recreation, good will, etc.) Why would a local dealer spend money to advertise the same commodity that the manufacturer advertises?

3. How many classifications of ads appear in the classified ad section? Are there any individual ads that offer suggestions for short stories or movie plots? Maybe you can find three 3-line ads that are worded clearly and fairly completely. Why not write a few classified ads?

4. Watch a particular classification for a week or two and see whether any particular ads are repeated regularly during that period. What conclusions might be drawn from this repetition?

5. From your local newspaper office, or from *Standard Rate & Data* at the library, obtain the newspaper's display and classified ad rates. Do you wish, as a class project, to compute the newspaper's income from advertising in a single issue?

6. Would newspapers be better or worse without advertising? Why?

E. *Industry and Culture*

1. Do you read the movie reviews in your daily paper? How about beauty hints, aviation or automobile news, book reviews, the Broadway columnist, advice on etiquette, comic strips, womens' club activities, the society pages? These are departments or features. Are they written like news stories or editorials? Are they impartial statements of fact or are they expressions of the writers' personal beliefs?

2. In addition to those mentioned, what departments and regular features do you find in your daily paper?

3. How much space is devoted to financial and market developments? Are these departments worthy of that space? Is there any relation or connection between the financial or market developments and some of the news stories appearing on the same day or on successive days?

4. Do you want to see if you can find features which appeal to the various members of a family that includes the following persons: a boy eight years old, a girl sixteen, a boy eighteen, their mother, who is active in P. T. A. and Ladies' Aid Work; and their father, who is an executive of a wholesale grocery company.

5. Would you consider the sports pages as a department or are they straight news pages? Why?

F. *Mirrors of Life*

1. Would you rather read a news story of an exciting event or look at a picture of it? Do you know if newspapers use more pictures now than they did ten, twenty, or thirty years ago? The library, or the newspaper office may have a file of the local paper's back issues which can be compared with today's issues.

2. Are some pictures used because of inherent interest or beauty or novelty, or must all pictures have a definite relation to a news event?

3. Why would newspapers use pictures similar to these:

   a. A movie star lying in a beach chair

   b. A little girl trying to put her bonnet on a puppy

   c. Sunset at Lake Lucerne

   d. A football huddle photographed from directly above

4. Where does a newspaper get its pictures? From your local newspaper office or from one of the books on journalism in the library, get information about national picture services, how they operate, how they are supported, how they sell and deliver pictures. Be sure to find out about pictures sent by telephone and radio.

5. Do pictures ever emphasize details of a news event that are relatively unimportant? If possible, find examples in the daily papers. Should newspapers follow this practice? Why, or why not?

6. Are cartoons more or less effective than pictures in attracting and holding attention? Why do many papers give space on the first page to a cartoon? Are cartoons always impartial, or may they be influenced by the feelings of the cartoonist or by the policy of the newspaper publisher?

7. Besides the difference in method of production, is there any difference between a cartoon and a picture? Should you have the same attitude in looking at both? Why, or why not?

II. Exploration

A. *Landmarks and Typography*

1. What is the most important story on the front page of today's paper? In which column does it appear? What is the second most important story? Which column does it occupy? During a week's time, are the most important stories given the same relative position on the first page?

2. Why is the third page considered to be the "second first page"? Why are right-hand pages considered better location for stories or for ads than left-hand pages? Have you ever noticed that display ads, as a rule, are placed along the outer edges of a page? Is this placement justified?

3. Why do many metropolitan newspapers have two or three sections, with subsidiary first pages, of fourteen or sixteen pages each, instead of one section of twenty-eight or thirty-two or forty-eight pages?

4. The head-line which goes clear across the top of the page is called a six- or seven- or eight-column line. Why should a newspaper gives this valuable space to one story when it might place the head-lines of several stories in the same space?

5. Why do different papers in the city on the same day emphasize different stories with eight-column lines? All papers have access to legitimate news material. Why should one paper "play up" one story and another paper a different story? Both papers probably print both stories. Is not the relative importance of both stories the same?

6. Do the head-lines in today's papers accurately summarize the stories they head? Does any head-line impress you as being excellently informative despite its terseness? Why not write head-lines from two or three news stories and compare them with those actually used?

7. Have you ever noticed that a newspaper may have only a comparatively few different styles of head-lines? For instance, one with an inverted pyramid over a three-line diagonal, one of four diagonal lines, one of three lines set squarely in the column, a two-column head-line of two or three diagonal lines, etc. Different sizes, and sometimes different kinds, of type are used to achieve variety in head-lines. You might try to get a complete set of head-line styles used by one newspaper.

8. Most newspapers are made up according to a plan or layout that is artistically pleasing. Very often, a page will be meticulously balanced, with the same sizes of head-lines in the same relative positions on each side of the page. Cuts—pictures—are also placed to balance each other. Look at your daily paper with this idea in mind, and see whether or not the various pages are symmetrical.

B. *An Easy Language*

1. Read a number of news stories and see if you can determine when the "lead" ends and the body of the story begins. It is interesting to follow one story through several editions of a paper to see how more important stories may crowd it out of a favorable position, or cause it to be cut down, or "killed"—eliminated. When a story is reduced, is it entirely rewritten, or are the final paragraphs pruned from the story?

2. Do you have any difficulty in reading and understanding news stories? Do they use strange words or familiar words? Involved sentences and elaborate constructions, or simple, easily grasped constructions? Are they trite and ordinary, or do they have some in-

dividuality and sparkle? Which kind of writing prevails—stiff, dull, and insipid, or original, smooth-flowing, and interesting?

3. Can you rewrite a news story or two in approximately the same number of words and tell everything as well as the news story does?

4. Do the stories and editorials in your newspaper seem to be deliberately written for people of meager intelligence? Why do some newspapers use capitals to emphasize words or thoughts, particularly in editorials? Do you approve of this practice or not? Why, or why not?

C. *A Well-marked Trail*

1. In order to discover how completely a newspaper covers an important event, trace the course of one story through several days' issues or as long as the story continues to appear. Sometimes the easiest way to do this is to begin when the story is at its height, when the first and second pages are used to present details concerning the event. You can then go back several days and find the first details of the event and bring the story up to date, and then continue with the story as long as it lasts.

2. Did the first story indicate the importance of the future developments? Or did the story break suddenly, with subsequent developments of an explanatory and amplifying nature? If the former, did the editor of the paper acknowledge the potentialities of the story by featuring it prominently? Or did he consider it a routine story and give it a secondary position?

3. If the story is of national importance, were the first news dispatches sent by one of the news associations or by a correspondent of the newspaper? If the latter, when did the news associations also send dispatches to the paper? In this connection, we may want to see how many stories in the paper are written and transmitted by the Associated Press, United Press, International News Service, or North American Newspaper Alliance? Are there any other news services used by your papers?

4. How soon after the event did pictures of it appear in the local paper? Were they taken by the paper's photographers or by one of the photo services? Which one? Were they sent by auto, plane, telephone, or radio? For how many days did the paper publish pictures of the event? Did it repeat the same picture? Do all the papers in your town use the same pictures of the event?

5. Has your paper published any editorials or cartoons or letters from readers which were a direct outgrowth of the news event? Does such publication indicate the responsibility of reporters and editors to present complete and impartial news stories?

D. *Interesting Inhabitants*

1. Merely from acquaintance with newspapers, can you classify generally the kinds of workers a newspaper employs? There are a few general classifications which will take in every one that works on even the largest newspaper.

2. Compare the classifications thus selected with those actually used by your local newspaper or by a newspaper in a large town near-by. A committee of the class might visit the newspaper plant and get an accurate list of the kinds of workers it uses. If possible, the committee may be interested in having an interview with some executive of the newspaper.

3. Is the newspaper one of a "chain" like the Hearst or the Scripps-Howard newspapers, or is it independent? With what national news services and photo agencies is it affiliated? How many newspapers in one town may be affiliated with the Associated Press, or the United Press, or any other association?

4. From newspaper executives or from books on journalism or on vocational guidance, find out the training and experience required for the different jobs in a newspaper plant. If you are planning to be a newspaper reporter, or a copy reader, or a pressman, or a circulation manager, or a compositor, what kind of school training should you have?

III. OBSERVATIONS

A. *Choosing a Guide*

1. Why should there be more than one morning newspaper and one evening newspaper in any city? Don't they all use the same news? Aren't they printed and delivered at approximately the same time? Should a newspaper deliberately cater to a particular group of readers, or should it present material which will appeal to every one? Why do newspapers have editorial policies, political leanings, different ways of presenting the same news matter? Is a newspaper a business enterprise, run for profit, or is it a welfare agency which places service to readers above financial gain? Should newspapers have a code of ethics? Do they have one?

2. Do all newspapers present the same news in exactly the same way? As an example, compare the Chicago *Tribune* with the Chicago *Daily Times* in their presentations of news stories concerning the Roosevelt administration. Or compare papers in different sections of the country, for example, the Kansas City *Star*, the Denver *Post*, the St. Louis *Globe-Democrat*, the Philadelphia *Public Ledger*, the *Christian Science Monitor*, the Seattle *Post-Intelligencer*. Is the same

news story presented in the same way by these papers? If people were to read only one newspaper regularly, would they get correct and complete information about all news events? If not, what would the result be?

B. *A Strange and Subtle Influence*

1. Read carefully for several days the financial news stories, the Broadway "column," and the Washington correspondent's dispatches in your daily paper. Do these features contain unbiased, scrupulously complete information? What about the society columns, book reviews, automobile news? Does the fact that most features of this kind are written with a "by-line" make any difference?

2. Do you like the daily Hollywood news and gossip printed in most large papers? Can you accept it as being fact, or do you think that it is partly rumor or partly guessing? Does it ever contain any adverse comment on pictures or movie stars? If not, do you think it is correct in eliminating unfavorable comment?

3. Have you ever done any photography work? Do you know whether or not it is possible to alter negatives so that the printed pictures may be better or worse than the subject photographed? Should newspapers influence opinion in news pictures by retouching negatives? We are not referring here to pictures published for their artistic interest or value, but to strictly news photos. Can you find any pictures so retouched? Many newspapers do not permit such distortion of truth, but some do.

C. *Publicity and Propaganda*

1. *Propaganda* is defined as "An institution or scheme for propagating a doctrine, etc., or the principles thus advanced." In today's issue of your newspaper, can you find any propaganda in the news columns? How many different stories? What are their subjects? Should a newspaper publish propaganda? Why, or why not?

2. Is publicity the same thing as propaganda? What definition do you find in the dictionary for publicity? Would any of the stories that you classified as propaganda be more correctly classified as publicity? Where does the publicity come from? Are there any general types of organizations or individuals who seem to desire publicity? Does your school secure publicity for its student activities? How?

3. Can you find any stories in the news columns which refer favorably to business or commercial organizations? Do these same organizations advertise in the paper? Should a newspaper publish publicity about its advertisers? Why, or why not?

4. It has been said that nearly everything published is propaganda

—that every one is trying to convert other people to his beliefs, or to urge them to pursue a course of action he favors: to buy his products, to vote the way he prefers, to advocate a closed season to protect wild life, to oppose his enemies or rivals, to attend a charity benefit, a play, a ball game or a dance, to be horrified at the actions of a governmental body, or to be overjoyed at the same actions of the same governmental body, and so on. What do you think of this idea? Is it true, is it untrue, is it partly true but only partly true?

D. *Struggle for Power*

1. You have probably seen advertisements for liability insurance or for automobile tires that featured pictures of horrible accidents. Perhaps you have read stories about little puppies that were lost in a bewildering city. Unscrupulous salesmen, particularly before the depression, used to steal money from people by selling them worthless stock in gold mines or in new inventions or in other things. They made the sales because they promised enormous profits almost immediately. During the World War, newspapers and magazines published pictures and stories which supposedly depicted how cruelly and inhumanly the enemy treated prisoners and non-combatants. In some instances, the same pictures were used by the governments whose soldiers opposed each other in the trenches. When published in France or the United States, the pictures would show the German atrocities. When published in Germany, the same pictures would show conditions behind the allied lines. All of these items were calculated to appeal to the emotions rather than to good judgment and intellect. Sometimes newspapers do the same thing. They try to influence us by appealing to one or more of the emotions—hate, love, greed, fear, etc. Should news stories make such an appeal, or should they endeavor to give us a full, interesting account of an event and let us judge whether the material presented is sound, ethical, and reasonable?

2. Do you know of any paper that bases many of its stories or editorials upon the emotions of its readers? Can you find half a dozen stories so directed in the issue of any paper? How do you know that its appeal is to the emotions rather than to the intellect? Can you pick out the factors that show this attitude? Try to rewrite one of these stories, using the same basic facts, but eliminating the emotional appeal.

IV. Last-minute Impressions

1. A newspaper is a complex organism, both in its physical, mechanical set-up and in its functions, purposes, and accomplishments.

2. A newspaper requires skill of a high type from a variety of workers.

3. News writing is terse, vivid, accurate. Much good writing is found in newspapers. There is also poor writing and there are undesirable attitudes on the part of writers and editors in selecting and arranging news material.

4. More careful attention to the editorials and to the editorial policy of a newspaper will help to evaluate the paper's news columns.

5. The modern newspaper could not survive without advertising, but on the whole, advertising is quite well kept out of news and editorial matter.

6. In addition to providing news, the newspaper offers a variety of special features and departments appealing to the interests and avocations of nearly every member of the family.

7. Pictures are powerful influences in the newspaper. They should, however, be viewed with detachment and appraisal, just as news matter should be.

8. Newspaper make-up is carefully arranged to present pleasing, harmonious, but attention-getting pages.

9. Head-lines have a great deal of influence in appealing to readers of a newspaper. They require skill and a little inspiration on the part of the writer.

10. A newspaper has great resources for gathering and distributing news, in fact one of the most highly geared and speedy organizations in modern industry.

11. Each newspaper has its own viewpoint, from which it considers everything that it prints. This viewpoint must be kept in mind when reading any paper.

12. Propaganda does not appear much in newspapers, unless one considers everything printed in it as propaganda. Publicity, on the other hand, appears to a considerable extent. The source of the story one reads should be considered in evaluating its importance.

13. Every story should be approached with a sensible attitude of determining whether it appeals to the better judgment of the reader or to his emotions only.

At the Evander Childs High School, New York City, Joseph J. Sexton directed the study of the newspaper as a record of human success and failure. The oral and written discussions growing out of alert reading revealed growth in critical thinking and power of expression.

Bringing Your Favorite Newspaper to Class [2]

The assignment for the first lesson had been: "Bring your favorite newspaper to class. Be prepared to tell why you enjoy it, and be ready to defend it against attack." Most of the class brought in tabloid newspapers. An honest statement of preference and reasons for the preference was made by each girl. The tabloid addicts preferred these papers because of features like beauty hints, movie news, comic strips, and because of the simple style of the news articles. They admitted that they had never tried reading another paper, except, in some cases the New York *Times,* which used "big words." Pupils who had brought in some of the better types of newspapers rose to the defense of their choice, and showed the "tabloidophiles" that every feature they mentioned appeared in evening newspapers like the New York *Sun,* the New York *World-Telegram* and the New York *Post.* They also showed, by the simple and forceful method of counting news columns, that the non-tabloid papers had more news; they showed that the advertisements were better, more reliable, more attractive. The class agreed to select one paper, the *World-Telegram,* for special study, to see if they couldn't find as many attractive features in it, and to find out whether the news columns and editorials weren't "easier" than the *Times.*

On the second day, the class, which had already been divided into five groups for other English work, received group assignments. One group (the superior group) was responsible for the editorial section, another for the front-page news articles, another for the theater and movie section, another for the woman's page, another for the columnists. Each group was given one copy of the newspaper from which to plan assignments. The chairman of each group divided the group assignments into seven parts; that is, each girl had a different columnist. The assignments were made for the following day's paper. The single copy given to each girl was used merely as a sample, and as an instrument to familiarize each pupil with the layout, etc. Every girl handled her group's copy, looked through it, *experienced* it. Each girl knew where she would have to look for her particular section in the next day's newspaper.

On the third day, the class met in groups. Each girl reported on the content of her section. She commented upon its reading difficulty, its interest. The group chose a representative to make a report on its section of the paper to the class at the next lesson.

[2] Reported by Miriam Rosenthal, Walton High School, New York City.

On the fourth day, a pupil from each group told the rest of the class about her section of the paper. She used clippings, pictures, etc. Discussion and questions followed. The class was then assigned to write a letter to the editor criticizing a particular feature, disagreeing or agreeing with a particular article, expressing each one's opinion of the paper as a whole from the point of view of a third-term high-school girl. The class arrived at standards for judging the letters, a possible outline, and a model form.

On the fifth day, letters were read and criticized in groups. The best letter in each group was read to the class, and the best one in the entire class was chosen. This best letter was sent to the editor.

This experience, carried on in three classes, yielded the following results. The letters written by the girls showed in many cases genuine enthusiasm. Many pupils volunteered the information that they had started reading regularly the newspaper studied in class. The girl in each class who wrote the winning letter received an answer from the *World-Telegram* which she read to the class. In the course of an examination of the newspaper, the pupils learned the difference between an editorial, a column, a news article, a feature, etc., in a genuinely functional way. All of the work in class was done with newspapers at hand. The girls had a chance to write a business letter for a real purpose. They were forced to be critical of their tastes. They were given another opportunity to participate in group discussion. They were introduced to some pressing current problems (many said that they had had interesting discussions with their fathers, while preparing assignments). They saw that editorials could not be understood if one were not familiar with the news itself, and they realized, as a corollary, that participation in adult conversation must be restricted in the same way for the same reason. The most gratifying result was the realization on the part of many that papers, other than tabloids, were readable, had "jokes," beauty columns, Hollywood news, and many pictures, and that news articles weren't all as "hard" as the *Times*. The inverted snobbery of "low-brows" had been somewhat dissipated.

The newspaper unit conducted by Stella Eliashaw with seniors in Evander Childs High School, also in the metropolis of New York, is reported only in outline, but the activities seem vital and the problems they illustrate seems important. The setting up of these problems by class discussion must be taken for granted.

THE NEWSPAPER AS A TOOL IN THE STUDY OF SOCIAL PROBLEMS [3]

Objectives

1. To make newspaper reading a regular vital process
2. To learn to evaluate a newspaper and the items within it

Activities

1. Discussing the importance of social problems in the life of the individual
2. Practising in class reading head-lines from the morning paper
   Fit each one into the life of the individuals in the class; for example, "City Relief Outlay of Two Years High Despite Reduction in the Rolls" (N.Y. *Times*)
   Implications: Increased cost of living
   Rent increase
   Meat strike
3. Discussing the coördination of events; necessity of a varied approach to a particular topic
4. Collecting news clippings over a period of several days. Recognize that material may be pertinent even though it is not on pupil's topic as he himself states it; for example:
   Problem—crime-prevention material may be found under *education, parks and playgrounds, housing, child labor*
5. Learning how to handle this material efficiently
6. Arranging material as a file; to each item, attach a statement as follows:
   a. Central thought
   b. Implications: e.g., Maine farmers, by class vote, rejected the federal government's plan to reduce the potato crop.
   (1) The government is trying to keep up farm prices by controlling production.
   (2) There is opposition to this in Maine.
   (3) Maine is not so solidly anti-New Deal in this as she has been in other matters.
7. Understanding some of the dangers of newspaper reading
8. Intensive reading of Odegaard's essay, *The Fourth Estate*
   Theme: The press is primarily a profit-making enterprise and cannot be relied on to present the truth.
   Development: *a.* Anti-labor policies
   b. Lack of decisive stand on controversial issues

[3] Reported by Stella Eliashaw, Evander Childs High School, New York City.

c. Sensationalism
d. Inaccuracy—head-lines
e. Increase in news and feature syndicates
f. Prevalence of propaganda

Through a discussion of these charges and of ways to counteract them, the reader's responsibility for critical reading is established.

9. Recognizing and evaluating propaganda
Definition: Refer to that given by Institute for Propaganda Analysis: (N.Y. *Times,* 10/9/37)
Forms: Analysis of clippings brought in by students
Dangers: Appeal to emotion
            Hidden nature
Distinction between democratic and undemocratic propaganda
—use in non-controversial matters (e.g., slum clearance; elimination of disease)

Appraisal

Some values of this unit will become evident when the teacher reads the pupils' essays handed in at the end of six weeks.

A READING COURSE IN MAGAZINES AND NEWSPAPERS [4]

I. *Objectives*

A recent survey of adult reading shows that 75 per cent of people beyond school age read magazines regularly, while only 30 per cent read books regularly. Probably 80 per cent to 85 per cent read newspapers regularly. Critical judgment and taste in such reading should be developed to the extent that:

A. There is contempt for the pulp magazine and tabloid newspaper.
B. There is distinction made between the good material and the poor material in mediocre magazines and newspapers.
C. There is some appreciation and enjoyment of the best magazines and newspapers.

II. *Scope of the Course*

A. Background
    1. Historical development of publications
    2. Country-wide survey of periodicals
    3. Classification according to types and standards
    4. Choice of representative examples for continual study

[4] Reported by Eula Baer, Ardmore, Pa.

B. The newspaper and news magazine as a basis for understanding the political, social, and scientific changes in the contemporary world; emphasis on the major news articles, the editorials, and the columns

C. The monthly magazine as a source of the best current lirerture, particularly the short story; the poem; the essay; the critical review of books, motion pictures, plays, radio programs

D. Special features in periodicals as a basis for fostering an intelligent understanding of art, advertising, hobbies or use of leisure time

III. *Possible Projects*

A. Newspapers
   1. Follow-up of a news story through several weeks; an election, a trial, a political controversy, a war. Guidance in tolerance and sane reasoning
   2. Information collecting for a current-affairs test

B. Magazines
   1. An individual unit in which each pupil becomes an authority on one magazine by analysis over a period of several months, or an authority on one subject (a hobby, perhaps) by following it through many magazines
   2. Class editing of a magazine anthology of the best magazine literature of the year

The following eight-day study of newspapers by students catches interest by class examination of the current issue of a local paper and brings out clearly the arrangement of newspaper departments and puts students upon guard for editorial bias. The time limit based upon actual classroom contact with a group of pupils may serve as a suggestive guide to teachers launching a newspaper unit for the first time.

READING THE NEWSPAPER [5]

Aim. To develop the habit of intelligent reading of the newspaper.

Activities. (The Roman numerals indicate the activities experienced in one class period.)

I. Used New York *Times* which pupils had ordered the week before delivered to school

[5] Reported by Miriam B. Booth, Board of Education, Erie, Pa.

A. A brief review of the make-up of the paper, resulting in conclusions by the class of emphasis on news stories, as follows:

Front page

a. Streamer head-line

b. Two- or three-column head-lines in upper right

c. Two- or three-column head in upper left

d. Center head of one or more columns

e. Heads to left and right of center

f. Heads on stories on lower half of page

g. Other methods of indicating importance: pictures, box; emphasis decreased as stories appear from front to back of paper, with the following exceptions: (1) first page of second news section, (2) classification according to departments

B. Rest of paper

The class is divided into sections, and using rulers, measures the column inches devoted to:

1. News—foreign, domestic

2. Features—Regular
   a. Columns
   b. Comics

3. Pictures

4. Advertising
   a. Classified
   b. General

5. Miscellaneous
   a. Stock quotations
   b. Weather reports, etc.

6. Editorial

The resulting totals are used with the total number of column inches in that edition to determine the percentage devoted to each of the divisions of material.

Assignment: The class, divided into sections, applied the same procedure to about eight to ten typical newspapers. The results in per cents were brought to class.

II. Discussed the use of space

A. Discussed assigned work, placing results on blackboard; class drew conclusions about amount of space devoted to each of the following and about what seemed to be the policy of the paper.

1. News (foreign—domestic)

2. Pictures
3. Comics
4. Advertising
5. Features

B. Gave the following special assignments (Each pupil selected one and had it ready in less than a week.)

1. Make a comparison of several metropolitan newspapers for the same day, by bringing to class the front pages, and indicating emphasis on types of news.

2. Show the type of reader a store expects to reach, by collecting and comparing advertisements of different merchandise in different newspapers for the same day. (As many as three types may be found.)

3. Make a collection of famous columns (national affairs, sports, humorous, etc.).

4. Make a collection, for comparison, of editorial pages.

5. Show how the same story is treated in several different papers by clipping and mounting the stories.

6. These materials, if sufficiently significant, may substitute for one of the above; otherwise, they are voluntary contributions.

  a. Foreign papers
  b. Small town papers
  c. Old papers (Lincoln's assassination, etc.)
  d. Papers of varying sizes (These are passed around in class or displayed as they are brought in.)

III. Discussed in class the business organizations of the paper

A. Contents
  News gathering
  Photography
  Rewriting
  Editing
  Make-up

B. Business
  Circulation
  Advertising
  Printing

C. Study of editorial page to discover
  Policies of paper
  Propaganda
  The typical editorial
  People's contributions

IV. Discussed the two papers
   A. Compared morning and afternoon issues of the New York *Sun*, previously ordered, for
   Make-up
   News emphasis
   Advertising
   B. Discussion of "Anybody's business becomes news if it is interesting."

V. Studied the development of the newspaper
   A. Brief history of the newspaper—special report previously assigned to reliable student—taken from Campbell and Thomas
   B. Discussion of methods of news gathering: reporters, photographers, foreign correspondents, city exchange
   United Press
   Associated Press
   Trans Radio
   Times news and picture service

VI. Made a general survey of use of newspapers
   A. Value of reading newspapers
   B. Possible influences
   C. Importance to students

VII. Took essay-question quiz on "Our attitudes and opinions are definitely influenced by the newspaper. Our stand on matters political, economical, and social may be the result largely of what we read."
   Discuss the foregoing statement referring specifically to two or more papers to prove this point. Be certain your answer shows a definite knowledge of newspaper content, make-up, and editorial policy.

VIII. Made trip to see how local newspaper is manufactured

The study of magazines follows the same principle as does that of the newspaper—analysis of make-up and comparison of the policies of different journals. Most experience-centered courses of the present day offer units in magazine reading. The following reports will prove suggestive either as points of comparison with what a teacher has already attempted or as a guide to what he may wish to try.

READING MAGAZINES [6]

With the flooding of the market with hundreds of magazines, good and bad, our eighth-grade literature class decided to attempt to evaluate a number of the most prominent ones and, if possible, come to some conclusions as to their readers and material. Consequently after a preliminary discussion on the reasons for the magazine's popularity, such as the busy American's demand for short, interesting story or factual material, the class went to work on the procedure we were going to use and decided what magazines we should include in our investigation.

Twenty-four titles of magazines of varied types were listed. Tactful and sincere discussion of the relative values of ethically and artistically acceptable magazines eliminated the offensive type of magazine from consideration.

The class was divided into six groups with four or five people in each group. Each group had a chairman who was responsible for directing a division of work among the members. When the magazines were apportioned to each group, opportunity was given for that group to investigate publications that were somewhat in line with its interests. For example, some of the boys did little reading of any sort. They were given the picture, outdoors, or sports magazines to report on. However, though it was expedient to work along the line of the children's interests, it was also possible to acquaint each pupil with unfamiliar magazines. Every group, therefore, read some new and some familiar magazines.

Our greatest difficulty came when we endeavored to set a standard of evaluation for such a different group of magazines. After discussion it was decided that each magazine was to be examined for these points:

1. *Cover*—its distinguishing marks, how made attractive
2. *General make-up*—number of pages, circulation, price, when published, where, by whom
3. *Departments*—articles, story, political, humor, editorial, current affairs, movie, foreign
4. *Type of illustration*—color, cartoon, photograph
5. *Arrangement of advertising*—all in one place, with story material, none (There was much interest in the cost of advertising.)
6. *To whom it is the most appealing*—to children, men, women, family

Though many of the above items are not essential, they lent interest to the discussion and the class displayed so much interest in

[6] Reported by Roland A. Gleisner, Board of Education, Ironwood, Mich.

such facts as advertising, how old the magazine was in point of years, changes in the size of the magazine to make easier handling, that they were included as given. Obviously, the consideration of what readers were appealed to yielded the most interesting findings.

Each group was given four magazines, and under the guidance of its chairman each member was to secure a copy of his assigned publication, investigate carefully all points given in our standard of evaluation, write out and organize effectively his report, and be prepared to give it orally when all groups were ready. Each individual was cautioned not to form his opinions too quickly, not to be dogmatic, but to try to give evidence for his statement at all times. This feature of the procedure necessitated a thorough examination of the magazine. In fact, some of the students looked through several issues in order to get a composite picture of the policies and general qualities of the publication.

Problems that arose were discussed at the beginning of each class period; otherwise, the class time was chiefly a laboratory period.

As each individual completed his written report he was allowed to practice orally outside of the classroom, in order to improve the effectiveness of the organization and to save time for the class. A stumbling, halting report would be of little value to a listening class.

After each group report was completed, a short period was used for a question and answer discussion, the committee being responsible for the answers to any questions brought up by the rest of the class. It was in these discussions that many interesting facts were brought out. In view of the fact that this unit was carried on during the time that a picture magazine made its sensational debut, the question arose as to the reasons for the instantaneous response of the public to picture magazines. It was obvious to the class that the old saying, "A picture is worth ten thousand words," was true, especially if such pictures were arranged so as to tell a continuous story. One student seemed to think that with picture magazines the rushing American could now save more time than ever!

After each group had given its report, a summary discussion was held to choose from the group of magazines examined the following:

1. The best news magazine
2. The best magazine for young people
3. The best factual magazine, not a news magazine
4. The best nature or sports magazine
5. The best all around magazine (family)
6. The best choice for subscription if a family could spend annually ten dollars, five, three, one

Naturally there was a sharp and lively division of opinion between the boys and girls when we came to choose on such a basis.

In conclusion, it is worth noting that having a large number of magazines in the homeroom stimulates pupils to read magazines pertinent to their interests. The number of times students have quoted from worth-while publications shows that the pupils had learned how to choose and to read magazines.

Access to magazines is important. In homes where the parents regularly subscribe to good magazines, the children show a very commendable knowledge of what is in them. Sometimes they hear them discussed and read them because their curiosity is aroused.

It is possible to lead children into reading books by the way of the magazine. If their interest lies in the detective story show them the difference between the poor, cheap mystery story and a good one. Finding a better detective story is more potent than merely criticizing the poor one which the pupil has read with enjoyment.

Public schools in Newark, New Jersey; Erie, Pennsylvania; New York, New York; and Baltimore, Maryland, and the parochial schools in Minnesota report vital units in reading magazines. In all accounts, these few points are common:

1. Pupils have a genuine purpose in reading.
2. A wide variety of well-selected magazines is used.
3. Standards of appraisal are developed inductively with the class.
4. Opportunities are afforded for reading magazines both inside and outside of the English classroom.
5. After the unit training pupils in discriminating selection and reading of magazines, many other units give occasion for boys and girls to apply their skills in reading periodicals for recreation and for information.

PHOTOPLAYS AND OTHER VISUAL AIDS

Out-of-school sources such as newspapers, libraries, museums, radio programs, and photoplays can stimulate boys and girls to read. Lambert Greenawalt tells briefly how photoplays of the sea sent his pupils to books and how appreciative reading of these stories of the sea deepened the experiences gained from the motion pictures. Here is his account:

PHOTOPLAYS AND BOOKS [7]

Mutiny on the Bounty was scheduled at a local theater. A com-

[7] Reported by Lambert Greenawalt, William Penn High School, York, Pa.

mittee of three was appointed to attend the show and to report to the class on the story, the acting, and the photography. A class period was devoted to the reports and a discussion during which was mentioned the fact that the authors of the book from which the photoplay had been adapted had written other books. Interest in these books was high, and the teacher had only to recommend *Pitcairn Island* and *Men Against the Sea*.

A check-up a week later showed that 70 per cent of the class had read or were reading one of the three books.

Several days later the teacher opened a discussion on sea stories. The class asked for a reading list. Each pupil was told to go to the library and find the names of books on that theme. In class the teacher helped to weed out undesirable books, giving in each case his reason for doing so. The list was then run off on the mimeograph and each pupil was given a copy for his own use.

The photoplays, *The Plainsman, Anna Karenina,* and *A Midsummer Night's Dream,* achieved the same results. It must be noted, however, that *The Plainsman* was used in an average tenth-grade class, whereas *Anna Karenina* was introduced to a twelfth-grade class of superior ability. In the latter case, the class was studying a unit of world literature. *A Midsummer Night's Dream* was found valuable to all grades as a stimulus for the reading of Shakespearean plays.

Though these projects were not checked against a control group, for obvious difficult reasons, it is possible to derive certain specific conclusions from them. A few of the conclusions are as follows:

1. Under guidance that is more subtle than direct, high-school boys and girls of average ability can set up criteria of a high order for the books they read.

2. Students thus led become their own best leaders, because of the absolute freedom of choice permitted them. This point would seem to contradict in no uncertain terms some of the tenets of formal education.

3. Life truths, in so far as adolescents have learned them, are held up as being basic qualities in literature.

4. A project conceived by the class, out of class needs, becomes absolutely vital to the students, as over against the artificial "assignments" of traditional teaching.

5. Life experience, reader experience, dramatic experience, audience experience were all involved.

6. Analysis of literary form became functional, not arbitrary.

7. A coöperative spirit entirely new to the class was evolved through meaningful projects of mutual interest.

8. A new momentum in reading was initiated.

9. These plans promise a fair measure of success under all circumstances that may be at least partially similar to the conditions in the foregoing.

The Technical and Commercial High School in Newark, New Jersey, reports the following guide to a photoplay-appreciation unit.

Enjoying Photoplays [8]

I. *Objective*

To learn to select movies intelligently so as to make them pay in enjoyment and education

II. *Activities*

A. In order to help you with later assignments, prepare a bibliography on varied phases of modern movies for the section of your note-book devoted to the cinema. Include books, pamphlets, and articles.

B. Draw from the library one (or more) title that seems significant to you. Bring these books to class. Write titles on the board. Members may add to their bibliographies. The chances are good that there will be books on scenario writing, costuming, make-up, acting, directing, development of the cinema, etc.

C. Report on the history of the movie industry. What part did Porter, Ince, Griffith, and Sennett play in the evolution of this art?

D. With the advent of Fairbanks what type of film became popular?

E. If possible, get information on

> *The Cabinet of Dr. Caligari*
> *The White Hell of Pitz Palu*

These are early foreign films. What influence did they exert on American films?

F. Think back over the films you have seen. Make a classification of types.

G. What do these names stand for: René Clair, Alexander Korda, Alfred Hitchcock, and Pudevkin?

H. What was the outstanding picture of each of the following: Vidor, Van Dyke, Capra, Cukor? Add other directors and titles to this list.

[8] Reported by the Technical and Commercial High School in Newark, N. J., through Alexandra B. Lewis.

I. What are the requirements of a good scenario?

J. Point out the differences between a stage play and a screen play.

K. State the factors that give the screen drama its appeal to the masses.

L. Do not be too technical, but come to class prepared to tell about one or more of the following:

How film is made

Kinds of films—positive, negative, reversal

Kinds of films—widths

Movies are the result of an optical illusion.

What is meant by "16 frames a second"?

How slow motion is attained

Explain "iris-out" and "flash-back."

Lens stops

Fade in and fade out

Lap dissolve—and wipe

Double exposure

Trick photography

How to take interiors with a movie camera

Sound track

Editing—cutting

M. Gilbert Seldes says, in *Saturday Review of Literature,* "Movies will never arrive at their highest level until they begin to create their own material as well as they have created their own methods." Comment on this.

N. Explain block-booking. Is it necessary? Why? What evils does it foment? Could producers afford to turn out pictures always on highest levels?

O. Do "stars" make the pictures, or vice versa?

P. What are the elements of a good review?

Q. Bring reviews to class clipped from magazines or from your local paper. (What is a blurb?)

R. State the esthetic principles of a good photoplay.

S. Ruth Bryan Owen once made this statement: "We must keep our trashy movies at home. They give foreigners a distorted impression of American life." Explain.

T. Did the coming of sound add or detract from the photoplay as an art?

U. Place a composite of the group's reactions on the black board. Have the group judge on these principles a picture the majority has seen. Use excellent (4), good (3), fair (2), poor (1), as indices. If the group has decided there should be six basic principles adhered to in the production of every picture, a top-notch picture that is excellent on every point would have a score of 24. Include such items as story and plot, acting, direction, photography, dialogue, sound, good taste; social, educational, inspirational values; settings, costumes, casting, diction, tempo, or timing, etc.

In the Baltimore, Maryland, English Course [9] for secondary schools, the theme of every literature unit from the seventh through twelfth grade has possible contacts with the movies. The teacher utilizes, therefore, what excellent relevant photoplays are being shown, have been shown recently, or will be shown in the near future. Thus many times during the school year the pupils' literary experiences may be enriched by discussion of the photoplay version of books they have read with enjoyment.

Other courses of study (see Appendix, pages 349–354) have carried out similarly the use of photoplays as stimulants to reading.

That visual materials facilitate interpretation of real and vicarious experiences is shown in a unit developed by Vinna R. Hill in the Ben Milam School, San Antonio, Texas, with a first-grade class. A visit of one pupil to a real farm started the others asking questions. The careful selection of pictures first by the teacher, then by the boy who had actually seen a farm, and later by all pupils enabled the class to take an imaginary trip to a farm. The class made use of pictures in magazines, advertisements, circulars, and textbooks. They drew pictures on etched-glass slides; made reels (pictures pasted on strips of window shades) and film slides of pictures taken with the teacher's camera on trips to farms and ranches. Supplementing these were word pictures in vivid poems and stories about farm life. When the trip was made—that is, when the pictures were shown—some of the pupils asked the "farmer" questions which he or one of his "family" answered.

The children's vocabulary was notably enriched. Their interest in farm products so heightened that informal conversation during lunch time for several days was devoted to topics connected with the farm unit.

Visual materials have also been tried with success as aids in

[9] *English Units of Work and Standards of Attainment*, published by the Department of Education, Baltimore, Md., 1934.

teaching pupils having serious learning difficulties. The following outline shows what one teacher accomplished.

VISUAL MATERIALS IN TEACHING READING [10]

I. *Types of Classes*
  1. Slow moving
  2. Underprivileged
  3. Mixed races
  4. Poor background

II. *Difficulties for Which Visual Materials Are a Corrective*
  1. Narrow span of recognition of words
  2. Inadequate experiences
  3. Ineffective eye movements
  4. Limited vocabulary
  5. Speech defects
  6. Timidity
  7. Lack of interest

III. *Procedure*
  1. Children made clay figures of the various characters in their basal reader.
  2. Clothes-pin figures were constructed by the children of characters from literature.
  "Tom Thumb," "Steadfast Tin Soldier and the Beautiful Dancing Lady," "Jack and the Beanstalk," "The Boy and the Wolf," "The Crow and the Pitcher," etc.
  3. Beaver-board construction work was used to illustrate other phases of the course of study.
  a. The children first drew figures on beaver board.
  b. These figures were then cut out and colored.
  4. Large illustrated booklets were made by the children of "Cinderella" and "Peter Rabbit."
  a. First the pictures were collected and mounted. Then the story was read and discussed with the children, after which the children retold the story and the teacher wrote the sentences under the pictures.
  b. The use of these illustrated booklets for class reading created interest in reading library books.

[10] Reported by Johnowene C. Menger, Ben Milam School, San Antonio, Tex.

5. Æsop's fables were dramatized in order that the children might learn the simple truths.

6. Through the use of stereoptican slides "Cinderella" was portrayed in moving-picture fashion.

   a. As each picture was flashed on the screen, the children told the corresponding part of the story.

   b. This practice created enthusiasm and desire to participate in the class activity on the part of the children.

7. Original poems were made by the children.

   a. Rhyming words were given children with which they composed poems.

   b. From this procedure developed the children's ability to compose poems.

8. The required poems of the course of study were presented by both newspaper cartoons and children's drawings.

   a. "My Shadow" by Robert Stevenson was typed under Skippy cartoons which showed the corresponding thoughts in the poem. These cartoons were flashed on the screen and read in unison by the children.

   b. The poem "Bed in Summer" by Robert Louis Stevenson was illustrated by children's drawings and then shown on the screen with the children reciting the verses.

9. The children made easel drawings of various incidents occurring in the basal reader.

   a. Similar stories were made by the children.

   b. These original stories were written under the pictures and used for class reading.

10. Original stories were made from the social studies.

   a. Each child illustrated his own story by a drawing.

   b. As the drawings were flashed on the screen, each child told his story.

IV. *Outcome*

The children grew in self-confidence and skill in reading and speaking.

RADIO

Teachers are introducing radio listening and discussion of radio programs into the English classroom for two quite distinct reasons. Some consider radio plays, monologues, and speeches just another form of literature, and are trying to refine their pupils' tastes and to encourage more discriminating choice of programs.

Others are also trying to use the radio as a lever to raise the level of interest in an appreciation of literature.

The first unit presented here is reported by Elizabeth Duane, Gillespie Junior High School, Philadelphia. It starts with discussion aimed at increasing the pupils' discrimination, and after bringing in almost all the speaking and writing skills concludes with a pupil broadcast over a commercial network. The actual radio experience is presumed to be going on daily at home, so that only the guidance of it falls to the school.

WHAT TO DO ABOUT THE RADIO [11]

Since the school population of today is of a new type, steps are being taken to adjust instruction to present-day conditions, and an effort is being made to bring pupils into contact with life as well as with books. The natural interests of children are being utilized in motivating teaching. Since one of the most absorbing of these interests at present is the radio, it is logical enough to have classroom activities tied up in a variety of ways with the radio.

Some very worth-while reactions were noted when radio was taken as the core for several units of work. In a preliminary discussion a large number of children admitted turning on the radio when they sat down to study their lessons, and then "letting it run," as they phrased it. Imagine it! So . . . . as Ed Wynn used to say, the horrified teacher thought something ought to be done about it. As a result, the following activities were engaged in to help pupils to listen to the radio with a certain amount of discrimination and, at the same time, to give them very definitely motivated instruction in English.

I. *Informal discussion.* What is your favorite radio program? Why do you like it? Do you *learn* anything from it, or does it merely *entertain* you? Are there any programs other than those referred to during this discussion which you should like to recommend to your classmates? (Time and station)

II. *Informal discussion.* Who is your favorite announcer or program broadcaster? Why? Do you like *what* he says, or the *way* he says it? What of his manner and voice? As to the latter, is it loud and shrill, or pleasing and well-modulated? Have you noticed his careful *e*nunciation and *pro*nunciation? What is the difference between these two words? (Dictionary work followed to elucidate this

[11] Reported by Elizabeth Duane, Gillespie Junior High, Philadelphia, Pa.

point, and to give pupils opportunity to look up the pronunciation of certain words which they had heard broadcasters use, and which had sounded rather "odd" to them. Incidentally, the broadcasters were not proved to be right in *every* instance.)

III. *Word study.* Pupils were asked to keep a note-book at hand when listening to the radio, and to jot down any words new to them or which they regarded as especially "vivid." They were also asked to make lists of words and phrases peculiar to radio (*static, microphone,* etc.). Lists were brought to class and studied in detail, with a marked growth in vocabulary as a result.

IV. *Research.* A pupil who had visited Radio City was asked to describe her trip to the class. The members of the class were permitted to question her upon various points concerning radio about which they were curious. The speaker was able to answer a number of the questions, but to some she replied, "I don't know." These unanswered questions were listed by the class for independent research. The reports made an interesting follow-up lesson.

V. *Debate.* Teams were selected from two classes of parallel grade to debate the following proposition: "That radio has been of greater service to the world than the motion picture." This proved an interesting topic for preliminary research, and motivated the development of paragraphs of contrast as well as intelligent use of transition words and phrases (*notwithstanding, on the contrary, on the other hand,* etc.).

VI. *Good usage.* Class was apprized of the station from which "Better Speech" broadcasts were to be given and asked to listen in. What was heard was reported in class and some follow-up drills were given by the teacher to drive home the points reported.

VII. *Sentence structure.* Since time is so important on the air, broadcasters must be masters of terse, vigorous speech. Pupils were asked to list good introductory sentences and convincing "clinching" sentences heard over the radio. Note was also taken of sentence *form,* that is, inverted, transposed, natural order, etc. Quite an interesting collection of these was made, and the written compositions and formal talks of pupils improved noticeably because of this work.

VIII. *Research.* The class visited the local broadcasting station. The manager personally conducted the group through the station, giving information and demonstrating the mechanics of radio, special sound effect devices, etc.

IX. *Written composition.* Topics assigned for written composition: "The World a 'Neighborhood' Through Radio," "Marconi's Contribution to the World," "The Joys of a Short-Wave Set," "What

Radio Has Done For 'Shut-ins,' " "Radio as a Teacher of Current Events," and "The Modern Miracle—Radio."

X. *Guidance.* A class discussion of the etiquette of radio: Consideration for the wishes of other members of the family regarding programs—"taking turns"—suggested; guarding against annoying of neighbors by the "late and loud" variety of playing; attention drawn to the delicate, fairy-like character of orchestral music when listened to with the radio turned down very low—pupils urged to try to cultivate a taste for listening to music in this way; attention drawn to the discourtesy exhibited to both program producers and visitors by turning on the radio and using it as a mere accompaniment to conversation; making guests in the home welcome to use of the radio for getting their favorite programs.

XI. *Oral.* A radio program was planned, and talks given in broadcast fashion by several members of the class. (An improvised "mike" was used and there was an announcer in charge of the program.) Members of the class gave constructive criticisms after the program was completed. The climax of a school drive for "better speech" was a radio interview in a morning assembly summarizing points emphasized during the drive.

XII. *Letter-writing.* Letters were written to the manager of a particular radio station, some expressing appreciation of certain programs, others making requests for the playing of favorite compositions, such requests having been solicited by the station in question.

XIII. *Advertising.* The attention of class was directed to radio advertising; cogent use of English, making every word "tell"; apparent sincerity of broadcaster's belief in value of product advertised; influence of voice and manner as elements of persuasion, etc. After informal discussion of this topic, the class was permitted to prepare a broadcast for morning assembly, setting forth the merits of the school paper and urging pupils to purchase.

XIV. *Dramatics.* As a climax to the radio unit a picked group of children prepared a playlet for a special assembly program, which they were later permitted to broadcast over a bona fide network.

Leon C. Hood, Chairman of the Radio Committee, New Jersey Association of Teachers of English, says:

Studies of the listening habits of school children show that they average more than two hours a day before their loudspeakers. Enthusiasts for the traditional literary forms lament the substitution of listening for reading. Yet, libraries have more than once been overwhelmed when a popular program has created a demand for books they cannot produce. There is ample observable evidence that current fashions of speech are presented and implanted by the radio and have an enormous appeal to our children. Colloquialisms and various modes of expression are quickly and unconsciously taken in by them. Surely radio listening as a means of experiencing literature is not to be ignored by the teacher of English. The uniqueness of radio technique, the timeliness of the broadcast, and the ease with which programs are obtained present a challenge to the ordinary materials of the school.

The unit which Mr. Hood reports also assumes the listening at home, and, in addition to discussion, makes use of much information about the production of programs—on the ground that such knowledge will engender discriminating appreciation.

This brief report by Evelyn Sprado, Richmond Hill High School, New York City, proceeds at once to employ radio in developing appreciation of literature.

EXPERIENCING ENGLISH THROUGH RADIO [12]

This term pupils by dramatization compared and contrasted short stories studied in class with other stories not found in the literature text. The Educational Radio Script Exchange, U. S. Department of the Interior, Office of Education, offers a number of scripts free of charge which can readily be adapted to this purpose. Among those used were "The Fall of the House of Usher," "The Legend of Sleepy Hollow," "Posson Jones," "Whistling Dick's Christmas Stocking," and "The Luck of Roaring Camp."

These scripts are fifteen-minute programs in which the average number of actors is ten. They do call for certain sound effects, but these can easily be worked out with the help of the *Production Manual,* and *Glossary of Radio Terms* (some of them pungently expressive) also offered by the Script Exchange.

Students had so much fun comparing the plots and structure of these stories with those they had studied in class and in working on these scripts that I utilized this same idea in the review study of *Silas Marner,* their rapid reading book. A summary of the plot and appreciation of character and dramatic incident were all accomplished by having the group work out a script for a half-hour program like those presented by the American School of the Air.

Later a number of club programs grew out of these activities— talks on programs, sound effects, production items, and broadcasts witnessed.

[12] Reported by Evelyn Sprado, Richmond Hill High School, New York City.

A library—classroom, school, or community—is an essential element in experience-centered English courses. Any extensive reading, any free reading, any integrated program emphasizes the need for many well-selected books classified and arranged so as to be quickly accessible to the pupils. Most English courses of study published since 1932, and a few earlier ones, list as term requirements specific library skills needed for the independent, intelligent use of books.

The units presented here are illustrative of how teachers are creating a favorable pupil-attitude toward books. Much material, however, that is classifiable in this section is incorporated in the division entitled "Free Reading." (See pages 51–76.)

Selecting books for a school library was the potent desire used by Marion Allen to encourage discriminating use of books. Having selected the books, her pupils then catalogued them.

SELECTING AND CATALOGUING LIBRARY BOOKS [18]

Origin of the project. To spend wisely fifty dollars provided annually by the Board of Education, for library books, a committee of two librarians and three teachers was appointed to compile a book list. It was agreed that children's judgment on fiction would be a more reliable index of interest than our adult judgment, and that by using various reference materials in the classrooms the usefulness could be better determined.

Procedure in selecting books. All new sample books from publishers were sent at random to the five buildings represented on the committee. Each fiction book was displayed. The purpose of the reading was made clear to the children. Individuals volunteered to read and report on each book. The class decided it would be necessary to keep these points in mind while reading:

1. To what age and type of child would this book appeal?
2. Are the characters lifelike?
3. Is the print suitable for ease of reading?
4. What situations especially appeal to you?
5. Do you consider the style of good quality? Why?
6. Are the illustrations interesting?
7. Do you recommend this book for the library list? Why, or Why not?

[18] Reported to Marion Allen, Kenwood School, Minneapolis, Minn.

In so far as possible, two or three children read each book and discussed it before recommending it for the list. One from each group made an oral recommendation to the class. At this time, questions were raised.

The reference books were used with various social-studies units. We compared the type of information given in each with texts and made further comparison with the information found in encyclopedias. Books were rated for ease of reading, variety of material, and interest.

At the second meeting of the Library Book Committee, the books rated very poor were eliminated. The remaining books were circulated in different schools and the same procedure followed.

A questionnaire was sent to teachers asking:

1. Is there any special field in which you feel the need of material?
2. Are more easy books needed?
3. Do your classes have any favorite books which you think should be included?

As a result of this questionnaire, we discovered that many people needed science material. Others requested good poetry anthologies, club materials, myths, legends, and plays. Many felt it necessary to have more books for easy reading to meet the needs of lower ability groups. A variety of individual titles was recommended.

With the help of the Minneapolis Public Library and the science supervisor, new materials were added to the trial group and used in the same critical fashion as the sample books.

Experiences in cataloguing. After Kenwood School had received books for two years, we felt the need of some means of cataloguing. (Cards and pockets had been placed in each book.) The 7B class visited a branch library where the cataloguing system was explained. The group observed the placement on the shelves.

The class wrote letters to invite the board of education librarian to visit Kenwood School to explain a simplified Dewey Decimal System that would be workable. She also explained the Cutter System for fiction. We decided to use a combination of the two for classification of our books.

The children divided the books into classes, wrote a slip for each book giving the markings to be placed on the binding. (Reference to the catalogue was necessary.)

The librarian made a second visit and taught the use of the electric stylus. After a committee of children marked all of the bindings, the books were shelved.

All were made familiar with the system by dramatizations and drill lessons in finding books on the shelves. Now each child writes his own card. When the books are returned, he cancels the card and returns the book to its place on the shelf.

How a first-grade group was introduced to a public library is told by Miss Buchanan.

A LIBRARY UNIT FOR FIRST GRADERS [14]

Realizing how a favorable attitude formed in youth can influence a whole life, we take our first-grade children to the public library. Here in their first visit to the attractive reading room for children they find the shelves housing picture books, fairy and animal stories, they hear a delightful story told by the librarian, and finally obtain a library membership card and learn how to use it.

Activities in the unit included the following:

1. Exploring the classroom library
2. Exploring home libraries
3. Planning trip to public library
4. Taking the trip to the public library
5. Discussing the trip
6. Playing library
   a. Pupils serve as "librarian" charging out and in books borrowed from the classroom library to take home.
   b. Pupils act as story-teller and entertain the children in the class as the librarian did.
7. Writing letters
   a. Pupils wrote to parents asking permission to make trip to library.
   b. Pupils wrote to librarian thanking her for pleasures of their visit.
8. Planning a Book Week program

As outcomes of this unit the pupils gained the following:

1. Familiarity with many good books—in the school library, at home, and in public libraries
2. Knowledge of the name, the location, and the purpose of the public library
3. Appreciation of what the city is doing for the children and grown people by having good libraries
4. Improved reading habits
5. Respect for public property

[14] Reported by Margaret C. Buchanan, teacher; Mrs. Bess S. Nash, Principal, Lamar School, San Antonio, Tex.

6. Learned to express their own ideas, formulate plans, and tell others about their experience
7. Safe conduct in traveling as a group
8. Courtesy to mothers, classmates, and library staff
9. Self-expression through art, music, dramatization, and poetry for the Book Week program

Winifred H. Nash of the Roxbury Memorial High School has used an extracurricular activity to build an attitude toward books, to furnish an outlet for book-talk and creative writing, and to open up writing and library work as pre-vocational activities.

THE BOOK AND QUILL CLUB [15]

The Book and Quill Club, organized 1932, is an extracurricular association open to members of the junior and senior classes of the Roxbury Memorial High School for Girls. Membership is limited to fifty. According to the regular club schedule, the group meets on the first and third Wednesdays of each month, but there are many impromptu meetings besides.

The purpose of the club is twofold: (1) to stimulate interest in the reading and discussion of books and magazines and (2) to provide incentive for creative writing and opportunity for helpful criticism.

The activities of the club may be grouped under three main headings: (1) the enrichment of the students' esthetic and social experience; (2) experiences with and through literature, and (3) experiences in creative writing.

Not all the activities listed below have been undertaken during any one year, but each year a goodly number of enterprises in each group have been successfully carried on.

I. *The Enrichment of Experience*

    A. Esthetic experience

        1. Visits to the Museum of Fine Arts
            Discussion of sculpture, paintings, periods of art, etc.
        2. Visits to the Isabella Stewart Gardner Museum; lectures by the guides; concerts in the famous music room of the Venetian palace
        3. Visits to the Boston Public Library
            Study of the paintings by Abbey, Sargent, and de Chavannes,

[15] Reported by Winifred H. Nash, Roxbury Memorial High School for Girls, Roxbury, Mass.

discussion of collections in the Treasure Room and the Fine Arts Department

4. Attendance at the open-air concerts on the Charles River Esplanade
5. Nature walks through the Fenway in the autumn and the spring
6. Picnics on Castle Island
   Snap-shots of the old fort; crab-fishers on the pier; coal-barges, fishing schooners, ocean liners, etc.

B. Social experience
1. Afternoon teas for the faculty and invited guests
2. Open meetings of the club to which parents are invited
3. Informal parties on Hallowe'en and May Day
4. Attendance at the Pop Concerts in Symphony Hall
5. Costume parties; for example, a Dickens' party at which club members and faculty guests were costumed like characters from Dickens' novels. Prizes were awarded to the person who named correctly the greatest number of characters, and to the person whose costume was most Dickensian.

II. *Experiences with and Through Literature*

A. Study of books and authors
1. Study of the works of one writer; for example, Jane Austen, by the club as a whole
2. Reports upon favorite authors by individual students
3. Informal discussion of books drawn from the club library or recommended for the club library
4. Stereopticon lectures upon an author's locale—Stratford, Abbotsford, Ayrshire, etc.
5. Dramatization of scenes from favorite books
6. Comparison of the photoplay version of a story with the original
7. Comparison of "books of the hour" with "books of all time"
8. Comparative study of magazines

B. Buying books for the club library
1. Visits to fascinating old second-hand bookshops
2. Visits to famous publishing houses
3. Visits to the authors' counter in department stores where on special days the author appears in person to autograph books for the buyer

C. Attending the Boston *Herald* Book Fair at which authors discussed their own books and literature in general

D. Public presentation of plays for the purpose of raising money to buy books

E. Lectures by invited guests
1. Upon several occasions journalists and librarians have ad-

dressed the club and have given valuable vocational information.

2. Louella D. Everett, co-editor with Christopher Morley of the new edition of *Bartlett's Familiar Quotations,* explained to the club in a very interesting talk some of the problems of the editor of a reference book.

3. A memorable event in club history was the address by Professor Charles Swain Thomas upon "Interpreting Life through Literature."

III. *Experiences in Creative Writing*

A. School correspondence

1. International correspondence conducted through the Junior Red Cross Foreign Correspondence Department—portfolios exchanged with schools in France, Belgium, and Hungary

2. Interstate correspondence—portfolios exchanged with Grover Cleveland School in Pasadena, California, and the Classen High School in Oklahoma

B. Manuscript meetings

1. At these meetings manuscripts are submitted under pen names. Each manuscript is read aloud and criticized by the club. The best manuscripts are submitted for publication in the school magazine.

2. The writing is purely voluntary. There are no restrictions as to type; poems, essays, short stories, editorials, radio scripts, or any other literary form may be attempted. The most ambitious project was a 15,000-word mystery serial that ran during five issues of the school magazine.

C. Prize competitions

D. Radio hours (all scripts original)

E. Dramatization of original sketches and short plays

The most recent project of the club was a Book Title Contest, which proved to be a simple and effective way of raising money for new books. Very little rehearsing was necessary, and the only expense incurred was the cost of the prize, two dollars.

Upon payment of a ten-cent admission fee, each member of the audience received a contest blank bearing the numbers 1–50. After each title was presented, time was allowed for the writing of the answer. At the conclusion of the contest, the papers were given to the club sponsor who later corrected the answers, with the assistance of a committee of club members. The prize was awarded at a public assembly next day.

In order to insure fairness, no club members took part in the contest. Furthermore, twelve of the titles were known beforehand only to the club sponsor, who gave the necessary instructions to the actors just before the title-number was called.

As a result of the contest, the club will be able to add about fifty new books to the club library. At present the club members are engaged in compiling a list of a hundred desirable titles, from which fifty will be selected by vote of the club at the next meeting.

What are the products of all these activities? These results are apparent:

1. A club library of about 250 volumes
2. Vocational guidance
   a. Two girls are happily employed in publishing houses.
   b. Several students are engaged in library work.
   c. Three girls are headed toward careers in journalism.
   d. Several free-lance writers are reporting an encouraging degree of success.
3. Educational guidance
   Students report that book reviews, reading programs, and composition work in the regular English curriculum are more profitable and enjoyable as a result of the club activities.
4. Quickened appreciation of literature as a means of interpreting life

How the Book Fair movement sponsored by the metropolitan newspapers enkindled new interests among her pupils is told by Miss Kerwin. Between the lines in her brief outline, may be read the guidance of a dynamic teacher.

A BOOK FAIR [16]

I. *Aims*

   A. To present regular and supplementary reading material in a new and attractive way so that there would be an urgent motive for reading books with understanding and enjoyment
   B. To stimulate thoughtful discussion of books read thus cultivating reading for a purpose
   C. To provide means for the acquisition of fresh information about books from new sources
   D. To afford training in effective expression in English
   E. To furnish opportunity for creative work

II. *Activities*

   A. Reading about the New York *Times* National Book Fair

[16] Reported by Luella M. Kerwin, Henry Snyder Junior High School, Jersey City, N. J.

and hearing reports from visitors, the pupils of the 9B classes decided to imitate it and to hold one on a small scale

B. Forming committees to
   1. Secure tables, book shelves, magazine racks, and exhibit booths
   2. Collect books on ninth-year list, as well as other good books read and recommended by pupils, from library and other sources
   3. Write invitations to parents, teachers, and pupils of other classes
   4. Secure guest speakers
   5. Prepare programs
      a. Write plays
      b. Write speeches of welcome, introducing speakers, and of guides explaining exhibits
   6. Prepare exhibits
      a. Model of setting of Ivanhoe country (Made in box of sand, with pieces of glass for river, cardboard forests, etc.)
      b. Maps of Ivanhoe country
      c. Model of Cedric's dining hall (cardboard)
      d. Model of medieval castle
      e. Dolls dressed as characters in *Ivanhoe*
      f. Charts of pictures of costumes, knights, homes, weapons, etc., of the period of *Ivanhoe*
      g. Small dictionaries of vocabulary of feudal times containing definitions of terms used
      h. Charts of lists at Ashby
      i. Lists of authors and their stories based upon the historical events of the same period as *Ivanhoe*
      j. Book reports with originally designed jacket covers
      k. Charts of newspaper clippings about authors
      l. Pamphlets on books obtained at New York *Times* Book Fair
      m. Magazines: *Modern Literature, The Scholastic,* etc.

C. Holding the fair
   1. Invitations were sent to visitors.
   2. Pupils acted as hosts and guides.
   3. The chairman of each class made a brief speech of welcome, explaining the purpose of the fair, and introducing the guest speakers.
   4. The guest speakers included:

      a. Principal
      b. Vice-principal
      c. Teacher
      d. Faculty poet
      e. Faculty adviser on school paper
   5. A scene from *The Taming of the Shrew* was dramatized.

III. *Outcomes*

  A. More requests for library passes
  B. Increased requests to borrow "Menus in Reading for Young People" by May Lamberton Becker
  C. Notes copied voluntarily on bulletin board—*Some Recent Books You Will Enjoy*
  D. Pupils have initiated plans for annual Book Fair.

PART TWO

Sharing Experiences Through Communication

SHARING EXPERIENCES THROUGH COMMUNICATION

LANGUAGE unifies all experience. To control the symbolism of language is to adjust to any social situation and to learn from life or from books. Words are the carriers of thoughts and emotions. The mastery of language is essential for personal happiness and for occupational success. Language is a mode of behavior, a response to a specific situation in speech or writing, or in inner thought.

A child's thinking and feeling will remain immature until he learns to use language symbols which will adequately convey his thoughts and feelings to himself and to others.

Stephens [1] summarizes well the social significance of language teaching in the following terms: "(1) the benefits that come to society because of the individual's greater intellectual efficiency reacting upon the social group, (2) those coming from his more effective membership in the family group, (3) those coming from his greater efficiency as a political and social unit in a democracy, and (4) those which come from his greater 'time-binding' power."

"The art of communication can be mastered only through experience in actual, normal communication, and mere practice in speaking and writing is valueless unless it arises directly from real communication and issues promptly in further communication. When pupils, for example, are preparing an assembly program, they see the need of good voices, clear-cut enunciation, accurate pronunciation, and correct usage, and are ready for some related habit-forming drill. On the contrary, practising voice and enunciation exercises and correcting pronunciation and usage errors accomplishes approximately nothing if pupils lack desire and determination to improve. When a boy decides to learn to play golf, he plays the game, goes in person or through a book to a professional for suggestions, practises driving, putting, and approaching, and continues to play the game. Practice swings and the advice of a professional will never make a skilful golfer out of a boy who

[1] Stephen DeWitt Stephens, *Individual Instruction in English Composition* (Cambridge, Mass., Harvard University Press, 1928), p. 10.

119

lacks either interest in the game or frequent opportunity to play real golf. Make-believe letters and other ordinary themes neither draw out the pupil's full power nor prepare him to meet the emotional and moral element in the real situations of life. Classroom experience that is itself real and is as close as possible to the reality of extra-school and post-school life, without deception or pretense, must be the actual basis of any realistic curriculum." [2]

The following illustrations from classrooms over the country give evidence that communication can and is being taught as experience.

[2] W. Wilbur Hatfield, chairman, *An Experience Curriculum in English* (New York, D. Appleton-Century Co., 1935), pp. 133–134.

VI

CONVERSING

IN THE FAST MOVING and changing world of ours, we cannot put too much emphasis on proper training for adequacy in social situations.

Even before the child enters school, he comes in contact with many personalities to whom he is expected to respond in conversation. He answers the telephone. He answers the door and greets callers. He purchases groceries from the neighborhood store. He goes on errands for his mother and some of her friends. He asks directions from the policeman. As he grows older, these contacts become more and more numerous.

What can the school do to help the child become more effective in social situations? The first provision requires that the classroom include situations which are life situations and which will function for the child. Most of the social situations can be grouped under the following classifications:

A. Social group conversing
B. Conversing over the telephone
C. Conversing after a formal and after an informal introduction
D. Social interviewing

The following discussion briefs the way a sixth-grade class attempted to work out the effective elements of each of the four types.

A SOCIAL CONVERSATION [1]

The class was given the first ten minutes of the period for free conversation, talking to another person or talking in groups of three or four about any topic which interested them. When the students were assembled for class work, they discussed what seemingly takes place when one converses. Out of this discussion we made an analysis of the attributes which make a good conversationalist. From this

[1] Reported by Elizabeth Wild, Teacher of Speech, Shorewood, Milwaukee, Wis.

analysis, we had six "golden rules of conversation" mimeographed for the class:

1. A good conversationalist is able to follow conversational leads.
2. A good conversationalist does not do all of the talking.
3. A good conversationalist is also a good listener.
4. A good conversationalist does not allow conversation to degenerate into a debate between two people, because conversation recognizes every person's right to his ideas.
5. A good conversationalist will attempt to include every one in the group.
6. A good conversationalist avoids a long, tedious account of the situation about which he is speaking.

The class was then divided into groups, and each group chose one phase of social conversation "which affects their lives" to present in some form to the class.

GROUP I

Aim: To show a situation in which there was too much "self" in the conversation. The following scene "On the Playground" was presented as a dramatization after the group had had one conference.

JIM [*throwing the ball*]. Butterfingers! You couldn't even catch a volley ball. Why, *I* pitched a "no-hit—no-run" game last week.
JOE. Yes, I know. Coach is helping me to correct my faults.
GLORIA. Jim, why can't you be more agreeable!
JIM. Why, I'm being perfectly fair and square.
JOE. Did you see on the sports bulletin that Bill Jones caught a "fly" with one hand?
JIM. Yes, I did and *I* think it was an unfair ruling on Coach's part. He dropped that ball in four seconds. Why *I* could do the same thing and hold it.
JOE. But the rules say if you hold the ball three seconds or more, it is considered legal.
JIM. Yes, I know, but I think those rules are crazy. [JOE *throws the ball to* JIM. JIM *misses it.*]   Oh, there goes the ball. Can't you throw a decent ball once in a while? [*They both run after the ball.*]
GLORIA [*to* LOUIS, *who has been watching the boys*]. Isn't Jim awful? He has lost nearly all of his friends.
LOUIS. And the only reason Joe plays with him is because he's so patient. It is always "I this— I that. I can do better than that. I—I—I all the time."
GLORIA. He can't do half as well as Bill Jones or Dave Harding.
LOUIS. S-s-sh, I hear them coming.

JOE. Did you hear that Dave Harding and some other boys have started a camera club?

JIM. Yes, and to hear them talk, you'd think they just saw the president or something. Why, if *I* were Dave Harding, *I* would have an organized club.

GLORIA. I think it's a pretty good organization.

JOE. Don Hutchins had a right nice speech on developing films.

JIM. It'll do.

JOE [*looking at his watch*]. Oh! it's 3:10 now and I promised Mom I would be home at 3:15. So long.

LOUIS. So long!

GLORIA. Good-bye!

JIM. Good-bye!

CURTAIN

GROUP II

Aim: To show a situation in which there is not too much "self" in conversation. The following dialogue was prepared and presented to the class.

JEAN. Say, Doug, we are working on a unit on conversation, and I am trying to organize my ideas into a talk for Monday. Would you be willing to listen to it and help me?

DOUG. Yes, Jean, I would be glad to help you. On what part of the conversation unit are you working?

JEAN. I am trying to show what happens when a person forces himself into the conversation.

DOUG. You really mean that you are going to talk about "self" in conversation.

JEAN. Yes, I will begin like this: "As you all know, people who have done things worth-while are spoken of by their friends and written about in the newspaper. In other words, it isn't necessary for them to speak about themselves. Their deeds have spoken for them. This illustrates the basic rule of personal conversation, which is, 'Do not talk about yourself.'

"The person who has done something worth-while, and who has not learned the rule given above, soon finds that his hearers think much less of what he has done when he keeps on referring to himself in the conversation; and he *may* become a bore, and even a failure, in their minds.

"When the subject being talked about requires reference to one's self, there is a right and a wrong way to do it. A person, for instance, who finds it necessary to comment upon some personal activity or accomplishment might better say, 'We found that this was the best way,' rather than 'I did it this way.' "

Well, Doug, how do you like my talk?

DOUG. Very good, Jean. However, I have one addition to make. See how you like this: "People are all interested in *themselves*. So the safest rule to follow in conversation is to talk about *the other person*, about what he has done, his accomplishments, his interests, etc., and leave it to general good sense for the others to bring 'you' into it. Never be guilty of pushing *yourself* into conversation."

JEAN. I think that makes a good ending for my talk. Thank you.

GROUP III

Aim: To show the advantages and disadvantages of talking too little or too much. This group decided that they would select a speaker who would address the class. The following report of the *group at work* illustrates a coöperative group attack to accomplish their aim.

DOROTHY [*chairman of group*]. We want to try to work out together the advantages and disadvantages of talking too much or too little. Now, how shall we begin?

MARJORIE. We could begin like this. "The advantages of talking too much are: 'Practice makes perfect'; that the more you talk the better you will be able to talk."

RUTH. Yes, and if you are a salesman, you want to win people over to your side.

DOROTHY. Let me see. Oh, I can't think of any more advantages. Let us think about disadvantages.

MARJORIE. If you talk too much, you may bore people.

DOROTHY. Yes, and you may show how little you know. Then, too, people who talk too much are very poor listeners.

RUTH. Sometimes people who talk too much do not think enough, and they often say things that hurt the other person's feelings.

MARJORIE. Now, let us consider some of the advantages of talking too little. Well, you certainly don't let people know how little you know if you don't talk. But a disadvantage of talking too little is that you lose opportunity to develop your personality.

DOROTHY. Ruth, we will appoint you as a group representative to talk to the class about the advantages and disadvantages of talking too much or too little.

CONVERSING OVER THE TELEPHONE

The class was assigned to analyze telephone conversations of their own and those which they could observe made by business men and women. Four points given below were suggested by the class members to be followed in reporting these analyses. A week or so after this assignment the reports of these analyses were given before the class:

1. How people answered the telephone
2. How the telephone conversation was concluded
3. How appointments were made
4. What abuses crept into the telephone conversation, such as calling at inconvenient times; talking very loud, very slow, or very fast; being discourteous; talking for a long time

Several students prepared as their reports monologues demonstrating good and poor telephone conversationalists. The following was selected by the class as an excellent example of an effective telephone conversation.

Nancy is sitting in an easy chair talking on the telephone.

"Hello!" Nancy speaks into the mouthpiece. "Why, hello, Dad! This is Nancy. I wished to tell you that Cousin Helen Bradley flew from Newark, N.J., this noon, arriving in Chicago this afternoon at five o'clock. She has probably taken the fastest train into Milwaukee. When she arrives, you are to get her and bring her to our house. Understand? . . . I have already called the Union Station and the latest train from Chicago arrives at 8:30. It is now 8:00. Please stay where I may keep in touch with you. Good-bye."

She hangs up the receiver and goes over to the couch to pick up a new magazine. She sits down and reads. Presently the telephone rings again. She drops the magazine and goes over to answer, saying, "That must be Cousin Helen now."

Nancy picks up receiver. "Hello, . . . no, he isn't." Then, recognizing the voice, she exclaims, "Why, hello, Cousin Helen! This is Nancy. I am so glad to hear from you. Are you in town? . . . That's fine. At what station are you? . . . The Union? If you will please wait near the telephone booths, Dad will come for you as soon as he is able. I am so glad that you have come to spend a few days with us! Good-bye."

Nancy hangs up. Then she gets straight to work dialing the phone for her father. Finally she has success. "Hello, is this Dr. Belknap? . . . This is Nancy again, Dad. Sorry to disturb you, but I have just heard from Cousin Helen. She is in town and is waiting near the telephone booths in the Union Station . . . Well, I'll be glad to do it again some time. Good-bye."

Hangs up. Then turns back to a restful evening of reading as curtain falls.

CONVERSATION WHICH FOLLOWS THE FORMAL AND INFORMAL INTRODUCTION

The class was in agreement that the most difficult conversation is that which follows an introduction to a person. At such a time, there are few common topics one can use which make an interesting conversation.

Before the class was divided into groups for group study of introduction, the members set up the standards which all of the groups should recognize:

1. The need for the person who introduces to speak very distinctly
2. The person to be presented when introducing ladies and gentlemen, older persons and younger persons, boys and girls
3. The present-day acceptance of (*a*) "How do you do" and when departing of "It's been a pleasure to meet you" or "I hope we may meet again" or such; (*b*) not shaking hands

This dramatization of a formal introduction presented by Bob's group is reproduced here.

SCENE I

[*In the school-room where* BOB, JUDY, *and a* CLASSMATE *are giving a skit of formal conversation*]

MOTHER [JUDY]. I just heard you were elected president of the H.H. Club and that Mrs. Green was —— [*Boy enters.*]

YOUNG SON [BOB]. Mother! Did you hear Frank won the —— [*Notices visitor*] Oh, pardon me!

MOTHER. Bob, I would like you to meet Mrs. Brown, president of the H.H. Club.

BOB. President of the H.H. Club! I am very glad to meet you, Mrs. Brown.

MRS. BROWN [CLASSMATE]. How do you do, Bob.

BOB. Mother, did you hear Frank won the highest score in spelling today?

MOTHER. The highest score in spelling! My, he must be very good.

MRS. BROWN. My little boy was telling me about that, too.

BOB. Would you excuse me while I ask Mother a question?

MRS. BROWN. Yes, of course.

BOB. Mother, do you know where my bat is?

MOTHER. No, Bob, I haven't seen it.

BOB. Well, I haven't time to look for it, and I am very glad to have met you, Mrs. Brown. [*Boy leaves.*]

MOTHER [*sighs*]. I am very interested in this H.H. Club. Is there anything I can do to help?

MRS. BROWN. Why, yes.

[*Curtain closes.*]

SCENE II

[BOB *and* JUDY'S MOTHER *is waiting for them.*]

MOTHER. My, the children ought to be coming home any minute now. [CHILDREN *rush in.*]

Bob. Mother, Judy and I had to give a little skit, a formal conversation, in school today.

Mother. That is interesting; what did you learn?

Judy [*going over and sitting down*]. Suppose you came home from school and found your mother entertaining some well-known person who is a stranger to you. After saying "Hello" to you, your mother probably would say "Mrs. Brown, I'd like you to meet my daughter, Mary."

Bob. And you would say, "How do you do, Mrs. Brown, I am very glad to meet you."

Judy. Mrs. Brown may ask you a few questions such as where you attend school and what grade you are in. You should always answer courteously.

Bob. Be very careful to use correct English. Always look at the person to whom you are speaking, and hold your body straight and tall.

Judy. It is not a good habit to finger buttons or fidget with anything, either.

Mother. Those are some very good points. Are there any more?

Bob. Yes. When the person leaves, you want him to feel that you are a very courteous and well-behaved child.

Mother. Well, you'd better go out and play while I get supper.

Judy. Come on, Bob! The kids are waiting for us.

Mother [*stands up*]. Now, what can I get for that hungry family of mine?

THE END

The Interview

The interview has become a very useful technique. With the present-day emphasis on the students' having actual contact with the activities about them, more of them will interview people in various fields of endeavor. A child is sent to arrange for a trip to a pet shop. A boy is sent to the telephone company to bring back a report. A group visits the judge of the criminal court. A student reporter goes to the theater to interview a famous actress. How are we training these students to interview individuals effectively and successfully?

Are we helping our students to ask important, direct questions, so that they can bring back the information desired? Are we stressing the necessity of quoting statements exactly as they were made? Are we insisting on courtesy at all times? Are we teaching students how to make a tactful and pleasing *entrée* and introduction to the person being interviewed?

After much class discussion on such points as listed, after some group practice, after considerable experience in interviewing people

for the purpose of reporting to the school paper, the following dramatization was presented as a culmination of the study by Mary's
group.

INTERVIEWING CONVERSATION

The first scene takes place in the ANDERSON *household.*

[*The door opens slowly.*]

MARY. Gee, have we got a tough assignment. [*Pause*] I don't know what
I'm going to do.

JACK. You said it. [*Looks in the paper*] Say, look here. It says that some
guests have come from England to stay at Mrs. Gray's house. We know
Mrs. Gray!

MARY. Sure.

JACK. Couldn't we interview them?

MARY. Why, that's a fine idea. Let's go now.

JACK [*after opening the door*]. I hope that they are home.

CURTAIN

[*The second scene takes place in* MRS. GRAY'S *house.*]

FRED. Say, aren't Americans a lively set of people?

CORA. Yes. [*Knock at the door*] I must answer the door.

MARY. Hello! Is Mrs. Gray at home?

CORA. No, she's not.

JACK. Will she be home soon?

CORA. No, I'm afraid not. But won't you come in and have a seat?

MARY. Thank you. Are you the children who just came from England?

CORA. Yes, we are.

JACK. We'd like to have an interview with you—a personal one. Do you
mind?

CORA. Why, not at all.

MARY. I'm Mary Anderson and this is my brother, Jack. What is your
name?

CORA. I'm Cora Phillips and this is my brother, Fred.

JACK. When did you come to Milwaukee?

FRED. We just arrived yesterday. We think we are going to like it here.

JACK. How old are you?

CORA. I'm thirteen.

MARY. So am I.

JACK. I'm fourteen.

FRED. I'm fifteen.

MARY. Were you born in England?

CORA. Yes.

JACK. We were both born in Milwaukee.

CORA. Do you like dolls?

MARY. Yes, I do. I have a Shirley Temple doll. Do you know about Shirley Temple?

CORA. Oh, yes. I've even seen her in several movies. But I've never seen a Shirley Temple doll. Does it look like her?

MARY. Yes, and there are many paper dolls made to look like her too, with clothes really just like hers. Not only that but dresses for girls are designed on her styles and are called Shirley Temple dresses.

CORA. In England all the girls try to be like Princess Elizabeth. The girls have Princess Elizabeth dolls. Some of them have doll houses copied after hers too. Do you admire Princess Elizabeth as we do?

MARY. I think that she is very sweet.

JACK. What are the boys in England interested in, Fred? I dare say you are scarcely the possessor of a Princess Elizabeth doll.

FRED. You are correct. We like sports, horse-racing, cricket, badminton. I like to collect stamps, too.

CORA. So does our father. He has a very large stamp collection.

JACK. I collect stamps, too.

CORA. I correspond with children from foreign nations for my hobby and Fred gets the stamps off the letters for his stamp collection.

MARY. Do you find the food over here better than in England?

CORA. We do like it better, perhaps just because it is different. Americans drink so much milk. Mrs. Gray says that we must drink milk with every meal. Fred likes it, but I do not care for it.

MARY. What do you plan to do when you grow up?

CORA. I want to be a pianist.

FRED. I want to be a lawyer.

MARY. I'm planning to be a nurse.

JACK. I'm going to be a baseball star. Have you ever seen Lou Gehrig? I have.

FRED. He is a famous player, isn't he? I haven't seen him yet, but I've seen *some* famous people. Cora and I saw King George riding in the park in a big coach, and we saw the Duke and Duchess of Windsor.

MARY. I suppose you've seen them changing the guard at Buckingham Palace too, and I envy you that. It's really getting late now. I think we must be going. I've had a very nice time.

CORA. I'm glad you did. We enjoyed meeting you. I'm sorry that Mrs. Gray has not come home.

JACK. Well, we really came to see you.

MARY. I hope that you will visit our school sometime. We think it is a lovely school. It is called Atwater School.

FRED. We would like to. Thank you.

MARY. I hope we will see you again.

CORA. We must plan to.

MARY. Good-bye.

JACK. Good-bye.

CORA. Good-day.

FRED. Bye.

JACK and MARY. Thanks for the interview.

CORA [*after shutting the door*]. How nice they are. I hope we see more of them. [*Sits down and picks up book*]

FRED. So do I. And I do hope that we will visit their school. I wonder what form Jack is in. [*He starts to read.*]

CURTAIN

If through experiences, and more experiences, such as these, training and guidance can make the features essential to good conversation functional for the child, the school contributes in an outstanding way to building poise and developing the personality of the child.

Developing the "daily-theme eye" is turned to good advantage in training pupils how to tell pleasantly an appropriate anecdote or experience in conversation. The outline which follows sketches briefly the procedure by which this goal was achieved.

SHARING EXPERIENCES THROUGH CONVERSATION [2]

Objective. To gain ease, poise, naturalness, and a sense of good form and breeding in everyday conversation, incorporating a school anecdote apropos of something that has been said

Activities

1. Listen to conversation at home, on the street-cars, in stores, at clubs, in the classrooms between or among your friends and acquaintances.

2. Try to imitate some of the good points you have noticed, such as, low soft tones, clear, distinct enunciation, pronunciation, phrasing, emphasis, etc. Strive to attain good posture while standing or sitting. Notice how the speakers move from one story or topic to another. Strive for this in your own conversation.

3. Observe the methods of some of the announcers or comedians on the better radio programs for their methods of telling a hu-

[2] Reported by William H. Blauvelt, Evander Childs High School, New York City.

morous story or anecdote. Pay attention to their plan for reaching a climax or making a definite point. Watch for the placing of emphasis and the effect upon the hearers, if there is a radio audience.

4. Select some historical, literary, or personal story or anecdote which you have enjoyed and which you feel sure others will like, and reproduce it for your friends, or tell it at the family dinner table. Notice the effect. Have you achieved the desired effect? In other words, have you made others enjoy your little story? If the result has not been satisfactory, try to locate the trouble. You might even ask your sympathetic friends for helpful suggestions. Have you added an appropriate story to the conversation?

5. Ask for new or interesting anecdotes from your friends or family. Gather stories you would like to repeat (from biographies you have read or from magazines). Get in the habit of jotting down worth-while items which you feel you may be able to use later.

6. Try these out with your friends and note the effect, each time trying to correct your faults in speech, emphasis, and coherence.

7. Attempt to achieve these results.

   a. Make your story apropos, that is, suitable to the time and fitting to the occasion.

   b. Work for smoothness and coherence in your conversation. (At first this will mean careful planning ahead of time.)

   c. Refrain from interrupting a speaker, but be ready to take advantage of a definite lull.

   d. Select something short and to the point.

   e. Refrain from attempting to explain the meaning after you have told your anecdote.

8. Try telling and retelling under various circumstances, many kinds and types of anecdotes and stories. Which can you do most easily? Which is liked most by your friends? Get in the habit of repeating interesting little things that happen in the classroom, or lunchroom, or halls. Observe humorous or unusual happenings on the way to and from school or at home. Keep awake to what is going on around you. Get in the habit of telling your friends about what you see and hear.

9. In the English classroom in groups of six or eight hold "conversations" in which the sort of anecdotes you have been preparing to tell will fit naturally.

10. Hold a discussion following the conversation activity to see what each member of the group was able to contribute and to learn from the period.

SHARING EXPERIENCES THROUGH CONVERSATION [3]

I. *Aims*

    A. To discover what is interesting or entertaining in the way of personal experience

    B. To learn how to communicate with others

II. *Activities*

    A. To record in a diary an event, a thought, an observation which seemed significant

    B. To look about constantly for interesting material

    C. To learn to speak in a way that will arouse the interest of others by

        1. Using adjectives

        2. Avoiding monotonous sentence patterns

        3. Eliminating the unimportant

    D. To learn to be an interesting conversationalist in a group, observing the rules of courtesy

        1. In telling a humorous anecdote

        2. In relating an adventure

        3. In describing a hobby

        4. In commenting on people

        5. In discussing books

        6. In discussing motion pictures

[3] Reported by Irene Jaworski, Evander Childs High School, New York City.

VII

LETTER-WRITING

"THERE IS NOTHING that will betray our crudeness, our insufficiency, our general inadequacy and wood-headedness as the test of the personal note.[1] . . . Yet," Tracy continues, "it is hard to see what excuse an ordinarily vivid person could have for writing a dull letter. Only one seems possible: mis-education. The idea that everything done with a pen is a task, not a pleasure; that words, when they are written, must somehow come dressed in stiff costumes—come not as they will but as they ought to; the idea that talking is one thing and writing quite another. . . . Things are alive when you say them, but dead *when you write* them." [2]

The failure in letter-writing and the paralyzing attitude toward writing which Tracy deplores are eliminated by the experience-centered activities which schools now set up.

Letter-writing is purposeful and pleasant. Opportunities are legion to write letters which have a destination and reach it. The following illustrations give evidence of the soundness of the statement that [3] "An epic or a system of philosophy is still attempted by very few of the human species, and a large, though diminishing, number of educated men and women end their lives without having written a novel or a sonnet. But we all practise letter-writing."

A PROJECT IN LETTER-WRITING [4]

Based upon the theory that the experience curriculum, utilizing the functional approach, contains definite provision for drill in the fundamental processes, the following project in letter-writing was developed with seventh-grade pupils.

[1] Henry Chester Tracy, *English As Experience* (New York, E. P. Dutton and Co., 1928), p. 299.

[2] *Ibid.*, p. 300.

[3] Walter Raleigh, *On Writing and Writers* (London, Edward Arnold and Co., 1926), p. 35.

[4] Reported by Nellie S. Willison, Allegheny Junior-Senior High School, Cumberland, Md.

133

Impetus for writing to favorite authors arose from a library-club activity. The club was compiling to present to the library a source book concerning present-day authors of junior high-school literature. Following the presentation of book reports, dramatizations, character sketches, and the reading aloud of favorite selections and poems, came the selection of authors to be included in the book. From the completed list, groups of four or five pupils each selected one author about whom they were to find biographical data concerning childhood, books written, hobbies, and interests. Books in the school and public libraries were suggested for reference, including *Who's Who, Living Authors,* and *Junior Book of Authors.*

Oral reports at the ensuing club meetings revealed varying degrees of success. Though many groups had found stimulating material, others reported that little information was available, and some, in dismay, stated that they had been unable to find any. Obviously, some other procedure was necessary. The question, "Wouldn't the publishers be able to give us some information?" was raised.

The suggestion was accepted as practical, and there followed in the regular English periods, a series of lessons on business letters, involving drill in which the following mechanical skills were developed: Letter form; the use of the comma to separate the date, city, and state, and after the closing; the use of the colon in the salutation, and necessary capitalization. Business letters brought from home and examples found in the textbook were studied as models of courtesy, conciseness, and definiteness, and for types of salutations and closings.

From a study of models, the pupils established definite standards, which were placed in a conspicuous place in the room, to be used as a guide in the writing and subsequent appraisal of the letters.

As three different classes were participating in this project, each row in each class constituted a group, all of whose members wrote to the same publisher. It was decided by the pupils that the best letter from each of these groups should be mailed. Rough drafts of letters were read by several pupils, and the contents discussed in the light of the standards previously developed. Under teacher supervision, the letters were then rewritten, and the best one according to the established standards of form and content selected by each group. A general discussion followed, in which each child made a statement regarding his weaknesses as revealed by the group comments upon his letter, and by his own diagnosis. The pupils were asked to keep their letters, to be used for comparison later. Several remedial lessons in letter-writing followed, based upon the needs as discovered by the pupils and the teacher. Another list of publishers was given, and the same type procedure as in the first writing was followed. Each pupil made a comparison of this letter with the first one he had written, and in the discussion of results, reported upon the progress he had made in correcting the weaknesses. Children needing further help were given individual remedial work.

A vitalized opportunity for teaching the correct method of addressing envelopes, and for folding business letters, was afforded, as well as for developing high standards of neatness and exactness. Most of the publishers responded generously, and the letters received were read in class. Pupils noted with pleasure that these letters measured up to the standards they tried to meet in their own letters.

It was with qualms and misgivings that we embarked upon the next step, that of writing to authors. Fearful of having really sincere letters interpreted as a mere device for procuring autographs, yet alive to the opportunities such a procedure afforded, I capitulated to the timid, but hopeful, "Do you think any of the authors will write to us?" The realization that we were writing to successful authors made the pupils try hard, and interest never lagged in spite of necessary drill at points where errors recurred.

Before any attempts at writing were made, the pupils read samples of friendly letters brought by the pupils, found in language and literature books. The pupils discussed possible adaptations to individual authors to be addressed and reiterated standards applicable to this type of letter. Types of salutations and closings were considered to find those appropriate to the pupils' relations with the correspondent. Correct forms of punctuation and capitalization needed in these letters were also reviewed.

Under teacher supervision, the first drafts of the letter were then written. In the following period, the letters were read aloud and appraised according to the standards previously accepted. Criticisms expressed by the group, although stated in non-technical terms, corresponded to the teacher's diagnosis made from her silent reading of the letters.

When the question, "Do you think we are ready to send the letters?" was asked, the general consensus of opinion was, "No, they aren't good enough."

An effort was consequently begun to have practice at this point of need. An attack was made on the use of adjectives and on sentence variety, two major weaknesses. Letters in which sentence structure was monotonous were written on the board and the sentences examined. It was found that the subject was placed first in most sentences, and that a noun or a pronoun was often the first word. Practice in transposing, in as many ways as possible, the order of the words and in supplying introductory words and phrases, was given. Examples of forceful sentences found in some of the letters and in books and newspapers were read, and the pupils rewrote the sentence that they recognized as especially weak.

Next came the teaching of adjectives from the viewpoint of their effectiveness in creating the exact idea. As a preliminary step, samples from the letters referring to entirely different types of books with the identical adjectives were placed on the board. The pupils saw that their words were not sufficiently accurate to be effective. Through several word hunts in the dictionary, in their recalled experience, and in books being read, adjectives assumed their rightful rôle in the pupils' "parts of speech consciousness." The boys and girls were ready to suggest apt adjectives to replace the ineffective ones which had been selected from their letters and placed on the board. Adjectives that would exactly shade the meaning and give the desired impression, were mentioned, and lists were developed of adjectives that might be applied to fit each pupil's letter.

After the letters were rewritten, and their contents judged satisfactory (this necessitated several rewritings on the part of some pupils), they were checked among the individual groups for grammatical correctness, letter form, capitalization, paragraphing, complete sentences, hyphenated words, and spelling. Each group selected in this manner the best letter. The letters were addressed either to addresses listed in *Who's Who* or to the authors' publishers.

Generous replies from such authors as Albert Payson Terhune, Jack O'Brien, Mrs. Martin Johnson, Rachel Field, Dorothy Canfield Fisher, Arthur Guiterman, Dan Beard, Elsie Singmaster, and Will James have been a real inspiration, and the mail man, these days, is a most popular person. The letters are read and discussed with keen enjoyment.

Continued use of the abilities developed in this project have been utilized in the writing to members of the groups out of school because of illness, a letter of sympathy to one of the teachers, and letters to pupils who have moved away.

The project has had gratifying results. Besides the satisfaction of participating in a real situation, technical skills have been developed, and techniques for self-appraisal learned in addition to an attitude toward authors as friendly, real people.

The completion of the project, that of assembling the materials for the book, involved practice in indexing, outlining, bibliographies, preface writing, and logical arrangement.

LETTERS IN NATURAL WRITING SITUATIONS [5]

In Bywood School our aim in written English through the sixth grade is for every pupil to be able to write an acceptable social letter by the time he leaves the junior high school. Though we have departmental organization from third through sixth grade, our work is so scheduled that language, penmanship, and spelling are in the hands of one teacher in each grade. It is her responsibility to develop such spelling and penmanship consciousness that the pupil will feel that these are an integral part of his English performance. Spelling no longer is just a list of words to be memorized; penmanship is not just a series of "push and pull" exercises (though drill is not omitted). The spelling list is employed in writing paragraphs and the measure of penmanship is the neatness and legibility of his daily papers. Not only in the English classes are standards observed, but frequently the English teacher calls for sets of papers in the social studies and checks them for their neatness, spelling, and letter formation.

In order that letter-writing may be natural, the teacher is ever on the alert to find real reasons for writing letters. Teachers have themselves felt so keenly the purposes for letter-writing that their pupils have sensed these purposes and, even in the first grade, ask if it wouldn't be well to write and thank so and so for his kindness to the class on their recent excursion! By way of digression it might be stated that since the introduction of manuscript writing, letter-writing in first and second grades has been definitely accelerated! Spontaneity is not lacking. Class letters (every child using the same sentences) after the middle of the first grade are not undertaken, except perhaps in slow-moving groups. There is class discussion of subjects to be presented in the letters and often groups will unite in discussing certain phases of the subject to prevent monotony for the recipient, but there is great variety in results! Proper attention is given to form and punctuation, and individuality and spontaneity of ideas are encouraged. Especially in the lower grades the letters are profusely illustrated with crayons and the results are colorful and delightful.

The following list indicates the kinds of letters needed to handle the natural writing situations which have arisen:

[5] Reported by Miss Marguerite Tennis, Bywood School, Upper Darby, Pa.

Letters to a sick or injured pupil or teacher
Letter of thanks to a firm for visit to plant
Letter inviting another class, or teacher or principal to visit the group
Letters thanking the group for their entertainment or program
"Get Well" cards, with original "sentiments" and illustrations (developers of individuality, neatness, balance and beauty)
Thanking for this courtesy
Letters to radio stars to thank for program (This activity was well developed in a fourth grade, and letters received in reply from the stars, formed an interesting exhibit as a climax to an activity.)
Letters to parents and interested adults to join in picnics and bazaars held to celebrate events.

One active Junior Red Cross Club in the sixth grade sends Christmas boxes annually to foreign countries and in each box is a letter about our school community and country. These letters are frequently answered and portfolios exchanged, bringing about reasons for writing letters.

Many teachers over the country report success in having their pupils correspond with boys and girls in foreign countries. Mrs. Adele Benson, Oshkosh, Wisconsin, was especially fortunate. Her pupils are exchanging letters with students in fifty different cities in Switzerland, New Zealand, the Philippines, the Hawaiian Islands, Mexico, and India. Kodak views, original drawings, and cartoons add interest to the writers' word pictures of things to see and to do in their native lands. Of course, the stamp-collectors in the class experience additional pleasure from the envelopes in which news for the class arrive.

BUILDING A VOCABULARY

"A word by our early magic was more than a name. It seemed to catch and to tell us as we said it, all the qualities we apprehended in the thing named. . . . This was our first vigorous construction toward forming a verbalized world. It was important because it *let us in* to things that other persons enjoyed. . . . It gave us power over things: lost things were found, wanted things gotten—by name." [6]

The game of words, once so entrancing, has its life quickened in the activities now conducted in English classrooms. A notable example of this kind of unit was submitted by Ruth M. Goldstein for

[6] Tracy, *op. cit.*, p. 176.

her 9A class at the Evander Childs High School in New York City. From an exploration of their present word stock, the pupils recognized how few words were carrying the burden of their communication. Next they cleared out shabby and overworked words by substituting vivid and specific words appropriate to the ideas they wished to express. Then they experimented with apt comparisons to replace commonplace expressions. To clarify meaning they learned to differentiate words they often misused. Finally they applied their word knowledge in purposeful writing which conveyed their meaning effectively and therefore gave them a sense of power over words.

Needless to say, vocabulary is also naturally built by alert reading. Many new words and new meanings of familiar words are picked up and assimilated through the reader's habit of responding to contextual clues and, where necessary, verifying in the dictionary the meaning guessed from the context. Many of the courses of study (see Appendix A) include both training in the use of contextual clues to word meanings and enlargement of vocabulary through conscious attention to new words as they are met in reading.

VIII

REACTING CREATIVELY TO LITERATURE AND TO LIFE

SINCE THE REAL PURPOSE of creative expression is the development of the child's capacity to react *creatively* to his own experience, the process is more important than is the product. The creative person does not sit behind his eyes, he sees with them.

Creative people are "lovers of the qualities of things. They are not engaged, as the learned say that all life is, in becoming adjusted to an environment, but they are engaged in becoming acquainted with it. They are possessed . . . by the wish to experience life and the world." [1]

VERSE WRITING

In every community from time to time some special occasion arises which may give purpose to creative activity of high-school students. In Baltimore such an event occurred on June 1, 1939, when the sculptress, Grace Turnbull, presented to the Eastern High School her memorial to Lizette Woodworth Reese.

The faculty, sensitive to what such an occasion could do for adolescent girls, let the English activities of two weeks preceding the affair take color from it. The following report is a brief statement of what one teacher of English did with her enrichment class of eleventh-grade girls.

CREATIVE APPRECIATION OF LIZETTE WOODWORTH REESE [2]

An occasion that was important to the entire school and to the community furnished the opportunity for lively and varied creative expression in an eleventh-grade class at the Eastern High School. Miss Grace Turnbull created a memorial to the poetess, Lizette Woodworth Reese. It is a marble shrine formed by a shepherd sur-

[1] Max Eastman, *The Enjoyment of Poetry* (New York, Charles Scribner's Sons, 1921), p. 6.

[2] Reported by Caroline L. Ziegler, Eastern High School, Baltimore, Md.

rounded by a group of eagerly crowding sheep. In his arms, the shepherd holds a little lamb. The whole unit is symbolic of the strength and tenderness of the shepherd's life. On the base beneath the bench is carved the poem "Come Every Helplessness."

Because Miss Reese had been a life-long resident of the community in which the high school is located, the memorial was placed in a slight meadow on the school campus where the shepherd can look out over the flowers and hills that Miss Reese herself has made immortal. The erection and dedication of this memorial was of interest to the entire school and community.

Preceding the dedication during the weeks in which the memorial was gradually taking shape on the school campus, we first directed the attention of the pupils to Miss Reese by reading aloud once or twice at assembly periods a few of her best known poems. In my own classes, because we happened to be having the literature unit "What Poets Write About," I supplemented this by reading a few of her poems. Gradually, as the interest increased, many of the pupils read widely in Miss Reese's poetry even after the literature unit was ended. The girls voluntarily sought out places mentioned by the poet—remnants of old lanes now nearly obliterated by city streets, old neighborhood houses with flowering shrubs and trees she talked of and loved. The girls looked with new eyes at their own school campus and trees, knowing that those were the very trees and fields mentioned in many of Miss Reese's shepherd poems. One day I invited the class to share their reading experiences with each other. They interpreted many of the poems they liked best, reading passages here and there, discussed new ideas they had gained, described places they had investigated because of references in the reading, mentioned what they considered some of Miss Reese's outstanding ideas, quoting passages to support their points and reading aloud poems they especially liked.

Earlier, when the date of dedication was announced, the school had been invited to write poems that could be used as part of the dedicatory exercises. This was entirely voluntary. In my class the writing was the outgrowth of their reading and the fact that several members of the class had been selected to read at the dedication some of Miss Reese's unpublished poems.

By this time, having watched the gradual completion of the memorial, the entire school was looking forward eagerly to the dedication. The ceremony consisted of two parts—the first took place in the school auditorium; the second around the shrine was impressive and inspiring. Immediately afterward when the class met for the regular English period, the impressions and emotions found expression in spontaneous though somewhat confused approval and delight.

A little later I asked the class to write their feelings and opinions about the dedication. Some wrote news articles for the school paper; others wrote letters to friends in different schools; still others voiced their feelings in diaries. This gave an opportunity for stating or reviewing and practising principles of organization and effective arrangement. Of course, the revision was another chance to practise sentence improvement and correct mechanics. More important than either, however, were the variety and amount of reading and oral and written expression which the class accomplished without realizing that they were "studying English." Then too, the ideas and feelings which were incoherent and almost inarticulate during the dedication became clarified and strengthened as the girls put them into words. (See page 143.)

A few samples and a copy of the program are appended as evidence of the vitality of this purpose for communication.

DEDICATION EXERCISES

LIZETTE WOODWORTH REESE MEMORIAL MONUMENT

Presented to the Eastern High School by
Miss Grace H. Turnbull, sculptor

June 1, 1939   *In the School Auditorium*

Scripture .   .   . Read by Jean Kuzmaul, President of the Eastern
High School Lizette W. Reese Memorial Association
The Lord's Prayer
Largo by Handel   .   .   .   . By the School
Three Poems by Lizette Woodworth Reese .   . Read by Betty Hill
    "The Shepherd Comes"
    "The Shelter"
    "The Shepherd"
Three songs (Poems by Lizette Woodworth Reese)
    "The Cry of Rachel"   .   .   .   . Music by Mary Turner Salter
    "Glad That I Live, Am I"   .   .   .   .   .   . A Latvian Carol
    "A White Lilac"   .   .   .   . Music by Jeannette Itzel Gruner
Two sonnets in memory of Miss Reese .   .Written by Anabel Hartman
Address   .   .   .   .   . Dr. Elizabeth Nitchie, Goucher College
"The Lord is my Shepherd"   .   .   .   . Glee Club
Address   .   .   .   . Dr. David E. Weglein

On the School Campus at the Shrine

"Unfold, Ye Portals," Redemption by Gounod . . .By the School
Tributes from the School
  "She May Return" . . . . . . Written by Alice Maginnis,
                                       Read by Jean Mencke
  "Inspiration" . . . . . Written and read by Helen Schneider
Poems
  "Come Every Helplessness" (This poem is carved on the monument)
  "The Shepherd Will His Vigil Keep" . Written by Mary T. Gallagher
"Lord Thy Glory Fills the Heavens," Beethoven . . .By the School

INSPIRATION

O shepherd, bent in tender silence there,
Thy look serene recalls the kindly heart
Of her whose poems, as a touching prayer,
Are cherished for the sweetness they impart.

To this dear one we proudly dedicate
Our shrine, enclosed with trees and daffodils,
In humble tribute for those songs that late
She sang of spring midst blossoming lands and hills.

A faith in God, a sense of beauty, too,
Entwine themselves as myrtle branches, tall,
In verses rich and full of meaning true
Which flowed as magic at her softest call.

Though marble's quiet stills thy eager tongue,
Thy poetry will speak to old and young.
                         —HELEN SCHNEIDER
            In memory of Lizette Woodworth Reese

                              1604 East 29th Street
                              Baltimore, Maryland
                              June 7, 1939
Dear Dot,
    You weren't with me, but I know you would have felt as stirred as I
was at the dedication of a memorial to Lizette Woodworth Reese. There
wasn't any sun. The day was cloudy and almost damp. There was a
shepherd and his sheep, there was an organ, and there were girls, many
of them. The first part of the exercises was held in our auditorium with
singing and reading of poetry, and sketches of Miss Reese's life. When
I got up to contribute my share in the dedication, my nervousness left
me and my pride increased—pride in being part of the audience before

me—pride in being able to help in some way—pride in a school and its leader selected for such an honor.

When we went outside to conclude our exercises, my impressions were vastly changed. There it was that I experienced sadness mixed with loveliness. In a beautiful setting of green trees and shrubs was the memorial with its shepherd and sheep, sturdy and peaceful. Surrounding it were many white-clad girls. Organ music completed the picture that compelled me to write to you.

But above it all I heard a bird trill a few notes, then fade away into silence. I saw the look of compassion on the shepherd's face that told of burdens borne and journeys traveled. I experienced a moment of regret that I had not known the woman to whom we were paying tribute. For some time, forgetting what I knew about her, I felt the spirit of Miss Reese hovering over the friends and places that she loved and I imagined her grief at no longer being able to wander in her hills and lanes. I was familiar with her desires to be safe in a fold, but in my ignorance of greater things, I forgot all knowledge that she had given me through her poems and mirrored in my thoughts my own desires. I guess in this instance the real sadness lay in me.

You once quoted these lines to me:

> "Sadness and loveliness went hand in hand,
> Trailing you close whene'er you walked about"

Now I'll say them back to you.

Love,

Betty Hill

Thursday June 5, 1939

Dear Diary,

Just four days ago, June 1, I had a new and thrilling experience. Upon our beautiful, rolling greens was placed a memorial which will be dear to the hearts of Easternites in the years to come. Diary, this memorial is lovely; so tender and sweet in its thought and yet so strong and stalwart in its material structure, that it filled me with a sort of reverence for the one to whom it was dedicated. The recipient of this honor, Miss Lizette Woodworth Reese, a Baltimore poetess, just like you has been my companion in lonely hours, a source of pleasant thoughts, and inspiration. In my solitude, a furtive glance at your pages or intensive reading of Miss Reese's poems gave me companionship; in my sadness, stealthy peeks at your amusing and happy-go-lucky sheets and heartening reflections upon Miss Reese's lighter poems gave me pleasure; and in the depths of despair, recollections of my previously inscribed happier days and thoughts of Miss Reese's climb to fame gave me encouragement. Yes, Diary, Miss Reese has certainly become an additional link in my chain of friends.

At your tender age, Diary, you couldn't know Miss Reese personally but I shall tell you what I have learned about her. Like the soft summer morn, like the shepherd and his flock, like the wise men of old, Miss Reese was a gentle, thoughtful, and intelligent women who possessed an enviable sense of humor. During her life she lived in the neighborhood of my Alma Mater, Eastern. She, too, attended Eastern in her high school days, after which she studied for the teaching profession.

Having received her diploma, she became a member of the faculty of Western High School. Yes, Diary, our friendly rival! Here she made many acquaintances who today cherish dearly their hours of friendship and companionship with her. Deeply interested in poetry, she started upon her rise to fame. Her poems were of a gentle and sweet nature; many were written about the shepherd and his fold.

These poems, such as "The Shepherd Comes," "The Shepherd," and "The Shelter" were the kind of poems which made the reader feel kind-hearted, helpful, and coöperative in dealings with others. They were exact duplicates of the character of their creator, Miss Reese. It would be helpful indeed in our everyday affairs, if we read such verse more often! Don't you think so, Diary?

In our dedication exercises some of her poems were so fervently read that it was inspiring to see how Miss Reese's poetry could envelop 2,300 girls in a blanket of silence. Diary, I was sitting in the balcony where it was very warm and uncomfortable, but during the reading I forgot the heat. I felt calm and contented and looking about me, I saw that my fellow-students seemed to have done the same.

Well, Diary, two years ago Miss Reese was separated by death from her beloved work. Since that time her poems have been even more widely read and warmly accepted. She has just been classed with world famous poets and her work is listed in Granger, Bartlett, and other reference books, with which we have recently come in contact, Diary!

Having told you about Miss Reese, how great she was and yet how humble, how famous she was and yet how human, I'm sure you're interested in the memorial. Its sculptress, Miss Grace H. Turnbull, chose a perfect site for it. It was placed in a woody glen, surrounded by beautiful trees and shrubs, emerald-green grass and daffodils, Miss Reese's favorite flowers. All this beauty will serve to reawaken year after year the sincere tenderness and love of beauty that was Miss Reese. The statue was exquisitely carved out of massive Georgia marble, giving a strong, substantial outward appearance. Yet when I looked at it, I realized there was a deep and tender theme hidden in the folds and curves of the structure. It portrayed a shepherd holding a lamb in his arms while the rest of the flock crowded close to him. One of Miss Reese's poems, "Come Every Helplessness," was carved upon the base of the monument. Diary, just the thought of the steadily increasing beauty of Eastern made me want to help to preserve and protect it; just as I do with your own precious pages.

Moreover in our library a lifelike portrait of Miss Reese has recently been placed. There was no evidence of overwhelming grandeur in her appearance; just a likeness of a woman, simple in taste, sweet in thought, and intelligent in looks, a truly great person to have for a friend.

In the dedication services, the heart-felt coöperation of the entire school was clearly evident. The beautiful readings, the singing by Dorothy Dittmar, and the impressive address by Miss Zouck increased my enjoyment and appreciation. But, Diary, that which impressed me most I have not heard any one mention.

When I think of poets I think of gray-bearded, aged, dreamy sort of persons who have lived long ago and about whom we learn only from our reading. However, at the end of the indoor services I had a new impression. On that stage I heard the direct words of those who knew Miss Reese, worked with her, and valued the friendship of the woman we were honoring. The fact that Miss Cairnes, Dr. Nitchie, and some members of the faculty actually knew her is almost awe-inspiring to me. For as yet, Diary, I have not gained the friendship of a truly famous personage and I admire those who have. Thoroughly impressed, I exulted in the thought that this woman whom we were honoring and whom the world will honor, was an Easternite. It gave me a thrill of joyous pride and hopefulness that some day I shall be successful in my chosen occupation.

At present my occupation is to inscribe upon your spick and span pages memories which I shall always hold dear, but this occupation appears to be at an end. And so until tomorrow night, dear Diary, good-bye, and I hope that you have enjoyed my chattering tonight.

LORRAINE KATZENBERGER

COMMUNAL VERSE WRITING [3]

As a means of introducing her class to poetry, a cadet teacher, who has since had a book of poems published by a first-rate publisher, led a class of twenty-five superior students in what we called "writing poems in concert."

She began: "Let us take some object. Let us think of it in as many ways as possible. Perhaps a narcissus bulb would do. Let us list all the qualities we can think of."

> "Brown"
> "Dormant"
> "Grows lovely green shoots"
> "Bursts into white flowers"
> "Brown ugliness develops into white beauty"
> "Life comes from it"

These suggestions came rapidly from the students as the idea grew.

TEACHER. There is an idea that is poetic. Since this is our first attempt,

[3] Reported by Ada M. Bing, Manual Training High School, Indianapolis, Ind.

let us write the simplest kind of poem. Our pattern should be the easiest in the language. I'll give you the first line. It is suggested by the way our ideas have grown here as we have talked about them.

"My thought is like a white narcissus bulb"

How is thought like the bulb?

PUPIL. It lies dormant for a while and then bursts into expression.

TEACHER. Who will say that in the rhythm that we have chosen?

PUPIL [*quick to see the development*]. That sleeps until its green shoots spring.

PUPIL [*suggests another*]. It is like magic.

TEACHER. A good comparison. How shall we say it?

PUPIL. And then like magic, bursting full of life.

PUPIL. Brings beauty to the world, a living thing.

A lively debate over the proper descriptive word in the last sentence, as well as the way to fit the words into the pattern enlivened the activity, but all were satisfied in the end with the composite of ideas.

So successful did the students feel their first effort to be that they were eager for a second trial. A newspaper story featuring the first airplane ride of an old man, eighty-seven years old, who in his youth had been a stage coach driver, suggested the subject for this trial. Growing more imaginative and at the same time more critical of their images, words, phrases, and rhythms, they disputed every bit of expression until the final repetition at the end.

This is the poem:

SOLOMON RIDES AGAIN

Old Solomon went riding, riding,
    Went riding through the sky.
"This is the first time in my life
    That I have been so high.

"Oh, I remember rutted roads
    And scattered cabin lights.
Oh, I remember wolves that howled
    Through long and lonely nights.

"Then the snail, but now the comet,
    And stars on heaven's ways
Are not more far apart than candles
    Sending forth faint rays.

"I seem to hear my horses' hoofs
    Among the hidden cloud;

> The muffled sound recedes from me
> Yet leaves me young and proud."
>
> Old Solomon went riding, riding,
> Went riding through the sky.
> "This is the first time in my life
> That I have been so high!"

More pretentious in its psychology, a later effort, "The House-maid Remembers," imagines the everlasting housemaid recalling her contact throughout the ages with the works of art and with the books of her cultured masters. Only for a second does she show a fleeting interest in what lies within the covers of the books she dusts. Someone calls her to dust another room and the glimmer dies.

THE HOUSEMAID REMEMBERS

> Endlessly I sweep, and endlessly I dust,
> Corridor and corner, statue and bust,
> Shakespeare in this room, Caesar in that
> And here is a chair where Napoleon sat.
> Endlessly I dust, and endlessly I sweep
> Following my broom, "We both are sheep."
> Little does it matter where I dust—
> Corridor and corner, statue and bust.
> Thus it has been since Troy's fame
> I dusted and swept there just the same.
> Lovely Helen rarely walked the halls
> Where I swept cobwebs from the walls.
> Troy and Oxford were the same to me.
> Only the gathered dust I see
> Here in the old professor's room
> On stacks of books in the morning gloom.
> But now I wonder what's in this book,
> I'll stop a minute or two and look
> To see what's hidden under these pages,
> Forgetting at last the dust of ages.
> Now someone calls for me to go
> And dust another room just so.
> Endlessly I sweep, and endlessly I dust
> Corridor and corner, statue and bust.

After a fourth trial in concert, called "Behind the Mask" and representing the wooing of a lady by Death at a fancy dress ball, the students began writing their own verses with more confidence and success than is usual.

The opportunity to browse through a set of papers entitled "Things I Love" led to request that the teacher, Miss Mulock, explain how she had secured effective verses. Here is her statement.

THINGS I LOVE [4]

The procedure in connection with the "Things I Love" papers was almost too simple to record. A class, not particularly brilliant, but delightful, had read Rupert Brooke's "The Great Lover" and was interested in the variety of things he mentioned. They pointed out particular things that they also loved, suggested other things, and out of that grew the assignment for the next day, just for fun, to list whatever they would include were they writing a similar poem. Momentary attention was given to the smooth phrasing of individual "loves" in the poem, but no special effort toward that quality was suggested.

The next day lists were exchanged, or read aloud, or skimmed through, and so many of them had delightfully smooth phrasing for occasional items that the whole class asked the privilege of bringing their papers in the next day "smoothed out."

That is the whole story. The four papers you selected, curiously enough, were written by a football player; a girl with no special ability, almost below average; a girl particularly interested in sports and out-of-door life; and a very serious-minded quiet boy, studious and not particularly articulate.

SHARING EXPERIENCES THROUGH VERSE WRITING [5]

In a seventh-term English class, in which I have planned to do some work in creative writing, I announced to the students, whose I Q's ranged from 117 to 143 and whose ratings in the previous term had been from 75 per cent to 90 per cent, that one of the things which we were going to do was to compose original poetry. This brought forth protests! I gathered, indirectly, some statistics:

1. Register 28
2. Number of girls who had ever attempted verses . 11
3. Number of girls who had had poetry accepted by a school publication 0
4. Number of girls who had never written poetry . . 17

[4] Reported by Mabel E. Mulock, Allentown High School, Allentown, Pa., to Angela M. Broening who read with genuine pleasure the entire set of papers and selected four to use as stimulants to her pupils' creative writing impulse.

[5] Reported by Florine Schwartz, Walton High School, New York City.

Despite their protestations that they would never be able to write well, we began a series of lessons in which we studied poetic forms, discussed ideas and themes for each, and actually began in class to write according to a fixed pattern (the quatrain, quintet, cinquain, roundel, and sonnet). Sometimes we all pooled our efforts and wrote one poem, and at others we worked individually.

At the same time, during literature periods, we were reading poetry for enjoyment from an anthology containing classic and modern poetry.

The following statistics were obtained directly after three and a half months' work:

1. Register 28
2. Number of girls now writing poetry 28
3. Number of girls now whose poems had been submitted to *The Fort*, the school magazine, or *The Log*, the school newspaper 23

Anne L. Cosse also reports an interesting experience in verse-writing. Her freshman group at the Richmond Hill High School, New York City, had read "Tartary." She asked them to write their own day-dreams in verse form. "If the verses do not come, write a paragraph containing picturesque words, vivid verbs, and figures of speech." She read aloud the verses always praising whatever good point was discernible.

Her invitation to the pupils to drop poems on her desk brought quantities. Most were amateurish, but many had one poetic idea or one memorable poetic image. The pupils enjoyed the process and as a result, after selecting editors from the group, prepared an anthology of the best verses contributed.

In the next account, a freshman group was stimulated to write verses after approaching poetry from the discussion of rhythm, meter, and figures of speech in a textbook available to the class.

SHARING POETRY [6]

As part of their literature work, the eighth grade read Longfellow's *Tales of a Wayside Inn*. Not all the selections were used; only those of interest and within the comprehension of eighth-grade pu-

[6] Reported by Cora Ebert, Supervisor, Western State Teachers College, Kalamazoo, Mich.

pils were chosen. The setting of the Inn today, pictures of the place, and other bits of supplementary information were discussed. After the poem or tale was read, particular attention was paid to the interlude, where the listeners commented on the story just heard, and how it gave a cue or lead for some other member of the company to introduce his story.

The teacher wished the pupils (1) to enjoy story-telling poems; (2) to enjoy good character descriptions; (3) to appreciate an historical landmark, such as the Inn; (4) to have an opportunity for oral reading of poetry; and (5) to realize the naturalness of such a situation as that at the Inn, and the fact that other authors have used the same idea.

No detailed analysis was made of any of the poems read, but just enough explanation was given to keep up interest and clear up any difficulties of understanding.

The prelude was read, of course, in order to get the setting and the characters. The familiar "Paul Revere's Ride" was also read because the children like it, and it was a surprise to them that it belonged in this collection as the landlord's story. The other tales read were:

> "The Falcon of Ser Federigo"
> "The Legend of Rabbi Ben Levi"
> "King Robert of Sicily"
> "The Birds of Killingworth"
> "The Bell of Atri"

A number of the students took their books home to read more of the poems. More time was spent in the study of "The Birds of Killingworth" than with the others. There was a little work done in connection with frequently quoted passages. Nine class periods of one-half hour each were spent in this part of the unit.

After the study of the *Tales* was completed, a class discussion followed about the naturalness of the situation of passing a rainy evening in story-telling, how one story leads to another, and how the common expression, "that reminds me of an incident," kept the ball rolling.

The class then decided to have an afternoon of story-telling similar to that held at the Wayside Inn. In carrying out our own informal afternoon of story-telling, fashioned after the *Tales*, the objectives were:

1. To become acquainted with a variety of narrative poems
2. To have an opportunity to select and to read poems of their own choice

3. To realize the qualities of good poetry reading
4. To have a little experience in improvising and sensing a fitness of theme and time for introducing their poems

The stories selected were narrative poems. A class period was devoted to making plans for this story-telling afternoon. Narrative poems were explained and illustrated. Many poetry books had to be obtained, and some suggestions were given, although the pupils made their own choices. Another period was given over to individual study of the poems. The pupil who had the duty of room host served in that capacity for the occasion. The chairs were arranged in an informal grouping around the host. There was no schedule or plan drawn up as to the time each student was to tell (read) his story, but it was his responsibility to watch for the appropriate time to introduce his tale. Then, too, his little introduction, tying up his story with the one that had just been given, had to be improvised. By listening carefully to the poem being read, he attempted to find some relationship between it and his selection, so he could say "that reminds me," etc.

It so happened that it was a cold, rainy day, so the host suggested that since they couldn't go outdoors for recess, they could entertain themselves by story-telling. By way of conversation, another child commented that the bleak, damp weather we had had so much of seemed to penetrate to one's very bones. That remark provided a good opening for a boy who had prepared to read "The Cremation of Sam McGee." He took up the last speaker's comment by saying, "You must have felt like Sam McGee, who was never warm after he left his state of Tennessee. Would you like to hear about his trip up North and his cremation?" Of course, the group was eager to hear it, for although some already knew it, it is always popular.

After the reading of this poem, another child saw an opening for her story, so she remarked, "Those last lines 'There are strange things done in the midnight sun by men who moil for gold' sound rather weird and tragic. It reminds me of another weird and tragic legend that the English people say recurs on winter nights. Have you ever heard of the 'The Highwayman?' " (Pupil read her poem.)

The story of "The Highwayman" reminded another child of a ride, not so tragic but famous, and he read "Sheridan's Ride."

And so the story-telling went on. The following indicates a few of the narrative poems chosen by the pupils:

> "Goethals, the Prophet Engineer"
> "Darius Green and His Flying Machine"
> "Lochinvar"

"Leap of Roushan Beg"
"Robinson Crusoe"
"The Ride of Caesar Rodney"
"Little Billy"
"How to Tell Wild Animals"
"Gunga Din"

Almost a whole afternoon of our school session was spent in this story-telling situation. There were twenty-seven students who participated and a number of the poems read were fairly long, so it required more than a regular class period.

Except where a few of the students probably read their poems through to a friend for their preparation, the poems were new to the majority of the group. Thus there was a genuine interest in the stories each told, and the situation was a very natural one.

An Experience in Writing Poetry [7]

After reading in their textbook the section on poetry which includes definitions of rhythm, meter, figures of speech, the pupils searched for figures of speech in the exercises in the book and wrote original ones. Then they read aloud the verses, stressing the rhythm. In their textbook they read aloud several poems, singly and in unison, emphasizing rhythm, and picking out figures of speech. Several poems with very marked rhythm were read in unison, with pupils tapping out the rhythm on their desks. Again the poems were read in unison but silently, with pupils tapping out the rhythm. After the teacher felt that the pupils had developed a feeling for rhythm, she asked them to bring limericks to class to read. Pupils then wrote original limericks. As a next assignment they were asked to write two lines about any experience they felt or enjoyed deeply. They were to emphasize "sense" impressions. In one line they were to tell about something that appealed strongly to one of their five senses and in the other line to tell how they felt about it. (It happened that at this time a very heavy snow fell, and many children wrote "snow rhymes.")

The rhymes were collected and the teacher read them to the class but did not tell the authors' names. The couplet that the class liked best was written on the board as the beginning of a composite class poem. A pupil went to the board and wrote lines to go with it that were suggested spontaneously by the class. After about thirty lines were written, the entire poem was read, and the "mood" of the poem

[7] Reported by Florence Guild, Department of Public Instruction, Indianapolis, Ind.

was agreed upon. The unsuitable lines were struck out. The class went over each line carefully, substituting more suggestive words, better rhymes, better meter, and stronger figures of speech. Since this work covered about three class periods, a class secretary kept a copy of the poem as it was written on the board and at the beginning of each class meeting she wrote it on the board in preparation for the class work.

As a result, a very attractive little fourteen-line "snow picture" poem grew from the composite efforts of the class. They enjoyed the activity so much that many gained enough confidence to hand in voluntary "poetic contributions." A class booklet was compiled of picture poems, jingles, couplets, rhymes, and limericks.

STORY-TELLING

Story-telling is a very old art and one that delights children both in the rôle of listener and that of story-teller. Of course, the content of the stories as well as the manner of telling contributes to the experience. That fairy lore fascinates young people is a fact established on the testimony of parents, teachers, librarians, and publishers of books for children. But what folk stories are yet unwritten, or what need to be re-told varies from community to community. The raw material, however, in life or in literature is present everywhere.

The following unit is an account of a delightful—to children, teachers, and visitors—experience in creative story-telling. The teacher, Miss Ritter, tells how this creative experience began and how it ended in a most satisfying climax.

Preparing for Publication a Modern Version of a Primitive Irish Tale [8]

The class. The fifth-grade class with which I work consists of a group of twenty-seven gifted children, ten and eleven years of age, with Probable Learning Rates ranging from 124 to 158 as measured by a group intelligence test. Rather than to speed them through school, an attempt is being made to provide for these children an enriched curriculum, increased cultural advantages, and problems which challenge interests and abilities alike. Recently this class has been engaged in preparing an ancient Irish tale for child readers.

[8] Reported by Eleanor M. Ritter, Teacher, Opportunity Class at Herbst School, Allentown, Pa., as an account of a creative-writing project.

The task, which provoked wide reading, spirited discussion, and frank criticism, proved, in the end, to be an experiment in creative writing as well as a useful exercise in analysis. It also provided some interesting excursions into history, geography, science, and even arithmetic, as will appear in the course of this account.

Getting the project under way. The teacher borrowed from the author an unfinished typescript of a number of Irish tales which had been rewritten for children. In preparation for the project, she read aloud the most amusing of these tales, "The Adventures of Manannan mac Lir." This story was received with such great enthusiasm that requests were made for other tales. The borrowed typescript was then divided into parts and distributed to the children with the comment that the work was unfinished and that the author would welcome their criticisms. The children read the stories silently and then discussed them critically. A little later the criticisms were written out at length. The titles of these stories follow: "The High Deeds of Moria and Maon," "The Triumph of Ailell and Etain," "The Nobility of the Fian," "Navigatio Brendani," and "The Vision of Bauheen."

As the criticisms developed, the children were told that the stories had been rewritten from ancient and medieval manuscripts, or translations from such manuscripts; that there existed similar material from which they might try to write a better story; and that, if they succeeded, the author would be glad to include it in his book.

Those stories that centered about humorous plights or brave deeds were universal favorites. At first the written criticisms were discouragingly short and incomplete. In order to evoke adequate criticism, the teacher asked many questions, attacking terse statements, such as "I liked the story" or "It was a good story but a little too difficult to understand," with the inevitable "Why?" At times, the resulting criticisms were class compositions; at others, they were individual or small group products. Several children exchanging ideas and working together usually evolved a fairly complete analysis of the story. The very definite progress in analysis and the expression of appreciation may be noted in two criticisms written by the same boy.

I think "The High Deeds of Moria and Maon" is good. I would make no changes. The only criticism I make is that the names of the people and of the towns are too hard to read. I think Lavra Laury was very cruel.
—P. L.

I think the map in "Navigatio Brendani" was very interesting. The part in the story which tells "Then the ships sailed on until they reached a small island where dwelt many black dwarfs and pigmies" shows that they reached the coast of Africa. It is interesting to know that the map of Brendan's last voyage was used until George Washington was a boy. Perhaps the Norsemen used this map when they reached the Coast of America.

I think the parts which tell of Brendan's visions are very strange. The sea cat, I believe, was a whale or shark.

—P. L.

Criticisms such as these from every pupil later served as a basis for criticizing, simplifying, and improving the tale of "Lu of the Many Talents," the story which the children helped to rewrite.

Later, when the teacher read excerpts from the translations of the tales used by the class as the source of the story they finally decided to prepare, the pupils noted variations in the stories of Lu and were curious about how they arose. The teacher told the children that all old Irish tales for centuries had been told or sung by bards, some of whom had inscribed their stories or parts of the stories they told on parchment made from the hides of animals. Gaelic bards often improvised. Because of this practice and because the tales were handed down by word of mouth, diversities occurred. One boy, who was very eager to make the teacher's explanation vivid, wrote down a sentence and then whispered it to the child nearest him. When the sentence had made its whispered round, the last child repeated aloud what he had heard. His statement differed greatly from the original sentence, which had been put in writing to furnish a check.

The children recalled that they had learned that many of the greatest poets and story-tellers used old themes. Grimm's and Andersen's *Fairy Tales, Arabian Nights,* and Lamb's *Tales from Shakespeare* were cited as examples of acceptable modern literature from old material. It so happened that the children had memorized Ariel's songs from *The Tempest.* The teacher mentioned that Shakespeare almost invariably employed old stories as sources for his plays.

Writing the tale. In writing the tale, the first choice of episodes was made by the teacher. These episodes, however, aroused much discussion and provoked keen written criticism. The episodes were criticized for suitability, necessity to the story, and interest. Those finally chosen had the approval of the entire class. Episodes chosen were as follows:

    a. The coming and proving of Lu
    b. The council
    c. The exploits of Doda
    d. Preparation for battle

e. The plan of the Fomorians to destroy the power of the Tooaha da Danann
f. The battle
g. Lu's victory over Balor
h. Counting the slain
i. The treatment of the conquered
j. Sword worship
k. Nooaha's restoration
l. Lu's name on the map of Europe
m. Lu's deposition and Lu's adventures in distant lands and his return to Ireland as High King
n. Memorial to Lu's foster-mother in Ireland

Episodes *l* and *m* necessitated the use of Shepherd's *Historical Atlas*.[9] The children were encouraged to point out *Londinium, Lugudunum,* and *Lugudunensis* on maps made from Caesar's maps, reproduced in this atlas. The class then pointed out *London, Leyden,* and *Lyons* on a modern map of Europe. The children were given a brief explanation of the derivation of words. Prefixes, suffixes, and genitives and possessives were studied. Some members of the class looked up the derivations of the words *mother* and *father* in an unabridged dictionary. This gave the class confidence in the idea of language as a changing and developing thing. With the teacher's assistance, one lad who had had some experience with languages (German and Hebrew) incorporated the information obtained about the derivation of the names *London, Leyden,* and *Lyons* in the form of an explanatory note.

The tale was outlined several times because the children disagreed about the length of the episodes. Several pupils suggested subdividing the story in imitation of the arrangement of "Navigatio Brendani." The story seemed to fall naturally into two divisions: first, how Lu became High King, and second, how he left his name on the map of Europe. Because of the unequal length of these divisions, all subdivisions were discarded, and the expression of Lu's importance in Ireland and, later, in other parts of Europe was relegated to the title which became "Lu of the Many Talents," "How Lu Came to Be High King of Ireland," "How It Was that He Left His Name on the Map of Europe."

Of their own accord the children decided to keep the odd tricks of language, for these amused and enchanted them. One little girl particularly praised the expressions, "Question me," and "Not hard

[9] William R. Shepherd, *Historical Atlas* (New York, Henry Holt and Co., 1929), pp. 34–35, 38–39.

to tell." These are her words: "Little children like 'Question me' because it was used in olden times. 'Not hard to tell' is an old saying which is easy to understand." "What was the number slain?" led to "How came Balor by this evil eye?" The first question is contained in the original, but the verb is in the present tense; the second question is not in the original material.

Some children objected to the monotonous use of "He said" and "Said he." Variations, such as, "Persisted Lu," "Undaunted, Lu replied," and "To that Lu replied," were substituted. At times the class could not agree upon words or phrases, so two or three were recorded. Two examples were "three enneads" and "belly." The former, discarded in the second revision for the simpler "thrice nine," aroused comments upon mystic numbers. "Belly," frowned upon by some as a vulgarism, was favored by a majority of the pupils, who appreciated its appropriate frankness in describing a humorous though vulgar character.

In addition to this, language bridges were made to emphasize or subordinate parts which appeared unimportant or disconnected. An illustration of this procedure may be found in the last paragraph on page 5. The simple sentence, "Yet were not all Lu's trials ended," strengthened the conception that Lu proved his boast of many talents. When the episodes were completed, the story was considered as a whole and some further connecting links were forged.

Preparing the glossary. The children had great difficulty with the pronunciation of proper nouns. One boy suggested writing the words as they sounded or translating the names. They used a pronouncing index in Gayley's *Classic Myths* to help them. Then proper names were changed, that is, rewritten phonetically or translated, as the following pupil-written account explains:

The children of the Opportunity Class have translated the original name, Lug Samildanach, as Lu of the Many Talents, so that other children and adults may read the name more easily. They translated names in the story because children and perhaps adults who do not know Celtic would find it difficult to understand and to pronounce the original names. For instance, *Lug Samildanach* or *Lug Lamfada* would be much more confusing to read and understand than *Lu of the Many Talents* or *Lu Longarm* is. Therefore three pupils of the class worked out a glossary for this story.

—G. S. and P. L.

What would other children, for whom the story was designed, want to know about these proper names? Two boys and a girl listed all proper nouns in the story and arranged them in alphabetical

order. Using the glossary in *Ancient Irish Tales* and the pronunciations in parentheses in Keating's *History of Ireland,* they compiled
a glossary which was arranged in three columns. The first, which
was called "Phonetic Spelling," contained proper nouns as the class
had written them; the second, entitled "Celtic," contained the original proper nouns; and the third repeated the phonetic spellings with
diacritical marks which indicated how pronunciations are to be arrived at. The children added a short explanation of each proper
noun. The few words which the children could not find were looked
up by the teacher.

The notes. Meanwhile, other members of the class prepared notes
to explain obscure or unusual things. Generally, two children worked
to explain a selected topic. The teacher suggested and supplied some
reference material, but she encouraged the children to search too:
histories of Ireland, *Ancient Irish Tales,* encyclopedias, and dictionaries were used. When information had been collected, it was rear-
ranged in interesting paragraph form. Paragraphs were submitted
for correction, but the notes were kept, as far as possible, in the
language of the child who gathered them.

If the topic made a general appeal, as did, for example, "The Well
of Slane," writing the note became a competitive class exercise. The
note which was finally selected as an explanation of the Well of
Slane was written by two children, a boy and a girl. The girl became
interested in plants which were and are used for medical purposes.
From her father, a physician, she acquired a long list of these plants.
She formulated questions and gave an interesting illustrated talk
before the science class. Many children drew pictures of the well.
Days afterward when the teacher assumed the topic had been almost
forgotten, one of the boys called attention to additional information
he had found about mineral baths.

Likewise, many children wrote descriptions about fairy mounds.
Some children illustrated their notes with interior and exterior plans.
The note actually used was a combination of two well-written para-
graphs and represented the work of three children.

The entire class also enjoyed reckoning the number of the slain,
and insisted on keeping this passage to puzzle other children. Some
commented on the difficulties of arithmetic with such an awkward
system of counting. The cataloguing of ships in Book II of the *Iliad*
was referred to as a similar literary example of ancient arithmetic.

Supplementary writing. In addition to the notes, much original
writing was accomplished. Character sketches were drawn under the
titles, "Ruadan," "Lu and His Foster-Mother," "Doda," and "Noo-

aha." "The Cat's Eye," "The Silver Arm," and "Balor of the Evil Eye" were enchanting subjects for short sketches. Several children pretended to be soldiers who wrote letters home recounting the details of the battle. Some dramatic moments of the story were selected as basic material for writing a play. One youngster dramatized Doda's feast; another wrote a purely imaginative scene entitled "Lu's Return." Several children attempted poems. One of the most successful was "The Ballad of Lu."

THE BALLAD OF LU

"Oh, High King Nooaha, I plead,
May I have ships and men to lead,
With a sword in every hand,
To find the unexplored land?"

"Lu of the Many Talents,
You are one of Ireland's gallants.
I, High King, your wish will grant
My flag in foreign soil to plant."

"Oh, come, my men, and get aboard.
Come, my strong and manly horde."
"We are coming, Lu the Great,
Bringing our spears of heavy weight."

—F. G. S., Jr.

It was by no means a finished poem in ballad meter, but its spontaneity and its clever conversational shifts rendered it acceptable. Another poem follows:

LU OF THE MANY TALENTS

By Lu Erin's battles were won far and wide.
Of this Celts boasted proudly,
Then showed enthusiastic pride
By cheering very loudly.

Lu used to travel quite a lot
And twice was Erin's king.
Toiltu, who raised him from a tot,
Was happy at this thing.

He left his name in Londontown,
In Netherlands, and France.
No man dared try to strike him down
With staff, or sword, or lance.

—H. F.

Finally, criticisms of the completed story, which the class voted best of all the Celtic stories they had read, were written. Two of these, one illustrative of the average reaction, the other of the individual reaction of an inconvincible skeptic, follow:

Lu Samildanach

Our story differs from other Celtic Tales in some ways. One story, for instance, was a love story entitled "The Triumph of Ailell and Etain." In it and in some of the other stories the hero was in love with a fair maiden. Our main character, Lu Samildanach, had love for no woman.

This story greatly resembles the story of the *Iliad* in so much as the Greeks fought the Trojans and the Nooaha Da fought the Formorians.

Most of the characters were warlike, brave, and noble. But Doda was a vain man with an enormous animal appetite. Many powers were attributed to the men. For instance, Deanhat wielded the power of healing; Luchta the power to supply the men of Erin with all the shields and javelin shafts they required. Some of the other heroes also wielded godlike powers to do different things.

I liked the story because of its fairy and humorous elements. I was thrilled by the tense moment when Lu met Balor of the Evil Eye and Balor told his men to lift his eyelid so that he might see the hero of the opposing army. Now Lu knew what would happen if that eyelid of Balor's were raised. Acting quickly, Lu got out his sling, put a rock on it, and let it fly. The stone whizzed through the air, then pierced Balor's eye, carrying with it the evil eye which fell at the feet of a host of Fomorians. Immediately thirty-nine Formorians were poisoned. Soon the entire army was in flight. What followed I think you can guess. The Nooaha da Danann carried the day.

The pupils all agree that "Lu of the Many Talents" is the best of all the Irish Tales which they have studied.

—G. T. S. and C. W.

Lu of the Many Talents

This story, although partly absurd, is also partly educational. For example, it tells that a flagstone that took one hundred and sixty oxen to lift was lifted by one man and hurled with such force and speed as to partly destroy a six-foot wall, while another character, Lu, not only brought back the stone, but repaired the wall. Impossible! On the other hand, our story tells of ancient man's belief in the supernatural, and it also illustrates his great admiration of physical strength.

To me it seems that this story is the most exciting and the least imaginative Celtic story we have read. It is imaginative, I agree, but not so fantastic as "Navigatio Brendani" and "The Vision of Bauheen."

—A. M. H.

Illustrating the book. The illustration and binding of the book were in charge of an inspiring and experienced art teacher, Mrs. Blanche Lucas. The children derived much pleasure from their efforts to make concrete representations of the characters with whom they had grown familiar. Their zest carried them through the disciplinary practice of much figure drawing, because they appreciated that in no other way could they express their ideas graphically.

The block printing of the book lining was a delightful experiment. Many block prints made by children in English schools and several books written, illustrated, and bound by Viennese children were brought to school and exhibited. Designs were cut from potatoes, daubed with pigment, and transferred to paper.

The finished tale. When the task was finished, the pupils decided to present a copy of the book to the Opportunity Classes in McKinley School. Their presentation letter follows:

> Herbst Opportunity Class
> Allentown, Pennsylvania
> May 26, 1938

To the Opportunity Classes
McKinley School
Allentown, Pennsylvania

Dear Girls and Boys:

It gives us great pleasure to present you with the first complete copy of our adaptation of the Celtic Tale, "Lu of the Many Talents." If you will put this copy of our book in your library, we shall be greatly honored.

We heard that you are writing some Pennsylvania German stories. We do not want to seem grasping, but we would appreciate something you have made this year in exchange for "Lu of the Many Talents."

> Yours sincerely,
> Victoria Pozza,
> *Secretary*

Presentation of a copy of the finished tale to the author of the tales that started this project. The children were so sure of their book's merit that they wanted to present it personally to the author who had started this project. At last, a committee of three eager children was chosen and set out with the finished book, and their delight at their handiwork was even greater when they returned than when they set out.

How vital teaching of expression and of legible handwriting sprang from children's spontaneous drawings is interestingly reported by Florence M. Smith of East Orange, New Jersey.

LEARNING THROUGH EXPRESSING EXPERIENCES [10]

Can we help a child to gain his written English through a series of written experiences in much the same way as he has acquired spoken English? A normal child at eighteen months is just beginning to use language, and two and a half years later he is using all the complex sentences of adult life. He has learned to talk by hearing people talk together, and he himself has talked. If written English is to be achieved in much the same way, each experience must be maturing in itself, yet constantly successful and constantly extending the achievement of the child to higher levels.

The idea that written English might spring from the everyday drawings of the child was first used in East Orange by Miss Ethel B. Hillman, a teacher in the first grade at Elmwood school. It is now being used by a number of teachers throughout the system, with results that are both interesting and revealing.

Every child has experience, no matter how poor his environment. He lives in a world where "Life" is seen and felt. His active mind is open to impressions, and he is displaying interest in all directions: seeing, feeling, hearing, smelling, and tasting things. He is doing certain things and is influenced by them without knowing why. Each day has some joy and some tragedy. He knows that "the world is full of a number of things," and by experimenting with some of these it is somewhat revealed.

A little child takes naturally to drawing. At first, he draws for the mere pleasure of manipulation, but as he matures, his drawings begin to take form. No technical ability is required to satisfy his execution of the things he puts on his paper—they tell something of the world he knows. "Only a part of the child's story appears in his drawing. Some of it remains in his mind. Sometimes the simplest drawing, which to the adult has no form, has a very significant 'story' attached to it which aids in understanding the child's personality (Dr. Sanders, Bellevue Psychiatric Hospital)." All that a child wants is an opportunity to tell his story.

Before we look at these stories for their possibilities for written English, may we look at their significance in helping the teacher to do the first great task of the school—namely, the development of the child in social living. First, there must be the adjustment of the child to his environment and group, and second, the adjustment of the group and its environment to the child. Before this can be done the

[10] Reported by Florence M. Smith, Supervisor of Penmanship, East Orange Public Schools, East Orange, N. J.

teacher must know the child. Many of his experiences and feelings are disclosed through these "mind stories" and in no other way could the teacher get these experiences and feelings except as the child dictates the stories for her to write.

The following stories give a better understanding of Jean and Edward. Both are children in the first grade.

> This is a house on fire.
> I saw it in Manchester Place in the night.
> I felt as though my heart was on fire.

Jean had filled pages with drawings similar to the one connected with this story. Not until she dictated this story, the first Jean ever gave, did any one know that her drawings were anything except for pleasure in manipulation. When her father saw this story, tears came to his eyes, and he said, "What terror the night must have held for her!" The incident happened when the child was three years old.

Edward's letter was written in February to his father in Puerto Rico. His mother had died the previous summer, and he and his sister had been sent to live with grandparents in East Orange since financial conditions did not warrant his father's coming to the States. Here is Edward's first letter.

Dear Daddy Tony,
> The cover has a picture of the white horse and me.
> You are coming soon.
> Have you still got your store?
>> With love,
>> BUDDY

The child waited for his father to return and when he did not return in May, Edward dictated this letter to his teacher:

Dear Daddy Tony,
> I hope you come here soon so you can ride me around on your back at night.
>> Love,
>> BUDDY

On the same day he wrote to his little friend who was out of school because of illness:

Dear Tom,
> Down in Puerto Rico at the beach a fish bone got in my foot.
> I wish you were here.
>> Love,
>> EDWARD

When a child comes to the teacher to have her take his dictation, his whole attitude changes. The teacher is doing something for him, something which he has asked her to do. He is all interest, as it is a "working" and "doing" time which he, the child, anticipates. He takes particular delight in telling his story to an understanding person who will take the time to record the story just as he tells it. He enjoys seeing his story about his picture.

As a little child vividly lives his experiences, he is not lacking in words to express himself. If handled properly, his first experiences with written English are joyful ones. He sees his spoken word as the written word full of meaning for him. He is unhampered with all the skills involved. Later he will be ready to begin some of the techniques.

The technique of written language is very difficult. It is made up of many complex skills, and whether a child learns any of them depends a great deal on whether he has a motive for learning.

By working with each child the teacher is able to sense more easily his wants and to give him the necessary help at the time he needs it. It may be a speech difficulty or the pronunciation of a word he uses. One boy called the conveyance that came for his injured friend an "umbelance." When he saw the word written *ambulance* and heard it pronounced, he looked at it, then at his teacher and said, "Thank you!" Many children do not hear the spoken word correctly or the initial sounds.

No child should be asked to perform beyond the level of his bodily development in the attempted learning of complex skills, or beyond the level of his insight in the attempted learning of mental-intellectual concepts or processes.

John, a boy twelve years old last December, has had to repeat every grade, principally because of his reading. A wholesome American boy from a very coöperative home, he has a remarkable memory and has acquired quantities of information from the radio, from conversations, and pictures. He is very observing, is a great "question box," and shows remarkable common sense. John's reading difficulties are the results of insufficient phonetic training, which seriously affects his spelling. Such simple words as *that* and *what* confuse him. All of this has hampered his written English attempts.

Whenever he has been asked to write, without help, on a given subject, his attempt has usually resulted in one or two simple sentences with very poor spelling. Because of the terrific effort expended and the meager results, each attempt has discouraged him greatly.

Through this new type of English work, John has improved considerably both in attitude and ability. To draw pictures and tell stories about them delights him. He is constantly making appointments with his teacher to dictate another story to be written in his book. He rejoices over two-page stories and is so pleased with the results that he finds great pleasure and satisfaction in reading his stories to others.

Many of his stories are about automobiles, the inspection, safe driving, smash-ups, and travel across drawbridges. Others are about lumbering, airplanes, sailboats, and the Niagara Bridge.

John has, at last, found something that yields him success. He always has a story or picture he is working on and boasts about the thickness of his book and his great number of stories.

Upon several occasions John has invited his mother to school to see his book. He always reads her his latest stories. Here is one of them.

On a Bridge

These cars are waiting for a drawbridge to close. The bridge is open to let a boat go by. When the bridge closes, all the cars will start to move.

They will keep in a single line. If they don't, there will be crash-up with the cars coming the other way. There are traffic cops all along the bridge to keep order.

The sun is setting. The people are hurrying to get home from the seashore.

—John

Another boy, Tony, almost thirteen, the youngest child of a very large Italian family, is the son of a shoemaker. English is never spoken in the home, and consequently the boy has found it very difficult to use the adopted language. Reading and spelling have always been extremely troublesome.

With this language handicap, one can readily understand why writing stories has been a bugbear. At first, Tony drew about half a dozen pictures, but acted as though he didn't dare touch the stories. Finally, one day, his teacher persuaded him to try. Little by little he warmed up and started to speak of the number of stories he had done.

One day, he brought his teacher a picture with a partly written story. She helped him finish his story by taking his dictation. Since then, he has written more and more of his own stories, going to his teacher for corrections. He finds great joy in using new words which he has found in the dictionary, the use of which has also improved his spelling.

From October until May he has written thirty-five stories. His subjects include automobiles, airplanes, trucks, boats, birds, cowboys, bridges, and swimming. Here is one of Tony's stories.

A SEAPLANE

My picture is about a plane. The plane is searching for four important men. They are at the North Pole.

The four men are scientists of the air. Russia wants to make her flying safe so she sent these men to study the weather.

The four men were on a big cake of ice. All of a sudden the cake of ice broke while the men were on it.

The Russian government sent airplanes and ice-breakers to find them.

—TONY

Carol, a first-grade girl, wrote her story without any help except to come and have *birthday* put into her dictionary. With a little help she had the word and she discovered the word *day* in it. Some children, like Carol, will need very little dictation after the first grade; others may need it longer, as Tony and John did.

MY BIRTHDAY

This is my birthday today. I got a new dress for my birthday. And I am having a cake too.

—CAROL

It is interesting to see other children steal up quietly to listen to the child dictating until there is a very intent group "listening in." That interest, as well as need is present, is evidenced by remarks such as, "Oh, I just love to hear other people tell their stories." "Isn't that a lovely thought of Jack's?" "Listen to this, please!" "I'd like to do this all the time." "That's good, John."

No two children have the same experience because of variation in native ability, depth of interest, previous experience, drives, and ambitions. Neither will they learn or develop at the same rate, but if a real interest in writing has been awakened, the creative process will go on, and "creative writing" will have many meanings.

As far as the skills are involved, the child learns the use of many of them by seeing the teacher use them and hearing her say, "I put quotation marks here because you said this" or "I am beginning this word with a capital letter because it starts the story." It gives him a meaning for all skills used and a greater willingness to accept their use.

Some of the outcomes from this approach to written English are listed below. Some of the objectives such as individual adjustment, right attitudes which function in everyday living, and appreciations have no objective measurements and only the judgment of the teacher can be given, while with the subjects involved we do have quite objective measurements.

A. *Attitudes and Appreciations*

1. Desire to express themselves in pictures and stories; desire to have stories written exactly as they give them (no words changed)
2. Experiences shared and discussed as an outcome of stories read
3. Sensitivity to the demands of individual and group welfare
4. Appreciation of stories told by other children
5. Pleasure in showing and reading their books to visitors
6. Friendliness and helpfulness toward the other members of the group; respect for and tolerance of other members' rights, feelings, and viewpoints
7. Beginnings of appreciation of literature as the subject-matter of everything that man has thought or felt or created

B. *Knowledge and Skills*

1. Vocabulary; the correct use and spelling of many words were learned
2. Story-telling as entertainment to group and as self-expression
3. Reading of their own and others' stories
4. The alphabet needed to arrange words in their dictionaries
5. Capital letters for names of particular persons, names of particular places, special days, first word in sentences, important words in titles, first word in quotations
6. Plurals of nouns and pronouns
7. *ing* and *ed* endings of verbs; forms of a few irregular verbs
8. Awareness of use of quotation marks, apostrophe for possession, apostrophe for contractions
9. Use of dictionaries
10. Handwriting, margins, indentations, spacing between words, letter forms

Although much of the teaching has been informal, it has been quite systematic—incidental yet not in any sense haphazard—and in classes with thirty or more children.

THE COÖPERATIVE STORY [11]

The coöperative story is one that is formulated from individual suggestions fused and welded together into a complete and literary whole by the activity of the teacher and the children working together. Its subject-matter comes either from one of the content subjects or from "imaginings" stimulated by real or literary experiences. In either case this kind of creative activity needs to be purposeful and concerned with significant ideas.

There follows a check sheet useful in planning a coöperative story activity, in appraising the effectiveness of work accomplished, and in revising procedures to the end that more worth-while outcomes may result.

I. *Stimulation*

    A. Was a purpose in writing established by the teacher? By the pupils?

        1. To add to chart stories which form a record of the children's experiences

        2. To add to note-books, and to be used for reading purposes

        3. To read to another group, another class, or to visitors

    B. Was a motive as to quality of writing established for the children?

        1. To show improvement over the last story written—specific aims mentioned

        2. To write as well as a story in a book is written

II. *Readiness of the Children*

    A. Are the children ready with the content of the story?

        1. Is the content true?

        2. Is it interesting?

        3. Is it in detail?

        4. Is it worth while?

        5. Are the children's ideas clear?

    B. Are the children ready with language for the story?

        1. Do the pupils use the words specifically related to the ideas correctly?

        2. Is there real meaning behind the words used?

[11] Reported by William R. Phipps, Supervisor of Schools, Talbot County, Md. For a detailed outline with concrete examples of coöperative stories by primary-grade children write to Sophie C. Camenisch, Chicago Teachers College, Chicago, Ill.

3. Has there been sufficient and varied experience with the ideas and with the words involved to make for an effective use of them?

III. *Informal Use or Recall of the Ideas Involved*

A. Did the teacher have the children recall the facts involved?
1. Did the pupils use key phrases and enlarge upon them?
2. Did the pupils interpret (not enumerate objects) a picture or pictures?
3. Did the pupils recall a whole experience, a process, a story, a visit, etc.?
4. Did the pupils explain drawings, sketches, charts, displays, etc.?

B. Did the teacher stress the use of meanings?
1. Did the pupils use ideas behind the words?
2. Did the pupils bring out comparisons and contrasts?
3. Did the pupils see end results rather than immediate facts?

IV. *Formulation of Ideas*

A. Did the teacher lead the pupils to organize and to evaluate the material at hand?
1. Was the development of a "single phase of an idea" urged?
2. Were the pupils helped to weigh and to sift the material so that only closely related material would be combined in the story?
3. Were the pupils helped to arrange the ideas in the best possible order?

B. Did the teacher lead the children to feel the continuity of the ideas?
1. Did they talk through the outline?
2. Did they make the sequence of ideas more impressive by referring to pictures, objects, displays, charts, and drawings?

V. *Actual Writing*

A. Did the teacher aim for a variety of expression?
1. By having several pupils give sentences related to the same idea?
2. By encouraging children to suggest other more effective ways of saying the same thing?

3. By encouraging the coöperative critical attitude rather than the personal critical attitude?

4. By supplying words or suggesting that certain words suit the purpose better—making sure that the pupils understand the use of the words?

B. Did the teacher make the enterprise coöperative?

1. Were the efforts of all the children encouraged and considered?

2. Were expressions from various children pieced together to make better sentences than those given by one child?

3. Were the pupils given the responsibility of following the outline or plan of work, and of suggesting the next logical part, rather than having all the initiative come from the teacher?

VI. *Judgment of the Finished Product*

A. Did the teacher help the pupils to judge the finished product?

1. Did the pupils read it over and notice its smoothness or lack of it?

2. Did the pupils notice gaps in the sequence of ideas?

3. Did the pupils notice any evidence of monotony of expression?

4. Did the pupils suggest changes for any of these defects?

5. Did the pupils notice good qualities in the composition?

6. Did they evaluate the product in terms of previous efforts to point out improvements or the need for additional effort along certain lines?

B. Did the teacher evaluate the finished product?

1. In terms of past work along the same lines?

2. In terms of improvement in overcoming previously realized shortcomings?

3. In terms of noticing present needs?

4. By making note of shortcomings and suggesting corrective measures?

VII. *Final Appraisal*

A. Was the coöperative method really used?

B. Was the greatest possible use made of each pupil's contribution?

C. Were the children given time to think about their contributions and about the contributions of other children?

D. Were the children forced to mold their ideas into a previously conceived plan which permitted little or no originality, and which lacked flexibility?

E. Was the teacher's authorship too evident, or was most of the expression the children's?

F. Are the children growing in power in using language to express their ideas?

G. Are the children ready with ideas and with language usage to express those ideas, or is the story drawn out of the children with too much effort on the part of the teacher?

H. Does it seem necessary to make any change in the type of presentation of material to be used as the basis of the coöperative story?

I. Does it seem necessary to provide for more experience with the use of ideas, and the pertinent language (following the initial presentation) before the children can be expected to develop worth-while coöperative stories?

J. What was the prominent and valuable feature of the activity?

K. What was the prominent undesirable feature of the activity?

L. What changes can be made to overcome the shortcomings evidenced in the activity both on the part of the teacher and on the part of children?

Relating imaginary experiences by means of a make-believe broadcast was a creative activity which brought pleasure and stimulated growth in expression on the part of Florence Guild's [12] seventh-grade pupils.

SCENARIO WRITING

PROJECTING *IVANHOE* AS A PHOTOPLAY [13]

A group of sophomores, after reading *Ivanhoe* and after seeing its great possibilities for moving-picture production, decided on a moviemaking project.

The first step was the decision concerning committees. The following were named: scenario writing; properties, including scenery and

[12] For details communicate with Florence Guild, Department of Public Instruction, Indianapolis, Ind.

[13] Reported by Merle J. Koch, 326 Lincoln Ave., Lansdowne, Pa.

costumes; and casting. Each member of the class chose the committee in which he was the most interested.

The second step was the decision concerning the scenes which were to be included. In this the entire class took part, acting as a cutting committee. After deciding upon the most essential scenes, they found that it was a big task to preserve continuity. Therefore, the decision was reached to divide the scenario-writing committee into two groups—one to write up the big scenes, about ten in a number, and the other to build up the informatory scenes. The difficulties encountered brought about intelligent discussion of what constitutes good drama. Their findings and adaptations they submitted to the entire class for approval. Each scene was acted out and commented upon for effectiveness, etc.

The properties committee, including scenery and costumes, did a considerable amount of research. The costumes and scenery groups used many books in their attempt to make as authentic as possible the scenery and wearing apparel. Those who could draw worked on diagrams of each scene. Their work also was presented to the class for the members' approval.

Finally the casting committee submitted its recommendations, in each case accompanying the name submitted with reasons for that choice.

Thus we finished the project, feeling that we had enjoyed Scott's romantic novel.

Coöperating on Our Own Motion Picture [14]

"Richmond Hill, To Thee" or "The Mystery of the Missing Pitcher" was an interesting experiment in ingenuity and coöperation. The writing of the scenario was launched as an assignment for every pupil. Although every member of the class submitted a script, the plot finally chosen was evolved by class discussion. Every person in the class had a job—self-imposed. Although in this project, as in others, the burden of carrying it through to successful completion was not evenly distributed, I have never had a class project in which work and enthusiasm were shared by all members of the class as they were in this—with the result that every one, not merely a few leaders, had the satisfaction of watching the film develop from a story on paper to the main feature of thirteen movie shows. Since coöperation was the key-note of the production, the class, making

[14] Reported by Miss Myra J. Adams, Richmond Hill High School, New York City.

coöperation the key-note of its commencement award, presented ten dollars to the student who offered the most satisfactory combination of high average in four years of English, high rating in Regents, and extracurricular activities in the field of English.

IX

PRODUCING A NEWSPAPER OR MAGAZINE

THE CLASS NEWSPAPER or magazine is a stimulating source of vital and varied writing. Techniques suitable to different grade levels are illustrated in the following descriptions of such projects as actually carried on by teachers. The needs of pupils and the opportunities of communities make necessary differences in the methods of development. However, in all of the plans there are provisions for (1) variety of subjects for composition, (2) pupil planning and direction, (3) functional teaching of language skills, and (4) pupil evaluation of results.

THE NEWSPAPER IN SIXTH-TERM ENGLISH [1]

Stimulated by the remarkable exhibit of sixth-term newspapers for the spring term, my pupils undertook to prepare newspapers attractive in appearance, artistically illustrated, original, and readable.

The three classes respectively separated into three groups, each being responsible for the publication of one of the required newspapers. To find competent typists and able artists in a group of twelve is a problem, but we divided up as equally as possible what talent we found. Our editorial staffs were chosen; dates were set for publication; and work began at once with a genuine spirit of competition evident. A blue ribbon was promised as a reward to the group producing the newspaper voted as best by the members of my sixth-term classes. The finished newspapers provided nine interesting club days when each student showed his part of the newspaper and read his contribution.

During the last week of school our newspapers were placed about the classroom and students allowed full freedom one day to inspect them. They had been instructed as to a rating scale and dropped their ballots into a ballot box provided for that purpose and un-

[1] Reported by Lillian Van Wormer, Richmond Hill High School, New York City.

175

opened until the close of the school day. The vote was overwhelmingly in favor of giving the award to *The Transcript*.

The paper reproduced in a six-page sheet the news of 1900–1905. It was published as a school paper of that period. The students had visited libraries or used papers preserved in their own homes to secure material and to find pictures to sketch, such as the styles of that day, Ford's early automobiles, and even the Wright brothers' first airplane. An editorial urged the reader to cease scoffing and to awake to the possibilities of future travel in the air. An interview with the operatic star, Madame Schumann-Heink, who died the week the paper was presented to the class, was an unexpectedly appropriate feature. It was during the chosen period that Richmond Hill, hardly more than a suburban town, built the high school of the dome. Naturally *The Transcript* painted that event with much delight. The paper was a student digest of a colorful period, written as a whole in good English of a journalistic style.

The paper which stood next on our voting was the third edition of *The English 6 Times*. This paper was published under the date November 13, 2036. Again Richmond Hill was entering a new high-school building, expressing all science could present in an up-to-the-minute edifice, fully equipped. Glass blocks instead of brick allowed health-giving sun rays; escalators carried happy loads up and down; visual and radio instruction was provided; student self-government left little for teachers to do except to act as animated reference books of superhuman intelligence. The humor column, however, smacked strangely of those tidbits which so delight students today. The one feature most enjoyed by the class, perhaps, was a drawing which represented the television apparatus in the school upon whose screen was shown a current football game in which Jamaica was going down before a sturdy R. H. H. S. team. It was with justifiable pride that Miss Stock and her group presented their paper to their classmates.

The last day of the term the students themselves summed up the newspaper project. In their opinion it was "a lot of work but a lot of fun, too." They liked the idea that their written work had a definite objective and could be compared with that of other students. They felt that it developed initiative, originality, and a sense of responsibility as well as revealed unsuspected talents and latent ambitions. To many it proved the most interesting event of high-school English and to a few of all high-school instruction.

Hortense Barten at Richmond Hill High School, New York City, also reported a dynamic unit during which her honor class in

English 2 published a forty-page magazine with many drawings and a literary contribution from every member of the class. The general theme of the magazine was winter sports; the title of the magazine *The Campus Constellation*.

SENIOR CLASS BOOK [2]

One of my senior class books consisted of biographical sketches of New Yorkers prominent in some activity, such as city government, social work, newspaper work, the arts.

The material for the essays was gathered by interviews as well as by reading whatever was available. If the first letter requesting an interview did not meet with the desired response, another person was chosen for the subject of the essay. Most of the persons, however, responded graciously; they granted interviews varying in length from five minutes to an hour. Heywood Broun granted an interview over the telephone, since he was too busy to arrange to have a student call on him.

The process of writing the book seemed of real value. Many of the students were thrilled with the opportunity of talking to a distinguished person. Some received inspiration which will likely influence their choice of career.

SCHOOL MAGAZINE [3]

Approach. During the first week of the semester a little booklet of poems by the pupils of another school lay on the library table. After a number of the class had shown interest in the poems, the teacher read several of the best ones and offered to bring in other poems by children. A discussion of the ability of children to write for publication began. The teacher suggested the possibility of printing a magazine if the children wished to carry the responsibility of furnishing the material, making selections and correcting copy.

Preparation. The class spent several days studying children's magazines, particularly *Child Life* and *Story Parade*, to note the make-up, types of material printed, and general character of the poems and stories. Two or three language periods were used in the discussion of the source of story ideas, types of material they could write, who was to constitute their reading public, the general organization of the activity.

[2] Reported by Miss Hortense Barten, Richmond Hill High School, New York City.
[3] Reported from Randall School, Madison, Wis. (Principal, Mrs. Alice E. Rood).

Procedure. An editor-in-chief was elected from the sixth grade. From each of the three classes editors were selected to have charge of departments. Thus there were three "story editors," three "school news editors," etc. The departments were not alike in all groups, as they were suggested by the pupils themselves. They included stories, poems, plays, news, puzzles, jokes, book notes, nature study, and social events. The editor-in-chief was responsible for writing an editorial for each issue.

An announcement of the magazine (written by class composition) was sent to every room in the building with a request for contributions. The majority of the contributions were to come from the sixth grades, however. Any pupil was free to use his language period any day for writing his contribution to the magazine. It was necessary, for the first issue, to spend some time stimulating story ideas by discussing how some of their own experiences could be woven into stories, and how possible stories might come from pictures. In no case did the teacher develop the stories completely, but rather suggested situations for stories and read poems to give ideas of poetic themes and of rhythm. Pupils who at the beginning were awed at the prospect of writing for publication soon made shy attempts and, on finding them welcomed, were eager to have a part in the writing each month. Pupils who found imaginative stories difficult were encouraged to report school news, boys interested in sports reported games, a model-airplane club wrote suggestions to other young makers of model planes. For the first issue the chief problem was stimulating the pupils to write; for the second issue and the third issue, it was leading the editors to a wise selection of material for publication and the maintenance of an increasingly higher standard for the contributions.

Contributions (first drafts) were given to the editors of each department for evaluation. In some cases several stories were read to the class and a selection made by vote. In case a story or article was rejected, general suggestions for improvement were given. No detailed criticism was permitted on stories of uninteresting content (interest from the pupils' viewpoint was the criterion). Pupils who wrote such stories were encouraged to write again but not to correct rejected articles.

When an epidemic of hair-raising mystery stories appeared, the teacher discouraged their selection. In several situations she thought it well to sacrifice some pupil responsibility to the necessity for influencing taste. In conversation lessons the class discussed a publisher's responsibility for the "tone" of his magazine and for its values to his readers. Except for a few such situations, the selection of contributions in each issue was the pupils'.

Standards for the contributions were set up by the editors. They emphasized interest, quality of expression, choice of vocabulary, and form of writing (in the order listed). Better quality was required for the third issue than for the first. Only original material was printed.

The editors were expected to proofread all copy. First drafts, after acceptance, were returned to the author with suggestions for improvement. Sometimes the author read his story to the class and received detailed criticism. In other cases, the author and the editor went over the material together. The teacher gave assistance when asked, but left the responsibility with the editor of each department. The author prepared a good copy (meeting the requirements of the editors as to form), and this copy, without the teacher's correction, was sent to the typist.

Publication was made possible by means of the Ditto machine. The cover designs were made with Ditto ink, as were the few illustrations used. The master copy was typed by a clerk. Pupils assisted with making copies.

Three issues were printed, one the last of October, one just before Christmas recess, and the last at the close of the semester.

The magazine contained from seventeen to twenty-seven pages. Eighty-five copies were made in order that each pupil might have one. A few extra copies were sent to people interested in the activity.

Evaluation of results. Each issue of the magazine was intensively and critically appraised by the classes as a part of their preparation for the next issue. Stories were read in the light of standards which had been set up. Form and language accuracy were judged on the basis of what might reasonably be expected of sixth-grade pupils. Improvement, not perfection, was the goal and evidence of growth in story quality was eagerly sought; standards for the new issue were set up in view of needs and accomplishments in the preceding issue.

Choice of subject was left to the taste of the individual, but suitability of his subject for the readers of the magazine and their interests came in for evaluation. Manner of writing received the bulk of the criticism. Such expressions as "He did not develop that part of the story enough, left too much to our imaginations" or "All of that first part is unnecessary. He ought to begin with the exciting part" were not unusual comments. The use of conversation to enliven the story was frequently suggested. Pupils were required to make constructive suggestions. The authors were always very much interested in these periods of discussion after publication.

Punctuation, capitalization, and paragraph indentation came to be more or less like good manners. A high standard on those points was merely "expected" of authors. Authors were quick to explain that such errors as were discovered were "misprints." They were reluctant to be found making the same mistake twice.

Outcomes evident in the work produced include:

1. Greater interest and information and better taste in magazine reading
2. Varied information from wide investigation on subjects for writing
3. Taste and judgment in considering subjects for writing
4. Greater clarity of expression, more variety in manner of expression
5. Effort made to suit vocabulary to subject and to reader
6. Better appearance and general form of written work
7. Improved sentence structure
8. More careful use of language tools, capitals, punctuation
9. Increased ability to select material of interesting content for publication
10. Careful planning of stories, better organization, and development of theme
11. Ability to evaluate own contributions and improvement
12. Practice in composing effective and correct letters
    a. To clerk to ask assistance in printing
    b. To other rooms in building to ask for contributions
    c. To contributors, expressing appreciation and encouraging effort
    d. To other schools to ask for an exchange
    e. To interested people, letters of transmittal accompanying copies of the magazine and asking criticism
    f. To school editor of *Wisconsin State Journal* asking her to come to talk about reporting news
    g. To editorial department of *Wisconsin State Journal*, thanking them for permitting the class to visit the plant
    h. To newspapers, expressing regret at discontinuance of school page

Along with the knowledge and skills came some wholesome attitudes including these:

1. Sense of responsibility on part of editors for producing the magazine
2. Satisfaction of accomplishment on part of contributors and editors
3. Realization of need for tact, in making suggestions and encouraging each other in writing
4. Sense of the ethical responsibilities of authors to readers
5. Willingness to accept graciously the decisions and constructive suggestions of the editors
6. Appreciation of abilities of others

7. Attitude of appreciation for assistance of classmates and teacher
8. Habits of promptness in meeting requirements as to time and for the acceptance of contributions
9. Ability to work together, willingness to sacrifice individual opinion for the judgment of the group when necessary
10. Appreciation of meaning of originality and the ideals of authors about it

Correlated activities included:

1. Excursion to newspaper plant to see the setting of type, the editorial department, and the printing of the paper
2. Construction of tests to check mastery of language tools
3. Wide reading of both poetry and prose of good literary quality

Developing Standards in Written Expression by the Use of Daily News Written by the Children [4]

Every day one child was selected to write a news item on the blackboard. He wrote on any subject which he thought might interest his classmates. After the class had discussed the news, it was copied in the News Book. This book was placed on the reading table and was in constant use. A few excerpts from what the children wrote between January 24 and May 4 will indicate what sentence structure, punctuation, and capitalization was experienced through this activity.

Jan. 24, 1938

Today is the first day of the term.

Dorothy T.

Jan. 25, 1938

We have some new children in our room. The other 2A's have gone to Miss Ryan's room.

Elizabeth H.

Jan. 27, 1938

Each morning since it has been cold we have been feeding the birds. They are waiting in the back yard when we get up.

Mary Elizabeth W.

Jan. 28, 1938

I saw a red bird yesterday. Seventeen of our children fed the birds yesterday.

Richard N.

[4] Reported by Lucinda B. Snyder, Fairbanks School, Terre Haute, Ind.

Feb. 2, 1938

Yesterday we put out a soap shaker for the birds. We put bread and fat in the soap shaker. Birds will come here on cold days.

CORDELIA ANN H.

Feb. 4, 1938

We read a story of the little old woman and the cakes. The little old woman was changed into a woodpecker.

DOROTHY R.

Feb. 7, 1938

I saw a chickadee Sunday afternoon. I fed the chickadee some bread and soon the bread got smaller and smaller.

WALTER T.

Feb. 18, 1938

Some children brought some more cotton to use for the Eskimo Village today.

DONALD M.

Feb. 24, 1938

Since we have made our bird cafeteria we have had a few bird friends. One was a pigeon.

JANE B.

March 1, 1938

When March winds blow we think of kites and other outdoor play things.

CORDELIA H.

March 2, 1938

Betty Elmerick and Norman Dean have made the background for our puppet show.

ELIZABETH M.

March 7, 1938

Last Friday we told Miss Kelly and Mrs. Kuhlman to come to our puppet show. Mrs. Kuhlman let some of her children read.

BARBARA V.

March 8, 1938

Our room played Thorn Rosa, a singing game, for the P. T. A. meeting.

RICHARD N.

March 9, 1938

We have some pictures of workers in our room. We get our report cards today.

VERN K.

March 17, 1938

We have a new girl. Her name is Delores Voges.

DOROTHY R.

March 24, 1938

We have frog eggs. One tadpole has hatched out. It is very little.

DOROTHY J.

April 13, 1938

Next Sunday is Easter. That is not very long from now.

DOROTHY M.

April 22, 1938

Emil Taxay is in the third grade. He went to Mexico this winter. He came and told us about Mexico.

BETTY McD.

April 25, 1938

Emil Taxay came in and told us that Mexicans said the word "serape" fast. He said that the Mexican people are very polite.

JOHN M.

April 25, 1938

There is a carnival in town. I went to see it last night. I rode a pony two times.

JOHN C.

April 28, 1938

The Mexican people sit under umbrellas and sell their wares. Chili and hot tamales are good Mexican food.

MARY R.

April 29, 1938

Mary is moving tomorrow. Elsa is back. Mary Elizabeth wrote the riddle. Today we are finishing our Mexican book.

MURIEL G.

May 2, 1938

We want to finish "My Mexican Book" today. Our poster is about done.

REGINALD G.

May 4, 1938

Bobby Simms brought two sombreros. We invited our mothers to come and see our Mexican Program.

BILLY G.

Among the outcomes of this activity which carried over into later pupil experiences are these: (1) a feeling for the sentence as a complete thought; (2) the ability to tell one thing at a time; (3) the ability to write a simple sentence without a copy; (4) growth in ability to express ideas clearly; and (5) joy in the feeling of successful accomplishment in written expression.

Producing a Newspaper in a Fifth Grade [5]

How the unit began. The basis for this unit really belongs in two periods. The little school newspaper began in a class of high fifth children seven years ago. It had its birth as an answer to a direct appeal made by the class of over-aged Mexican children. They wanted a school paper and asked for it. I told them we had no equipment but, if they really wanted a paper and were willing to do the work necessary, I would do all I could to help them. Various names were suggested, but when *La Prensa, Jr.* (*La Prensa*, a local Spanish newspaper) was suggested, the vote was unanimous. An editor, reporters, and stencil cutter were elected. The editor wrote the copies in longhand. Members of the class made duplicate copies in a laborious manner. The newspaper slowly improved in form and content.

The second period came this year when interest had reached the point where the class really wanted to make an intensive study of newspaper work. Our little paper is now typed on a stencil and mimeographed. All work is done by the children.

What the unit aimed to do. The wish for an organ of expression in which the whole school could join was the initial object. Then this year the aim was to find out how real adult newspapers were handled. From the teacher's standpoint the purpose was to provide vital subject-matter about which the class would wish to express themselves in effective and correct oral and written English.

What materials were used. The most intangible but most valuable of materials was the interest which has never waned. For the actual materials we use a typewriter, stencils, mimeograph, rolls of paper (newsprint), red and green ink, pamphlets on newspapers, reference books, excursions, and talks by men experienced in the business.

How the unit was introduced. As an introduction to the unit immediate interests were used. When the class had decided that they wanted to study newspaper work, a printer, who had a little girl in

---

[5] Reported by Angie Weibling, Teacher, and Dora Mabrito, Principal, Sam Houston School, San Antonio, Tex.

the class, brought type, spacers, and other materials. He gave a talk in preparation for the excursions which were made later.

How excursions stimulated expression. The entire class made excursions to two newspaper publishing companies, one an English daily, the other a Spanish daily (*La Prensa,* in whose honor our paper was named). Every phase of the work was seen and many samples were brought back to school: raw material, type, matrix, metal columns, stereotype plates, copy, proof, and printed columns. Two newspapermen from *La Prensa* came to the class and added to the knowledge actually acquired by further explanations. The children asked questions and made responses which taxed their power of clear oral expression. Their vocabulary was growing rapidly. The printers of our little paper made another excursion to a printing shop for further information. Committees of children were sent to a printers' exhibit, a high-school printing shop, and the public library. Where the entire class was not permitted to enter, committees representing the class gave reports on their return. This involved correspondence for appointments, notes in preparation for the trip and for the talks to the class. The preparation of each monthly issue of the newspaper became a vital part of the development of the unit.

What written English grew naturally from unit. A scrap-book was made as a class activity. Short, clear sentences told what had been learned. Pictures of famous newspaper men were cut and pasted, among whom were Gutenberg, Franklin, Gail Borden, and O. Henry. A vocabulary list was made of all new words learned. A second activity came as a program originated and given by the class. They had been much interested and amused at the maxims from *Poor Richard's Almanac.* The class was divided into about six groups each of which dramatized one of these maxims. Examples: "A penny saved is a penny earned." "Waste not, want not." As O. Henry is of local interest, one of the girls made a clay replica of his home in San Antonio as it is today. Another girl gave a short account of a visit to his home in Austin.

What was accomplished.

1. School spirit is definitely promoted. Every child is asked for contributions to the monthly issue. The primary grades send in simple sentences and drawings. Any primary grade may call for a reporter from the low or high fifth grades to write up an activity they may wish to contribute. This stimulates an interest in oral and written English throughout the school.

2. Sympathetic understanding between classes and individuals is kept alive. Each class knows what the others are doing.

3. A tie is formed between school and home. If a child's name appears in connection with a worth-while enterprise, the parents are naturally pleased.

4. An opportunity is given for more respect for the culture and personality of a Spanish-speaking community. The children were happy to know that the faculty and visitors were interested in the newspaper received in their homes.

5. A bond is made between the big Spanish daily which serves our community and the little *La Prensa, Jr.* which serves our school. The big publishing company has been most kind and sympathetic.

6. An interest is fostered between ex-students and present-day pupils. Often students who have been out of school some time wish to be subscribers.

7. The staff is given a motive for application to duty. Some of our boys who have worked on our school paper have become printers and newspaper men. One boy who has recently graduated from high school is now editor of a magazine in English on the activities of Spanish-speaking people in San Antonio.

8. Opportunity is afforded for using good judgment in selection. The low and high fifth furnish the staff. It is done by election.

9. Responsibilities are given to the staff.

10. Free expression is encouraged in art. Talented children are not the only ones contributing. Unusual talent often is discovered and recognized.

11. English composition is not wasted. Our mailing department sends out its letters along with copies of the monthly paper. Letters of thanks for favors and notes of invitation stimulate English expression. Correspondence includes exchange of newspaper between our school and other schools in our city, our state, and other states.

12. Original work in stories, poems, riddles, school jokes, and editorials is encouraged.

13. A felt need is created for acquiring a skill in proper form and a well-organized, rich content in English expression. The children throughout the school realize that the members in their school, their community, and friends on the mailing list read the articles published.

14. Children are trained to express their thoughts in the fewest words possible. If articles exceed a prescribed length, the editor returns them to the contributor to be cut down.

15. Business training is provided. The copies sell for one penny

each. No one is obliged to buy and no pressure is put upon any child who is unable to buy. Copies are also kept on classroom library tables. The business manager and collector turn in all money collected. The amount must tally with the papers printed, and returned. Then the total is entered in a book kept for this purpose. The money is taken to the principal's office where it is rechecked and the book audited. The new balance is brought forward. At the end of the year a clear statement is left for the incoming business manager. Any expenditures necessary for carrying on the publication of the paper are deducted. Such expenses are having the roll of paper cut to the necessary length, and red and green ink for special numbers. Just before Christmas, 1936, enough money had been collected to allow one dollar for each class to spend as it saw fit. Discussions as to wise choice were held in each class. The committees were chosen. These committees were instructed as to the wishes in general of the classes and then sent to town to use their own judgment as to detail. Games, books, and balls were bought. Then the committees visited the other classes and showed the results of their shopping expedition.

16. Opportunity to stress need of and interest in records is furnished. A copy of each issue of newspaper is kept on file. Children refer to paper filed in order of months and years.

How the unit facilitates integration.

1. Language arts: correspondence, grammar, spelling, form, original stories, and poems; stories of other newspaper men

2. Literature: reading O. Henry's children stories

3. Science: use of lead and antimony in connection with newspaper work, function of printing machinery such as the linotype machine and press, source of paper

4. Fine arts: illustrating articles, original cartoons, selection of songs for program

5. Social studies: countries from which necessary materials are obtained, history of newspapers

6. Reading: reference material

7. Mathematics: financial responsibilities in collecting funds and spending funds gave practice in decimals

What the faculty learned from unit.

1. Anecdotal records: give teachers and administrator opportunities for learning child's inner life

2. Curriculum: furnishes suggestions for school and community enterprises

3. Coöperation: spirit of entire school (children, teachers, and principal) greatly influenced; administrative efforts become coöperative enterprises

4. Public relations: closer relationship with patrons of school and other members of the community

A very useful summary of the objectives and activities in producing a school newspaper has been supplied as follows by Helen C. Ormond.

A Unit in the Production of a School Newspaper [6]

I. *Objectives*

A. To give each pupil an opportunity to assist in a piece of creative work

B. To heighten the appreciation of steps and problems in planning any newspaper

C. To give the student a grasp of the fundamentals of layout

D. To teach the elements of
 1. News reporting
 2. Editorial writing
 3. Feature writing

E. To give practical experience in
 1. Preparing copy
 2. Proofreading
 3. Making a dummy

II. *Materials*

A. Reference books on journalism and style books

B. Copies of old issues of the New York *Times* and the New York *Herald-Tribune*

C. Patterns of newspaper writing as provided by the New York *Times* and the New York *Herald-Tribune*

III. *Preparatory Work for Issuing Paper*

A. Layout (3 days); explanation that the last step in the preparation should be visualized before doing any writing
 1. Sketch of four-page paper on board
  a. Proportion of height to width 5 : 3
  b. Symmetrical balance

[6] Reported by Helen C. Ormond, Girls Commercial High School, Brooklyn, N. Y.

    c. Estimate of number of words indicated by column according to height of type front

    d. Head-lines indicated by spaces

    e. Consequence of leading in altering number of words

    f. Estimate of words by page with deduction for pictures, cartoons, cuts, etc.

    g. Recognition of the relative space and position to be devoted to each article according to its importance and interest to readers

  2. Assignments

    a. Make a model of page one to exact size

      (1) Give dimensions

      (2) Cut out blank pieces of paper the width of a column and the length that the estimated number of words will need

      (3) Pin or paste articles in proper spaces on front page like a jig-saw puzzle

    b. Make a second model exact size

      (1) Cut out head-lines and articles from real newspaper

      (2) Paste to make up dummy

B. Newswriting (7 to 10 days)

  1. Use of five W's in the lead

  2. Variety on the construction of the lead

  3. Inverted pyramid writing

  4. References available

C. Editorial writing (5 days)

  1. Getting started

    a. Bring to class an amusing editorial

    b. Excerpts to be read to class

    c. Analysis of devices

      (1) Striking contrasts

      (2) Use of allusions

    d. Classification of editorials

      (1) Serious

        (*a*) To achieve some improvement

        (*b*) To effect some reform

      (2) Humorous: to amuse

      (3) Link to cartoon on editorial page

      (4) Avoidance of preachiness

  2. Writing editorial on school topic

  3. Writing editorial in a lighter vein on a school topic

4. Planning layout of editorial page with allowance of space for masthead, cartoon, fewer words in editorial column with 10 pt. type, feature article and possibly poem
5. Finding references available

D. Feature writing (4 days)
1. Sports articles from standard dailies
2. Fashion articles
3. Interviews
4. Columns
5. Write an example of one kind of feature writing after several series of clippings have been made
6. References available

E. Head-lines (3 days)
Note: No head-line with all its decks should ever be longer than one-fifth the length of the article.
1. Sketch and illustrate examples of different types of head-lines
2. Point out use of lower point letters on lower half of page
3. Note the length of leading article
4. Indicate use of captions
5. Use references available

F. Directions for typing copy
1. Style sheets
2. Proofreading of copy

IV. *Production of Paper*

A. Scheme for assignment of articles on blackboard
1. Complete list of all possible sources of news within the list (sheet attached)
2. Board marked:
Assignment covered by: typed by: estimated words: actual words: date received: total
3. Listing of articles and reports made by student editors
4. Very brief list of articles to be kept on file
Note: Whenever the name of a school officer or member of faculty is used in an article, he (or she) must initial the correctness of facts reported.

B. Use of folder for final copy, one section for each page
C. Directions for cuts and pictures
1. Requests to art department for illustrations to fit exact dimensions as planned on layout

      a. Cartoon to link with editorial which must be sent to artist as early as possible

      b. Ears for front page

      c. Fashion sketches to accompany article which also must be sent to artist

      d. Cross-word puzzle

  2. Pictures

      a. Appointment to pose for photographer

      b. Development of glossy print

      c. Indication of scaling for engraver

D. Assembling copy

  1. Copy-editing

  2. Retyping by staff

  3. Final estimate of words

  4. Plan of blank layout for real dummy of issue: similar to first assignment except that articles are in final positions

  5. Placing of advertisements on "dummy"

  6. Sending of copy to printer on deadline

E. Return of two galleys from printer

  1. Proofreading galley read and marked

  2. Dummy galley numbered by column each inch

  3. Dummy galley cut in strips and pasted in proper spaces allotted to articles

  4. Head-lines written and keyed to articles and positions on pages with five indications:

      a. Family of type fonts

      b. Height of fonts in points

      c. Upper- and lower-case letters

      d. Number of lines to deck

      e. Width of column or columns (cf. III., E)

  5. Page proof checked and corrected

V. *Business details managed by a separate staff which handles*

A. Securing of advertisements

B. Layout of individual advertising cuts

C. Circulations

  1. Advance publicity

  2. Advance orders

  3. Collection of subscriptions or G. O. stubs

  4. Paying of bills

  5. Keeping records of accounts

Most teachers find it easy to vitalize expression by having their pupils develop newspapers covering the contemporary scene. A few artistic teachers can so teach the literature of the past that their pupils experience the story with the keenness of reality. That a vicarious experience, when potent enough to captivate children's imagination, gives as strong a motive for communication as does a real experience is evident in a report from Miss Corinne Oertel, Richmond Hill High School, New York City. She had presented an historical novel so vividly that her pupils identified themselves with the characters and situations. They discovered the "human interest," "feature," and "news stories" in the thrilling events and the emotional conflicts in *Ivanhoe*. When their teacher exhibited modern newspapers written by older pupils, the ninth-graders "got an idea," and developed *Ye Ashley Gazette, The Crusaders,* and *Sword and Shield.* "The Inside Story of the Challenge of the Palmer and the Templar," "Ivanhoe's Account of the Tournament," "The Archery Contest," "The Capture of Torquilstone," "News from the Crusades," "Fashion Hints," and "Rowena's System for Keeping Beautiful" were among the topics projected and written up by different pupils. The activity as conducted was neither fantastic nor dull. What anachronisms occurred did not detract from the sense of reality in the pupils' experience in re-creating, as they read, Scott's *Ivanhoe*.

X

BROADCASTING

THE RADIO has opened new opportunities for speech development. Educational broadcasting stations and many commercial stations are providing students with time for programs. The periods of preparation for such programs are full of possibilities for effective teaching. It is rather generally agreed that the real broadcast should be a finished performance of a quality satisfying to both participants and listeners. Careful and thorough rehearsal, complete scripts, and even transcriptions on phonographic records are used to assure the smooth and effective quality essential to programs that are sent out on the air.

Such programs are in their beginnings at the present. The experiences of classroom teachers reported below suggest problems and procedures that may be helpful to other teachers who may wish to attempt the use of radio in speech training. Though opinion differs on the question as to whether broadcasts in which children appear should be rehearsed, most workers in this field find that the purposes of broadcasting school programs are usually better realized when they are rehearsed. In the account which follows Miss Thomas and Miss Davies report excellent results from a non-rehearsed program in which they attempted only to have a radio audience "listen in" upon a regular class period of oral reports followed by class appraisal.

AN ENGLISH CLASS GOES ON THE AIR [1]

Undeniably the radio world is glamorous. In the opinion of many a high-school student, persons who speak over the air—whether questioned for a few minutes in a quiz program or known nationally because of frequent broadcasts—are set apart from other mortals by an aura of distinction: their voices have been heard through many

[1] Reported by Muriel I. Thomas, Central High School, and Hazel L. Davies, Head of the English Department, Central High School, Scranton, Pa.

193

loud speakers. In the life of the twentieth-century adult, as well, the ubiquitous radio exerts a compelling influence; it furnishes entertainment, admonition, and information.

Why cannot this genie serve both the student and the citizen interested in the school? Why should not high-school students have the thrill of speaking into the microphone? Why should not the radio give parents unmistakably direct information about their children's school day? So wondered a teacher, who was determined to put a solid foundation under his air castle. The tangible corner-stone was laid; Central High School went on the air.

The school auditorium was wired for the first broadcast, an assembly program during which the championship basket-ball and swimming teams were presented by their coaches. A week later the school's musical organizations broadcast another assembly program. On both occasions the student audience, overjoyed at the almost incredible realization that they were witnessing and participating in an actual broadcast, had never been more quiet than they were when the announcer said, "In another minute we'll be on the air." No disturbing sound was heard throughout either half hour, but after the announcer's last words had died away against the background of the softly hummed "Alma Mater," and a wave of his hand had indicated that the school was off the air, a gusty sigh manifested both relief from tension and satisfaction in a new experience.

The broadcasts were still prominent subjects of conversation when a new venture was tried, the broadcasting of an actual class in vocational guidance. With the aim of keeping the situation "natural," the class work was unrehearsed; the students did not even know in advance that case study would be discussed. So natural and so successful was this first attempt at classroom broadcasting that another was considered, this time presenting a class in sophomore English.

The sophomores whose section met during the period that the local broadcasting station found convenient to schedule the program were astonished to learn that two days later their scheduled oral themes were not to be heard and judged as usual by the familiar audience of thirty or forty, but were to be addressed to many unseen listeners. Some of the prospective speakers looked pleased; some were frankly startled.

It was known that twenty-five minutes of the broadcast time could be devoted to the actual speaking of the pupils and to class comments. As the average talk lasted approximately three minutes, there would be time to hear not more than ten students at the most, providing, of course, that the uniqueness of the experience should not cause some of the speakers to be more brief than usual.

Because only one-third of the class could participate and because some seemed reluctant and others eager, the fairest plan was to let the students decide whether or not they wished to take advantage of the opportunity. They were told to consider the proposition and to indicate their wishes. The following morning slips of paper informed the teacher which boys and girls were eager to talk over the air and which were not. Twenty wanted to face the microphone. A representative group of ten was chosen, including average pupils as well as excellent, for the broadcast was to be typical. The other ten aspirants were told that as many more as time would permit would be given a chance to talk.

The nature of the work of the English class differed from that of the vocational-guidance class which had preceded it on the air. In the latter there had been a rapid give-and-take of ideas. Each individual had had the assurance that the conversational ball would be caught quickly by some one else. In the English class, however, each pupil faced the responsibility of speaking, uninterrupted, for several minutes, without help of notes or script. "Mike fright" could make him mute if he had never spoken into the mechanism before. Therefore, the authorities of the broadcasting station thought it wise that those students should have the experience of speaking into a microphone before the actual hook-up was made.

The ten who had been chosen went to the broadcasting station's studios after school and for the first time faced the microphone. They spoke conversationally on any topic they wished to select and although they knew that they were heard only in another room, not in the world at large, their voices quivered with excitement during this first attempt.

The pupils learned how near they should stand to the microphone and how to interpret the signals of the operator, made mute by the control room's curtain of soundproof glass. In itself, the visit to the studio was epochal. No mechanical detail missed observation.

On the morning of the broadcast the class trooped from its room to the auditorium stage, on which a rug had been spread to eliminate disturbing sounds. When all the members had been seated, the stage curtains were drawn to make the "room" even more soundproof. The ten who were definitely to speak sat in semicircles around two microphones; the other members of the class were grouped behind them. At a table between the two semicircles sat the teacher and the radio station announcer, with a table microphone between them.

No movement of the technicians escaped the observation of the engrossed class; not a fraction of the trial microphone test was missed. Then came the statement of the announcer: "In two minutes you'll be on the air," a cool sentence, but electrifying in its effect.

The announcer's voice intoned, "Ladies and gentlemen, you have just heard the opening of a class in sophomore English in Central High School in Scranton, Pennsylvania. The lesson for today is oral English. The students will assume that they are in life situations, addressing audiences, arousing enthusiasm, selling products. The next voice that you hear will be that of the teacher."

The assignment for the oral compositions that morning had offered the pupil a variety of situations from which to choose: he might pretend to be an after-dinner speaker at a reunion of his class ten years after graduation, a salesman trying to persuade a reluctant housewife, a pep speaker in a school assembly, a teacher addressing students, or a radio speaker. The talks were not to be written out, learned, or read but delivered orally from such mental notes as the student could make in advance. To prevent possible memorizing, the official at the broadcasting studio on the previous day had warned that to memorize a radio talk was dangerous: ideas might leave the speaker's mind entirely, and having depended upon definitely learned paragraphs, he would be tongue-tied.

Evidently the warning had been heeded. The salesmen extolled their products convincingly; the speakers at reunion dinners recalled events that had occurred when their class was still at Central; the pep speakers tried to arouse enthusiastic support for prospective football games. Thanks to the experience of the preceding afternoon in speaking over the microphone, each pupil spoke calmly. The class commented as they would have on any oral theme day. In short, the work moved forward as it would have against the familiar background of Room 9 or in any of the English classrooms anywhere in the country. An observer would probably have thought that the microphones were not connected with any device which transmitted sound outside the school walls.

Yet the class differed in two ways from the customary situation. The speakers talked for a shorter time than usual. Consequently, there was time for three more pupils who had written on their slips, "Please call on me." The second difference was that the criticisms of the themes were more complimentary and less directed at improvement than ordinarily. The comments which listening parents heard were: "His vocabulary is very good," "She would have made me buy that," "He knew what he was talking about." No one was censorious enough to say, "The beginning was too slow," "He mispronounced a word," "The end was abrupt." The critics were conscious of an unseen audience, and they did not want classmates to appear to a disadvantage; adverse criticism might be made in the privacy of a classroom but not in the universe.

Surprisingly soon the announcer handed a paper to the teacher: "You have ten seconds left." She summed up the last comments of the class. The announcer concluded the broadcast. There was a sigh. The students who had spoken were overwhelmed with compliments.

Echoes of the broadcast were heard for several days, not only in the commendatory comments of citizens who had heard it and in the conversations of the students, but also in the student's written themes. Those pupils who had been spectators wrote detailed accounts of the set-up on the stage or explained some aspect of broadcasting; those who had spoken described their reactions.

I had often wondered what it felt like to speak over the air, even on a "Quick Quiz." (One wrote.) I thought that it must give one a very excited feeling to know that one's voice was being heard by thousands of people. Of course I never thought that I would have occasion to speak over the air, but the thing one never expects to happen always happens, doesn't it?

Our English teacher told the class one morning that an English class was to broadcast over WGBI. "How nice for some one," passed fleetingly through my mind. And then—she said we were to be the ones. . . .

Next morning when we finally assembled on the stage of the auditorium, never did seconds pass so slowly. Finally the cool, assured voice of the announcer opened the program. After him the teacher spoke. How could they be so *un*excited? Should I be called on first? Pray not. No, it was some one else. Who, I don't know, the relief was so great. Then finally my name was called. I rose fearfully. My knees didn't collapse. Was I too near the microphone?

Look at the teacher. Smile; be calm. There's nothing to be afraid of. This is just an ordinary classroom period. These thoughts passed through my mind, but I wasn't comforted. I gazed at the "mike" as if hypnotized. My voice rang in the silence. It quavered and shook. My breath came in gasps. Did any one notice? No, every one was intent upon himself. I sat down just as my knees were about to give way. It was over! But then came a strange feeling. I wanted to do it again. It was really fun!

Another pupil wrote of similar despairing feelings and concluded, "When you have finished and sat down, you remember to your horror that you have not said half the things you intended to say, but you realize what a marvelous thing radio is, and you are glad you had a chance to broadcast."

"Mike fright" was described by one who has the heaven-sent ability to laugh at himself. "When I had finished," he chuckled, "I realized I had forgotten half of my talk. I still think the point of my speech was good."

The self-condemnation of these pupils was really undeserved. Despite the understandable tension they spoke with assurance and coherence.

All who wrote about the experience decided enthusiastically that it had been delightful and advantageous. One summed up the opinion of the group by declaring, "It gives classmates a thrill to know they have spoken or are going to speak over the air. . . . It develops the idea of becoming a program announcer or a speaker. . . . The thrill of the parents listening at home for the voice of their son or daughter is something to encourage the continuation of this kind of broadcast."

From these four experimental broadcasts it is planned that more shall grow. Every Tuesday evening, now, a fifteen-minute program, as the announcer says, "presents your high-school reporters." Five students, one from each of the city's senior and junior high schools, give a running commentary upon classroom and extracurricular events in their own schools. The news is gathered by the staff of the school publication, and the radio script is written by a student. The program is already popular with both pupils and parents.

A full year of weekly half-hour broadcasts, like the four already given within the school walls, is contemplated. It will give all five senior and junior high schools a voice and will be varied: through the medium of the air waves the public may, if it wishes, "come" into the assemblies, classrooms, and shops; it may be entertained with music or plays presented by the pupils.

The advantages of school's going on the air are obvious. Broadcasting school activities interprets to the public, more graphically and convincingly than any other way, education's aims and methods. Broadcasting also provides a spur for the student to do even better curricular and extracurricular work. An unseen audience is exacting. Most important of all, broadcasting provides a link between school and life experience. Radio is one of the twentieth century's most magical devices. Students enjoy waving that sorcerous wand for their own and others' pleasure and instruction. The radio may well join the devices and methods which schools have long been employing to make learning vital and to inform the taxpayer of what he is getting for his school taxes.

Radio in the English Curriculum [2]

Clifford J. Scott High School in East Orange, New Jersey, has copied the techniques widely used in motion picture appreciation. A club is set up consisting of persons interested in various phases of radio. After a period of study and training they go into various English classes and assist the teachers in presenting a unit in radio appreciation or in leading discussions on particular broadcasts. The following outline suggests a procedure found useful in both clubs and English classroom.

I. *Preliminary survey of radio tastes and listening experience*

II. *Broadcasting*
- A. Scope
  - 1. Historical development of broadcasting
  - 2. Regulation
    - *a.* Federal laws
    - *b.* Station policies
    - *c.* Commercial requirements
    - *d.* Technical limitations
  - 3. Chain broadcasting
  - 4. Studio set-up
    - *a.* Facilities
    - *b.* Personnel
  - 5. Program-building
    - *a.* Conception of program ideas
    - *b.* Script-writing
    - *c.* Publicity
    - *d.* Directing
    - *e.* On the air
  - 6. Future developments and improvements
- B. Activities
  - 1. Trips to studios, study of books about radio, study of scripts, script-writing, talks by visiting artists, script-writers, and others associated with radio; actual par-

---

[2] Reported by Leon C. Hood, Chairman of the Radio Committee, New Jersey Association of Teachers of English.

ticipation in radio broadcasts, "broadcasting" over the school's public-address system. (The latter activity, since it can include every step in program-building and presentation, is the best means of giving understanding and consequently appreciation of all the phases of the broadcasting art.)

III. *Listening to Broadcasts*

   A. Scope

      1. Radio manners

         a. Consideration for others

         b. Active listening

         c. Fidelity of tuning

         d. Boiler-factory ears

      2. Choice of program

         a. Information from listings and reviews

         b. New programs for variety and discovery

         c. New stations

         d. Daily schedule of listening

      3. Analysis of broadcasts

         a. Types of programs

         b. Elements of programs

            (1) Style

            (2) Personality

            (3) Technique

         c. Evaluation

            (1) Technical perfection

            (2) Authenticity

               (*a*) Honesty

               (*b*) Naturalness

            (3) Effectiveness

               (*a*) Colorful and interesting

               (*b*) Not too complex

               (*c*) Not oversimplified

               (*d*) Motivating

         d. Surveys

            (1) Crosley ratings

            (2) Advertising agency analysis

            (3) Polls by periodicals

            (4) Local polls

         e. Comparison of standards

            (1) Between pupils

  (2) With standards of advertisers, educators, broad-
    casters, government, and others
  f. Comparison of styles
  (1) Books
  (2) Stage
  (3) Movies
 4. Effects of listening
  a. Personal
  (1) Social
  (2) Economic
B. Activities
 1. Making scrap books (clippings from radio magazines,
  newspapers, and station news services), reading radio reviews, conducting radio column in local or school newspaper, use of transcriptions borrowed from broadcasters
  for detailed analysis, writing letters to broadcasters

IV. *Final Survey of Tastes and Listening Experience* (A comparison between this and the preliminary survey will serve as a
basis for an individual evaluation of the effectiveness of the
study.)

V. *Essentials for a Program for Developing Radio Appreciation*

A. A progressive, enthusiastic adviser for radio club activities
B. A radio appreciation club consisting of pupils of above average ability in English (Radio study can originate in the
club and expand into curricular activities in English.)
C. Books on radio, library of actual scripts used over the air,
radio, magazines, program listings of stations which can be
heard locally, access to at least one broadcasting station for
attendance and occasional participation in broadcasts, a
portable or permanent public-address system, radios for
school listening, and useful, although not essential, transcriptions and reproducing equipment
D. Classroom discussions of particular programs or types of
programs led by club members
E. Study guides and detailed information of programs that are
to be broadcast
F. A course in radio appreciation given either intensively in
two weeks or spread over several weeks
G. Development of cordial relations with the librarian to set
up a reading program related to radio listening

H. Coöperation with other associations in the community and state to promote the interests of this study and listeners in general

That radio can be used to stimulate improvement in oral English is the contention of Anne Ray in the report which follows.

ENGLISH THROUGH RADIO [3]

One means of acquiring speech skills today is through the radio, for every listener may become a discriminating critic, and the critic may in turn become the speaker. Damrosch uses its magic to train boys and girls to recognize tone qualities and the range of orchestral instruments. So too, training in critical appreciation of beautiful diction, and of the range and flexibility of vocal tones may serve to stimulate personal achievement. The primary objective of this unit is to develop freedom from self-consciousness, not to establish diction-consciousness, though at first awareness of good qualities may facilitate their acquisition.

Objectives.

1. Appreciation of diction, style, and voice as an index to personality
2. Appreciation of literature on the air
3. Knowledge of radio techniques
4. Skills in choral reading, dramatization, and story-telling

Procedures.

1. Listening to teacher-recommended programs in which superior diction, style, and voice control will be heard
2. Establishing criteria for discrimination between the worth while and the mediocre
3. Studying radio techniques, including signals, scripts, sound devices
4. Reading old ballads, using a solo part followed by chorus
5. Choral reading of such selections as "The Highwayman," "Billy Boy," "The Barrel Organ," "The Congo," "A Frog Went a Courting," "The Bombardment"
6. Dramatizing materials prepared professionally for the radio and then those prepared by pupils
7. Story-telling, by a narrator and cast, of well-selected short stories having a dramatic quality

[3] Reported by Anne Ray, Murphy Junior High School, Atlanta, Ga.

XI

DRAMATIZING

CREATIVE ENERGY that overflowed into a voluntary after-school activity is described by Mary Johnson. She tells how the dramatic impulse of her young pupils was directed into making a play that was play, not work, to her primary-school group.

WHEN WE MAKE A PLAY[1]

One might think the day's work was over for a busy teacher at dismissal time. Such is not the case in my classroom. In some school buildings children are kept after school but in my room they linger from choice. "May we work on our play tonight?" some one asks. If the answer is in the affirmative, the atmosphere becomes suddenly charged with animation, eagerness, desire. "May I stay too, oh please, may I stay?" They crowd around me in excited little groups fairly clamoring for the opportunity to participate in an activity, which, for want of a better term, we shall call creative.

When permission has been given, our school-room is transformed at once into a perfect beehive of industry. A few children hurry to get precious manuscripts containing the plays, poems, or stories they are writing. Some one covers the tables and floors with newspapers and sets out the paint jars and brushes. Several rush to get our "tool"—that is, the saw, hammer, or plane we have been fortunate to borrow from home. Our district is not a wealthy one. The children have very few things that they can bring to help with such an undertaking, so the child who has brought the tool is the one, if he can, who will be granted the privilege of doing the necessary carpenter work.

With all in readiness, two children who have earned this coveted privilege bring out from behind the cloakroom door our masterpiece —a large panel which is to be used as a section of scenery for our latest play. Then the painting begins—"Oh, isn't it pretty?" "May I paint next?" "I just love to paint with such bright colors." Such

[1] Reported by Mary T. Johnson, 2413 First Ave., Minneapolis, Minn.

comments are expressive of the sheer delight these half-grown young-sters experience in handling materials.

Our sets are made from old pieces of wooden crating nailed to-gether and supported by laths. We secure large cardboard cartons, mattress covers and other large pieces from furniture dealers. These are measured, cut to fit our wooden frames, and then tacked on to the wood. This cardboard makes a very good surface for painting the landscapes we desire. Alabastine, a dry, colored powder, mixed with water is the medium used. We work with large brushes.

Wooden buttons are nailed to the top and bottom of the back for the purpose of tying the pieces together. Although very light and easy to handle, they are strong enough to stand by themselves. Ef-fective backgrounds are thus made for the programs and plays we give.

Of course, we write our own scenarios. Sometimes they are scenes written to portray ideas gleaned from social studies. Often they are made for special days. Thanksgiving, Christmas, and other holidays inspire numerous themes. Frequently they represent the culmination of a unit of work. "Marion Visits the Dentist," was a purpose play designed to increase the percentage of pupils who had completed all necessary dental work. "Fairies and Flowers" was an original play written after the class had studied wild flower conservation. Usually, however, our plays begin with the dramatization of a scene from a book we have enjoyed together. It was the story of the Vikings which appealed to us most this year. We wanted to experience the joy, the freedom, the daring of those bold rovers. We read several juvenile books on the subject. Then we delved into their mythology and be-came acquainted with their gods. A social-studies unit supplied the geographic background while natural science explained the basic concepts necessary for understanding life adjustments in the land of the Midnight Sun. Art, music, and dancing contributed their share to the enjoyment.

The original dramatization outgrew itself. We added scenes, wrote imaginary dialogues, runes, and songs until we had an original pro-duction consisting of four scenes. Our imagination carried us back into the Icelandic home of Leif Ericsson's ancestors, where we listened to a skald entertaining his audience with hero tales of the Norse gods. Our own young verse-makers were the authors of the sagas he recited. Icelandic children themselves were rune-makers. Their runes were about the world of nature as they knew it. Our rune-makers had to project themselves into a far-off time and a far-off place in order to re-create such scenes. Encyclopedias, maps, and reference books were freely used for authenticity. Some might call this research. We called it play.

A play is never a play without an audience. The greatest reward of creative effort is reached, without any doubt, when the dramatist hears the "oh's" and "ah's" of appreciative listeners. Their part, too, is creative.

They must enter into the illusion. When the curtain is drawn back on the third scene of our play, and the excited children behold our ocean scene—the sky dark and low'ring, the waves angry and dashing—they must forget that the loud crash of thunder is handmade back stage by a boy with a dishpan. They must believe, for the instant, that the blinking of the electric lights is actually lightning.

When our huge Viking boat rolls out across the stage, they must become oblivious of the fact that the cardboard boat stands upright and moves because it is attached to a coaster wagon and is pulled across the stage by ropes. They must experience, vicariously, the terrors of a storm at sea in a tiny open boat when Leif stands up in the prow of his ship and shouts.

This extra hour of ours is the happiest time in the day. Inhibitions loosen and fall away from the timid child. Strong pupils grow in executive ability. The average child unfolds and grows in a normal happy way. Creative experiences and the learning process are one and the same. In our lives, this making a play is a very vital part of our learning.

Abby Wager, Norristown, Pennsylvania, reported an excellent use of dramatization in grade two in a rural school.

OUR PUPPETS, WHAT FUN! [2]

Objectives. The pupils wished to make hand puppets for U. S. soldiers' and sailors' children confined to hospitals. (This was one of the pupils' Junior Red Cross activities.) The teacher desired to utilize this well-motivated constructive activity to encourage correct and effective oral and written English on the part of her pupils whose parents were not born in the U.S.A. and who still spoke the foreign language in the home.

Initiation of experiences. The student teacher invited six children, boys and girls, to meet with her to discuss what the group might make as their Junior Red Cross contribution. Dolls were suggested. The teacher showed them a recent, well-illustrated booklet on hand

[2] Reported as a fourth-grade unit conducted by student teachers under the guidance of Dorothea Lindenau, Portage Agricultural School, Portage, Mich.

puppets, manipulated with the index finger, inserted into a hole left in the puppet's head.

The main part of the toy is the head which may be made of a great variety of materials. The boys carved heads of wood. The girls made stocking heads. The next day they made dolls from shoe trees and used bits of fur for hair, eyebrows, mustaches and beards.

By this time the news had spread and other children asked to participate. They modeled each other and achieved some good likenesses in clay.

Now all wanted to join. There were now thirty-eight children, all intensely interested, making puppets of papier-mâché. The pupils cut newspaper strips, and the student teacher made a lime-water mixture which, when poured over the paper, made a very easily workable material for modeling puppet heads. After the heads had dried, they were painted, and by this time each child had decided on a specific character which his puppet was to represent. We had been reading about famous discoverers, explorers, and colonizers, so some chose characters from history, some from literature, and some made Negroes, Indians, and clowns.

Before the puppets were delivered to the boys and girls for whom they were made, several playlets were written by the pupils as individuals and as groups. These playlets concerned safety rules and historical events. All the while good training in oral and in written English functioned in helping the pupils to communicate their ideas to an audience.

Preparation of an exhibit of puppets. To exhibit for the Junior Red Cross, the pupils needed to do these things:

1. Make labels which indicated the character part and a few sentences of the speech.
2. Select representatives who would explain the making and the purpose of the puppets.
3. Choose the best articles written as summary of the work done.

Outcomes. From the language and constructive activities the following results were obtained:

1. Attitudes

Writing is a very useful skill.
Careful expression facilitates production.
Correct expression is necessary in order to be understood.
Willingness to read carefully for exact information is necessary.
Coöperation with one's fellows in work or play is fun.

2. Skill

Capitalization of proper names, *I*, and first word in sentence

Neat handwriting

Correct spelling

Planning before speaking or writing

Correct use of *see, saw, seen; did, done; these, them; isn't, aren't; have, got*

Punctuation of sentences, salutation and complimentary close of letters, and dialogue

XII

CHORAL SPEAKING AND ORAL READING

LITERATURE is experienced more deeply by many people when it is heard or said than when it is merely read silently. Poetry especially takes on added charm when its rhythm swings its vivid imagery and emotional tone into the memory of the reader or listener.

The radio has brought back to the masses some of the joys of oral literature. The classrooms over the country likewise are finding that choral reading can be a means of immediate personal pleasure and of social entertainment. Activities that once were carried by the picked, best student in a class or in a school now have greater audience response and educative value through utilizing every individual *in his appropriate part* either as a member of a speaking choir or of a class group trained to read well orally as a group.

Between the lines in the accompanying reports is evidence that the mood and the idea of a literary selection can be caught and interpreted more adequately by both mediocre and gifted when the literature makes its appeal through all the senses.

THE 4M's ENJOY GOOD READING [1]

Merely by creating an audience situation, we cannot make good oral readers. Bad habits must be obliterated by specific training in the basic rules of oral interpretation.

In the 4M class we were embarking on an oral reading unit, the purpose of which was appreciation and enjoyment. Our outcome was to be a finished presentation entering the "art stage"—poetry, a description, a selection containing much feeling, or a humorous situation.

We started our project by reading a selection orally, after a very careful silent reading. To the dismay of many of our number, they were deprived of their turn when they had read the first few sen-

[1] Reported by Edith Mae Smith, teacher of speech, Elementary School, Shorewood, Milwaukee, Wis.

tences. They learned that it was not fair to take the time of the group unless they could offer something worth listening to. They were anxious to put forth an effort to improve their performance. They said, "How shall we do the thing better?"

The children did not let their bodies help in expressing what they were to read. They were told to recall the good speaker they had heard in the assembly the day before. Donald said, "His mouth opened wide and set firmly." Carol added, "His head moved vigorously, and he used his hands to gesture." It was agreed that if such a bodily participation was used by a speaker to express himself, surely then, we could not eliminate it in our reading performance.

How could we learn to develop a natural bodily expression? We found that simple pantomimes were helpful. Slips were passed out to every one upon which were written such directions as, "You are one of the King's guards. You shall ring the bell to announce his wedding feast." Afterwards, the class discussion included, "Did he ring the bell hard enough for the whole village to hear?" "Did he express his happiness and the importance of the occasion in his face?" After much work of this kind, we understood how effective bodily participation could be and we did experience it in our oral reading.

However, some of our class were reading too rapidly and with extremely tense bodies, whereas others were careless with their speech. We undertook to remedy these faults by dividing the class into groups: those who needed to relax and those who needed to be more particular about how their words came out of their mouths. We used speech drills and games applicable to each group's particular difficulty. There are few children who will not profit by being made a little speech-conscious.

We talked and learned together about word grouping and good reading rhythm. We took phrases from our selections, put them on the board, drew graphs of them. We discovered that all phrases have "ups and downs," and that if we recognize them, we get real expression from the words. We beat the rhythm of the phrases and sentences with our pencils. This rhythm beating was firmly guided by the teacher at first, but soon members of the class could take the position of leader. Plays and stories full of conversation proved helpful in developing good reading rhythm, because dialogue contains short clear sentences and colorful words.

The 4M's were then made to realize that these same techniques functioned whenever they read orally a literary selection, a news clipping, a bit of information, or the like. Thus the children began to feel a personal interest in the stories and read with much more feeling than before. Each child became critical of his own rendition.

After much practice, individual and group, we discovered that definite standards were needed by which to criticize one another's work. The following, which were discussed and put upon the board, really "worked":

1. Read the selection over orally. Look up each word which sounds queer as you pronounce it. You tend to pay little attention to words read silently that may bother you when read orally. Be sure that you know how to pronounce each word correctly.

2. On the second oral reading, pay attention to word groups. Are you pausing after each thought-grouping to allow yourself to get a breath and to take a rapid silent preview of the material ahead? Are your pauses long enough to allow your audience to comprehend and appreciate the thought which you just gave to them? At first, underlining thought groups may help you in controlling the place to pause. Later on, you will find that familiarity with the thoughts of the selection controls the pause.

3. A third oral reading is necessary. During this reading watch for a certain word or words in a thought which need to be colored or intensified. If you underline the word or phrase to be stressed, you will be sure to remember to give it more force, or to change your tone of voice if necessary.

4. A fourth reading is necessary to check the parts of the selection which should be read faster—such as an exciting part of the story and the climax; the parts which should be read slower—the words of a selection which are so powerful in their meaning that each must stand out and be fully comprehended by itself, or a beautiful description, or the closing paragraph of a selection.

5. A fifth reading is needed, to help you become very familiar with the selection and to check your enunciation and tone. Do you think your tone is pitched so high that it will be rasping to the audience? Do you change the range of your voice when needed? Do you read some parts of the selection naturally and easily? Do you need a deeper tone or a higher, softer tone for certain parts? Are you enunciating clearly, or do you tend to slur certain sounds and to skip over word endings? Slowing your tempo and relaxing your jaws and tongue will help you decidedly.

6. During the sixth reading pay attention to your body. Do you find yourself looking up from the book a great deal? If not, practise reading the selection doing this. You cannot look from the book to the audience unless you are so very familiar with the selection that a mere glance is all that is needed to tell you the next word groups. You will need to watch your audience with your eyes.

Is your body in a relaxed, pleasing, assured position so that your audience will have confidence in you and be ready to listen? Is one hand free for the needed emphasis, to point, or use the palm according to the way your interpretation of the selection directs you?

7. Now read the selection over as many more times as necessary to make you feel that (1) you know it so well that there is no word you cannot place after a single glance; (2) your audience is going to like it; (3) you have so much confidence in the way you interpret it that your body will be relaxed and natural, your tone free to change as you make it, your eye free to watch your audience.

As a result of this intensive analysis and practice the 4M's read orally frequently just for the pleasure of making others enjoy their selection. They did not think of criticism at this stage. A group prepared a poetry assembly, each member reading a favorite poem. Another group read a story to a lower grade and still another read individual passages for an older class.

Our "grand finale" was an oral reading assembly which was done so perfectly that our audience enjoyed it as they do a dramatic production.

The children's interest remained high. Their growth in ability to interpret, in appreciation, and in self-confidence was very gratifying to them and to their teacher. And what was more, each child in the 4M class became "a personality." He had acquired that poise, "that something" which we say a person has when "he gets himself across with an audience."

Sharing Experiences through Reading Poetry Aloud [2]

We began our reading of poetry by sharing with each other a few of the poems that we already knew and liked: simple easy verses from Emily Dickinson back to Milton. Then we decided that daily, as an outgrowth of that day's reading, each pupil would post on the bulletin board on a 4 x 6 slip the best findings of that day's reading. The second period used yellow paper, the third white, and the fifth blue. The posting might be anything from one line to a sonnet. If the choice was more than fourteen lines in length a proper cutting was made.

At first the students posted verses that they liked. Then we began looking for ideas, strong metaphors or similes, unusual verse forms or sound effects, examples from the imagists. After the first few days, when the critical judgment of the students began to show real discrimination, we gave daily awards for the best poem posted in each class. Frequently poems of outstanding merit or unusual qual-

[2] Reported by Edna L. Sterling, Lincoln High School, Seattle, Wash.

ity were read, each to a part of the class gathered about the round table for a reading period.

Each slip that was posted gave the following information: the title of the poem, name of the author, in the lower left-hand corner the date, and in the lower right-hand corner the pupil's name. This information made possible student records, and these slips furnished material for very interesting study of the quality and extent of the pupils' reading and taste. In order to direct the work along certain lines the teacher from time to time read to the class poems that would touch different ideas or moods from those the pupils had selected. Oral reading heightened appreciation of the music of the verse and interpretation of the idea of the poem. A noticeable improvement was made by the pupils in their skill in using oral language to convey an emotional idea.

Choral-Speaking as an Extracurricular Activity [3]

I. *Objectives*

    A. To bring together a group of poetry lovers among the pupils

    B. To increase their enjoyment of poetry by permitting self-expression

    C. To increase their familiarity with good verse

    D. To strive for pleasing voice effects

        1. Much richer tones can be procured through a group than with a single voice.

        2. Tone variety can be played with in different styles of poetry.

        3. Solo and chorus effects can be used in certain poems.

II. *Activities*

    A. A group was formed consisting of forty members.

        1. All interested were admitted, regardless of voice qualifications. (A selected group would give better results but would defeat some of the objectives.)

        2. The voices were divided into high, low, and medium.

    B. A meeting was held every Friday afternoon.

        1. Various poems were read aloud by the group and experimented with for the most pleasing voice effects.

        2. Suggestions were made by the pupils as well as by the adviser.

        3. After selections of poems were made, the large group was

[3] Reported by Mary Moore Parrish, Eastern High School, Baltimore, Md.

divided into smaller ones. (Better effects were usually obtained in a group of fifteen voices.)

4. Eventually the poems were memorized, but this came more through repetition than through conscious effort or requirement.

5. Gradually preparation was made for a recital before the school.

C. The choral-speaking group appeared before the assembly
   1. The following program was given:
      a. Psalm XXIV—by the whole group, with antiphonal effect of low and high voices
      b. Traditional May song
      c. "The Apple Orchard"
      d. "The Ballad of the Oysterman"
      e. "Days"
      f. "Lochinvar"
      g. "Break, Break, Break"
      h. "The Barrel Organ"
      i. "The Golden Journey to Samarkand"
   2. Lighting effects were used
      a. Though these are not necessary in a choral speaking program, and some say unsuitable, the lights were available and, when tried out, proved effective.
      b. In the spring poems, sunshine effects were used; in "The Ballad of the Oysterman," there was a change for moonlight in the first part to a ghastly effect for the last stanza; in "The Golden Journey to Samarkand" we strove for an Oriental atmosphere.
   3. Simple Greek costumes were used.

III. *Outcomes*

A. Among the participants
   1. An increased enjoyment of poetry
   2. An increased self-confidence
   3. An improvement in diction—temporary, if not permanent
B. In the audience
   1. An apparent enthusiasm and appreciation
   2. An increased interest in poetry

A more technical approach to training a speaking choir is presented by Bess Wright. She explains the preliminary speech activities which served "to release and to discipline" voice and body.

This teacher has, of course, also developed effective programs with non-Biblical content.

UNIT IN THE TEACHING OF CHORAL SPEAKING [4]

The purpose in reading verse is to give adequate expression to an experience which has been written in chosen terms. The reading to be satisfactory and successful necessitates not only the reliving of the experience by the reader, but the projection of it so that it reaches an audience in its right form.

Exercises which release and discipline the voice and body will make them flexible, plastic, vital, and responsive in attacking selections so that something is actually relived and communicated to an audience. Less injury is done, and there is less danger of discouragement, if an early practice is done on exercises other than the poems which we wish to polish. This does not assert that such may not be learned in the process of doing a selection, but some of the early "butchering" may be avoided.

In the final performance the reliving comes first and expresses itself in pantomime that precedes and colors speech. The skills which must be acquired are these:

1. A sense of sound
    a. The ability to hear and produce vowels and consonants with correct formation and placements
    b. The ability to modify sounds in their combination with other sounds
       (1) Proper aspiration and unaspiration of p, t, k
       (2) The voicing and unvoicing of voiced consonants
       (3) Lengthening of vowel, diphthongs, and consonants
2. The recognition of strong and secondary stress and a knowledge of correct weak forms and how to use them in connected speech
3. Observation of breath groups and accurate attack of sounds at the same time, pause for breathing and for the pantomiming of the thought
4. A sense of the basic melody of English
5. Adequate voices with power and control

After training in sound control, attention needs to be directed to reliving the experience in the selection to be read. With the help of the open, natural children the group may be led into recalling experiences based on the senses and in giving them expression in series of pantomimes. Then a few lines which appeal to each of the senses

[4] Reported by Bess Wright, Public Schools, Indianapolis, Ind.

might be taken from prose or poetry. Plan from the beginning for the pantomime to precede each breath group and also plan the stressed and unstressed syllables and melody. Presently the pattern of pantomime and speech blend. Selection based on senses may logically be attempted. One for sight might be "The Juggler" by Bliss Carman; for touch, "Khamsin" by Clinton Scollard; for hearing, "The Train" by G. B. Crandall; and for smelling, "Smells" by Christopher Morley.

Emotional reactions must come out of the reliving of experiences, or there will be no pantomime and no responsive vocal coloring. Situations in which various emotions are awakened may be pantomimed. Pupils may add their own words as they come to them spontaneously. Then the same sequence may be followed with words already given to them except that they will be working backwards, so to speak, and the words should be assigned their proper place, which is last not first. A pupil must have the confidence that it is quite normal to respond emotionally to nature, to people, to situations, and to the world about him. That the undesirable thing is the lack of control and direction of these emotional reactions. The next step is the ability to recall and transmit these responses, by means of voice and body, colored by his own individuality, and that this giving to others is a normal and desirable thing to do, too.

Movement or bodily expression should be only a reaction that precedes the words spoken and has a definite purpose. At no time is it decorative or in the way of thought. The sustained rhythmic quality of the verse itself may be helped by a constant flow of rhythmic response through the body. Very simple exercises will aid breathing, walking, turning, and the constant "feed" from the feet up through the entire body as well as the relinquishing of head and arms, and of a consciousness of one's self that leads to the outlining of individuals in the group. Cues for beginning, keeping together, and pausing may be given through this sense of rhythm. I use the term *rhythm* to mean the "going-on-ness" of thought, body, and voice, and when there is no voice or movement, this fundamental thing still goes on.

In a ten-minute reading dealing with the periods of the life of Christ: His birth, boyhood, the periods of His life spent as a carpenter and a minister, and His crucifixion we use the following poems: "Mary, the Mother" by Theodosia Garrison, "Judean Hills Are Holy" by William Stidger, "The Carpenter of Galilee" by Hilda Smith, the Beatitudes with accompanying verses found in the volume *Christ in Modern Poetry* compiled by Elvira Slack and published by The Woman's Press, New York. It was necessary to establish and sustain a spirit of unity of purpose throughout the group during the ten minutes, and it was also necessary to move on the stage in view of the audience. Platform levels, as many as are needed to form a pyramid with the madonna at the apex make an effective stage. We used four lifts with the top one just large enough for one person; the next one projected enough to permit two angels to kneel at the sides and to allow them to walk up from the back and down in the front. The others were arranged on the other levels to the floor.

I have found that a group moving together into a picture strengthens the whole performance; yet it takes a much longer time to prepare it. First shoes have to be discarded, bare feet being better than sandals or socks, so that the whole foot functions in carrying the weight, and thus tottering or any inability to move and climb steadily is avoided. In this case, where a state of being must be attained by each pupil in tune with the spirit typified by Christ, the moving harmoniously and rhythmically tends to induce a state of being, unadorned, simple yet strong, beautiful not pretty. The enlarging of spirit seems to come just as much through movement as through repetition of beautiful words and great thought.

The problem of aiding each member in attaining the feeling of the axis through the body and of moving and turning on it was facilitated by studying famous paintings of Christ and of the Madonna. "The Transfiguration" by Raphael, "The Immaculate Conception" by Murillo, "The Assumption of the Virgin" by Titian, "The Magdalen" by Titian, and "The Descent from the Cross" by Rubens, all illustrate the flowing, linking relation of bodily positions. The unbroken, sustained, concentration of thought, movement, and words, I find, are helped by certain foundation exercises which, of course, have to be done by the teacher with the group. The body is enfolded as though over an arc with head relaxed first and the enfolding going gradually down the spine—the tip being held down as a starting point for unfoldment up. Shoulders must be down and relaxed and the hands and arms hanging; the back of the neck and head, open. Knees should be relaxed yet resilient not sagging. Repetition of this to music, such as "Ave Maria" by Schubert, over and over, is necessary until heads cease to pop up, self-consciousness is lost, and the group may walk together, out of the rhythm established. Strong feet with a sense of weight centers, and legs, elastic and firm, are necessary for sustained moving. Arms may move as the torso becomes strong enough to carry them up, out, down, or where feeling may lead them. If a group is nervous, jittery, or unstable, the closing of the eyes until they can draw upon themselves from a center is helpful. The record of "Ave Maria" was used as an accompaniment as the group entered, but the music was allowed to die out completely as the words were spoken.

In the actual presentation of the unit the Madonna approached from behind the platforms and climbed to her position at center; the two angels came from either side and knelt while the group followed closely and arranged themselves on the platform levels. They came to a bowing position with feet, legs, and tip of spine under so they might have strength and leverage for rising. The arms and hands came to the bowed heads, then as they lifted, the arms were outstretched to the Virgin. As they came up, she spoke the first line, her movements folding into the suggestion of the babe in her arms. The whole selection was given with a soloist carrying the lines spoken by Mary and the group speaking in unison the other lines. The group sank slowly into sitting position and held a sympathetic and responsive attitude during the next selection.

"Judean Hills Are Holy" was done by a soloist who spoke from her position in the group. The girl had an adequate, well-supported, sustained, and modulated voice; otherwise, I should have arranged it for group. The group rose for the next selection not as individuals but as a unit in harmony with the thought they were giving.

"The Carpenter of Galilee" was done in unison.

As a part of the movement of the group, the Madonna descended the steps before the solo, "Judean Hills Are Holy," and sat and spoke with the group. A boy took the place occupied by her during "The Carpenter of Galilee," and lifting his arms, gave the opening, "And seeing the multitude, He went up into a mountain and when He was sat, His disciples came unto Him, and He opened His mouth and taught them, saying."

He also spoke the Beatitudes with the group. If a strong boy is available, or a girl with a deep quality of voice, they may be done as a solo, and the whole group might give the verses. As it was, the whole group did do the last verse, and lifted their arms out on the last two lines. The bringing of them down, wrists leading of course, made a smooth transition for "The Ballad of Easter."

The Beatitudes and the responsive verses were done by the deep and lyric voices respectively. The Beatitudes seemed difficult to do, and I mention it, particularly, because the difficulty lay in a lack of the observation of weak forms. There was a tendency, as there is so many times, to stress too many syllables so that the really important ones are lost. The general unresponsiveness of the group to the ideas was due to their failure to see the balanced construction of the Beatitudes, the quality being named first and the reward last. Transition and coloring finally came.

"The Ballad of Easter" was done in unison except for the two soldiers, two women, and two angels. One of the women was, of course, Mary, who fell up the steps as she said, "My son, my son, my son."

The two groups left from each side of the center group on a triumphant note with a Halleluiah chorus, as an accompaniment. The music must blend with speech or the rhythm of the whole is lost. The two angels came down the steps, and the Madonna rose, caught their rhythm, and went out with them. The center figure followed.

The question of costumes may arise. We have two sets of choir robes: flowing cheese-cloth ones in light blue, gray, and bluish lavenders (subtle shades have to be dyed), and sateen ones in princess style with tight sleeves and plain round necks in a dark red, dark blue, and purple. We used one set of costumes for one performance; and the other set for another. The Madonna wore a white robe with a clear blue cheese-cloth thrown over her head, and a gold piece draping from shoulder low in the arm. The color scheme for the first was blue, white, and gold, and for the last, the warm tones of the old masters. No boys appeared in the first presentation, and in the second they wore grayish tan robes, long and belted with cords. The angels were in yellow cheese-cloth robes made with a bodice and very full, long skirts and enormous sleeves banded at the wrist. Since the feet are bare, dresses are all to the floor.

XIII

USING ENGLISH FOR PRACTICAL AFFAIRS

ENGLISH AS A TOOL has a place in the experience-centered curriculum. To every pupil of any age, learning what he needs in a practical situation is motivated and tested by experience itself.

The units that follow show that the practical affairs of school and community activities, and of vocational training have the immediacy which Tracy [1] describes as characteristic of the situations in which children first learn the magic of language as a control over their environment.

SCHOOL AND COMMUNITY ACTIVITIES

The daily routines as well as the extraordinary occurrences in school and in community life furnish boys and girls with purposes for communication. Skilful guidance by dynamic teachers of English, however, is required in order that these pupils gain in power to speak, to write, and to read effectively and correctly as they use English in everyday life.

AN EXPERIMENT IN CREATIVE EXPRESSION [2]

This creative-expression unit is based upon the idea that student activities should originate in the classroom and grow into extracurricular activities. The unit also satisfies four teen-age desires— namely, (1) to do constructive thinking, (2) to invent outlets for dramatic impulses, (3) to gain teacher and pupil approval for correct and effective informal and formal communication, and (4) to interpret imaginatively all he sees and hears. Each creative activity set up for classroom work has focused on one of these normal creative impulses. The best of these individual attempts find their way to public performances.

Relation with the local paper. Here is how this creative program is developed in grades seven through twelve. Awakening and guid-

---

[1] Tracy, *op. cit.,* Ch. IX.
[2] Reported by Mildred C. Schmidt, 710 Albion Ave., Fairmont, Minn.

ing constructive thinking grow from the classroom unit of composition to editorial writing for local daily city paper. The creative dramatic unit begins in the short story, drama, poetry units, supplementing the declamation contest, and becomes an artistic prose and poetry festival for the public. Book-Week program of original plays also comes from their dramatic impulse. Extemporaneous speaking contests grow out of class speech units and modern problems in social-science classes. Not just to win but to command the material and convince the audience has been the contestants' aims. Class composition grows into a semester school magazine.

For the creative-writing projects, materials appropriate to each year of students are chosen. Because ideas are reorganized with assistance, word meanings checked in the dictionary, and papers read and reread for effectiveness and correctness, the pupils' control of technical English shows improvement. These paragraphs grow into stories and essays. At the end of the selected writings, they are published as a school literary magazine.

Relation to local history. During the fall of 1937 in the creative-writing project we capitalized on the fact that the Lovelaces had just published their novel about Fairmont, *Gentlemen from England.* This novel relates the early settlement of the English and Germans in this locality. The 1937 fall number of the literary magazine became an early Fairmont number. Students interviewed, investigated, and wrote their own family pioneer histories. Art classes illustrated the accounts. One art student, after the topography of early Fairmont had been reconstructed, produced a picture map of the vicinity. A girl who lives in one of the early English settler's frontier mansions mentioned in *Gentlemen from England* wrote the account of the house as it was when her father purchased the place. Many German frontier stories were accumulated. After the material was assembled, the staff of the school paper took over the publication and the distribution of it.

Relation to school programs. Creative dramatic activities are evident in several units. Outlets for this impulse are present in interviewing, telephoning, and conversation and are used in dramatization of short stories and classroom plays. November Book-Week programs also grew out of classroom activities.

In the poetry units, oral reading is used to develop appreciation through putting across to the class audience the poet's idea and his feeling about his idea. Boys experiencing the rhythm of "The Congo" or "The Santa Fe Trail" volunteer to show the rest how the idea swings. Choral reading comes out of such beginnings. The choir uses books in reading and memorization of best liked verses comes usually at the close of the unit. The class and the teacher listen, judge, discuss the quality of the reading. After class eliminations are made, private coaching begins and at a preliminary try-out in the dramatic studio, four readers from each grade are chosen to read in an evening public performance. Thus the classroom project has become extracurricular. Two weeks are allowed for practice before junior and senior eliminations are made individually. Selections may be changed for each meet. To eliminate the competitive idea and to keep interest focused on the artistic skill of performers, rating charts and ballots are passed to every member of the public audience on the final night. Ballots are marked *superior, excellent, good, poor.* Rating charts indicate specific items to note as selections are read. No rivalry appears, and the audience seriously considers the charts. Because we feel that high-school people should hear only the best, these best readers change their selections again and read later to the assembly.

In the effective-speaking unit in senior high, English teachers work with the social-science teachers. Students have practice in speaking with us, but they have vital problems in social science that stimulate extemporaneous speaking. For this assembly activity pupils use material from periodicals. Students talk about a modern problem. The best two speakers are selected by students of each class. Two speakers from each year in senior high, six altogether, meet an hour before the auditorium program to draw up their topics. The assembly gives a fitting outlet to this valuable speech activity.

From Portland, Oregon, Nellie Fawcett, reports that her eighth-grade pupils find opportunities in school and community projects to speak and to write effectively. Some of these occasions include advertising a class play, selling tickets for the annual football game between the all-star players of the high schools, and the season's champion high-school team. This game is sponsored by the Portland Firemen's Association to raise money for supplying milk daily to the children of indigent families and consequently makes an emotional appeal.

SERVING ON A TRAFFIC SQUAD [3]

Some time ago, Portland Schools organized safety traffic squads to guard children while crossing busy streets, and in Glencoe School, service on the squad is a coveted honor for the 8B class.

[3] Reported by Ella P. Roberts, Glencoe School, Portland, Ore.

Discussion in the civics classes brought about further desire for service, and traffic squads for hall duty were organized. Officers were chosen from both 8B sections, one class taking duty at dismissal and the other at change of classes.

Before putting the plan into operation it was discussed in English classes. Methods of getting the coöperation of the whole school were discussed. Talks were prepared which were given to each class in the school, explaining the plan, showing the arm band in the school colors which the officers would wear, and asking the coöperation of all in more orderly movement in the halls.

The officers of each class met and elected a chief and a secretary. Regular meetings are held at which reports are made and traffic problems discussed.

The officers have learned to speak courteously to children violating traffic rules. They occasionally go before a class to compliment it for improvement or for especially good behavior. When it is necessary to report a child to his teacher or the principal for flagrant or repeated violation of rules, they have learned that the proper tone of voice and friendly manner get the results desired.

Occasionally a joint meeting of both groups is held, and the principal and both assisting teachers are invited, and asked for suggestions, but the responsibility for conducting the meeting is placed on the children and is admirably handled by them.

COMMUNITY SURVEY AS A LANGUAGE ACTIVITY [4]

I. *Objectives*

1. To learn one's relations to his community and to practise techniques of adjustment to community living
2. To understand the meaning of the concept "community"
3. To form a basis of judgment concerning community life
4. To prepare for community participation in work and leisure
5. To achieve those language skills necessary for satisfactory participation in community life

II. *Activities*

1. Making up an ecological map of the community, showing clubs, recreation centers, schools, churches, Y's, playgrounds, etc.
2. Bringing in a report on community recreation facilities
   a. Talk on the nature of leisure and recreation

[4] Reported by Leon Mones, Central High School, Newark, N. J.

b. Debate on the values of commercialized recreation

c. Letters to the press on moving-picture programs

d. Themes on a day in park, playground, etc.

e. Writing newspaper reports on community social and sporting events

f. Preparing posters, notices, tickets, etc., for community concerts, etc.

3. Bringing in a report on community tastes, reading, movie programs, radio preferences, sports, etc.

4. Preparing talks for community celebrations

   a. Preparing a calendar of coming community celebrations

   b. Preparing talks for fund-raising, support, etc.

   c. Preparing newspaper reports

   d. Writing letters to organizations for support

   e. Giving radio accounts of the celebrations

   f. Preparing a community *Who's Who*

5. Writing letters on matters of community business

6. Writing biographies of community heroes

7. Bringing in surveys and reports on community politics, business, shopping habits, street improvements, transportation, etc.

8. Making collections of community slang, legends, etc.

9. Representing one's community in a classroom federation of various communities

10. Preparing a community newspaper or periodical

    a. Appointing an editorial board

    b. Determining on newspaper procedure

    c. Assigning to different positions

    d. Discussing newspaper content

    e. Writing of community news, gossip, social activities, etc.

    f. Rewriting, correcting, typing, illustrating, etc.

III. *Appraisal of Growth*

1. How much better do the pupils understand the mores of their community?

2. How well do they know what are the wholesome, free, or inexpensive recreational facilities in the community?

3. How well can the pupils use language to participate courteously and effectively in the life of their community?

4. How many of the resources of the community do the pupils use since making the survey?

ENGLISH CORRELATED WITH COMMUNITY ACTIVITIES [5]

How the unit originated. One day a letter was received by the fifth-grade children of the Campus Training School from some fifth- and sixth-grade children in a rural school about seventy miles from Kalamazoo. This letter asked for information on how paper is made. The teacher knew nothing about the correspondents, but since Kalamazoo is a paper-making city, she thought that it might be possible for her pupils to use this request to learn something themselves about paper-making.

How the unit developed. After the letter was read by the children, discussion followed as to how the letter might best be answered. These were some of the questions that were raised: "What do we know about the making of paper? How can we find out what to tell them? What would we like to know?" One child suggested that the class should go to a paper mill to get first-hand information. This met with the approval of the group, and a committee was sent to find out whether they might visit a paper mill and when it would be convenient.

After plans were made to visit a mill, the question arose as to how they should get ready for their visit. They decided that each child should make a list of questions he would like to have answered. It soon became apparent that some of them felt that they did not have enough information to ask intelligent questions, so it was suggested that they read about the making of paper before they went to the mill. Much time was spent in finding material, reading, and in wording questions.

As the time for the excursion approached, several parents who have lived in Kalamazoo for many years, but had not visited one of the paper mills, asked permission to join the group. The plan of going in a school bus was changed, and on the appointed day five mothers and the teacher took the children in private cars to the Kalamazoo Vegetable Parchment Paper Mill where they were met by three guides. At the close of the trip an envelope of illustrated material and a book of information were given to each child.

The next day a general discussion took place in which there was much worth-while exchanging of ideas, checking statements, and the raising of many new questions. Again the children were forced to return to their books and pamphlets to gain more information in order to answer some of the questions that had arisen.

---

[5] Reported by Miss Florence E. McLouth, Campus Training School, Kalamazoo, Mich.

The next problem was to choose the form in which to send their information to the children in the rural school. The group decided that they would compile a book on paper-making in which each child would write on a different topic. This work occupied a number of days, for it was to represent the best work of each child. Three children arranged an exhibit which showed the making of paper from wood pulp. One child prepared a map showing the paper centers of the United States. It was suggested that some of the printed material which was given to them at the mill should also be enclosed. After all the material was written and approved, a committee was chosen to arrange the book and to make a table of contents. The material was later bound in a cover which had been made by one child. Another group had the task of wrapping and mailing the package.

Integration with various subject-matter fields. The opportunity for work in English was far-reaching since it included many types of written work as well as much oral discussion. A letter was sent early to the rural children telling them that information would be forwarded to them as soon as it could be assembled. Outlines, questions, sentence and paragraph work, and organization of material were some of the important phases of the written English. Silent and oral reading were also emphasized because much information and exchange of ideas were necessary. From this study a question was asked as to how paper mills happened to be located in Kalamazoo. This led to work in geography and history. The children had been studying the New England states and knew that paper was manufactured there.

The request for information made purposeful the pupils' reading, observation, and writing of letters and reports. The importance of answering a request encouraged more effective and correct penmanship. The habit of proofreading all written work which was to be read by others or preserved was strengthened. A knowledge of the work of the community as well as an interest in it was fostered.

How a teacher utilized the launching of the first air-mail service between Albert Lea and Minneapolis is illustrated in the following outline.

NATIONAL AIR MAIL WEEK [6]

I. *Speech Experiences*

A. Telephoning
   1. Encouraging friends to mail letters on "special flight"
   2. Asking for appointments for interviews

[6] Reported by Sybil Yates, Public Schools, Albert Lea, Minn.

        3. Arranging for public-library visitations
- B. Conversing
  - 1. Sharing airplane experiences
    - *a.* Rides
    - *b.* Airports
    - *c.* Air circuses
    - *d.* Newspaper articles
    - *e.* Airplane movies
    - *f.* Airplane library books
    - *g.* Airplane poems
    - *h.* Airplane magazines
    - *i.* Airplane letters
    - *j.* Types of aircraft
  - 2. Sharing hobbies
    - *a.* Airplane craft
    - *b.* Stamp collections
    - *c.* Cachet collections
    - *d.* Pen pals
- C. Interviewing
- D. Reporting on interviews and conferences with
  - 1. The postmaster
  - 2. The pilot
  - 3. The designer of the local cachet
  - 4. The chairman of the Junior Chamber of Commerce
  - 5. Pioneer mail men
  - 6. Pioneer residents
- E. Introducing adult speakers with aviation experiences
- F. Giving airship sales talks
- G. Discussing and planning
  - 1. Vocabulary list of words concerned with aviation
  - 2. Spelling list of above words
  - 3. Radio program

II. *Writing Experiences*

- A. Social and business letters
- B. Original poems, short stories, etc.
- C. Reports on
  - 1. How is air mail handled in larger cities?
  - 2. How are airplane hostesses trained?
  - 3. How are pilots trained?
  - 4. How are mechanics trained?
  - 5. How are airship pictures made?

6. How are air-line pamphlets and bulletins secured?
D. Newspapers
   1. Editorials
   2. Announcements
   3. News stories
      a. Real
         (1) City's special flight
         (2) City's air mail history
         (3) City's coöperation
      b. Imaginary
         (1) Realization of a trip
         (2) Narrow escapes
   4. Bulletin board of current aviation news re-written
E. Bibliographies relevant to airplane interests
F. Outlines of group accomplishments

SOLVING LOGICAL PROBLEMS

Developing the language skills needed in the logical solution of social and personal problems has been a goal of the pupils in English VII under the direction of Flora L. Taylor.[7] The students appraise their progress by asking themselves these questions at the close of the unit:

1. Do I see more clearly the exact questions to be answered in order to solve a problem?
2. Do I know how to find what information is available on any phase of a problem?
3. Do I realize more fully that all information is not of equal value?
4. Do I know how to tell which information is trustworthy and which is not?
5. Have I a better idea of how to organize my material logically?
6. Am I more critical and thus less likely to be misled by one-sided information and false logic used by others?
7. Can I recognize the factual from the emotional in my reasoning?
8. Am I sensitive to the presence or absence of logic in editorials, sales talks, advertisements, and the like?

VOCATIONAL TRAINING

The teacher of boys preparing to become automobile mechanics is challenged to adjust the expressional activities of the English

[7] For further details write Flora L. Taylor, Evander Childs High School, New York City.

period to the present and immediate future needs of his pupils. How such a teacher managed to work *with* the grain of these boys and how he utilized their school shop experience to anticipate real life is illustrated in the following account.

English and Vocational Training [8]

Thirty boys preparing through the schools for a life as automobile mechanics require as specialized work in English as do those who intend continuing education after high school. Not professional English, to be sure, but English suited to their own specific and known needs. In a large senior high school in a northern Ohio industrial city I had such a group. Their curriculum included half a day spent in the automobile shop working on cars and parts and studying theories of machine construction, mechanics, and all fields specifically needed for their future life work. The other half of the day was spent in hour-long classes of history, mathematics, and English, the former two distinctly vocational in nature. The English had not been.

The group, averaging well below the twenty-fifth percentile on the Ohio State University Intelligence test, included five boys whose scores on the test were under fifty per cent. More than half of the group were retarded at least a year, several up to three years. Writing, speech, and behavior—all offered distinct problems. Moral and social questions were of real interest to most of the group, not technically but practically. Several had court records, one overage boy having at least six acquittals for major delinquencies of which he was prone to boast and the others to talk.

What to do? No standard test, either in speech or composition, would be practical. It would be too disheartening. For the pupil who was average or below (in the class), a vulgar tongue learned around the factories, in the homes, and near railroad centers served as English. Even up-to-date-slang, unless found in popular songs, was beyond them. But they had an interest in automobiles.

The first week was spent largely in exploratory talks on speed of cars, design of bodies for various purposes, stream-lining, tread of tires, good and bad qualities of various makes of cars, what the high-school course should mean to the group, possibilities of transfer to aviation mechanics, and other similar topics introduced by the class. Rather naturally, the question of the value of English appeared, heatedly at times. Why should a mechanic be able to read

[8] Reported by George H. McClellan, State Teachers College, Frostburg, Md.

novels? Why should boys be required to learn to write when all they think they would ever need to write would be check sheets and bills? What purpose could learning to spell serve them? Why should they be grammatical if none of their companions were? The questions were almost endless, and the answers came almost entirely from members of the group, the better ones serving as temporary jury in the trial of English.

That preliminary discussion took place after the second day as prepared talks before the class and served, incidentally to my purpose if not to theirs, as excellent oral composition. Out of it grew the course outline, for at least one of their two final years of English. Spelling of words which the boys themselves deemed essential to their purpose. Grammar of a functional nature was to grow out of their difficulties in speech and writing. Reading was to follow interests outlined by members of the group and could well include at least one long-time assignment by the teacher of some type of material he thought would be of interest and value to the class. Writing was to be as professional as possible, except for occasional personal experiences that would be discussed before they were trusted to black and white. Talks were to be almost as frequent throughout the year as they had been during the first week, but should be better planned. Standards for each variety of activity were to be worked out as the course proceeded, but for oral expression they should at least start promptly.

The set-up looked perfect. The intelligence scores, school records, and court judgments were not final. Intelligence of an active sort was demonstrated, as was definite interest in sharing experiences within the group. Committees began at once to set up the various tasks the class had determined to undertake. As the work advanced, however, interest flagged. Energy was required and unwillingly given. Behavior problems arose that appeared habitual. The three worst boys, those whose intelligence scores were the lowest and whose retardation was the greatest, asked permission to handle discipline in their own way. It was to begin as admonitions, continue as threats, and end with any required out-of-school physical persuasion. The principal and teacher, quite unwilling to go so far, did permit the first step. As a result the erstwhile ringleader in disorder served for a time a most useful purpose in carrying on activities in English class.

The committee on spelling was the first to turn in a workmanlike job. Six boys decided that the beginning of the speller should naturally grow out of their manual and work sheets in automobile mechanics. Reading for a purpose, in a little over two weeks, each committeeman had prepared a list of difficult, unusual, frequent, and easily mistaken words in the 300 pages of print and mimeograph. Alphabetizing and mimeographing of the resultant list was simple, with occasional teacher help in arrangement and spelling. Next came the task of keeping records of words misspelled on *all* written work done by the boys, work in other classes as well as English. Whenever a word appeared three times on the key list, it was transferred to the master list which was to be mimeographed and included in the speller. That list ended in June with slightly over 1500 words. The making of the list served its purpose, for through repetition or pride of ownership, the spelling of the group was vastly better before the end of the year. On written work, errors in spelling were reduced from a preliminary average of eleven per page to a resultant average of less than two.

Grammar proved a greater difficulty with its larger variety of errors. Spelling, they could watch. Grammar, they did not know how to attack. One member of the language-usage committee suggested that language was my job, and the committee should not be bothered. Others suggested a committee check on all papers after my reading of them, to make a list of frequent errors. Of course I agreed, for that prevented my having to make a similar list for each pupil and offered excellent opportunity for at least the committee to learn detail.

Before the first spelling list was completed, and after several orders for automotive supplies and letters to manufacturers were written, a preliminary list of usage difficulties was ready for attention. Agreement of verbs with subjects, agreement of pronouns with antecedents, the principal parts of several irregular verbs, the lack of logic in using double negatives, the case of personal pronouns and *who* and *whom*—those, as usual, were the chief causes of difficulty, and the committee recognized the fact. Correcting or preventing recurrence of these, however, was beyond the group. But their preliminary work and their demonstration of the errors to the class made an excellent starting place for instruction in grammar. Not only the committee but all members of the class could see that work was needed on these simple errors, and the group was willing to spend the time necessary to prevent their recurrence through understanding them. Of course all could not be tackled at once. Instead, a review of the grammar the group had studied in previous years and a discussion of the first and third types of errors listed led to a direct attack on them. *See, do, give, some, lie, set*—these and the whole traditional list could be taken, one at a time, learned in context, discussed, and checked on. This start on verbs led the parade toward more correct language usage, which continued throughout the year. To be sure, the result was neither as positive nor as measurable as was that in spelling, but both in speech and writing the specific difficulties which had been met at the first of the year were largely missing in June. *Come* no longer was past; *who* seldom introduced the clause in which it served as object; and *don't* infrequently followed immediately after a third-person singular pronoun, even in conversation. The committee's preliminary and follow-up work saw to that, for that small group realized the advantages inherent in constant checks.

A third committee started the year more happily than did any other group. Its task was that of scouring magazines in the school and public libraries for articles and reviews that should prove of interest to class members. At first they limited themselves to technical or semi-professional articles, but merely leafing through the *Reader's Guide to Periodical Literature* and the digest type of magazine directed their interest into fiction that should appeal to most boys. National Council of Teachers of English reading lists were searched; library bulletins and lists played their parts. As a result, the committee and the majority of the class did far more reading than could logically have been expected of them in any regular school course. Naturally pulp magazines came in for their share of interest, as many of them appeal directly to the mechanically minded boy. Their attraction, however, paled before the delights of the more definitely intriguing and sophisticated material listed on the board each week by the enthusiastic committee. Quite naturally oral and written reports were forthcoming, and heated debates could well grow out of technical or non-technical points of interest. Reading was required, a minimum amount each week. Few were the boys, however, who did not regularly read beyond the minimum. The committee thought it an excellent game to read vast quantities of material and almost dare the others to do as much. Best readings each week were discussed by committeemen or by others appointed by them. The discussion was brief, factual, suggestive. Before the next discussion, the majority of the class would have read each of the suggested articles and sampled one or more of others listed. Each member of the class kept a note-book record of his readings, in bibliographical form with notes, and showed his book to the teacher as occasion permitted. Many of the books served as a diary, with frequent personal comments sensibly made after the regular entry.

Some, of course were exceedingly poor, but the average notation at the end of the year showed a definitely professional interest and curiosity in the reading done.

The last two committees, made up largely of the weakest members of the group, wanted to work out assignments for writing and talking. As the work of the other groups led so largely into that of these two, their task was actually much lighter. Letters, both personal and business, attracted the interest of the writing group. Form, attack, purpose, language, and varieties of letters drew their attention and led to much class writing and discussion. Interviews between "mechanics" and "customer" concerning repairs, equipment, complaints on service, and the like gave opportunity for practice in a life use of English. Papers on topics suggested by shop work, materials from other academic courses, and the activities of the other committees grew out of their meetings. The "talking committee" acted on similar principles, but also drew up standards for talks and for discussion of both content and manner of the talks. Between these two groups, communication of many varieties was instigated, checked, improved; interest in beginning and continuing discussions on the floor and through writing was stimulated; reading and writing of many varieties were motivated.

Not to be outdone by the academic classes in the school, the boys felt the need of textbooks which were strangely missing. The regular blue grammar had not appeared, nor the required weekly papers. In the second semester, other classes were allowed to read *Ivanhoe*, *The Idylls of the King*, and *As You Like It*. Not so, these. Other classes could spend six weeks on each of the books. A group discussion persuaded the teacher that these boys were missing something which they should have. It led to ordering copies of *Modern Literature* [9] for the semester. Completely unconnected with the purpose set up for the course by the group, the bi-weekly magazine appealed first because they had something the others did not have and then because the contents was engaging. They read avidly. Each exercise was worked out, each story and essay and poem read with a will. The fact that much of the material was beyond them, intellectually, did not seem to matter. They were growing in ability and in application.

Hearing other sophomores discussing *Ivanhoe* made them want to read that book. Its difficulty, for more than five or six of the group, however, appeared too great. Instead, they were urged to go beyond

[9] Now *Everyday Reading*, American Education Press, 400 South Front St., Columbus, Ohio.

the academic pupils again. Instead of *Ivanhoe,* they could have their choice of 125 historical novels in the school or public library. Of course *Ivanhoe* was included in the list. Would it dare be left off? And of course it was read by several boys. During the six weeks in which part of the time was given to discussion of novels as such, each boy read at least four of the books on the list, many reading a book for the first time in their lives, if confession can be believed.

In retelling, the course sounds better than it was. Discipline, application, attendance, interest—all caused problems that had to be solved. Coördinating the tasks of committees, keeping them at work and willing to work, and seeing that the results they achieved were worth while may have taken far more time than was deserved. Definite needs in each of the areas covered during the year were still obvious in June, but spelling, grammar, punctuation, organization of materials for writing and speaking, reading of many sorts—all these showed a definite improvement over what had prevailed when the boys entered "automobile English." Attitudes were better; interests were broader and more definite; behavior was much less a problem. The very exacting sharing of experiences that grew out of group planning and carrying forward of plans had served its purpose: to improve the boys' skills in writing, talking, and reading in the English classroom, in other school subjects, and in life itself.

Another phase of adjusting English to the vocational needs of seniors is revealed in the following outline from the Allentown, Pennsylvania, High School.

How to Graduate from School into a Job [10]

Following the writing of applications for positions, discussion centered upon how to secure the right job through a personal interview. The pupils listed what to them seemed the difficulties. The teacher suggested that the class dramatize these business situations in order to anticipate what problems would likely arise. This the pupils did.

The class divided into groups of two, three, or four pupils. Each group was to select a situation from real life and to present it to the class. Two versions were acted: a what-to-do and a what-not-to-do version. Appearance, approach, technical knowledge, personal characteristics were appraised by accepted standards. The two most skilful stenographers in the class recorded everything said and done. The transcriptions of their notes furnished excellent material for

[10] Reported by Mrs. Mary E. Herbert, Allentown High School, Allentown, Pa.

appraisal of such situations as an interview for a position, an interrupted dictation when the employer was called on the telephone.

The pupils were enthusiastic not only over their success in a lifelike situation but over having a chance to see themselves as an employer might. The teacher saw many points at which the pupils needed guidance. Later activities helped pupils to well-founded assurance that should help them graduate into a job.

"Looking Forward" is the descriptive title given by Tom Miller [11] to a unit in which seniors through discussion, interviewing, reading, and writing answer these questions about their future: (1) What would you like to do if you could? (2) What college would help you attain your goal? (3) How do you expect to earn a living? (4) How can you spend your leisure time?

A similar unit was developed by Margaret W. Boutelle assisted by Dr. Alfred Crago and Dr. E. W. Garris.

A New Outlook on Life [12]

Activities

1. Reading poetry
2. Writing autobiographies
3. Searching for material on vocation in which one is interested
4. Taking notes on material found
5. Listening to lectures on vocational fields
6. Visiting plants to study occupations
7. Interviewing men of achievement in chosen field
8. Organizing material for presentation
9. Writing paper including findings
10. Making a bibliography that would be helpful to others
11. Making a note-book (scrap-book) of material that was found helpful
12. Reading books and magazine articles on character and personality
13. Reading and discussing biographies to learn more of traits leading to achievement
14. Class discussions to clarify thinking and to enlarge understanding
15. Reading and listing poems expressing one's philosophy of life

[11] For details write to Tom Miller, 971 Lancaster Avenue, Syracuse, N. Y.
[12] Margaret W. Boutelle, P. K. Yonge School, Gainesville, Fla.

16. Discussing novels, plays, and essays which reveal character and personality
17. Making an analysis of one's self in order to develop further an effective personality
18. Deciding what to do about unsatisfactory findings
19. Rating personal traits to lead to self-improvement
20. Taking notes on reading on a 4 x 6 card, to record exact sources and number of pages read, and to comment on the the books and articles read

Outcomes—vocational and personal

1. An appreciation of the importance of the work
2. A knowledge of work and working conditions
3. An awareness of the effect of the work on the worker
4. A knowledge of opportunities associated with the vocation
5. An acquaintance with the training needed for the vocation
6. A knowledge of the personal qualifications needed in the vocation
7. A knowledge of the range of wages
8. An appreciation of the advantages and disadvantages
9. A self-survey to assist in finding the right job
10. An appreciation of leisure-time activities as recreation from work, an enrichment of personality

XIV

PRESERVING THE SOCIAL AMENITIES

PARENTS AND TEACHERS are often shocked at the discourtesy and irreverence of youth. Yet all too often these apparent shortcomings represent only a lack of skill in the choice of words, not insensitivity to the feelings of others.

The same facts can be transmitted in a telephone call or letter without irritating the recipient of the news. A favor can be requested in a way that affords pleasure to the donor. Appreciation can be expressed without strain on the energies of the person who received a letter, a gift, a favor, or the pleasure of an excellent speech, recital, radio, or screen performance. It need not be easier to express sympathy in gifts than in words.

The opportunities in every school day for direct and indirect teaching of language as a means of getting along with people—of preserving the social amenities—are so numerous that all that is needed is a well-mannered teacher who is sensitive to the flavor of words.

LANGUAGE AND THE SOCIAL AMENITIES

Language facilitates or inhibits pleasant social relationships depending upon the speaker's choice of words. Many schools are attempting to assist boys and girls in using language to help them get along with people.

A. T. Krider at the La Porte High School made a study of the social needs for language and then set up problem situations in which the student attempts to meet the situation. The class and teacher help him to appraise what he did, and through practice he grows in spontaneous, effective use of language.

The teacher has typed the "problem situations" on cards and deals them out for both extemporaneous and prepared solutions.

The following list of problem situations in which a telephone is used indicates the spirit of these activities. Similarly this teacher has handled introductions, letter-writing, and interviewing.

SOCIAL BEHAVIOR THROUGH LANGUAGE TRAINING [1]

Using the Telephone (For freshmen and sophomores)

1. Your mother is out of town and you are left with the responsibility of preparing the meals over the week-end. Call the grocer and order what you need.

2. You have been invited to go with a group of your friends on a skating party. On arriving at your home, you find that you have guests, two cousins your own age. Call the person who arranged the skating party asking to be excused from going.

3. You have been invited to attend a small after-game gathering at the home of a friend. A cousin arrives at your home unexpectedly. Call your host and ask that your cousin be included.

4. Your father has offered to take you and several of your friends to an out-of-town basket-ball game. Call those friends and invite them.

5. Your mother has gone down town shopping. Your father is out of town with the car. She has asked to have a taxi waiting for her at 5 : 30 at the corner of Chestnut and Maple streets. Call the taxi office.

6. Your mother feels that you are too young to have dates. One of your classmates calls asking you to go with him to the high-school mixer next Friday night. Refuse the date tactfully.

7. A friend of yours has offered to teach you to swim. Call him suggesting next Saturday afternoon for the first lesson.

8. Your mother feels that you should begin to assume responsibility in the kitchen. For dinner Sunday there will be six people at the table. She has asked you to order the meat for the Sunday dinner. Phone the butcher.

9. You are at home alone and discover a leak in the bathroom plumbing. Call the janitor in the apartment house.

10. You notice a roof fire on the house across the street. Call the fire department.

11. Your little brother's clothes have caught fire. After smothering the flames with a small rug, call the doctor.

12. You are on a basket-ball trip, and forty miles from home the bus becomes stalled in a snowdrift. The group takes refuge in a farm house. Call your parents and assure them of your safety.

[1] Reported by A. T. Krider, La Porte High School, La Porte, Ind.

13. Your father is attending a convention in Indianapolis. Your mother has just been taken to the hospital with an attack of appendicitis. Call him at the English Hotel and take care not to alarm him unduly.

Using the Telephone (Juniors and Seniors)

1. You are giving a dinner party at the Hotel Rumely. You call the head waiter and make all necessary arrangements with him.

2. A child is lost (Lincoln Way). You go into the drug-store and call her father at his office and inform him of what has happened.

3. A man has been struck by an automobile at the corner of Monroe Street and Lincoln Way. You go to a near-by drug-store and call the doctor.

4. You are calling a girl for a date for a coming school dance. There is a possibility that she has already bought her own ticket planning to go unescorted. You wish to find out whether or not she has a ticket so that you will know whether or not to buy one for her.

5. You are treasurer of a school club to which the captain of the football team belongs. He is the only member who has not paid his dues and you wish him to pay. You don't know him very well and wish to avoid offending him.

6. A girl has persisted in calling you. When you arrive home after school, you find she has called again and has left her number with the request that you call her. During the course of the conversation explain politely the embarrassment caused by her frequent phoning.

7. Your sister has been invited to a dinner. At the last minute she becomes ill. Call the (host) hostess and decline for her.

8. The mother of your best friend has just died unexpectedly. Call your friend and offer your condolences and services.

9. As social chairman of your class, you are charged with the responsibility of securing an orchestra for a coming class dance. You call the office of the Music Federation of America in Chicago and arrange for an orchestra.

10. You happen to know that the most popular girl in your class does not have a date tonight. This is noon and you decide that you want to ask her to go to a show with you tonight. You wish by all means to avoid giving her the impression that she must be unpopular not to have a date.

11. A teacher has given an involved assignment. When you settle down to study at home, you realize you do not know just what is required. Call another member of your class asking how he understood the directions.

12. A mechanic, a good friend of yours, has done some repair work on your car. You discover that the defect has not been remedied. Call him and inform him of the fact.

13. You have stopped overnight at a tourist home. The next morning, ten miles down the road, you discover that your watch is missing. You think that you have left it on the dresser in the tourist home. Call back and ask the landlady if it is there. If the landlady cannot find the watch, offer a reward to have her maid try to find it.

14. You are involved in a motor accident which is a clear case of negligence on the part of the other driver. The damage to your car amounted to $50. The other driver at the time of the accident was vehement in declaring the accident to be your fault. He is a hot-tempered individual. Call him to inform him that unless he is willing to settle for the amount, you intend to put the matter in the hands of your attorney.

15. You and a close friend have quarreled childishly over a disputed point in a game of bridge. You are sincerely sorry for the difference and call to confess your willingness to let bygones be bygones.

In the smooth running of any modern school there are countless opportunities to experience English as a means of getting along with people. Excuses, complaints, requests, greetings, sympathy, congratulations, thanks, acceptance, regrets, inquiry, and order are but some of the kinds of purposeful oral and written expression which are necessitated by living together in a social institution guided by some sort of regulatory routines concerning attendance, punctuality, and use of property.

When adolescent boys and girls, participating in student government, feel that the "faculty is really running things," they need to learn how to use language to obtain more privileges or to secure information essential to their appreciation of why the faculty is doing what it is.

Discussion that is significantly pointed, genuinely sincere, yet comfortably courteous is the result of a thoughtful choice of ideas and of words.

A typical instance happened in the Forest Park High School in May, 1939, when a home room section of the junior class was restive under their junior class adviser's selection of an orchestra for the Junior Prom. The adviser had acted with and through a student committee. The disgruntled group had sent no representative to

the meeting. Because the teacher of the home room section over-
heard the ill-humored discussion among a group before school, she
brought the discussion out into the open. All real and imaginary
grievances were aired. Attention was given to all possible explanations of *why* the adviser had not selected "a name orchestra" which
this group desired. Then the home room teacher, who also taught
English to the group, recommended that the class present their
case in a letter to the adviser of the Junior class.

The experience of composing this letter of complaint was one
long to be remembered. From the offensive tone of the first boy's
suggested opening sentence the group progressed through forty-
five minutes of thinking and feeling until a sincere yet courteous
letter was composed.

The psychological value of writing out their grievance and
then reconsidering it from the point of view of the person to whom
the complaint was being made was a new experience to these
eleventh-grade pupils. The adviser received the letter and, as requested, stopped into the class at his convenience to tell the facts
which this group needed to know. So helpful was this activity that
not only were disorganizers turned into loyal supporters, but a
group of intellectually keen young boys and girls went to the prom
and danced happily to the music of the orchestra which they had
falsely concluded, without evidence, would not be acceptable.

Dozens of instances happened with this and other groups in
which language was used to relieve emotional tension, *yet before
the letters were mailed* the writer had found a way to express his
grievance without offense to the recipient of the letter.

Another type of letter useful in preserving the social amenities
is one written to visitors to the class. Nowadays every school is
open to parents, taxpayers, local and out-of-town teachers and administrators. Children of all grades can be trained to serve as hosts
and hostesses, every member of the group having a turn. In addition to this experience in oral courtesy, is the possibility of helping
a stranger into a comfortable and rapid adjustment to whatever
is going on in the classroom. This type of letter is composed co-
operatively in the class. It is altered at the end of three weeks when
a unit is completed. Incidental to the experience in courtesy to a
visitor, is understanding the objectives of the units well enough
to summarize briefly the scope of each one in the term.

Two examples are attached. The January letter shows how the letter sums up a term's work; the February letter illustrates how a letter projects a term which is just beginning.

Forest Park High School
Baltimore, Maryland
January, 1939

Dear Visitor:

Welcome to Forest Park High School and especially to our English class. Realizing that you are not as yet acquainted with our work, we are listing for you the six units which we plan to complete in the first term of the eleventh grade.

Unit 25— Responding to Challenging Ideas
Unit 26— Changing Styles of Heroes and Heroines
Unit 27— With the Men and Women Who Do Things
Unit 125— Producing a Newspaper
Unit 126— Enjoying Photoplays
Unit 127— Increasing Mastery of English Usage

We have completed Unit 25, during which we surveyed periodicals for challenging ideas, read essays for fun and information, and became acquainted with writers who have an appealing personality.

In Unit 125 we learned how to write all kinds of articles, to work in committees, and to produce a class paper.

In Unit 26 we discovered what characteristics of the heroes and heroines of the days of King Arthur still function in our modern world.

During Unit 27 we developed a formula for success through reading about "Men and Women Who Do Things."

At the present time we are engaged in Unit 126. In this unit we plan to learn about photoplays in order to select better movies and to enjoy more those we see.

Along with these units we are carrying on such individual drill in the fundamentals as reading and language tests show we need.

Will you kindly write your name and address on the enclosed slip? We like to remember our guests by name. We hope that you will enjoy your visit and come again very soon.

Sincerely yours,

BARBARA DEMAREST
Hostess, 1302
HERMAN ALLEN KERNGOOD
Host, 1302

Forest Park High School
Baltimore, Maryland
February, 1939

Dear Visitor:

It is a pleasure to welcome you to Forest Park. We are glad to have you in our English period.

In order to give you a background for what you see today, we are listing the six units in 10A English.

Unit 22: Understanding an Eccentric Person
Unit 23: Romance
Unit 24: Are they the same at home?
Unit 122: Making the Expression of Ideas Clear
Unit 123: Painting with Words
Unit 124: Discussing Interesting People

We are now engaged in Units 24 and 124. While we are reading biographical sketches of famous men and women, we are on the lookout for why they are remembered, what they accomplished, what personality traits contributed to their public success and to their being a companionable person in their homes, what difficulties they encountered, and what personality pitfalls in their career they escaped or fell into.

Through our reading we plan to become acquainted with some people worth knowing. Having seen how professionals write biography, we expect to try our pen at depicting the life of a person in whom we are especially interested.

We are also following up with individual drill the results of diagnostic language and reading tests which we were given on September 15 and 16, 1938, and January 3, 1939.

Will you please write your name and address on the enclosed slip so that we may add it to our file of guests.

We hope that you will enjoy your visit and will come again whenever you can.

Sincerely yours,
Frances Bartlett
Hostess, 1252
Marjorie Franklin
Hostess, 1252

XV

SHARING EXPERIENCES IN AN INTEGRATED PROGRAM

INTEGRATION that capitalizes a genuine pupil interest, which touches the whole world, is excellently illustrated by the unit reported by Miss Noyes of California. Rich evidence in pupil and teacher approval, quantitative data concerning the number and kinds of books read, the quality of the pupils' speaking and writing and their test-measured growth in reading skills—all this evidence points to the values of the course.

To give the flavor of the unit an excerpt from Miss Noyes' narrative precedes her outline of the activities engaged in by the pupils.

BUILDERS TOGETHER [1]

A Tenth-Year Adventure in World Friendship

"To build understanding of and sympathy with the various peoples who have contributed to the cultural growth of America; to learn what those contributions have been and to understand the backgrounds that enabled these peoples to contribute; to be able to believe in and to work for the ideal; to build by the aid of all these elements a 'Creative Americanism' that shall be satisfied with nothing but the best for every American, whether he be American by birth or by choice."

With this goal 100 sophomores in Santa Barbara High School started gaily on their year's adventure last September. They were not a picked crew; they represented, therefore, a good trying-out field for the new course. They were under the guidance of three teachers, all volunteer.

In all the planning for this course (done at Stanford during the summer under the guidance of Holland D. Roberts) two ideas were kept in mind: first, that world friendship is highly desirable; sec-

---

[1] Reported by E. Louise Noyes, Santa Barbara High School, Santa Barbara, Cal., from whom bibliographies and other data are available.

ond, that youth can "serve its world" in doing something about such friendship. Two groups in the high school were kept particularly in mind through all the planning, those who have always had life made easy for them and who therefore take for granted that life is such for all people and those who come from the groups thought of as immigrants to this country. Each group had much to give and also much to learn.

Santa Barbara may perhaps be particularly fortunate in the variety and type of her foreign-born citizens, but it seems that almost any community could find a large amount of material at hand for such activities. Every one was friendly and interested in the work the youngsters were doing. In itself this brought grown-ups back to school with a growing interest and belief in world friendship and appreciation of what other cultures contribute to American life. During the study of Italy, classes visited a city park which was the former home of Dr. Franceschi Fenzi, the great Italian botanist, a man of world-wide reputation. They visited also one of the city parks in which almost every tree is a rare specimen brought here by this same Dr. Fenzi. Individuals visited two of the large city fish markets, both run by Italians of long residence in the city. They learned there of the fishing industry of the city. They learned that it was largely manned by this same group. A Montecite estate which is a perfect replica of an Italian garden was visited. Since one world famous Italian sculptor is a resident of the city, this lent point to the discussion of that branch of art.

The study of the Scandinavian countries found a number of residents ready to help the students. A physician was very willing to talk of his boyhood days in Norway; another man was willing to share with them very beautiful snap-shots taken on a trip back home just the year before. Many people brought books and pictures sent from the old country. Luncheon at the Viking restaurant, whose proprietor was most generous, proved a high spot in the experience of one group. A Swedish Christmas party was a culminating activity for another.

Finally came the question, "What kind of a community do we wish Santa Barbara to be?" And after that, "What kind of state, nation, world do we wish for the future?" How have foreign-born groups helped to build American culture, and how may they help in the future?

One large part of the year's work has not yet been mentioned, even though it has been started first and then carried on through the entire year. The first six weeks spent in definite work on the improvement of reading skills. This work was begun, but all the teachers concerned in the experiment wish the next term to begin the work of the course first. This plan will permit the students to begin reading along their own special lines of interest and to use much of their reading as testing material for each individual.

Suggested Activities

I. *What Is Our Community?*

Trace your own background through both great-grandparents, if possible, at least through grandparents.

Bring an anecdote of your background to share with us all.

Find some one way in which your parents or grandparents had a share in building the community in which they lived. Tell us about it.

See how students are helping to build this school, this community.

What plans, if any, have you for your share in building the community in which you hope to live?

Find out, through a census, what the racial make-up of the present 10B class is.

Plan the questions for this census and discuss your plans with other members of this same group.

Plan, as a class, for the same type of census of the whole school.

Tabulate the material obtained. Work for accuracy.

What work are people doing in Santa Barbara to build a better city? List the people who are best known for such work. Are they the only ones who are thus working? Who are some of the unnamed ones who are contributing a full share?

Through what agencies are these people doing their civic work?

Plan interviews with some of the people in each of these groups. Let various church groups, that is, plan a collective interview; possibly carry it out collectively. This same type of thing can be planned for the school community.

Make a map or a graph, or both, of our community for racial elements and for contributing elements, churches, schools, etc.

II. *What Is the Background of Our Peoples and Relationship to Us?*

The what and why of an immigrant. Distinction between immigrant and emigrant.

Find out why your ancestors left their homeland. Find out why they chose to come to America rather than to some other country. Discuss the meaning of "The Land of Promise" and of "America, the Melting Pot."

Find out what agencies and situations in New York helped them to think of this country as the land of their dreams and what things, if any, disillusioned them. (Edmund Steiner is good here; also rather specially "They Who Bring Dreams" and Schauffler, "Scum of the Earth.")

How and when did your ancestors make their way to California? Did the journey add to their dreams or take from them?

Plan an exhibit of things brought from the homeland. (Culminating activity) Discuss how the home in the Old World influenced the one in the New: furnishings, habits, attitudes, etc.

There are said to be five main ways in which immigrants have contributed to American culture: Manual work (see Panunzio specially), old customs, the fine arts, science and invention, and journalism. Can you think of other ways in which immigrants have contributed to our culture?

Newcomers have perhaps a harder time, with more obstacles to overcome, in getting an opportunity to help build than do oldtimers (natives). Discuss some of these obstacles. Find out how people you actually know or know of have overcome them. Fnd out what has helped.

Try to construct a whole community built just of immigrants. What nationality would you choose as the best for each piece of constructive work? Build a composite citizen. Build a composite town. (This is a good culmination for the whole work.)

Study the musicians, painters, sculptors, actors, producers, writers, etc., of our town, then of the nation, who are foreign-born. Try to see what their contributions have been to our culture. A modern problem is those who come over as "guest artists" only. Investigate a bit on this. Find out whether we are now sending American-born artists of all sorts back to other countries as "guest artists." Try to contrast the results, both on the countries and the artists.

Make a similar study of scientists and inventors.

Make such a study of newspaper men, of whom there has been a surprising number (Bok, Bennett, Schurz, McClure, Pulitzer).

Read biographies of immigrants to our country. There are many of them. Read from two angles: for the type of work that the person did after he came to America, and for the type of struggle that the person had in adjusting himself to America.

Make a list of such books, with comment appended of your opinion on each.

Write a story of yourself as an immigrant to one of these countries; make it accurate by finding how such countries receive immigrants; try to see yourself in this situation as the immigrants you have been reading about were in our own country.

Make a bibliography of books about immigrants by talking to friends and neighbors who are of foreign descent. Try for both biographies and novels. Try for both individual and collective biography, for both individual and collective experience. Such novels, for instance, as Bojer's, *The Emigrants;* Cather's *My Antonia;* Rölvaag's *Giants in the Earth* and *Peder Victorious* give collective experience. Books are legion on these topics; you will enjoy asking people what ones they have read and liked in addition to going to the card catalogue for your facts. Some of you may be able to read a book in some language other than English that bears on this same problem.

Many of our holidays and our manner of celebrating them have much that has come from the old countries. Choose some one or two, such as Christmas or Easter or Thanksgiving and show some part of our celebration that has come from one of the older nations.

We take many conveniences in our homes for granted today. Find out for which of these we must thank some nation other than ourselves. Compare and contrast modern ways of housework with those of earlier days and with those of the countries from which your ancestors came.

Many people today are keenly alive to the beauty (or lack of it) in our natural surroundings and in the conservation of our natural resources. How have foreign-born helped in this? Are we ahead of or behind other nations in our attitude toward such things?

Write a story of a typical day in the old country home and then one of such a day in the new country for some family.

Plan, if possible, a festival day in the country of your greatest interest. Perhaps you will be able to exhibit a real costume from your country or at least to draw a typical one.

Compare and contrast our treatment of the aged poor with the treatment accorded the same groups in some other country.

Compare and contrast the local governments of two towns or cities.

Plan a picnic in ———— and in Santa Barbara. Perhaps you can prevail on some of the cookery classes to help you supply a little of the actual food for us, enough for samples.

Go to church in the two countries, in ———— and in Santa Barbara, and tell what was different. Go to a Christmas service particularly.

Go to school for a day in the two countries.

Go to a Boy or Girl Scouts meeting. Compare and contrast. Perhaps some of you have actually belonged to such groups somewhere else or have been to a Scout Jamboree.

Go to a wedding celebration in ———— and in Santa Barbara, with all the old ceremonies carried out as they were in the old country.

Illustrations of all the above, either crayon drawings on the board or bulletin board ones large enough to be seen from a distance, or large tempera paintings will be always helpful and welcome.

III. *What Kind of Community Do We Wish Ours to Be?*

Men have always striven for an ideal community. Find out about some of them. Perhaps some of your ancestors helped at Brook Farm or at the Oneida Community in our country. Some of you will like to look up something about one of the earliest stories of an ideal community. It is written by a man name More and is called *Utopia*. Modern writers also have played with the same idea. See what you can find about such communities.

One basic idea is at the back of all such ideas. Can you guess what that idea is? Must it be at the back of any plan for a planned Santa Barbara? Find out whether we have already taken any steps in that direction.

Many agencies are at work to make Santa Barbara the kind of city we wish it to be. Do all of them agree as to what is best?

Foreign-born groups have already made many contributions to the growth of Santa Barbara. Find out about all of these. Are they all working in the social field? In the religious? In the civic? List and evaluate as many such contributions as you can.

If any groups are working today, find out about them also. Do you know what the Tokalon Club is? Do you know the work that the Sons of Herman are doing? These are only examples. Find others, just as many as possible. Are all these groups working alone, or is there any unifying agency?

What is a community survey. Is one desirable here on this problem? Can we as a tenth-year group do it? If so, how? Can we help actually to make Santa Barbara a better place in which to live?

Reading and expression skills are integrating forces in the unit program developed by Helen Ackermann in Davenport, Iowa. Diagnostic tests disclose in which skills the pupils need corrective teaching. The literature units feed out into social studies, science, and the fine arts.

In Hudson, Wisconsin, Evelyn Jerdee has used reading as a core for unifying the pupils in school and out-of-school activities. One of the testimonial cases which Miss Jerdee describes is quoted as illustration of her evidence that her plan worked.

READING AS A UNIFYING EXPERIENCE

One instance might be given of a boy in our school two or three years ago who seemed to care for nothing except football. It was a problem to get him to read even his daily assignments and we began to feel that he never would learn to read anything without constant urging. One day when the English III class was beginning a novel unit, I suggested as a sort of final resort that this boy read *Giants in the Earth* by Rölvaag, and I gave him a copy to look at while I tried to tell him a few interesting things about the people in the book. I hoped that the portrayal of the real life of the pioneers in our section of the country would appeal to him. I knew also that his background was Scandinavian and that he enjoyed reading stories that pictured true-to-life characters and background. From the very first chapter, this boy read the book with enthusiasm. From time to time I asked him a thought question based on the reading in order to bring out some points that he might otherwise have missed, and he responded enthusiastically. He went through the book rapidly, only to ask when he had finished it, "Say, did this man Rölvaag ever write any other books?" Well, he went on to read several books of Rölvaag's and then to other pioneer stories; needless to say, my reading problem with this boy was solved. Again and again he would ask, "Have you a good book for me to read?" He still considers the reading of *Giants in the Earth* a milestone in his literary progress, and he often tells other boys about it. Some other book might have been even a better choice, but in this case the book recommended worked out very satisfactorily.

In a unit [2] tracing the influence of the monastery on civilization in the Middle Ages, Elizabeth M. Lincoln's sixth-grade pupils made use of photoplays, pictures, history texts, fiction, poetry, and excursions to libraries and museums. The profusely illustrated booklet of original stories and poems gave evidence that the children had experienced literature.

Growing out of visits of the school nurse and her examinations of a group of fifth-grade pupils, Angie Weibling developed an interesting unit, "Pioneers in Health." Her purpose to help pupils understand and practise simple rules of health led to wide reading and vital discussion. The accompanying outline indicates how well she achieved her purpose.

PIONEERS IN HEALTH [3]

I. *Materials*

    A. Reference books, pamphlets, posters, pictures in school and in public libraries

    B. Visits by committees to City Hospital, Red Cross Headquarters, City Health Department

    C. Talks by school nurse and Red Cross Nurse

II. *Activities*

    A. Talks by school nurse

    B. Questions from pupils

    C. Reading in reference materials to answer questions

    D. Looking up words in dictionary

    E. Writing letters

       1. Requests for materials

[2] For details write to Elizabeth M. Lincoln, 226 Union St., Leominster, Mass.
[3] Reported by Angie Weibling, Sam Houston School, San Antonio, Tex.

  2. Invitations to speakers
  3. Thanks
 F. Constructing scenery, costumes, stretchers, medicine cabinet used in playlets and later for practical purposes in the school
 G. Dramatization of four incidents significant in developing better health conditions in the world
 H. Making scrap-books for children in city hospitals

III. *Outcomes*

 A. Stimulating a desire for good health and clean living
 B. A knowledge of the contributions of science to health
 C. Appreciation of the work that is being done in this and other countries to promote better health
 D. Coöperation of social welfare agencies and school
 E. Value to the entire school
  1. Assistance of two student nurses from the upper grades to the regular school nurse
  2. Value of coöperation in making Christmas gifts
 F. Value to the community—These children have gone home and passed on helpful suggestions. Parents have responded very graciously. Some have expressed interest in an adult training class in home nursing.

IV. *Articulation with Other School Activities*

 A. Language arts
  1. Oral expression
  2. Dramatization
  3. Letters for material, note of thanks, etc.
  4. Literature—stories of people important in health promotion, poems such as Longfellow's "Lady of the Lamp."
 B. Mathematics—measuring in construction work, problems related to the activity
 C. Science—knowledge of what countries have contributed
 D. Physical education and health—importance of exercise and following health rules
 E. Fine arts—music related to unit, poster-making and modeling clay maps
 F. Industrial education and home-making—construction and use of simple, helpful materials, selection of first aid materials to be kept in medicine cabinet
 G. Social studies—citizenship, history, geographical information involved

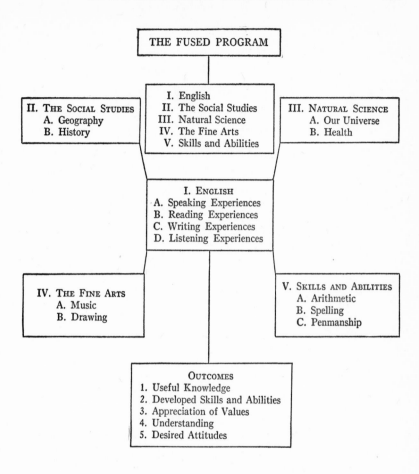

A suggested guide for the daily program.

APPROVED: MAUDE L. KNOWLTON
F. R. SHINGLE   Supervisor of Intermediate Grades
                                 Public Schools of Syracuse, 1937

To show how one school interprets in the classroom the general plan of integration illustrated in the chart on pages 252–253 the report on pages 254–255 is presented.

ENGLISH AS AN INTEGRATING EXPERIENCE

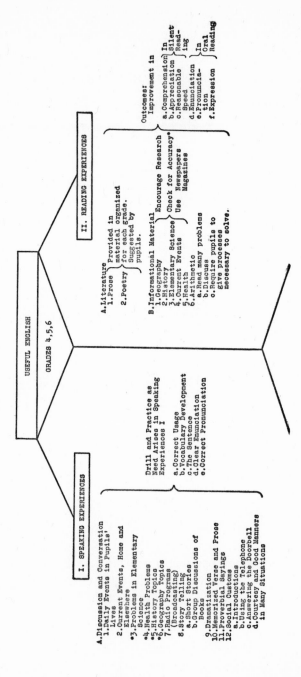

USEFUL ENGLISH

GRADES 4,5,6

I. SPEAKING EXPERIENCES

A. Discussion and Conversation
1. Daily Events in Pupils'
   Lives
2. Current Events, Home and
   Elsewhere
*3. Problems in Elementary
    Science
*4. Health Problems
*5. History Topics
*6. Geography Topics
7. Radio Programs
   (Broadcasting)
8. Story Telling
   a. Short Stories
   b. Group Discussions of
      Books
9. Dramatization
10. Memorized Verse and Prose
11. Proverbial Sayings
12. Social Customs
    a. Introductions
    b. Using the Telephone
    c. Answering the Doorbell
    d. Courtesy and Good Manners
       in Many Situations

Drill and Practice as
Need Arises in Speaking
Experiences I

a. Correct Usage
b. Vocabulary Development
c. The Sentence
d. Clear Enunciation
e. Correct Pronunciation

II. READING EXPERIENCES

A. Literature
1. Prose } Provided in
2. Poetry } material organized
           for each grade.
           Suggested by
           pupils.

B. Informational Material Encourage Research
1. Geography
2. History
3. Elementary Science Check for Accuracy
4. Current Events Use Newspapers
5. Health   Magazines
6. Arithmetic
   a. Read many problems
   b. Discuss
   c. Require pupils to
      give processes
      necessary to solve.

Outcomes:
Improvement in

a. Comprehension } In
b. Appreciation } Silent
c. Reasonable } Read-
   Speed } ing
d. Enunciation
e. Pronuncia- } In
   tion } Oral
f. Expression } Reading

252

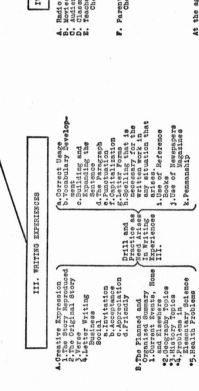

III. WRITING EXPERIENCES

A. Creative Expression
  1. The Story Reproduced
  2. The Original Story
  3. Verse
  4. Letter Writing
    Business
    Social
      a. Invitation
      b. Acceptance
      c. Appreciation
      d. Friendly

B. The Planned and Organized Summary
  1. Current Events, Home and Elsewhere
  *2. Geography Topics
  *3. History Topics
  *4. Problems in Elementary Science
  *5. Health Problems

Drill and Practice as Need Arises In Writing Experiences III.

a. Correct Usage
b. Vocabulary Development
c. Building and Expanding the Sentence
d. The Paragraph
e. Punctuation
f. Capitalization
g. Letter Forms
h. Spelling that is necessary for the written work in any situation that arises.
i. Use of Reference Books
j. Use of Newspapers
   Magazines
k. Penmanship

* In schools where the departmental plan is followed, the teacher of each subject is responsible for the accuracy, the research activity, and the sequential arrangement of all subject material, that is starred under the major experiences, I, II, III. The English teachers' task is to improve English—oral and written.

IV. LISTENING EXPERIENCES, SELECTIVE, PURPOSEFUL

A. Radio Programs—Check by oral resume
B. Movies " " " " "
C. Audience Reading—Check by class discussion
D. Classmates' Reports "
E. Teacher—Guidance
    Check by — a. Attention of pupils
          b. Interest " "
          c. Effort " "
          d. Growth " "

F. Parent—Guidance
    Check by — a. Getting acquainted with parents
          b. Discussing with parents the work-play attitude of their children
          c. Seeking to understand the parent—child relationship.

At the age levels of pupils in the middle grades, Reading is the medium by which the child's interests may be best observed and his growth accurately tested. Therefore Reading is the very core or major interest-center of the English curriculum.

The activity may precede a unit or a problem, or it may grow out of either.

Maude L. Knowlton
Supervisor of Intermediate Grades
Syracuse Public Schools — 1937

Chart Showing English in Relation to the Entire Curricular Experiences of Pupils in Grades 4, 5, 6, Syracuse, N. Y.

A STUDY OF LIFE IN THE EARLY AMERICAN COLONIES THROUGH
BOOKS, STORIES AND POEMS WRITTEN ABOUT THIS PERIOD [4]

I. *Objectives*

A. To develop through a directed reading program a realization
that around the truth of history a wealth of fiction has been
written

B. To discover the types of people who played an important
part in the development of our country

C. To know that former environment and geographical location
determined types of homes and mode of living in various
Colonies

D. To recognize the fact that faith, courage, perseverence, fore-
sight and hard work are essential to the successful completion of any worth-while venture

E. To appreciate a standard of living which made it possible
for adults and children of this period to have happy times
though they had none of our modern ways of amusement nor
mechanical conveniences

II. *Activities*

A. The teacher for several days before launching the unit, read
without comment, short portions from different stories descriptive of life in the early days, such as, an account of a
spelling bee, a description of a Colonial kitchen, a few lines
from "The Courtship of Miles Standish" which tell of the
building of John Alden's home for Priscilla, etc.

B. The teacher displayed on the reading table eight new books
from a local book store and others loaned by the public library.

C. Pupils wrote letters.

1. A letter to the Paramount Studios asking for posters from
A Maid of Salem which some of the children had seen and
thought the others would enjoy

2. Letters such as might have been written by business men
of the Colonies ordering supplies from London

3. An exchange of friendly letters between children who
might have lived in the South with those of the North
(An understanding of the home, school and church experiences was noticeable in these letters.)

[4] Reported by Winifred E. Brownell, Principal, Thomas W. Meachem School,
Syracuse, N. Y., from whom an interesting bibliography may be obtained.

4. An invitation to a New England party written to mothers of the class and children of the 6–1 grade

D. Some pupils wrote verses about Colonial life.

E. Pupils gave impersonations of interesting characters found in their reading.

F. Pupils discussed the old word forms found in the stories.

G. A New England party was held. Mothers of the class and children of the 6–1 grade attended.

H. A host and hostess were chosen by the class who welcomed and introduced guests, and with their "children" carried the party to a happy conclusion. Refreshments consisting of maple sugar, popcorn, and apples were served.

I. A trip was taken to the replica of a frontier fort located near our city.

J. The children brought in dolls dressed in Colonial costume— little canopied beds—a real powder horn—pewter dishes— etc.

K. Some individuals drew pictures and made miniature representations of objects used in Colonial days.

III. *Outcomes*

A. English skills and abilities were improved through written and oral compositions about topics of vital interest to the pupils.

B. Children have inquired what they are to study next and some have read stories about happenings in the Revolutionary period.

C. Four of the new books have been chosen by the class to be purchased and added to the room library.

D. Children realize that both fact and fiction play an important part in the enjoyable understanding of the long ago.

An Integrative Experience through Puppetry [5]

How the unit developed. A puppet show given time after time for two days by a group of pupils from the Joseph E. Brown Junior High School in Atlanta was the culminating activity in a project which integrated the work of art classes, creative writing, oral English, home economics, industrial arts, and photography.

The project originated in the art classes when a group of pupils,

[5] Reported by Cornelia M. Neal, Joseph E. Brown Junior High School, Atlanta, Ga.

inspired by the presentation of a Puppet Club show, wanted to make more and bigger and better puppets.

The pupils soon found that the number, size, costumes, and characteristics of their puppets would naturally be determined by the selection of a play for production. Finding difficulty in making this selection, the pupils sought the advice of the creative writing class. After a few days this group submitted "The Night of the Colored Lanterns," a Chinese story by Frances Jenkins Olcott. This they felt was a colorful story, suitable for dramatization, with opportunity for marked differentiation of characters as well as artistic costumes and stage settings.

The story was accepted and the creative writing group put it into dramatic form while the art classes made sketches for characters, designed costumes and backdrops, drew plans for the stage and stage settings and determined the scale for furniture. With these details completed, the boys in the wood shop were called upon to construct the stage, the electric shop to wire it, the girls in the home economics classes were invited to make costumes, while the students in the art classes made the puppets, furniture, and stage settings.

Manipulating the puppets and learning dialogue came next, and the boys and girls spent many happy hours rehearsing speaking parts and pulling strings, being in turn manipulators, stage directors, or audience.

One day the complaint came from the audience that the words behind the curtains were muffled; the old man did not speak like an old man; the pantomime did not coördinate with the spoken word. What to do! Straightway the class took its problems to a teacher of oral English. They needed oral English! With such motivation, the work of the next few weeks had to be successful. The class plunged headlong into a study of pronunciation, enunciation, voice placement, resonance, pitch, modulation, and character portrayal by synchronization of voice and gesture.

Practices began to improve; audiences ceased to complain; characters and understudies were finally determined. More practices, more polish, more manipulating, more lights, more tacks, and the "Wooden Headed Theater" was ready for its "first night" which came at 9:30 one Friday morning in the exhibition room of the Georgia Education Association Convention in Atlanta. In the next two days a series of performances were given by the several casts who enjoyed their hidden parts quite as much as did their appreciative audience of teachers.

After this successful "run" the theater moved back to the school where the casts were called upon to repeat their performances again and again.

What the unit accomplished. To evaluate a project of this kind is quite difficult for besides the knowledges and skills acquired in the art, home economics, industrial arts and English classes, there are other learnings not so apparent but often of deeper significance to the child.

Before this project was completed, the boys and girls experienced many difficulties which they overcame or found a way around. The art of working together and the feeling that each had an integral part in the completed whole was another lesson learned. The consciousness of a pleasing voice and of good posture revealed itself as the actors unconsciously lost themselves in character portrayal, and poise before an audience grew after each performance. Pupils not only learned to do simple research work but delved into the study of the people, their costumes and their customs.

To see how carefully the pupils watched the setting up of each part of the stage, how gently they arranged a bit of stage furniture, how tenderly they handled each puppet doll made one realize just what the project meant to each boy and girl and made one understand why the demand for more puppets next year is so strong.

How the puppets were made. The wooden head string puppets designed and executed by the elective art pupils were from eighteen to twenty-four inches in height.

The bodies were cut out of white pine scrap pieces, varying from three-fourths of an inch to two inches in thickness. The legs and arms with one exception, were cut from dowel sticks. Ting Ling, the father in the play was the most complicated puppet of all as his body section was carved from soft pine, the hands, arms and legs fitting tightly into sockets.

The heads were formed of plastic wood as were some of the hands. The former took a good portion of the allotted time as they were first modeled from plastic clay from which sectional molds were made out of plaster of paris. Next, one layer of paper towels torn in long strips and soaked in water were carefully molded over each of the mold sections. Before the paper dried out, plastic wood was carefully pressed into the mold about one-half inch thick. After the plastic wood had set the two head pieces were put together with additional plastic wood and following complete drying were ready for sanding and painting.

PART THREE

Solving Teaching-Supervisory Problems

SOLVING TEACHING-SUPERVISORY PROBLEMS

AFTER ABSORBING the point of view of English as experience, after building literature units around themes, and after selecting communication centers for language-composition units, teachers and supervisors then need to decide: How shall the units be graded? Articulated? How shall growth be appraised? What corrective teaching will be needed? What instructional equipment will be required to put into effect the experience-centered course developed locally? That these problems can be solved locally is evident in the concrete accounts which follow.

The solution of specific problems of concern to teachers and to supervisors can be located by consulting the index, page 379 and following.

XVI

DETERMINING GRADE PLACEMENT OF UNITS AND PROVIDING FOR ARTICULATION

THAT THE SOLUTION of grade placement of units must be evolved locally was the wise conclusion reached by the Experience Curriculum Commission.[1] This Commission reported and illustrated principles which can be applied anywhere. It recognized that deliberations of local committees have a strong educative and unifying influence upon the school. Throughout this earlier report, therefore, the Commission reiterated that it was offering a *pattern* curriculum, a pattern not itself to be worn but merely to serve, as "an instrument to assist in the cutting—often with allowances for the individual peculiarities of the wearer" [2]—of the local English curriculum.

To assist others in making such local adaptations as the Commission anticipated, an outline is presented of the procedures used in a city, a county, and a state system in adapting locally the pattern curriculum.

EMPIRICAL EVIDENCE IN CLASSROOM

In Baltimore City, Baltimore County, and New York State the local programs were developed coöperatively by teachers and supervisors. Teachers were invited by questionnaire to indicate the phase or phases of English in which they were most interested, the problems they wished to investigate, and the type of experimentally developed materials they were willing to test out in their classrooms. Directed readings and discussion at departmental, city-wide, county-wide, and state-wide conferences along with mimeographed bulletins summarizing significant relevant research

[1] See W. W. Hatfield, and others, *An Experience Curriculum in English* (New York, D. Appleton-Century Co., 1935), p. v.
[2] *Ibid.*, p. v.

findings orientated the teachers to the problems involved in developing a local course built on the experience philosophy.[3]

Having absorbed the point of view of the experience curriculum, the supervisors and teachers in city, county, and state departments studied the "experience strands" into which each major phase of the course is divided and the units—"the beads or links of which the strands are composed"—centering upon specific types of experience. The adjustment of the pattern curriculum to each of the local situations involved the following activities: (a) building literature units around themes; (b) selecting communication centers for language-composition units; (c) determining grade placement of the units in each strand; and (d) providing for maintenance of skills.

As in the case of the basic philosophy underlying the experience curriculum, the point of view as to why, what, and how in experiencing literature in each of the local courses is consistent with the National Council's report. The specific names of the literature units and the specific titles listed under each unit show adjustment of the pattern to the local personnel and equipment. An outline of the Baltimore City course follows as an illustration.

An Interpretation of the Intensive and Extensive Treatment of the Required and Related Readings in the English Course, Baltimore [4]

In every unit there are *required* and *related* readings. *A pupil who has special reading difficulties and for whom a remedial program is provided need not actually read all of a required book. He will become acquainted with the selection through his reading of the easiest and most interesting parts and through his participation in the class*

[3] Cf. *Course of Study in English,* Grades 7–12, Baltimore, Maryland, 1932, pp. 7–13; 224–236.

English Units of Work and Standards of Attainments, Department of Education, 1934.

Course of Study in English, Board of Education of Baltimore County (Baltimore, Warwick & York, 1934).

New York State Syllabus in English (Albany, New York, 1934).

Marquis E. Shattuck, and others, *The Development of a Modern Program in English, Ninth Yearbook* of The Department of Supervisors and Directors of Instruction of the National Association (Washington, D. C., 1936), Chs. V. and VI.

[4] Cf. *English Units of Work and Standards of Attainment,* Grades 7–12, Baltimore, Md., 1934.

discussion of the more difficult passages. The "related readings" provide a range of books to cover all levels of reading abilities and interests. The teacher, as shown in the mimeographed assignment sheets sent to the schools, helps each pupil to select an appropriate book. The slow readers read only an easy book, the more skilful readers read the more difficult books. Pupil reactions to their related reading are incorporated in the class discussion of the required reading. A pupil also supplements these suggested readings from his own free reading which often takes direction from the stimulating theme of the literature unit.

In each term some *required* reading is handled *intensively;* other, *extensively.* This has been done to give pupils experience in reading

METHOD OF TREATING REQUIRED READINGS IDENTIFIED BY LITERARY TYPES

(Every unit suggests also extensive individual reading on the unit theme.)

Unit Theme	Intensive Method	Extensive Method
	7B	
1. Adventures on the High Seas	novel of adventure	
2. Answers to Thousands of Why's		myths and legends
3. Faithful Friends		novels of adventure
	7A	
4. Everyday Magic	lyric poetry	
5. Ideals of Work		stories and poems about work
6. Thinking of Others in Relation to One's Self		stories and poems of service
	8B	
7. Love and Friendship	long narrative poem	
8. Some People Worth Knowing	autobiography	
9. Ideals of Home Life		poetry and prose of home life
	8A	
10. What About a Dog?		novel of adventure
11. In the Days of Good Queen Bess	five-act comedy	
12. Arm-Chair Traveling		literature of travel
	9B	
13. Enjoying a Good Story		short stories
14. Wanting to Be Somebody Else		novel of adventure
15. Political Intrigue	Shakespearean tragedy	

Unit Theme	Intensive Method	Extensive Method
	9A	
16. The Lure of the Middle Ages	historical novel	
17. Vagabonding through Poetry		narrative poems
18. Wonders of Science		literature of science
	10B	
19. Story-Telling Ballads	ballad poetry	
20. A Sea-Faring Vagabond		sea poetry and prose
21. Adventures in the World of Science	literature of science	
	10A	
22. Understanding an Eccentric Person	novel of character	
23. Romance	Shakespearean comedy	
24. Are They the Same at Home?		biographical sketches
	11B	
25. Responding to Challenging Ideas	Essays—formal and informal	
26. Changing Styles of Heroes and Heroines	poems of chivalry	
27. With the Men and Women Who Do Things		essays and biographies of achievement
	11A	
28. What Poets Write About		lyric poetry
29. Misdirected Ambition	Shakespearean tragedy	
30. American Life in Literature		regional literature
	12B	
31. Groups in Conflict		historical novel
32. Creating Public Opinion	argumentative speeches	
33. Poems of Courage and Glorious Adventure	lyric poetry	
	12A	
34. Looking Into the Past	historical novel	
35. World Friendships		stories and essays from world literature
36. Best Sellers of the Ages		survey of the best-sellers of the ages

for recreation as well as for study. The intensive method is characterized as the detailed study of a piece of literature with respect to its thought and its literary style. The *extensive* method is characterized as *rapid reading* of a comparatively large amount of literature with general questions and class discussions of a conversational nature. In connection with the units which are treated extensively, more library reading is possible than with those units treated intensively.

Training in reading and library skills is provided in each grade.

A Phase of Integration: Showing How Time in Composition Units Is Saved by Utilizing Background of Ideas Gained from Literature Units [5]

Always after a unit of technical English frequent opportunities occur to apply what has been learned. All literature units provide oral and written English activities, but the literature units in parenthesis are not used as content background for entire composition units.

The unifying activities for the language-composition units are consistent with the functional centers discussed in the experience curriculum. Grammar is made instrumental in improving the correctness and effectiveness of oral and written communication. The themes used to unify the readings in the literature units are suggested by the intrinsic experience in the selections read in the unit.

Language-Composition Units	*Literature Units*
Seventh Grade	
Writing Letters That Will Be Answered	Unit 1—Adventures on the High Seas
Story-Telling	
Developing a Sentence Sense	
Learning the Magic of Words	
Conducting a Club	Unit 4—Everyday Magic
Using the Verb Effectively	

(Other Literature Units: 2—Answers to Thousands of Why's; 3—Faithful Friends; 5—Ideals of Work; 6—Thinking of Others in Relation to One's Self)

Eighth Grade	
Preparing an Assembly	
Writing Effective Sentences	
Getting Acquainted with People	Unit 8—Some People Worth Knowing

[5] Cf. *English Units of Work and Standards of Attainment*, Grades 7–12, Baltimore Md., 1934.

Gaining Control of Nouns and
   Pronouns
Story-Telling   Unit 10—What About a Dog?
Producing a Play
(Other Literature Units: 7—Love and Friendship; 9—Ideals of Home Life;
   11—In the Days of Good Queen Bess; 12—Arm-Chair Traveling)

Ninth Grade

Story-Telling   Unit 14—Wanting to Be Somebody Else
Using Phrases and Clauses
Conducting a Club   Unit 18—Wonders of Science
Building Word Pictures   Unit 17—Vagabonding through Poetry
Understanding the Verb and Its
   Functions
Reviewing and Reporting   Unit 16—The Lure of the Past
(Other Literature Units: 13—Enjoying a good story; 15—Political Intrigue)

Tenth Grade

Story-Telling   Unit 20—A Sea-Faring Vagabond
Gaining Sentence Variety
Preparing an Assembly
Making the Expression of Ideas
   Clear
Painting with Words   Unit 23—Romance
Discussing Interesting People   Unit 24—Are They the Same at Home?
(Other Literature Units: 19—Story-Telling Ballads; 21—Adventures in the
   World of Science; 22—Understanding an Eccentric Person)

Eleventh Grade

Producing a Newspaper   Unit 25—Responding to Challenging Ideas
Increasing Mastery of Current
   Usage
Enjoying Photoplays   Unit 26—Changing Styles of Heroes and
                              Heroines
(Other Literature Units: 27—With the Men and Women Who Do Things; 28
   —What Poets Write about; 29—Misdirected Ambition)

Twelfth Grade

Winning an Audience   Unit 32—Creating Puplic Opinion
Improving Control of Current
   Usage
Preparing an Assembly
Interpreting Experience through
   Conversation and Letters   Unit 35—World Friendship
Producing a Play
Interviewing and Reporting
(Other Literature Units: 31—Groups in Conflict; 33—Poems of Courage and
   Glorious Adventure; 34—Looking into the Past; 36—Best Sellers of the
   Ages)

Simultaneously with allocating the units, the teachers in Baltimore [6] investigated the problem of articulation. The procedure used is perhaps more interesting than the results since teachers everywhere can use this method of discovering locally an answer to the query: "How can skills be maintained from grade to grade?"

Every teacher kept careful records of what individual pupils and groups were able to accomplish during a unit. Standardized and teacher-made tests and observational data concerning pupils' emotional and oral responses were studied. Specimens of pupils' writing prepared under known conditions were accumulated and analyzed. From all these, a tentative list of attainments grade by grade was set up. Then through conference of 7B teachers with 6A, 7A with 7B, 8B with 7A, etc. on up to 12A with college and with placement counselors, the grade lists were analyzed for overlapping. Items in the list for a given grade were then starred to show what teachers of that grade should like entering pupils to have mastered and what the promoting teacher reported as attainments of her pupils. For example, 12B teachers reported that they should like entering 12B pupils to know how to get the main point in reading so as to discuss it intelligently with or without questions being asked on the material read. The 11A teachers reported that the pupils they were promoting could meet this requirement with reading content within their maturity and interest levels. Objective test material and titles in the literature units of the 11A course were cited as concrete evidence of attainment of this promotional standard.

The teachers, of course, understood that they were responsible for greater achievement from pupils who entered their class at a higher level than indicated for the grade. They knew, too, that any pupil who was promoted with less than the agreed upon minimum would require extra time and more individualized guidance from the receiving teacher.

Certain of the goals, the teachers realized, continued throughout the grades, but became more advanced skills when applied to more difficult reading materials and more mature language experiences. Teachers, therefore, decided to work toward pupil growth commensurate with all the factors influencing each pupil's learning.

[6] Cf. City of Baltimore, Department of Education, *Course of Study in English,* Grades 7–12, 1932; *Units of Work and Standards of Attainment,* 1934.

Care was taken to set up learning situations which yielded simultaneously these skills and wholesome personality development. Specimens of pupils' work demonstrating each of these skills were mimeographed and sent to all teachers.

In planning the correlation of English and other school subjects, it was understood that the strongest motive for mastering English is its application in getting, articulating, and sharing experiences of intrinsic interest to the learner at his present level of maturity. The program of studies in the junior and senior high schools is full of vital content—experiences of individual and social significance useful in the vocational and avocational education of adolescents. When what is taught in English is applied to the assignment the student has to do anyway in his other subjects, he gets practice in the skill and mastery of the knowledge. The subject teacher is then freed to guide his interpretation of data and to develop the specific skills other than language controls which his subject contributes to the education of the student. When English is attacked in this way it is "human experience," a good thing to be shared, a game of words entrancing because it helps the pupil to see specifically, to articulate accurately and vividly what is perceived and to organize and evaluate knowledge so as to apply it in new situations.

The corrective phase of instruction, another aspect of providing for articulation, depends upon the psychological fact that "every error is a potential source of motivation for learning," but unless the error is brought to the attention of the learner, it will not stimulate him to engage in a learning activity. "If "rambling responses" are accepted outside of the English classroom, the student will not stretch himself to "talk on the subject." If the teacher "helps" him by several supplementary questions, he will not make himself analyze the first question to get the answer by applying the appropriate technique developed in the English classroom or by the subject teacher. Therefore, teachers of other subjects have studied the grade attainments set up in the English course and attempt to hold their pupils responsible for putting into use what the teachers of English have taught. As a return courtesy, the teachers of other subjects call to the attention of teachers of English serious weaknesses of individual pupils and also the opportunities in their subject field for creative writing, for the preparation of source papers, and for socialized discussion.

As a means of gaining the coöperation of all subject teachers and pupils in Baltimore County, standards of appraisal for each type of communication were mimeographed and supplied to both teachers and pupils for evaluation as to their desirability and attainability.

This process of enlisting the intelligent enforcement of standards is as educative as the standards which are quoted here. (See also pp. 273–4 for illustrations of the standards developed in Baltimore County.) It is through cumulative standards of appraisal that effective articulation is provided from unit to unit and from grade to grade.

In determining grade placement in Baltimore City, Baltimore County, and New York State, evidence gained from careful observation of how children learn, of how they enjoy the process of learning, and of how they apply what they have learned was utilized. Such empirical evidence revealed at what maturity (grade) level specific material was teachable without waste of energy on the part of the learner or of the teacher.

TEST RESULTS

Teacher-made and standardized objective tests [7] revealed what the pupils were accomplishing in English and what needed immediate attention from the teachers. Whether or not the instructional material was inappropriate, the learning experience beyond the maturity level of the pupil, or the teaching method ineffective was discovered in test-controlled situations. From all data assembled it was then possible to regrade experiences, materials, and procedures to fit the interests, abilities, and present level of achievement of the boys and girls for whom the experience-centered course was planned.

Tests of any kind (silent reading, outlining, English usage, spelling, literary appreciation, or any other) revealed such a range of differences among pupils of the same chronological age, mental age,

---

[7] City of Baltimore, Department of Education, *Course of Study in English for Grades 7–12* (1932), Chs. II and V.

English Units of Work and Standards of Attainment (1934), Ch. V.

John L. Stenquist, "Fifteen Years of Testing," *Baltimore Bulletin of Education,* March–April, 1938, pp. 1–10.

or grade level that the units to be experienced in any grade required materials and activities varied enough to educate pupils of all sorts.

Though the philosophy and the pattern of the experience curriculum was potent in shaping these local courses, the final sanction for grade placement of the units came from an analysis in test-controlled situations of pupils' actual response to these experience-centered units.

CUMULATIVE RECORDS OF PUPIL GROWTH

The cumulative record of pupils' voluntary and assigned reading, of diagnostic and achievement test results, and of observational data revealing personality adjustments gave incontrovertible evidence as to whether or not from the learner's point of view the English offered was experience.

Throughout the country, moreover, as the word *records* in the index of this volume shows, dynamic teachers have found ways and means of gathering data relevant to these queries about pupils of a given age-grade level: how and why children succeed, what and why particular books appeal to boys and girls, and what and why certain usages prove difficult for pupils.

XVII

APPRAISING PUPIL GROWTH

"MEASUREMENT OF THE GROWTH resulting from the experiences in the curriculum is desirable. . . . Such measures must cover something more than progress in the mechanics of composition and the incidents in and facts about literature; they must measure composition power, social spirit and poise, perception of beauty, and habitual choice of worthy literature. The use of such dynamic, if vague, tests of growth as are included at the bottom of each expanded unit in this pattern curriculum is preferable to entire dependence upon standard tests in mechanics of composition, reading, and literary knowledge." [1]

Of course, the process of developing such "dynamic tests of growth" as are recommended by the Curriculum Commission is in itself an educative process. When teachers come together to study seriously *what* they are grading, *why* they are grading, and *how* they are grading pupils' work, every one present gains from the discussion. Pupils also benefit when teachers ask themselves in conference: "Can a pupil from my class adjust fairly rapidly to the standards of any other teacher in the department? Can a pupil who comes to my class from other teachers in this school adjust fairly rapidly to my standards? Is any greater uniformity desirable? Is any greater variation desirable?"

Translating teacher-determined criteria of pupil growth into standards of pupil self-appraisal is a very important step in the teaching process. The following reports show how teachers have done just this.

PROVISION FOR PUPIL SELF-APPRAISAL

In Madison, Wisconsin, teachers have been working for several years toward the development of personality adjustment along with language ability. One phase of this excellent program was the

---

[1] W. Wilbur Hatfield, and others, *An Experience Curriculum in English* (New York, D. Appleton-Century Co., 1935), pp. 8–9.

formulation by pupils of the following standards for directing their activities when considering how a group of people can help solve a given problem through group discussion.

PUPIL APPRAISAL OF INDIVIDUAL CONTRIBUTION TO GROUP DISCUSSION [2]

1. Talk from brief, well-organized notes.
2. Use large pictures and charts whenever possible to make ideas more concrete.
3. Bring out definite points by personal experiences.
4. Frequently interest your listeners and bring them into the discussion by direct questions.
5. Use descriptive gestures to make words more vivid.
6. Be prepared both to ask questions of others and to answer questions yourself when asked.
7. The leader will tie up all material so that a unified picture of his group's research may be presented.
8. Every one should be happy and enthusiastic, and show the class how eager he is to talk.
9. The group should challenge each speaker by alert attention, encouraging him to express his opinions by polite and fair consideration for each speaker's ideas.
10. Let the audience as a unit find a solution for the whole problem, making definite suggestions based on the mass of information before the group.

In Baltimore County, Maryland, standards of appraisal for each and every type of communication were mimeographed and supplied to both teachers and pupils for evaluation as to their desirability and attainability. The process of enlisting the intelligent achievement of such standards is as educative as the standards which are quoted here. Space permits a sample only of the complete set of standards listed in the Baltimore County Course of Study in English.[3]

STANDARDS OF APPRAISAL FOR SUMMARIES AND REPORTS

Grade 7	Grade 8	Grade 9
ORAL		
1. Did my summary or report include the important ideas and omit the unimportant ones?	Standards for Grade 7 plus: 1. Did my report show that I understood	Standards for Grades 7 and 8 plus: 1. Did I have my subject well in hand so

[2] Reported by Ethel Mabie Falk, Madison, Wis.
[3] Warwick and York, 1937.

STANDARDS OF APPRAISAL FOR SUMMARIES AND REPORTS

Grade 7	Grade 8	Grade 9
2. Were the ideas arranged in the best order for clearness? 3. Did my summary (or report) have an introductory and a concluding thought? 4. Did I use such necessary aids as maps, charts, graphs, or pictures to make my talk clear? 5. Did I show interest and enthusiasm? Did I speak clearly? Was my posture good? 6. Was my English free from the gross errors on which the school has been working? 7. Did I make use of the words which we have learned during the unit?	my materials and did not merely repeat the words of another? 2. Did I give emphasis to the most important ideas?	that I used my notes sparingly? 2. Did I make clear to my audience through transitional expressions each new division or phase of my topic? 3. Was the introductory sentence thought out carefully beforehand? Did it catch the interest of the audience? Was the closing sentence appropriate and effective?

WRITTEN

Grade 7	Grade 8	Grade 9
1. Does the summary or report include the important ideas and omit the unimportant ones? 2. Are the ideas arranged in the best order for clearness? 3. Have I made use of the words which we have learned during the unit? 4. Is my English free from the gross errors on which the school has been working? 5. Are spelling, punctuation, capitalization, and manuscript form satisfactory?	Standards for Grade 7 plus: 1. Does each paragraph develop *one* idea? 2. Does my report show a common-sense order of paragraphs and of details within each paragraph? 3. Is the material written in sufficient detail to be useful for reference? 4. Am I making use of the vocabulary of the subject?	Standards for Grades 7 and 8 plus: 1. Have I used enough illustrations to make the report interesting and clear? 2. Do the transitional expressions make clear to the reader each change of topic? 3. Are introduction and conclusion appropriate and effective?

PROVISION FOR TEACHER APPRAISAL OF PUPIL GROWTH

The practice of making observations of individual pupils in a class and of recording from time to time subjective evidences of growth is increasing in popularity. Teachers are aware of the inadequacy of objective measures of many of the more important phases of language ability.

Charts, alphabetized card files of pupils, and individual folders are means used for keeping such cumulative records. Their value is increased if the study carries over from year to year so that each teacher sees the continuous development of the pupil along specific lines.

The chart on page 276 is used by prospective teachers who are being trained at the East Texas State Teachers College to study the needs and activities of children in the elementary school and to record their observations so as to plan educative experiences for the children.

The use of this chart is illustrated by the following record of language activities made by a student who observed pupil B.J.A. in the third grade, during the first period of the day at which time the children were free in their activities.

I. Activities involving the use of language
   A. In getting information
      1. Hunts pictures to use in drawing
      2. Looks in the encyclopedia when told to do so
      3. Asks questions freely of both teacher and classmates
      4. Looks at books a great deal
      5. Reads stories and poems silently
      6. Listens intently to children and teacher, telling stories and explaining their contributions during conference period
   B. In giving information
      1. Explains pictures she draws
      2. Tells the group stories she reads in books
      3. Writes letters to absent teacher and classmates
      4. Gives account of trips made over the weekend
   C. In trying to influence others
      1. Gives suggestions to others for improving their work
      2. Carries on animated conversation with classmates
      3. Persuades others that she is right in her criticisms or suggestions
      4. Tries to get her work approved by showing it to others often
      5. Works with group in planning a panel to improve the appear-

OBSERVATION IN LANGUAGE LEARNING [4]

	Function A To Get Information		
Activity Observed	Language Needs Observed	Language Ability Observed	Provision for Meeting Language Needs Observed

Function B To Give Information

Function C To Influence Others

Function D To Keep Records

Function E To Make Plans

Function F To Share Experiences

Function G to Express Esthetic Emotions

[4] Reported by Anne Workman, Director of Observation, Upper Elementary Grades, East Texas State Teachers College, Commerce, Tex.

ance of room, and in planning means of expressing sympathy to a classmate when his father died

D. In keeping records
   1. Helps make rules of politeness
   2. Contributes ideas to class story of excursion to fire house and power plant
   3. Keeps first copy of all of her written work

E. In making plans
   1. Makes plans for her picture before drawing it
   2. Plans what she will do next day at free period
   3. Helps plan her Christmas costume with the student observer
   4. Helps plan the excursion to the power house
   5. Helps plan the panel

F. In sharing experiences
   1. Enjoys taking part in program
   2. Often contributes to class discussions some experience she has had
   3. Brings a few pictures for the bulletin board
   4. Shows her work to others
   5. Helps draw picture for the decorative panel

G. In expressing esthetic emotions
   1. Takes great pleasure in working out panel of the history of the world
   2. Enjoys making Christmas gifts
   3. Wraps presents attractively
   4. Enjoys giving readings at club meetings
   5. Enters into Christmas program with enthusiasm
   6. Enjoys wearing her costume
   7. Works diligently with care of pets
   8. Models a great deal in clay
   9. Enjoys hearing stories told
   10. Enjoys listening to poetry
   11. Chooses very bright colors in making panel

II. Needs of pupil observed when engaging in the activities listed
   A. In getting information
      1. Needs to keep lips closed when reading silently
      2. Needs to feel more at home in school-room; improving in this
      3. Needs to read more books, other than texts, to get information
   B. In giving information
      1. Needs better posture in standing before class
      2. Needs better usage of verbs and pronouns ("It ain't no good," "I ain't gonna do that now," "He come to see us," "Curtis, he," says "uh," "and," "but," constantly when talking, are some of the mistakes made.)

3. Needs more distinct enunciation
4. Needs habit of punctuating headings, addresses, and complimentary closings of letters
5. Needs control of the spelling of a great many words
6. Needs to contribute more during conference period
7. Needs to tell more of her experiences that would be of interest to group
8. Needs to have better breath control when talking to group
9. Needs to reduce nervous habits of speech

C. In influencing others
1. More power in making others see her way
2. More care in writing. Untidy papers and letters
3. More poise in relating experiences
4. Closer relation in points of explanation
5. More confidence in her own work
6. More attention to one thing at a time

D. In making records
1. Needs better handwriting
2. Needs encouragement to work alone

E. In making plans
1. Needs to talk more freely in group planning
2. Needs to believe in her own ideas more
3. Needs to make more plans. Works often without planning

F. In sharing experiences
1. Needs clearer enunciation in giving readings
2. Needs better knowledge of pronunciation of words
3. Needs encouragement to tell more of her unusual experiences, for instance: Going to school in a bob sled in Illinois

III. Language skills, habits, and attitudes shown in activities listed above
A. In getting information
1. Can follow printed or written directions
2. Can get thought from printed page
3. Can write well when she tries
4. Can find information in encyclopedia without much help
5. Can select appropriate materials to read aloud
6. Can understand what others read orally
7. Can keep place without pointing
8. Shows gradual elimination of lip movement
9. Can interpret main ideas of simple passage
10. Can express herself clearly
11. Can find answers to questions
12. Has mastery of sufficient reading vocabulary
13. Can memorize easily

14. Can find titles in tables of contents
15. Can ask good questions
16. Draws good pictures
17. Reads independently in school library

B. In giving information
1. Uses what she reads in content subjects
2. Selects appropriate materials to read aloud
3. Holds picture she is explaining so all can see it
4. Has a pleasing voice with good tone qualities when talking to group
5. Considers the audience
6. Makes others understand when she is reading orally
7. Usually has something to say worth listening to
8. Has good ideas in drawing
9. Has adequate vocabulary to express ideas
10. Is able to write a very good letter
11. Can stay on the subject
12. Can talk in assembly and in a large audience

C. In influencing others
1. Has adequate vocabulary
2. Gives good suggestions when encouraged by teacher
3. Explains her pictures in good conversational tones
4. Very forceful if she is sure of herself

D. In keeping records
1. Draws well; has contributed a great deal to the wall panel
2. Can write better than she does
3. Memorizes well

E. In planning
1. Ability to plan has increased
2. Beginning to plan for longer periods of time
3. Is getting acquainted with materials, and plans to use more of them
4. Gets started quicker every morning
5. Offers help in small group planning, but says scarcely anything in large group work

F. In sharing experiences
1. Tells more of her experiences than formerly
2. Is becoming well-acquainted with others in class, and more communicative

G. In enjoying esthetic experiences (Has grown in power to express ideas with clay, water colors, crayons, and in dramatic play.)

IV. How the supervising teacher is meeting the needs of the pupil observed
A. In getting information

    1. Corrects errors in speech without making her self-conscious
    2. Uses excellent English herself
    3. Has pleasing, well modulated voice
    4. Encourages B. to read with lips closed
    5. Makes B. feel at ease in classroom
    6. Supplies many interesting easy books on low open shelves
    7. Asks B. questions that need finding answers in encyclopedia
    8. Tells her to hold book farther from her

B. In giving information
    1. Teacher is helping her to feel more at home
    2. Draws her into conferences and plans
    3. Gives individual help in spelling
    4. Compliments her work whenever she can

C. In influencing others
    1. Teacher asks questions to hold her on the subject until one part is explained fully before going on to the next

D. In keeping records
    1. Teacher uses B.'s copies for the bulletin board
    2. Encourages neat handwriting
    3. Mounts and displays pictures
    4. Keeps class records of experiences on large chart
    5. Prints class compositions on large charts
    6. Prints rules of politeness, and library rules on charts

E. In making plans
    1. Teacher encourages her to make suggestions
    2. Often accepts her suggestions
    3. Often asks: What do you plan to do next?
    4. Prints class plans on large chart

F. In sharing experiences
    1. Teacher puts her on programs
    2. Asks her questions about her trips
    3. Calls her before the group

G. In expressing esthetic ideas
    1. Gives ample freedom to child
    2. Supplies many mediums of expression
    3. Provides periods of play
    4. Uses her pictures
    5. Puts her on programs

George Lawton at the Evander Childs High School, New York City, also developed useful criteria in appraising pupil growth.

The teachers of English in the Cheltenham Township High School, Elkins Park, Pennsylvania, tried to develop an accurate and a definite method of evaluating and recording pupil progress.

After a study of the reasons that the usual letter and numerical grades were unsatisfactory, they developed a workable plan. The process of development was as valuable as the results.

A PLAN FOR EVALUATING AND RECORDING PUPIL PROGRESS IN ENGLISH [5]

The result of discussion in meetings of teachers was the separation of English into six major divisions, three relating to literature and three to composition. These are: (1) literary comprehension; (2) free reading habit; (3) literary background, or knowledge of facts *about* literature; (4) mastery of the mechanics of spoken and written English; (5) organization and presentation of material; and (6) development of the creative faculty. These, then, were to provide the principal headings for the new type of recording. Another heading, not relating specifically to English, was also included— work habits. Much finer division, of course, suggested itself, but too great detail, it was felt, would produce confusion and prove cumbersome in use. Furthermore, the descriptive type of recording affords opportunity for the inclusion of specific traits and abilities under the headings provided.

Sample sheets bearing the above headings were drawn up, and these were filled out experimentally for selected pupils. In a subsequent meeting, these were read aloud and compared until a somewhat uniform style of recording was agreed upon. It was decided to issue the reports in triplicate: one copy for the office files, another for the teacher's own records, and a third to be sent to the parents. Actual test scores might be included on the office and teachers' copies, but not on the forms sent to parents. In order to apprise the parents of the purposes and mode of operation of the plan, and to enlist their coöperation, two meetings of the parents were held in the high-school building at which explanations were made and an open discussion of the workings of the plan was conducted.

The plan has now been in use in selected classes for one year. It is still decidedly in an experimental stage. However, with very few exceptions the response to its use, from both pupils and parents, has been wholeheartedly favorable. After the issuing of the first report, many parents wrote letters commending the school on the new type of report. Some parents declared that the report embodied the first definite and understandable statement of their children's school progress that they had ever received.

[5] Reported by Albert E. Weston, chairman, Cheltenham Township High School, Elkins Park, Pa.

The teachers using the report were supplied with a carefully worded exposition of each term and of how to use it when evaluating pupil's progress. A specimen of one pupil's report is attached.

CHELTENHAM HIGH SCHOOL

ELKINS PARK, PENNA.

DATE————————

STUDENT . . . .

English

1. *Literary Comprehension*

(Critical understanding of materials read)
His comprehension of the more practical kinds of literature is excellent. However, owing probably to hasty reading, he misses many of the implications of literature. He reads too rapidly, hitting only the high spots, and leaving much splendid material undigested.

2. *Free Reading Habit*

(Appreciation, acquaintance, scope)
Appreciation of prose exceeds that of poetry, and is really excellent. Favorite forms of reading seem to be biography, travel, and scientific works. His general acquaintance with literature, as measured by standard tests, is slightly above the average of his group. He reads much in newspapers and magazines.

3. *Literary Background*

(Literary biographies, criticism and history)
Historical background in literature is woefully lacking, but he devours literary criticisms on modern books. Is well versed in the lives of a few older authors and reads everything he can get concerning modern ones.

4. *Mastery of Mechanics of Spoken and Written English*

Tests reveal that his mastery of mechanics is very imperfect, and his own papers bear additional evidence to the fact. He is particularly weak in sentence structure, using a dashing choppy style. Most mistakes in grammar are probably attributable to carelessness. Oral expression fluent but poorly organized.

5. *Organization and Presentation of Material*

As to organization, I am tempted to say there is none. Although he observes quite well, his impressions are scattered pell-mell throughout his papers. There is a graphic impressiveness and occasional brilliancy to his phrasing, but little logical consecutiveness.

6. *Development of the Creative Ability*

He has a creative flair in words and phrases. Is excellent at short characterizations of real or imaginary persons. Recently wrote a commendable paper on his visit to a bird haven, and another in Chemistry on atomic weights.

7. *General*

(Work habits)

Generally good, though his efforts are often superficial. He is constantly "busy" and has a great zest for learning, but needs to learn to concentrate his efforts on one thing at a time and keep at that until it is mastered.

TEACHER . . . .

In appraising pupil growth, teachers find objective, standardized, and objective and subjective teacher-made, and even pupil-made tests useful. Whether one type of test or another is preferable depends upon which of the following purposes [6] in testing is paramount at the time:

1. * To classify pupils according to learning capacity, cultural interests, and achievement levels
2. * To discover the teaching point, i.e., the present status of the pupil in respect to a specific function
3. * To diagnose specific difficulties within a given area of learning
4. To measure pupils' growth in respect to the objectives of the grade and term
5. To focus teachers' and pupils' attention upon the basic concepts, significant habits, and emotionalized attitudes which are the outcomes desired in the course
6. To facilitate pupils' recall of significant facts and application of skills in new situations (stimulus to habit of reviewing and organizing knowledge, and applying, wherever relevant, what skills the pupil has)
7. To equalize pupils' opportunities for accurate evaluation of their achievement (An "objective" test can be scored by any type of marker; a "subjective" test is unreliable when scored by "an easy marker" or a "hard marker.")
8. * To validate teacher-made tests
9. * To assist in appraising a new method or new instructional materials

[6] In the list of purposes, an asterisk is used to show purposes for which standardized tests are available; for the other purposes teachers need to make their own tests.

In Baltimore, Maryland, the teachers of English in secondary schools have developed tests covering the following appreciations, skills, and knowledge:

I. *Appreciation*

A. Literary elements—(spoiled-version technique—best-answer type—tested on passages not studied in class, as in College Entrance Board "Power" Test)

Prose—
    Plot consistency
    Character consistency
    Sound basis of emotion
    Poetic justice
    Word imagery

Poetry—
    Imaginative thought
    Metrical effect
    Emotional tone

B. Qualities contributing to excellence in pupil's written compositions—(spoiled-version technique—best-answer type) specimen spoiled for one factor at a time—
    Grammatical correctness
    Vivid words
    Sentence structure: unity and coherence
    Paragraph structure: unity and coherence
    Capitalization
    Punctuation
    Spelling

II. *Skills*

A. Compositional (all tested objectively in quarterly test; subjectively in pupils' writing of themes and in notebook work during the quarter)
Recognizing purpose in writing
    Selecting ideas relevant to topic
    Organizing ideas
    Expressing ideas
    Reading for technical errors and ineffective words

B. Reading (all tested objectively in series of quarterly tests—best-answer, matching, completion, etc.; during the entire quarter, however, oral discussion of assignments in literature and language books gives evidence of how well pupils are reading for specific purposes)
    For exact meaning
        Central idea
        Answering specific questions
    Skimming
    Reading rapidly

Remembering what is read
  Outlining
  Making a précis
  Recognizing sense-appealing words and apt comparisons
  Building a meaningful vocabulary
C. Library Skills: use of
  Card catalog
  Title page—preface—table of contents—index
  Unabridged dictionary
  Atlas
  Magazine indexes
  Encyclopedias
  Dictionaries of biography and of history
D. Spelling words on the grade list

III. *Knowledge*

A. Literature
  From the three literature units in each term, a selected list of contemporary and classic authors and titles of works read, selected passages, essential content of books as part of the literary experience gained from the units, the characteristics of literary types, and sources of literary materials

B. Language-Composition
  Grammar, punctuation, capitalization and spelling rules as aids to revising individual's own writing; essentials of outlining; précis writing.

PROVISION FOR TEACHER SELF-APPRAISAL

The final phase of appraisal is what the teacher herself *feels*, *thinks*, and *knows* (because of empirical or experimental evidence) has happened to the boys and girls in her class. Looking back over a unit of work while details are fresh enough to be recalled accurately yet with the perspective of a completed experience gives a teacher the courage to repeat or to abandon the unit with another group of pupils. Three examples of appraisal are offered as indicative of this wholesome kind of teacher appraisal.

EVALUATION OF UNIT TEACHING [7]

Conferences

1. Did the conferences help pupils to see the immediate and remote values of the subject-matter?

[7] Developed in Baltimore, Maryland, by the teachers coöperating with Angela M. Broening in building the *Course of Study in English for Secondary Schools*.

2. Is there evidence that the knowledge, skills, and attitudes gained in these conferences will be used later?

3. What opportunities were afforded for individuals or groups of pupils to raise questions, give suggestions, etc.?

4. How effectively did the teacher provide for the future use of these pupil suggestions?

5. Did the conferences utilize and further develop the special abilities and interests of pupils in projects of social significance?

Unit Assignment Sheet

1. To what extent was the assignment sheet stimulating to the abilities and interests of every individual?

2. Did it utilize sufficiently the pupils' previous knowledge, habits, etc.?

3. Was the language clear? Was the unit divided into workable sub-units?

4. Did it make clear what written records were required?

5. Did it challenge bright pupils to enriched experience through special reading, additional observation of first-hand data, etc., without discouraging the less bright pupils?

6. Did it emotionalize scholarship goals by having them function in situations of immediate satisfaction to the pupils?

7. If the teacher visited is not the *author* of the assignment sheet, did he use it with flexibility and intelligence so that it was adapted to the class he was teaching? Was he able to evaluate critically the assignments as his class used them?

Practice Tests

1. Were they so arranged as to be self-administering and self-corrective by the individual pupil?

2. Were the associations being drilled upon *important* enough to warrant their being made automatic?

3. Were they so arranged as to help pupils see how near they were to the goals set up in the unit and to help them diagnose where they needed to straighten out their facts and improve their skills?

4. Did they provide ample "repetition with satisfaction" so that the desired associations were established by every pupil?

5. Did they provide practice of the various reading skills needed in the subject?

6. Did they give satisfying repetition of the habits of correct writing? Which?

7. Were they constructed so that the bright as well as the average and less-than-average pupils felt an urge to perform them?

"Real Tests"

1. Were they adequate measures of what was being measured?

2. Could they be scored objectively by the teacher?

3. Were they applied at a time and under conditions favorable to the pupil's success?

4. Did the teacher utilize the results as incentives to pupil effort and achievement? As incentives to more individualized teaching?

Records

1. Were the laboratory graphs kept up-to-date and posted conspicuously enough to keep the pupils informed of their individual and group progress on the unit?

2. At intervals of different lengths did the teacher check with the pupils their efforts and successes as recorded in their notebooks and evidenced in their special individual and group projects?

3. Was help given pupils in developing responsibility for budgeting their time so that more adequate returns in progress were secured?

TEST-DETERMINED TEACHING OF READING [8]

I. PURPOSES

    A. To show how test results may be used by both teacher and pupils to motivate and to direct learning

    B. To demonstrate individualized drill within a class organization

    C. To reveal what an observer may be able to discern when visiting a class engaged in reading to improve their skill

II. ACTIVITIES DEMONSTRATED

    A. Using test results to motivate and direct each pupil's learning

    B. Using a letter to the students about reading to give them an overview of the reading problem from their own point of view

    C. Training the class as a whole in how to handle the reading practice

    D. Segregating individuals and groups according to what the test results show they need most urgently

    F. Showing pupils when and how to use the key to practice exercises and how to keep records of their progress

III. OBSERVER'S GUIDE FOR APPRAISING THE LEARNING ACTIVITIES DEMONSTRATED

(Check any statement for which you see evidence in the lesson observed.)

    A. *The Pupils*

      — 1. The pupils see reading in relationship to life in and out of school.

      — 2. They show a desire to improve their reading.

      — 3. They know what to do in order to improve.

[8] This appraisal sheet was developed for use in connection with a demonstration lesson given for teachers and supervisors interested in reading.

— 4. They begin their practice with alertness and attention.

— 5. They make enough progress within this initial period to establish a favorable attitude toward their reading activity.

— 6. They know where to begin again in the next period to be devoted to reading for skill.

— 7. They are aware of one method of reading for a given purpose and can apply this method at once if the same purpose occurs in their home reading tonight.

B. *Instructional Material*

— 1. Reading material is selected from contemporary and classical sources of intrinsic appeal to secondary-school pupils.

— 2. It is adequate follow-up of the test results used to diagnose pupils' needs.

— 3. It is graded according to difficulty and grouped to provide continuous practice in developing a specific skill.

— 4. Each section is prefaced by clearly stated instructions for developing the proper technique in reading for a given purpose.

— 5. Provision is made for reading work-type and literary materials so that the pupil will develop the skills required in a well-rounded, individual reading program.

— 6. The practice material is arranged so as to focus the pupil's attention upon a specific skill appropriate to a specific reading purpose thereby enabling the pupil to develop the habit of reading in this matter whenever he experiences this purpose again.

— 7. It utilizes all relevant motives for learning.

— 8. Keys are furnished to enable the pupil to take care of his individual needs while the teacher is in conference with other pupils or while the pupil is working at home on the remedial practice.

— 9. The material is so arranged as to offer simultaneously a challenge to the bright, the average, and the below-average pupil. It provides for individualization within a class organization.

C. *The Teacher*

— 1. The teacher believes that reading is an important tool and a source of recreation.

— 2. She helped the pupils to see the immediate and remote values of improving their reading.

—3. She and the pupils felt a purpose in the activities of the period.

— 4. She used the instructional material with flexibility and intelligence, so that it was adapted to the class she was teaching.

— 5. She was genuinely interested in helping the pupils help themselves to improve their reading.

— 6. She utilized whatever opportunity arose to foster a pleasant pupil attitude toward the reading program. (Remember Robert Frost's warning: "We should not make a pain out of what should be a pleasure.")

— 7. She conceived the reading practice periods as periods when the pupils must be allowed to read silently, to check their answers, and to secure her help when they cannot help themselves. (She visualizes her job as coach, umpire, and cheerleader in the pupils' game of reading to improve their skill.)

IV. SUMMARY

A. Do you consider that this period was time usefully spent by the pupils?

B. What would you plan as the "next step" in teaching these pupils how to read?

C. How practical does "individualized reading within a class organization" appear to you?

D. In what way will the improvement of the pupils' reading skills through training in an English class facilitate your teaching of these pupils?

E. In what ways does your subject furnish purpose for reading?

F. What reading problems which you have met in your classes would be partially solved if your pupils knew how to discriminate as to the reading method appropriate to the reader's purpose and the available material?

Teachers of English and of the social studies have much in common. The appraisal sheet which follows shows (1) how a teacher of social studies utilized and extended the language skills developed in the English department, and (2) how the English teacher can make use of the experiences boys and girls have in the social-studies class.[9]

COÖPERATIVE THINKING THROUGH DISCUSSION BASED ON INDIVIDUAL AND COMMITTEE RESEARCH

Unit: *Large-scale Industry and Problems of Labor*

I. *Purposes of the Demonstration*

A. To show how pupils are trained for the experiences of active membership in democratic institutions, viz.,

[9] Demonstrated March 2, 1939, by Grace D. Broening with 12A students of the Forest Park High School, Baltimore, Md.

1. Ability to organize for mutual welfare
2. Open-mindedness toward wholesome changes in the social order
3. Independent and intelligent analysis of problems
4. Discriminating search for, and evaluation of, data
5. Tendency to base one's generalizations on facts
6. Experience in coöperative thinking
7. Training in the method of discussion

B. To demonstrate why and how a teacher selects instructional materials and learning activities appropriate to the goal of active membership in a democracy

1. This unit is vibrant with unsolved problems which are the source of controversy among economic and legislative groups in our democracy and which the present high-school generation must meet realistically as the workers, consumers, and citizens of tomorrow.
2. The nature of these problems necessitates and invites coöperative thinking based on careful research to find, digest, and appraise available data.
3. The nature of these problems will touch off pupils' loyalties and prejudices developed from parental political convictions and economic status, and propaganda in press, on radio, and on screen.

C. To reveal what an observer may be able to discern when visiting a class engaged in discussion based on a research study (Observers may wish to check outcomes evident in period. See IV below.)

II. *Activities before March 2, 1939*

A. First period

1. Listing problems from an extensive view of the contemporary scene involving large scale industry and the problems of labor— These problems came from
   a. Teacher's discovery of trends during years of intensive study and extensive reading on the problem
   b. Teacher's accumulation of "pupil-discovered" problems during recent years of teaching the unit
   c. Statement of problems by the present group of pupils engaged in investigating their solution
2. Suggesting bibliography and providing for pupil's use of pupil-discovered additional bibliography
3. Projecting plan of committee work
4. Selecting committee members (Pupils chose each other on basis of congeniality and of dependability.)

B. Second period

1. Discussing pupil-proposed plans of work, teacher helping

pupils to eliminate wasteful procedures and to set up feasible, efficient techniques

   2. Beginning work as committees

C. Third period—pupils worked on their plans with the teacher available to counsel regarding sources of information, method of reading, of note-taking, and of budgeting time

D. Fourth period—took stock of home and school study to help pupils analyze their findings toward sound interpretation, to modify reading method to fit reader's purpose (rapidly to locate specific, pertinent reference, then carefully for exact data, then thoughtfully to draw conclusions or to define problem upon which further data are needed before making generalization)

Note: Periods intervening have been devoted to individual committee and class conferences in which the teacher helped pupils to discover and to interpret significant data, to appraise sources, to differentiate personal and quoted opinions so that listeners can identify sources of data and of interpretation.

III. *Activities Demonstrated March 2, 1939.* Coöperative thinking based on research study of these problems

A. Why was it possible for an industrial civilization "to vanquish" an agricultural civilization in the Civil War?

B. Why did industry become "large" after 1860?

C. How has the "problem of labor" come about?

D. What are the social consequences of expanding industry and reducing the importance of human labor?

IV. *Outcomes* (Check any for which you see evidence during the period.)

A. Development of basic understandings

B. Respect for the democratic method of discussion, based on careful research, as a means of solving problems

C. Sense of individual "belonging" to the contemporary social scene

D. Sense of responsibility to think straight in the midst of conflicting propaganda

E. Habit of utilizing the experiences of the past in interpreting the present; alertness to legislative measures which are directed at maintaining or at changing the social order

F. Ability to evaluate sources of historical evidence

G. Ability to use books, including pictures, charts, maps, and graphs, radio, screen, and the daily press with critical awareness of propaganda vs. truth

H. Experience in historical method

I. Experience in using oral language to clarify thinking and to influence the opinions of others

J. Experience in using various visual aids to supplement words as a means of communicating ideas

(Though Dr. Eells on page 7 in *Evaluative Criteria,* Coöperative Study of Secondary School Standards, 1938, offers the following criteria for consideration only of subject-matter offerings, these standards may be applied to the instructional procedures as well as to the content experienced in a unit.)

V. Check which you find applicable to the unit as demonstrated on March 2, 1939.

— 1. Emphasizing significant contributions of racial culture to present-day life
— 2. Promoting pupils' understanding of present-day society
— 3. Stimulating pupils interests and satisfying their needs
— 4. Promoting the spirit and understanding of democracy
— 5. Promoting desirable social relations because of habits, understandings, appreciations, and attitudes developed
— 6. Selecting material having potential value in adult life
— 7. Engaging in a wide range of experiences for extending pupils' interests
— 8. Making adaptation to the tastes, interests, and abilities of individual pupils
— 9. Stimulating continuous growth and improvement of pupils throughout school life
— 10. Finding reference and illustrative materials and other teaching aids
— 11. Helping pupils to find reference materials
— 12. Stimulating continuous development of independence and power by all pupils

(Observers may wish to list here the basic understandings which the pupils derived during the discussion.)

XVIII

PROVIDING FOR CORRECTIVE TEACHING

In TEACHING or in supervising English, the primary objective is growth of the individual pupil's power to use English as a tool and as a source of recreation. Consequently, in setting up a program of preventive and remedial instruction—called *corrective teaching* in this monograph—every phase of English in which skill is desired must be duly considered. This kind of teaching must begin with a specific attack on particular difficulties and with content at the social-maturity level of the learner. Whenever objective, diagnostic tests, and dynamic practice materials graded in respect to difficulty are available, a teacher need not create her own testing and teaching materials. In discovering the environmental and temperamental factors influencing learning, however, the teacher has to depend upon observational and interview techniques.

Success in corrective teaching is dependent upon the pupil's will to succeed, his self-analysis of his difficulties and of his progress toward his goal, his alertness in applying in real-life situations the skills developed while using practice materials, and his satisfaction from receiving approval from his peers and superiors.

The accounts that follow in this chapter sample the excellent teaching through the country in establishing skills in reading, usage, and speech. The key ideas guiding these actual classroom "success stories" are: test-determined, differentiated, and integrated teaching of English as experience in the present-day life of the pupils.

READING

Corrective teaching is a broad enough concept nowadays to include building experience before beginning to read as well as rebuilding experience when tests reveal that boys and girls lack a meaningful vocabulary essential to skilful reading.

In the report which follows, a first-grade teacher tells of a reading readiness program which built the background of experience so necessary in the learning-to-read process.

A READING READINESS PROGRAM [1]

Our reading readiness group was drawn from first-grade classes. The children who composed it had very scanty vocabularies and lacked a background of suitable experiences which would aid them in learning to read, to express themselves orally, and to manipulate materials. There were also children who did not speak or understand English. Our main objective was to supplement their home experiences.

We wanted the children to be able to follow directions. Their coordination was to be developed. Materials were to be used with comparative ease. They were to gain some specific knowledge, such as the names of colors and objects that were encountered in their work or in their daily life. An opportunity to do problematic thinking was to be provided. They were to be trained to keep a series of events in mind in their proper sequence. Experiences that many children have at home and that are often assumed by teachers, these children were to have.

Their vocabularies were to grow. We wanted words, oral and written, to have meaning for them. Stories they were to hear and read would not then be so abstract. Conversation was to be carried on in simple English sentences with correct enunciation and pronunciation. Above all, the desire to read and to tell others of their own experiences was to be developed.

The children were to become acquainted with the world about them and feel at home in it. They were to become adjusted to the school situation. They were to develop responsiveness and good working habits. They were to develop desirable attitudes toward their classmates, teachers and themselves. They were to become more stable emotionally.

All these outcomes were to be achieved by enriching the lives of the children. Our means for enriching their lives were excursions to various places in the school and neighborhood, handwork, drawing, painting, picture books, conversations.

A typical excursion was the trip to market. We were going to buy a pumpkin. In order to get to the market it was necessary to cross a busy street where traffic signals were located. A chance for prob-

[1] Reported by Margaret Cook, Public Schools, Gary, Ind.

lematic thinking thereby was presented. Were we to cross with the red light or green? We talked about it, and the children learned why we should wait for the green light. This was valuable information.

Personal contact was made with the children while walking. The child who was the teacher's partner found himself talking enjoyably with her. (The partner changed with each excursion.) Others would, at times, join in the conversation. Sometimes songs or poems were made to the rhythm of our footsteps, as on this occasion. We chanted over and over,

> Green light says go.
> Red light says stop.
> Green light says go.
> Red light says stop.

Once at the market, the children were interested in stall after stall of fruit, vegetables, flowers, and poultry. We talked about the carrots. They were orange. They were long in shape. They were vegetables and could be eaten. We went from place to place talking about the things we saw. We found the pumpkin that was larger than the rest and purchased it. Each child had a turn to carry it part of the way back to school.

The following day we made the pumpkin into a jack-o'-lantern. The children sang songs to the jack-o'-lantern, and learned a poem about him. A story was told. Everyone wanted a jack-o'-lantern to take home. So, following oral directions, they made large orange paper lanterns with scissors and paste.

A dramatization of the trip to market was given for the older children in the auditorium along with a few of the other trips. This required recalling a series of events in their proper order and the use of effective English.

Later a vegetable book was made. Each day a new picture was drawn with crayons on manila paper. The choice of color and drawing was directed. Some time later, a vegetable and fruit department was added to the store in which we were playing. The fruit and vegetables were made of clay and painted.

When the library was visited, the pictures and books which attracted interest were those about which the children knew something.

There is no doubt that low mental ages, according to tests, have been made higher because children have acquired a wider speaking vocabulary and much valuable information. Their experiences have surely made them feel closer to one another and to their teacher.

They are eager to look through books or magazines and to talk or ask about the pictures they find. They like to work with their hands because they can make things that are satisfactory. They can follow directions. The non-English speaking children talk with other children. They find friends.

The children now are able to tell a story fluently by looking at a sequence of pictures. They are able to color well and within quite a small space in their workbooks. They are able to use the color directed by the teacher. They know what the pictures are about because they have seen and talked about the objects represented in them. In other words, they are ready to learn to read.

Dramatics as a means of experiencing is advocated by a teacher of special reading classes.

EXPERIENCING NEW WORDS [2]

It appears to me that the value of teaching remedial reading, or in fact, any subject, through the medium of dramatics cannot be over-estimated. Deep down in our hearts, we all love to act and to imitate. If we do not, it may be because of some inferiority complex which might easily have been overcome with opportunity for self-expression.

It is upon this truth that our special reading group is conducted, with particular stress upon dramatizing everything possible in connection with the printed word or thought.

Every word, phrase, sentence, paragraph, or story that has any dramatic possibility is "acted out" by the children of our special reading class. Children search for words that they may illustrate, and there is keen competition among them to discover which child can learn to use and dramatize the largest number of new and unfamiliar words.

Observe the difference in a child, who, for instance, reads the word *rebuke* in a rather perfunctory fashion and reasons about it abstractly and the child who is given an opportunity to dramatize it by being permitted to rebuke his classmates gently and to have them rebuke him. "Rebuke" becomes part of the active and living vocabulary of the child who has participated in the illustration.

This "Let's Pretend" program serves a three-fold purpose. It tends to create expressive reading in an habitually monotone reader; it helps to relieve the emotional distress of timidity or shyness that

[2] Reported by Bertha Dorothy Brown, Public School 26, Staten Island, New York.

frequently manifests itself in children who are below grade in reading; and it aids the children actually to live and experience new
words.

A group of girls and boys whose reading ability and low I Q's had
kept them from progressing at a rate consistent with their chronological ages were gathered together as a pre-vocational group.
Their teacher made a three-way attack on the pupils' reading difficulties: (1) using graded reading material, (2) using illustrated
newspapers, and (3) using interesting library books. Her story is
summarized below.

A REMEDIAL READING PROGRAM WITH A PRE-VOCATIONAL GROUP [3]

Here was an opportunity to test my theory that slow students
even after seven or more school years of continuous failure in reading could be taught to read. The group was a pre-vocational class
of twenty boys and fifteen girls ranging in chronological ages from
fourteen to sixteen and having a median intelligence quotient of 88.

Their ability in reading was that of a slow, ten-year-old child, but
their interests were those of their own age class. About five students
could read haltingly a short paragraph from a fourth-grade reader.
Two could read fluently the same material. The other twenty-three
could not or would not try to participate in any oral reading. My
two problems at the end of the first week were: (1) to get every
student reading aloud in an intelligible manner, and (2) to raise the
silent reading comprehension to the seventh-grade level.

Reading graded material. To achieve the goals established, I devoted the first two of the three weekly reading lessons to silent reading of an elementary-grade reader new to the pupils. The selections
of stories and articles were followed by short lead questions to be
answered. Each reading lesson included three stories as the goal.
Only a few pupils completed all three. Most finished two, and a de-
creasingly small number completed the first only.

Reading illustrated newspapers. The other period was used to read
for information in newspapers. One of the first resources tapped was
the rotogravure sections of the Philadelphia and New York newspapers. Each student brought in his own picture section and exchanged it for a neighbor's or my part of the *Times.* He had a chance

[3] Reported by Carmelita C. Rettaliata, Tilden Junior High School, Philadelphia, Pa.

to see the pictures first and then silently read the short caption underneath. The style was simple and the vocabulary easy to comprehend. Then the best readers as reporters were assigned for each paper. They interviewed their readers and secured volunteers who read aloud the most interesting item on their page. Before long everyone was contributing at least one item.

In all other projects I had the most intelligent students assist me in teaching the others how to read. I explained the situation in advance to the reporters who were the best readers. During the lesson they called for volunteers and frequently asked them to read an entire page at a time. Once the shock of hearing his own voice was over, the slowest could be persuaded to read first a few words, a sentence, and later a short paragraph intelligently. No one ever read unwillingly. The questions always were: "Who wants to read today?" "How many boys want to pace the girls?" "Who likes to read conversation?" "Who wants to start the story?" "How about a paragraph team?"

Once the confidence of the class was gained, I had 100 per cent coöperation in reading response. This was the greatest factor toward raising the class level to seventh-grade comprehension. The newspaper again supplied the material in the form of sports and news headlines that I had cut from the papers. All the information down to the small news print was supplied for the lesson. The reporters distributed the headlines. The students had two minutes to read silently. Questions were briefly stated. What? Who? Where? When? Slips of paper were distributed. The best readers analyzed from seven to ten items, while the slow averaged three per period. In the beginning the students referred to the clippings, but later on the material had to be recalled by memory.

Reading library books. The next aid was a set of books borrowed once a week from the school library. Several copies of *Tom Sawyer, Huckleberry Finn, Smoky, Jimmie the Bear Cub,* and Andersen's *Book of Fairy Tales* were distributed after each pupil had made his own selection from a long list of choices. Each week as librarians, the class recorded the number of pages read, title, date. No check was made on the reading, other than this page count. Any pupil who disliked his story could change to a book on the lending library shelf in my room. Once the first two chapters were covered, the student usually wanted to finish his book. Frequently the desired book was taken out over the weekend, to be read at home. By the end of the term the average number of completed books was three. The best had finished five, while the slow were still on the first book.

Very few of the same students had ever read a book before in their entire school life.

Perhaps the biggest test of the class improvement came late in the term. A pupil suggested our having a play. In the reader at hand, we found a very easy version of "The Prize Zinnias." After ten minutes of silent reading, the cast had volunteered and the various characters read their lines. Modified stage directions were read by a chorus. Our first informal production was a success.

Final estimate. Last February this class graduated from junior high school. During their final term their English teacher remarked at a departmental meeting, "Most of my 9B pre-Vocational students read better than many of the 9B's in regular class." This, plus my personal experiences in teaching the group, led me to believe that slow students can be taught to read after seven or more years of concentrated failure to develop an interest in books.

Corrective teaching, in the broadest sense of the term, includes teaching that aims to develop correct habits and skills. It is with such an interpretation of the term that Elizabeth G. T. Smith [4] and Mabel Goddard [5] submitted excellent exercises for developing skills in the use of the dictionary, the card catalog, encyclopedia, indexes to periodicals, and anthologies of poetry and of prose.

LEARNING HOW TO LEARN THROUGH READING [6]

In 1931, Syracuse, New York, instituted the system of guided free reading in the ninth-grade English course of one of its high schools. Soon it was established in the tenth grade of a second school. It has since spread till now it is carried on in eight schools with more than half of all our ninth- to twelfth-grade pupils. In the second school to adopt it the teachers discovered within a few weeks that the pupils could not read well enough to make use of the opportunities afforded them by the new system. Our study of the prob-

[4] For details write Elizabeth G. Townsend Smith, Department of Education, Oklahoma City, Okla.

[5] For details write Mabel Goddard, Arsenal Technical High School, Indianapolis, Indiana.

[6] Reported by H. C. Newton, Head of English, Public Schools, Syracuse, N. Y.

Syracuse, New York, makes a positive attack on the reading problem by a planned series of tests, experiments, and experiences calculated to help pupils discover the kinds of learning that school and their (tentatively) chosen vocation will demand of them, and their abilities and disabilities. The work described is for grades IX, X, or XI.

lem and efforts to do something about it have resulted in the development of an entirely new plan of attack upon the problems of ninth-year English and the incorporation into the course of a program of activity whose objective is expressed in its title, Learning How to Learn—especially through self-improvement in reading.

Our program is not remedial for selected pupils. It aims at increase in all pupils of the power to learn by reading. We are thus working on the problem which by common consent of educators and on the basis of criticism from the public and from colleges is the most difficult and vital and most neglected of all educational problems. Our program is essentially one of guided individual and social experience of such a nature as to result in self-analysis, self-understanding, self-measurement, self-improvement. It changes attitudes, generates new interests, develops new abilities and purposes, all to the utmost extent possible considering the individual affected, the instruments used, and the *teacher*—who cannot be lesson-giver, recitation-hearer, examination-maker, but must be an understanding, skilful, inspiring guide of working pupils.

Our program is divided into six units, each consisting of experiments and experiences out of which develops a new realization which we aim to fix as a determining force in life. As you read each of these six statements, think of it as a realization resulting from several weeks of testing, experimenting, and of guided experience aimed to establish this realization as a life-shaping factor.

Unit I. I learn by doing, by observing, by listening, by reading, by reflection—and always in proportion to my concentration upon the effort. I can and must improve myself as a learner by every method.

Unit II. I can greatly improve myself as a learner in high school by systematizing my life.

Unit III. I learn most and most easily about those things in which I am most interested; therefore, I must control my native and determine my acquired interests in order that I may be most interested in those things knowledge of which will do me the most good.

Unit IV. Because reading is outstandingly the most-used method of learning during high-school years, I must do my best to become the most efficient reader I can possibly become.

Unit V. I should choose, at least tentatively, a vocational goal and should shape all my educational experience to reach it.

Unit VI. I must train myself purposefully and determinedly to overcome all physical, mental, and moral handicaps and to develop the habits and powers that will help me to succeed.

Challenges to Meet at the End of These Experiments

1. Am I reading more than I was six weeks ago?
2. Have I developed ability to read more efficiently as to both rate and comprehension?
3. Am I using less total time for the reading necessary in preparing lessons—and yet learning more efficiently?
4. Am I concerning myself with finding good reading for each of the three purposes enumerated?
5. Am I habitually reading more intensively—with greater concentration and vigor?

The program consists of thirty-four "practices," four of which are standardized tests. Several furnish motivation, seven explain each a reading skill, others cumulatively demand practice of these skills. The procedure is self-managing and completely individualized. For each individual the steps are as follows:

1. Read a passage—taking 1 to 6 minutes, record speed, and hand speed score in on nameless slip of paper.
2. Fill out questionnaire—taking 2 to 10 or 12 minutes.
3. By use of key, check answers, determine score, and hand it in on nameless slip of paper.
4. Study errors to discover reason for each, and record it in a lengthening (or shortening) list of "Reasons for My Failures in Reading."
5. While slower workers are still busy at 3 or 4, some who have finished are arranging initial scores, then comprehension scores in a column on the board, and marking median and quartiles.
6. Bring progress graph up to date.
7. Discussion of subjectmatter in passages read, of reading-improvement problems, of opportunities for and ways of utilizing skills developed, of the advantages of maximum-efficiency reading, etc.

By use of the entire program we have produced more than double the normal ninth-year increase of reading ability as measured by the Iowa Silent Reading Test—Advanced.

If pupils are to be successful in school, they must be able to find their way about in books. For a ninth-grade remedial reading class the following game was helpful. In addition to providing experience with the encyclopedia, it gave excellent practice in purposeful reading.

Miss Rosenfield explains that her unit on the use of the encyclopedia was preceded by six short units entitled "Locating Information." In these units the pupils used the textbooks from various subjects which they were pursuing. For the majority of her group, Miss Rosenfield said, getting acquainted with the encyclopedia was the discovery of new materials. The pages of the unit were arranged to match the particular volume of the encyclopedia in which the answers to questions were to be found. In formulating questions, she made an effort to select not only material that had some intrinsic interest for first-year high-school students, but also such material as might give background for subjects such as civics and science. After an exercise on each separate volume, she gave general questions requiring the pupils to determine the appropriate volume.

LET'S PLAY PROFESSOR QUIZ! [7]

Have you ever played any of the question-answer games so currently popular on the radio? They are lots of fun, especially if you know the answers and can win a prize. Radio games have many different names such as: True or False, Yes and No, Professor Quiz, guessing games, and many others.

We are going to play Professor Quiz, with this difference. Instead of answering Johnny-on-the-spot, you will be given time to go on a treasure hunt for the answers to the questions. The reference books about which you have been studying contain the required information.

You will be given your questions on sheets of paper. You must complete each set of ten questions in one period as no more time will be allowed for that set. As you read, you write in your note-books the facts you want to remember for the answers. Here are a few hints:

1. Keep your question clearly in mind.
2. Select the key word in the question.
3. Search for this word in its particular volume.
4. Jot down the volume and the page number of the reference book in which the answer is located.

Each question counts 100 points. Answers partly correct will receive part credit. At the end of the game, the girl making the highest score will receive a grand prize of a book that you all would love to have. To the girl with the next highest score a second prize of a pen and pencil set will be given. The winners' names will be posted on the English bulletin board. Are you all set? Let's go!

[7] Reported by Augusta Rosenfield, Girls Commercial High School, Brooklyn, New York, as a phase of a remedial-reading course.

To make the thing easier for you, we are going to use a reference book which has large print and lovely pictures to help you understand. Always look at pictures and their headings, for they may contain the very information you need. The key words of the first five questions have been underlined.

Exercise I— questions based on volume A

1. What other name is given to the *Arabian Nights?*
2. Why do *alligators'* teeth always show?
3. How did a cruel robber chieftain give *Antwerp* its name?
4. What is the chief product of *Akron,* Ohio?
5. Name two of the prehistoric *animals* that lived long ago.
6. How do ants communicate with one another?
7. The famous Greek mathematician Archimedes was about to be killed. What were his last words?
8. What great scientist first used antiseptics in operations?
9. Which character in Miss Alcott's *Little Women* represents the author herself?
10. Where is the longest aqueduct in the world?

Philadelphia makes use of teacher-made materials and books published for the purpose of developing pupils' reading skills. Growth—as measured by the objective, standardized Philadelphia Reading Test and pupils' increasing ability to succeed in all school subjects requiring reading as a study procedure—encourages the teachers and administrators to continue to give attention to instruction in reading.

This city [8] has the following six types of organization of remedial reading classes.

1. Remedial Reading Club
    1 to 2 periods per week
    1 to 3 classes organized in each school replacing club activity
2. Remedial Reading Study Class
    1 to 2 periods per week
    1 to 3 classes organized in the school replacing a study class assignment of pupil
3. Two-period per week remedial reading substituted for appreciational reading and/or written expression in standard Course of Study in English

[8] For details see Bulletin No. 487, Division of Educational Research, November, 1938, prepared by Dr. Philip A. Boyer, Director of Research, Board of Education, Philadelphia, Pa.

4. Program in remedial English, largely remedial reading, replacing regular English Course of Study
5. Five-period remedial reading substituted for a failed term of English (with credit) or substituted for some other major subject in which pupil is ahead of his grade classification
6. Part of remedial English program which also includes written and oral work in other fields of English. 1 period per week replacing free study period

The pupils for these classes in the different schools are selected by one of the following methods:

1. On the basis of Philadelphia Reading Test. Grades 4–6
2. Names are proposed by English teachers
3. Reading record and opinion of English teacher
4. Philadelphia Mental Ability Test I Q
5. All non-accelerated groups
6. On the basis of normal I Q's and low reading quotients
7. Reading for comprehension lessons given previous term, plus judgment of social studies and English teachers at close of term, plus standard test given in September
8. Reading record of Educational Record card verified by reading test
9. On the suggestion of psychologist
10. On advice of medical inspector (for sight)
11. All 10A pupils who did not achieve E or G in junior high school or elementary school English

In Allentown, Pennsylvania, a remarkable remedial program [9] has also been developed. From the results of Form A of a diagnostic reading test, the specific weaknesses of each pupil were discovered. During the school term, one period each week was devoted to the improvement of the reading skills of the various pupils with special emphasis upon specific weaknesses shown by individual pupils. At the end of nine months, Form B of the same test was administered. The last month of the school year was spent by the instructor in giving attention to individual pupil improvement of those skills not yet sufficiently rectified. The median reading score of 328 tenth-grade pupils so instructed showed a gain of 3.4 years in ten months. A few of the many interesting individual growth records are quoted as evidence that dynamic teaching focused upon learning needs of pupils does produce growth gratifying to both pupils and teachers.

[9] For further details write to Superintendent William L. Connor for Bulletin No. 38, School District, City of Allentown, January, 1939.

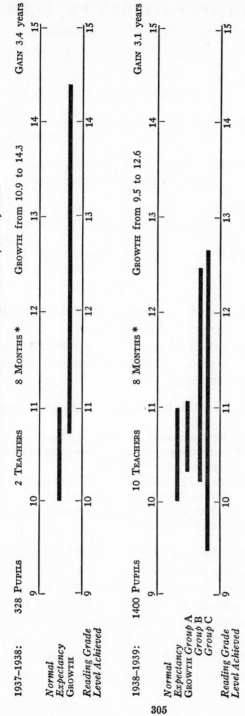

TENTH-GRADE REMEDIAL READING *Allentown, Pennsylvania*

1937-1938: 328 PUPILS · 2 TEACHERS · 8 MONTHS * · GROWTH from 10.9 to 14.3 · GAIN 3.4 years

Normal Expectancy
GROWTH

Reading Grade Level Achieved

1938-1939: 1400 PUPILS · 10 TEACHERS · 8 MONTHS * · GROWTH from 9.5 to 12.6 · GAIN 3.1 years

Normal Expectancy
GROWTH *Group A*
Group B
Group C

Reading Grade Level Achieved

Group A used special practice material, *ungraded.* GROWTH 10.4 to 11.1 GAIN .7 years
Group B used the "psychological approach" with the ordinary classics included in the course of study as practice material. GROWTH from 10.3 to 12.5 GAIN 2.2 years
Group C used the "psychological approach" with special practice material, *carefully graded.* GROWTH from 9.5 to 12.6 GAIN 3.1 years

* The interval between standard tests was eight months, although the school term was ten months.

305

Pupil 1 I.Q.   78 Standard Test A—Reading Score   6.
                Standard Test B—Reading Score 14.4
                        Gain   8.4 years
Pupil 2 I.Q.   94 Standard Test A—Reading Score   8.
                Standard Test B—Reading Score 13.3
                        Gain   5.3 years
Pupil 3 I.Q.   99 Standard Test A—Reading Score   8.0
                Standard Test B—Reading Score 14.4
                        Gain   6.4 years
Pupil 4 I.Q. 106 Standard Test A—Reading Score   8.
                Standard Test B—Reading Score 15.0
                        Gain   7.0 years
Pupil 5 I.Q. 112 Standard Test A—Reading Score 10.0
                Standard Test B—Reading Score 14.4
                        Gain   4.4 years
Pupil 6 I.Q. 139 Standard Test A—Reading Score 12.0
                Standard Test B—Reading Score 15.6
                        Gain   3.6 years

The approach to the reading problem in the senior high school in Allentown was purely psychological. That is, it was made in terms of reading skills, or lack of them, universally recognized to be of value in doing work, in school and out, which requires reading. For example, pupils were taught

1. To discover the central idea in paragraphs and longer passages
2. To answer specific questions
3. To outline with a view to remembering what had been read
4. To recognize sense-appealing words and apt comparisons with a view to quick visualization and permanent recall
5. To skim newspapers and periodicals for specific information
6. To read rapidly, alert to the demands mentioned above
7. To discriminate between poor and well written paragraphs
8. To use the library and library materials

The practice materials used were well graded and required the pupils to climb rapidly from difficulties characteristic of work in the elementary school, through difficulties characteristic of work in the secondary schools, to difficulties experienced by college students and by adults doing professional work in the world.

Through formal tests and through his failures and successes in his daily work, each pupil was made aware of the skill or skills he needed to emphasize most, thus motivating the work in an unusual way.

From time to time pupils were encouraged to write out brief statements of their own notions of the progress they were making and of the difficulties they were experiencing. Teachers used these statements in helping to individualize the work in building on the part of each pupil a personal desire to succeed.

During the second year, the remedial reading program was extended to include *all* pupils in the tenth grade. In general, the plan followed the plan of the first year except in that the approach was made universally through specific skills known to be useful in doing work in school and out, but without regard to any *one* specific set of practice materials; that is, during the second year, approximately one-half of the pupils (Group C) were taught by the plan and with the materials used the year before; one-third of the pupils (Group B) by the outline indicated above, but without any formal practice material; and the remainder (Group A) by a wholly different plan and with different materials. (See chart on p. 305.)

The results during the second year were not as spectacular as those of the first year, except in the case of the teacher who had done best during the first year. Her pupils, using the same materials and following the identical plan used the year before made an average gain of 4 years. On the whole, the experiment seems to indicate the importance of a well-conceived plan emphasizing practice with well-graded practice material on the list of skills mentioned above, and using both standard and informal tests to aid the teacher in pointing out to the pupil his specific need.[10]

From Baltimore, Maryland, comes the report on pages 308–309 of a survey of 20,000 high-school pupils' reading purposes and the skills required to achieve these purposes. This survey resulted also in the construction of well-graded, dynamic practice exercises which provide pupils in grades 7–12 with adequate training in each of the skills and necessary practice in discrimination as to which skill is needed for a specific purpose. From their experience in reading this wealth of content selected from every subject field and including all types of literature, the boys and girls developed the skills listed.

A study of these purposes, skills, and required written responses will reveal to any teacher of any subject and any grade in the secondary school an attack of reading which will prevent wasteful study habits and emotional frustration due to a lack of reading skill adequate to the pupils' avocational and vocational needs.

[10] From unpublished report of work in Allentown, 1938–39.

SURVEY OF 20,000 HIGH SCHOOL PUPILS' PURPOSES AND NEEDED
READING SKILLS, BALTIMORE, MARYLAND

High School Reader's Purpose	*Skills Needed to Achieve Purpose*	*Written Responses Required*
1. To get main points in reading so as to discuss it intelligently	*Discovering the central idea*	Author-title-pages Statement of main idea Outline Précis
2. To settle differences of opinion or conflicting evidence between readers and authors, or one author and another	*Discovering the central idea*	Statement of main idea Outline Précis
3. To read for fun (fiction or non-fiction) on a subject one is interested in	*Discovering the central idea* (Unifying mood)	Any way the individual wishes; all of the above are suitable
4. To supplement from other sources data found in one reference	*Discovering the central idea*	Statement of main idea
5. To answer questions assigned before the material is read	*Answering specific questions*	Exactly worded statements
6. To follow directions	Answering question: "Exactly what am I told to do?"	Whatever questions asks
7. To find things to do and how to do them	*Answering specific questions*	Outline or diagram
8. To keep up with current events in school and out	*Skimming* newspapers and magazines, bulletin boards	Key words and source-page-column
9. To find places to go	*Skimming* movie bulletin, club notes, etc.	Key words
10. To find something to eat or drink at a limited cost	*Skimming* menus, ads	Key words
11. To find news about self, friends, schoolmates, etc.	*Skimming* headlines	Source, page, column
12. To make reports on collateral readings	*Reading rapidly*	Author-title-publisher, Gist of material
13. To prepare assembly or club programs	*Reading rapidly*	Author-title-publisher
14. To see "what the author is up to"	*Reading rapidly*	Key ideas Key ideas
15. To raise questions for conversation or formal discussion	*Reading rapidly*	Gist, key words, striking quotation

16. To prepare bibliographies	*Using library skills:* card catalog, magazine indexes, book indexes, encyclopedias, dictionaries of biographies and of history, books of quotations, anthologies of literature	Author-title-publisher-date-pages-annotation which will recall reason for selection of item
17. To find data in several books on same topic	*Using titlepage,* preface, contents, list of illustrations, index of book	Same as in 16 above
18. To look up definitions	*Using the dictionary* after getting contextual clues as to meaning of word	Meaning which applies in context
19. To find locations, routes, etc.	*Using maps,* diagrams, floor plans	Key words or sketch
20. To interpret graphs, charts, etc.	*Reading legend,* scale, etc.	Key idea or facts

USAGE

In stating that in the teaching of correct usage the aim is habit formation, not knowledge of correct forms, the Curriculum Commission responsible for *An Experience Curriculum in English* was realistic enough to add: "Diagnostic, practice, and mastery tests, which make goals visible, enable the pupil to measure his own progress, and make education a game in which a score is kept, help to arouse a desire to use correct English. A good slogan in corrective teaching is, 'Every lesson a test, and every test a lesson.' " [11]

The following narrative, *Tests That Teach,* gives a concrete picture of how a program of test-determined teaching of correct usage can be made easy for the teachers and efficacious for the pupils.

TESTS THAT TEACH [12]

Teacher once was described as a person who sat up half the night marking the written evidence of her failure. But that was before the advent of the diagnostically coded, machine-marked answer sheet. For us, the interval between those days of teacher-marked, subjective examinations and these of machine-marked objective tests covers the dynamic story of how the scientific measurement move-

[11] W. Wilbur Hatfield, Chairman, *An Experience Curriculum in English* (D. Appleton-Century Company Inc., 1935), pp. 243–244.
[12] Reported by Angela M. Broening, Baltimore Public Schools, Baltimore, Md.

ment is transferring teacher energy from laborious test scoring to creative teaching on the basis of valid and reliable test results.

Teacher-made, machine-marked tests. To a teacher interested in improvement of learning there is no greater thrill than the experience of seeing her pupils' reactions to their machine-marked, diagnostically coded answer sheets. This sheet is for each pupil the electric signal which starts learning and keeps it going in the direction of worth-while, attainable goals. The writer, during her teaching of hundreds of boys and girls and her supervision of the teachers of thousands of pupils examined four times a year with departmentally prepared *Tests That Teach,* has never witnessed such a dynamic effect upon learning as during the period, *the day after a test was taken,* when a pupil's answer sheet is returned to him. Whether he passed or failed—the only fact which most pupils stopped to discover on the old-style, hand-marked test—is not even a minor attraction. He is fascinated by seeing, as never before, exactly why he is right or why he is wrong. There is no exhausting debate with the teacher over any item in a test; no laissez-faire reaction after seeing a passing grade; no confusion as to "what the teacher wants, anyhow," the emotional response of all too many pupils who in the past hovered just above or below a teacher-set standard of promotion. It is surely front-page news when *a pupil gets his test paper back the day after taking the test and immediately knows exactly what he has right and why, and what he has wrong, and why.* Because he finds on this answer sheet an accurate diagnosis as to what specifically he must do, he is on his way to gain sufficient control of English to convey his thoughts and emotions to others and to understand what others desire to communicate to him. Here, indeed, is a new educational instrument which combines these aids to improvement: "interest in the work, interest in improvement, significance, problem-attitude, attentiveness, absence of irrelevant emotional excitement, and the absence of worry." [18]

Of course, this type of answer sheet has "learning magic" only when it is made to fit a valid and reliable test of significant learning products. The answer sheet reproduced on page 312 aids improvement because it fits a test of 104 items which measure validly and reliably a pupil's mastery of the technical knowledge and skills known to be essential to effective and correct English. These test items cover in four different ways an adequate sampling of English usage, sentence unity and coherence, paragraph unity and coherence,

[18] Edward Lee Thorndike, *Educational Psychology—Briefer Course* (Teachers College, Columbia University, 1921), p. 214.

recognition of the elements of a sentence, sentence structure as an aid to clearness and to style, knowledge of the technical vocabulary useful in discussing how to revise one's writing, proofreading for coherence, applying rules for current usage in revising, proofreading for punctuation errors, and proofreading for capitalization errors. Both paragraphs and single sentences are used in the test. All errors which appear in the test have been checked against an inventory of the serious errors made most frequently by the high school pupils.[14]

The pattern of the answer sheet on page 312 illustrates also the important fact that the teacher did not make a test to fit an answer sheet. Instead she determined from course-of-study objectives what was to be measured, set up the most valid type of testing situation for each objective, and then made an answer sheet to fit the test.[15]

The day after a test in English. On September 15, 1938, every pupil in the school was given the F.P.H.S. Every Pupil Language-Composition Test (Form A-938). At three o'clock that afternoon 2500 answer sheets were machine-marked in the Bureau of Research in less than an hour. On September 16, 1938, in his English class every pupil was given his answer sheet and the diagnostic sheet to be used with the coded, machine-marked answer sheet. (See pages 312–313.) Briefly this is what happened in the period:

Teacher: Read the "Directions to the Pupils" shown in red on the answer sheet. Do you understand how you will know when your answer is right?

Pupil: When the red circle and my X coincide, my answer is right.

Teacher: How will you know when your answer is wrong?

Pupil: When my X and the red circle do *not* coincide, my answer is *wrong.*

Teacher: How many pupils got the first question right? [Hands are raised.] The first question wrong? [Hands are raised.] What letter in red is typed below the number of the first question?

Pupil: Capital R is typed below I.

Teacher: Now look at the diagnostic sheet to find capital R. What explanation is given?

Pupil: Unity is secured through every sentence developing the topic of the paragraph.

Teacher: Any pupil who got this question wrong, that is, who did not cross out square 1 and square 5, should write in his notebook this statement

[14] A coöperative research study made by the heads of the English departments of the Baltimore Secondary Schools.

[15] Any type of objective question can be used. Occasionally, we have used also questions which require the pupil to write words or numbers instead of crossing out squares. The correct answer then is typed in red beside the space in which the pupil wrote his answer. In every case, however, the answer sheet has been coded to furnish a diagnosis.

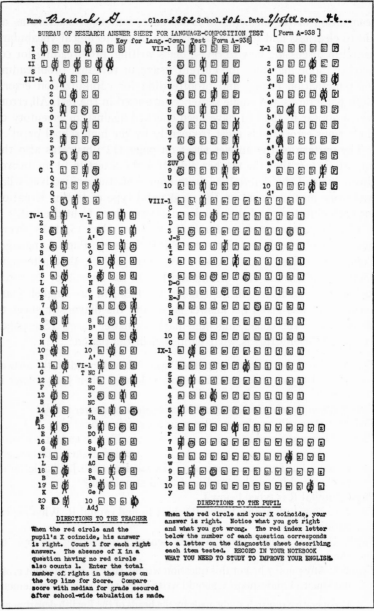

PHOTOGRAPH OF ONE PUPIL'S ANSWER SHEET AFTER IT HAD BEEN MACHINE-MARKED.

The circles around squares, *Directions to the Teacher*, *Directions to the Pupil*, and the index letter under the number of each question appear in red on the actual, machine-marked answer sheet.

DIAGNOSTIC SHEET
EVERY PUPIL LANGUAGE-COMPOSITION TEST (Form A-938)

Use with class when marked answer sheets are returned to pupils.

The letter to the left of each item corresponds to a red index letter below the question number on the marked answer sheet.

Each pupil should record in his notebook the specific language fact which the test shows he has not mastered. He should practice on the battery of drill exercises prepared to remedy his weakness.

CORRECT USAGE (A–N)

A A pronoun should agree with its antecedent in gender, number, and person.
B A verb should agree with its subject in number and person.
C Every pronoun should have an unmistakable antecedent.
D A participle should refer clearly to the word or words to which it is related in thought.

___

RECOGNITION OF ELEMENTS OF SENTENCE (O–P)

O Simple subject is that part of the sentence about which the sentence asserts something. (It is incorrect to repeat a subject by using a pronoun after a noun as an extra subject.)

___

PARAGRAPH UNITY (R)

R Unity is secured through every sentence developing the topic of the paragraph.

SENTENCE SENSE (S)

S A sentence is a group of words having a subject and a predicate and expressing a complete thought.

KNOWLEDGE OF TECHNICAL TERMS (T)

___

PARAGRAPH COHERENCE THROUGH (U–A')

U Correct order of details (logical or psychological)
V Internal punctuation where needed

___

DICTION (B')

___

PUNCTUATION (a–z)

a Place a comma after an introductory adverbial clause when it is long or when a comma is needed to avoid confusion.
b Place a comma after an introductory adverbial phrase only if it is long or strongly parenthetical.
c Use a comma to separate two independent clauses connected by a coördinate conjunction if there is danger of misunderstanding.
d Use a comma to separate items in a series. (The comma may be used or omitted before the conjunction.)

___

CAPITALIZATION (a'–f')

a' Proper nouns are written with capital letters; common nouns with small letters.
b' First word of a direct quotation is written with a capital.
c' First word of a sentence is written with a capital.

___

NOTE: The complete diagnostic sheet covers two sides of a paper 8½ x 13 inches. The broken lines indicate where items were dropped out in order to reveal on one side of the sheet the scope of the entire diagnosis.

about paragraph unity. How many pupils got question II wrong? [Hands are raised.] Right? [Hands are raised.] What letter is typed in red below II?

Pupil: Capital S is typed below II.

Teacher: Find capital S on the diagnostic sheet and read aloud what the explanation is.

Pupil: A sentence is a group of words having a subject and a predicate and expressing a complete thought.

Teacher: Any pupil who had this question wrong will copy in his notebook this explanation.

This procedure was continued, the teacher securing from pupils oral examples illustrating the correct application of the rule. When pupils could not give such examples, the teacher supplied illustrations. No use was made of any material in the Every Pupil Language-Composition Test.[16]

Summary of individual diagnosis disclosed on answer sheet on page 312. This pupil's answer sheet shows him that four times out of eight (B on the diagnostic sheet) he did not make the subject in the sentence agree with the predicate in number and person. In IV, when he was faced with selecting one of two forms to be used in filling in blanks in a sentence and where the context should have aided his decision as to which verb form was correct, he failed to select the correct verb. In VIII, when he had to pick out from groups of four sentences the one sentence which he considered best, he did not choose correctly. Though he did not have to tell *why*, the best sentence in the group numbered 3 was best because its subject and verb agreed in number and person. In his response to III, he revealed a lack of the knowledge useful in proofreading and in revising his own writing for agreement of subject and verb. He was unable (see O and P on the diagnostic sheet) to identify—not by definition, but merely by selecting the word in the sentence—the simple subject and simple predicate in the sentence. Whenever an interrogative sentence was used, the boy was completely confused as to which word was subject, which verb, and which object. Furthermore, in connection with the habit of having subjects and verbs agree, his answers in VI revealed that he did not have *a functional under-*

[16] After three or four months of follow-up practice on the pupil's specific needs, he is ready to be retested. The same test can be administered again because no discussion was given of the actual sentences or paragraphs in the test. The practice effect of taking the same test will be eliminated by the lapse of time and by the fact that the pupils were not expecting to be retested with the identical test.

standing of verb, predicate, phrase, clause (T on the diagnostic sheet).

So too, his efforts failed when he tried to find a direct object in a sentence. (Q on the diagnostic sheet and items III, C-1, 2, 3, and DO, VI-5. See p. 313.) He showed he lacked both an understanding of the term and a knowledge of the case form required of the noun or pronoun used as a direct object.

Neither was he able to put the subject of a verb in an interrogative sentence in the nominative case (M).

He was not aware of how to select the tense of a verb to convey accurately the time of an action (N).

In the matter of a dangling participle (D on the diagnostic sheet; V-4; Pa, VI-8; and U, VII-3, 6. See p. 313.) he lacked an understanding of the function in the sentence of a particple and of how to revise a sentence to eliminate a dangling participle.

He knew no aid to improving paragraph coherence except the use of connectives. In fact (U and A' and a, c, n, p on the diagnostic sheet), he was unable to use the correct order of details, proper subordination, parallel structure for ideas of parallel value, or internal punctuation to express clearly and effectively his ideas.

His one error in capitalization was made because he assumed that an adjective used with a proper noun was a "title." (He wrote *dear old* with a capital in the expression, dear old Forest Park High, giving as his reason that a title used with a proper noun needs to be capitalized.)

This boy's remedial work [17] was very definitely mapped out for him. If he is to improve, he and his teacher must see to it that he develops the concepts behind the technical vocabulary which the authors of textbooks and practice material use in teaching correct usage and which teachers employ in composition marking and in pupil composition revision. He must have more practice in seeing and hearing simultaneously the correct and the incorrect forms of verbs and nouns so that, when he writes or speaks incorrectly while he is trying to improve, he will be sensitive at once to the correction

---

[17] This diagnosis is available whether or not the boy's correct responses are totaled. Only when tests are used to rate a pupil's work is it necessary for his score to be counted. When a pupil's score is needed as a part of his school mark. it is easy to determine the "passing mark" on the basis of pupil difficulty. After each pupil's score has been counted, a distribution is made of the scores for the class. From the distribution of all classes at the same grade level, medians are derived. Then the raw scores are weighted for each grade level so that they may be averaged with other marks given on a basis of "60" as a passing grade.

TEACHERS CLASS ANALYSIS CHART PRODUCED BY STEP-UP PROCESS

IOWA SILENT READING TESTS

ADVANCED TEST: FORM A *(Revised)*

This illustration shows thirty-three pupils' answer sheets "stepped-up"—that is, arranged with overlapping top margins—to show the summary results for the entire class. Since the name and score of each pupil is written at the top edge of each answer sheet, this step-up produces a tabulation without any copying and the final result becomes, in effect, a facsimile of the Teachers Class Analysis Chart which was formerly made by the process of transcribing the results on a single large chart. When the answer sheets have been thus stepped-up, a copy may be made by any one of several photographic processes. Besides the saving in time and labor, transcription errors are completely eliminated. But more important still, he must make. He needs much habit-forming practice on eighteen of the sixty elements measured in this test. Unless he is allowed to practice only on the eighteen which he personally needs, he will be over-learning what he already knows and under-learning what he must practice in order to secure that mastery of English usage which is attainable at his level of social and educational maturity.

Were space available to show the diagnosis for the other forty-three pupils in the class, it would be evident at once that no uniform class drill material will bring about improvement. All pupils need some drill, but they need drill on different items. This individualized drill is becoming a practical classroom procedure through using *Tests That Teach* and through allowing each pupil to work on the specific steps in his mastery of language at which these tests show he lacks skill.

Summary. It is worth remembering that the machine-marked answer sheet with the "step-up" device has these advantages: (1) The detached answer sheet, by coding the questions, can be made a diagnosis for both pupil and teacher of the specific weakness (and strength) of the individual pupil. Throughout a term this individual *pupil-analysis chart* is useful in diagnostic teaching. (2) Tests can be returned to pupils while their interest in the results is at its maximum. (3) This diagnostically coded, machine-marked answer sheet focuses the pupil's attention on what was the cause of his failure on a test item instead of on his total score in the test. (4) The machine-marked answer sheet can be used for all of the following learning products: (*a*) Taste (by best-answer type of question), (*b*) skills (all types of questions), (*c*) knowledge of understandings or facts (all types of questions). (5) By means of a "step-up" device on the edge of the answer sheet, a class distribution is derived immediately by inspection and in an hour a school distribution can be tabulated. The "passing mark" can thus readily be set in terms of pupil difficulty disclosed by the test results instead of teacher judgment formulated in advance of seeing the test results. (6) Use of a battery of practice exercises, labelled so as to correspond to the areas tested in the diagnostic achievement test, makes individualized drill possible in a class organization. A pupil works only on the specific skill in which he needs to improve. (7) A record of the raw score and grade level or percentile rank on the test record card makes permanently useful the data from a specific test. (8) The teacher uses a symbol on her seating chart to remind her of the specific needs of her pupils below grade in control of English usage. (9) Time previously consumed in hand-marking an objective (or subjective) test is being used by teachers in preparing valid and reliable *tests that teach.*

The problems of setting standards and of improving the mechanics of composition are always with us.[18] Only a device that takes into account the individual need can be successful. Evelyn Sprado's report describes how she made her pupils aware of their individual errors in order to focus their learning and to secure improvement. The motivation of earning a good grade was incidental to the pupils' purpose of learning how to speak and to write effectively.

A Compositional Error File [19]

Keeping a composition error file is an old but rather effective device. For every student in my English-6 classes I kept a filing card on one side of which I jotted down his salient defects in written composition, and on the other his most flagrant defects in oral composition.

The "getting-acquainted" talk and composition during the first eight days were most revealing. In written composition I was able to note immediately those who were inveterately bad spellers, who habitually wrote half or run-on sentences, who punctuated with lordly liberality, or who showed no attempt at organization of material. On each student's card I noted the errors which I considered most serious, and, in correcting his work, I pointed out the error on which I wished him to concentrate first. Before the next composition was written, I explained the importance of eliminating one serious error at a time—but eliminating it permanently. Students were told that on the second theme more than two errors of the type noted would automatically entail an F. On the third composition,

---

[18] Though the weight of experimental and empirical evidence is in favor of teaching grammar as an instrument of communication, R. G. Vanderlip, of Central High School, Washington, D. C., has investigated the question once more. He compared teaching grammar (to an experimental group) as a need arose in the pupils' speech and writing with teaching (to a control group) a grammar unit as planned in a modern textbook.

The median score of the control group was a gain of .5 year, as measured on a standardized usage text, whereas the median score on the same test for the experimental was a loss of .1 year.

Mr. Vanderlip calls attention to the small number of cases he used, to the limited type of test he set up as a criterion, and to the fact that modern textbooks themselves present grammar as an instrument of communication.

[19] Reported by Evelyn Sprado, Richmond Hill High School, New York City.

more than one error of the type meant a failure. When one error was eliminated and others persisted, I pointed out the next error on which attention should be concentrated; and the same procedure was followed.

An important point in this program was the conference after class when special remedial work was done.

In the case of oral composition, special defects were noted on the card during the first talk (enunciation, "and" habit, "uh" habit, posture, carrying quality of voice, memorizing, poor development of topic, etc.). Before the next oral composition the cards were distributed, each student noted the comments on his card, and then returned it to me. The grade on the second talk was then determined by progress (or the lack of it) in eliminating the errors noted in the first. Interest in improvement was strengthened by the desire to pass the third term's work and promotion depended upon "passing" in oral composition.

In many cases it was necessary frequently to add to the list of errors on a card; but it was also possible to draw a red line through many of them. In order to keep each student informed of his progress (or his need for better work), a conference with the instructor was required at the end of every quarter.

This method helped me to set up minimum essentials for the individual as well as for the group and aided in raising the standards of work for D and F students in particular.

That teacher-training institutions are using the experience approach is encouraging when results obtained are as significant as those reported by John P. Milligan, field supervisor, New Jersey State Teachers College at Newark. Here the students, through directed observation in actual classrooms, come to know the teaching-learning problem at first hand. Then in the follow-up discussion with the instructor of the course, "The Teaching of English," the students project solutions for the problem discovered in the classroom. Later visits to the same room give them opportunity to see whether the teacher in charge planned as they did and whether this solution (or another, if hers were different from their projected one) worked. Such activities as collecting pupil-written material and analyzing it for types of sentences, clauses, phrases, parts of speech gave the students a knowledge not only of how and what the children were doing but also of what technical English the prospective teachers needed to review in order to teach these children.

PUNCTUATION AS AN AID TO COMPREHENSION [20]

Primary Objective. To improve paragraph comprehension by developing recognition of punctuation marks and their correct usage

Enabling Objectives. To realize the need for punctuation marks as aids in overcoming misunderstanding in the interpretation of sentences and paragraphs; to develop the ability to group words correctly through the aid of punctuation marks; to realize that oral expression aids comprehension; to recognize the incorrect use of punctuation leads to misunderstanding both in silent and oral reading

Activities

A. Informal discussion to review the punctuation marks that enter into the ability to comprehend sentences and paragraphs
    1. Discussion of uses of punctuation
        a. The use of the comma as an indication of a slight break in thought and in the grouping of words.
        b. The use of the semicolon as an indication of a larger break in the thought.
        c. The use of quotation marks as an indication of a break in the continuity of the narrative form.
        d. The use of the apostrophe as an indication of a break in the form of a word.
        e. The use of the dash as an indication of a break in the continuity of the thought.
    2. Recognition of incorrect use of marks in order to avoid incorrect comprehension and oral expression.
B. Individual silent reading of the paragraph
    1. The student is given one minute in which to read the paragraph in its incorrect form. (If the group is very slow, the length of time should be extended.)
    2. The student is given a test of ten questions to check his comprehension and memory.
C. Individual silent correction of the exercise
    (The student is given ten minutes to make all corrections. For the first few lessons in the unit, tell the student the number of errors in each line so that he does not become discouraged at his inability to note errors.)
D. Oral correction of papers

[20] This unit was developed by Emma J. Bender, Hammond, Ind., in an attempt to make practical the suggesiton found in *An Experience Curriculum in English,* pp. 242–245.

1. The corrections are given orally.
2. The corrected sentence is read orally with whatever inflection and grouping the reader thinks it should have.
3. Criticisms of the reading are made by members of the class.
E. Correction of a comprehension test to check lack of punctuation marks, incorrect punctuation, or general sentence meaning

Materials. This unit consists of ten lessons (or more) consisting of original paragraphs so constructed that they contain practice on common uses for punctuation marks; practice in proper reading "by eyefuls" by drawing attention to the mechanical devices—phrasing and punctuation marks.

Each student should have an individual graph sheet on which he may record his scores each day in order that he may become more interested in his "rise or fall."

A mastery test should be constructed and given at the completion of the unit.

In the construction of the paragraph these items should be noted:

1. They should be short enough to be read and corrected within the given period.
2. Their content and the questions over that content should be quite simple at first but should gradually become more provoking.
3. They should not contain too many errors—seldom more than two in a line.

Appraisal

A. Have the students become conscious of the value of the correct construction of the sentences?
B. Is their comprehension improved by their realization of the use for punctuation?
C. Have they become more accurate in their writing and speaking?
D. Can they read more effectively silently and orally?

Corrective teaching—based upon diagnostic testing, motivated learning, individualized drill, and natural opportunities for applying acquired knowledge and skills—is well illustrated in the following unit developed by Miss Caroline L. Ziegler.

Making the Expression of Ideas Clear [21]

As a first step in the unit, *Making the Expression of Ideas Clear,* the pupils were led to discover causes of confusion in several anec-

[21] One unit in a series of 36 developed in a curriculum research program conducted by the heads of the English departments in Baltimore, Md. This specific unit was developed by Caroline L. Ziegler and tried out in every high school.

dotes, advertisements, pupil accounts of personal experiences, and letters. The pupils soon realized that lack of organization, the use of inappropriate connectives between sentences and paragraphs, and confused sentences (due to faulty position of modifiers, lack of parallel structure, incorrect subordination of ideas, vague reference of pronouns and incorrect or omitted internal punctuation) were causing the readers to miss the writer's intended meaning.

In "Organizing Your Thoughts in a Plan," the second step of the unit, the pupils learned how to think through or analyze an idea within their own experience. Such questions as "Why did you select a certain course in high school? Why are you planning to go to a certain college?" gave pupils practice in analyzing a situation to discover reasons or causes. They next learned how to analyze the thought further by finding supporting reasons or ideas for each main reason. To do this they considered subjects of vital interest in the school, for example, "Why our school should have a movie club," and after stating the main reasons, they answered the question How? or Why? with each reason. These answers gave the supporting reasons or illustrations. After the pupils had gained some skill in thinking, they were shown an accepted method of numbering main reasons and designating supporting ideas and further details. As a check-test of their knowledge and skill, they criticized and corrected a series of student plans. As a mastery test the pupils constructed a complete outline of a new topic. In both the practice material and the mastery test each pupil chose his topic from a list made up of subjects concerned with vital in-school and out-of-school activities.

In the third section, "Revealing Thought Relations through Appropriate Connectives," the pupils learned first that certain relations exist between ideas. They became familiar with the most usual relationships, for example, the relations of contrast or difference between ideas, cause, consequence or result, and time relationship. In doing this they also discovered that ideas are not all of equal importance but that some are subordinate to others. They improved their skill in showing accurate thought relations between the parts of a sentence; then they learned to reveal the relationship between the larger units, paragraphs and sections. As a check-test the pupils discussed and then improved a number of student-written paragraphs.

The fourth section of the unit developed the pupils' skill in "Making Clear Sentences" (1) by arranging modifiers carefully, (2) by using parallel structure for similar construction, (3) by subordinating ideas and selecting exact connectives, (4) by having clear reference of pronouns, and (5) by using appropriate internal punctuation. In each part, the pupil discovered in several sentences of confused or doubtful meaning the cause of confusion and the principle for improving clearness. Then through practice in clarifying the meaning of sentences culled from pupils' papers they learned how to revise their own writing. As a check-test on each phase of this section the students measured their ability to make clear sentences by recognizing and correcting all errors in themes of three to five paragraphs each.

The pupils developed in the fifth section of the unit an awareness of the significance of *internal punctuation* in making their meaning clear. For each mark—comma, semicolon, colon, quotations, apostrophe—through reading carefully selected unpunctuated and punctuated sentences, the pupils discovered the rule which they later practised in sentences secured from natural writing situations concerning pupils' life activities. Graded in difficulty and varied in content and form, these exercises prepared the pupils not only for the mastery test on all internal punctuation but also for proofreading their own writing.

As a final check on the pupils' growth in making the expression of their ideas clear, each pupil selected one topic from a list of thirty-five correlated with science, with literature, with economic geography, and with personal reactions. Then he organized a plan for his explanation; wrote, revised, proofread, and appraised his growth in clear expression.

Corrective teaching of spelling is ingeniously handled by Lena A. Shaw in a spelling booklet in which each pupil picks and chooses exercises which may contribute to his growth in ability to spell correctly. Though Miss Shaw does not list the spelling words themselves, she does sketch the procedure whereby 6B pupils learned to spell correctly.

What Words Do You Use for Writing? [22]

To the Pupil: This spelling booklet was written for many children. Perhaps you don't need some of the words in this book. Per-

[22] Reported by Lena A. Shaw, Assistant Director, Handwriting-Language Education, Detroit Public Schools.

haps you need some words which are not here. This is an exercise to help you discover useful and interesting words which *you* need to know how to spell in order to write compositions, letters, or reports.

You may wish to write words that you do not know how to spell. If you can pronounce a word, you may be able to find that word in the dictionary. Discuss this problem with your teacher. Plan to use the dictionary to help you spell any word you wish to use in your list that you do not know how to spell correctly.

Below is a list of words that are often used in writing about farming. Copy the list of words given below. Then make a check mark after each word that you find in the "Spelling Vocabulary." On another piece of paper, write the words that you did not find. Label them *Extra Words*. Keep this paper so that you can add other words to your list. (The list which followed is not reproduced here.)

Problems

1. What did you find about the words in this list?
2. What words did you write in your list of extra words?

PART 2

Make your own list of words that have something to do with travel such as *planned, trip, train,* etc. Your list may consist of twenty or twenty-five words.

Place a check mark after each word that you find in the "Spelling Vocabulary." Add the words you did not find to your list of extra words.

Problems

1. How many words did you find in the "Spelling Vocabulary"?
2. How many words did you add to your extra list?

PART 3

Here are other suggestions for which you may prepare lists of words. Your lists may consist of ten to twenty-five words. Do the same with these lists that you did with the lists in Part 1 and Part 2 of this exercise.

    a. Things that run on wheels
    b. Foods that the farm produces
    c. Words that tell all the things that boys and girls can do such as talk, hear, etc.

d. .Words used in some unit of work you are studying in social science or reading

e. Choose your own topic for a list of words

Problems

1. How many words did you have in your list of extra words?
2. Compare your list with some other pupil who has finished this exercise.
3. Can you spell all the words in your list of extra words?

PART 4

Write all the words in your list of extra words in alphabetical order. Have your partner dictate this list of words to you.

Problem

Plan to learn to spell all the words that you did not know how to spell in your list of extra words.

Other exercises concern original writing in which of course spelling will function. The topics concern airplanes, birthdays, trips, safety rules, and others of interest to sixth grade boys and girls.

With the point of view that the best way to make any desired skill automatic is to use that skill frequently in real situations, Edna M. Heilbronn [23] developed a course in oral and written expression for grades one to six. She utilizes purposeful activities but at various points provides for practice with attention on specific items which cause individual pupils to speak or to write incorrectly or ineffectively. The instrumental grammar point of view of the Experience Curriculum Commission has guided Miss Heilbroun in her choice of content and method.

SPEECH

Corrective teaching in the field of speech education is no longer merely repair work with children having speech defects which completely impair normal communication. Speech activities at the present time make a direct attack on the oral language of every pupil in school and include training in the effective use of the voice, gesture, and posture in addition to careful pronunciation and enunciation. Even when these activities are handled by a special "speech

[23] For details write Edna M. Heilbronn, Central State Teachers College, Mt. Pleasant, Mich.

teacher," what the child has to say and why he is speaking at all are of as much concern as is his manner of speaking.

"BETTER SPEECH, BETTER BUSINESS" [24]

Point of View. "Better Speech, Better Business" is a new discovery of this century. Jesse Rainsford Sprague, himself a business man and a spokesman of the new order, assures the ambitious young man and woman that in the business world there are "dividends in diction," and so urges them to perfect their speech.

The first week is spent in a getting acquainted assignment through having students tell about themselves or classmates. These informal discussions give opportunity for the teacher to disclose that good speech is a key which admits its possessor to the company of the leaders of men and that poor speech in school means poor mathematics, poor history, poor chemistry, and poor English.

I. *Objective.* The objective of this course is to develop the personality of the student through the improvement of speech habits. More specifically stated the objectives are: (1) to improve the powers of expression through voice and action for the purpose of communicating ideas and emotions, (2) to eliminate undesirable mannerisms, (3) to develop a knowledge of correct social conduct in business or social contact, and (4) to attain self-confidence in public and private situations.

II. *Procedures.* (1) Discussion of the speech qualities which contribute to success, (2) through pantomime, improving posture and poise, (3) talking before the group, (4) improving voice control through demonstrations, analysis, and practice in enunciation, articulation, pronunciation, and control of voice volume; (5) studying dress and manners appropriate in business situations, (6) conducting business interviews in person and by telephone, (7) practising introductions, (8) telephoning for all business purposes, (9) experiencing parliamentary procedure, and (10) oral reading for enjoyment and as corrective measure.

Each teacher has some little device for cultivating an awareness of language habits and for breaking bad habits. The device described below probably worked because the suggestion originated with the children.

[24] Reported by Ethel Kaump, East High School, Madison, Wis., as an eighteen weeks' course for 11A Commercial Students.

An Experience in Corrective Speech [25]

Last fall I found a way to correct language errors without injury to feelings. This solution of the problem "when to correct and how" arose very naturally and with no plan on my part. I was reading a story about the early Pilgrims. The story said the Pilgrims did not want to stay in Holland because their children were adopting Dutch ways—even in speech. Later on in the story was an account of a Pilgrim school in America where the master was trying to eliminate the Dutch words from the children's speech. Each morning he placed a little metal object on his desk. The first child who used a Dutch word was given this metal button. It was considered a disgrace to have it; so the child listened carefully to the speech of his schoolmates. He could pass it to the first one he caught using the forbidden words. The child who held the button at the end of the day was given a flogging. The children liked this story very much and several of them said, "Oh, I wish we could do something like that." One boy said, "But no one here speaks Dutch."

Then I said, "Well, we don't always use good English. Sometimes we make mistakes." They asked if I would give a button to the first one who made a mistake. I found a large, green coat button in my desk and we began the game as soon as I heard the first mistake. The children watched their own speech very carefully and the speech of the others. No one resented receiving the button. Of course we omitted the flogging. The child just left the button on his desk over-night. This even carried over into the homes. Soon whole families were playing "pass the button." One mother said, "I'm glad. I didn't realize how careless we were getting."

One mother told me she spent a very uneasy half hour. She had a caller whose speech was very careless. The mother said her small son sat listening to the conversation. Every time the visitor made an error the boy's eyes went to the family button which lay on a near-by table. Of course being a well-trained boy he only glanced at the button, but the mother was afraid he might want to include the visitor in the game.

The little device which arose from a school-room story did more to make the children speech-conscious than anything we had tried; yet it did not detract in any way from the children's fluent expression.

[25] Reported by Gladys Penton, Grant School, Watertown, S. D.

XIX

PROVIDING INSTRUCTIONAL EQUIPMENT

SCHOOL BUILDINGS need to be as safe, sanitary, and sense-appealing as modern architecture and school budgets permit. But the essential education of youth comes from their contact with creative teachers and dynamic instructional materials. An excellent teacher as well as one who is mediocre needs tools, such as dictionaries, reference books, anthologies of literature, individual classics, language-composition texts, and practice materials in the English classroom. Evidence of the creativeness of a teacher is not that she teaches without books but that she so teaches with books that her pupils develop independent study habits essential to continuous self-education.

CRITERIA FOR SELECTION

Individual teachers and book selection committees have found the criteria which follow helpful in selecting language-composition books, anthologies of literature, and practice material.

CHECK-LIST OF QUESTIONS FOR CONSIDERATION IN THE SELECTION OF A TEXTBOOK IN COMPOSITION [1]

Directions: 1. Place a "3" on the line in front of each item to which you can answer an unqualified "yes" for the textbook under consideration.

2. Place a "o" before each question to which you must answer an unqualified "no."

3. If your answer is qualified but nearer "no" than "yes," put a "1" in front of the item.

4. If your answer is qualified but nearer "yes" than "no," put a "2" in front of the question.

5. Total your points within each of the sections indicated by the roman

[1] Prepared by a Committee of the National Council of Teachers of English, Dora V. Smith, chairman. Reprinted by permission of *The English Journal.*

numerals. These figures may then be compared with the ratings of other textbooks for the same section. It is the consensus among members of the committee that no textbooks should be considered for adoption which average less than 2 on the points starred.

—I. *The Viewpoint of the Textbook*

— * A. Does the author recognize that composition is a social activity?

— * B. Does he recognize the uses of composition in everyday life?

—II. *The Author's Style*

— A. Is the style stimulating, suggestive, vigorous?

— B. Is there sufficient concrete detail to develop general concepts?

— * C. Is the exposition clear, accurate, and simple enough to be readily understood?

— * D. Is it suited to the age of child for whom it is intended?

— E. Does it address itself to the pupil?

—III. *Proportion and Organization*

— A. Does the author give adequate attention to

— 1. The motivation of expression?

— 2. The stimulation of interests and ideas?

— 3. The selection and organization of ideas?

— 4. The development of power of expression?

— 5. The habituation of correctness in speech and writing?

— * B. Does the author give to oral composition the proportion of time dictated by its prominence in the activities of everyday life?

— * C. Does he give to letter-writing the emphasis demanded by its practical importance in everyday life?

— D. Does the author stress the subordinate and contributory function of correctness in speech and writing in relation to the larger purpose of expression?

— E. Does the author organize his material into sectional divisions large enough to stimulate interest, to give perspective, and to promote well-rounded growth?

— * F. Does the author organize his materials in such a way as to

— 1. Care for pupils of varying abilities and interests within the same class?

— 2. Make both pupil and teacher conscious of the ends toward which they are working and the degree of progress attained?

— 3. Provide for flexibility in adapting the assignment to to the individual classroom situation?

—IV. *Motivation*

— * A. Does the author create in the pupil the desire to express himself?

— * B. Does he identify the composition work of the classroom with the expressional activities of life both within and without the school?

— C. Does he keep before the pupil the purpose of each activity in which he is asked to engage?

— D. Does the author stimulate observation and interest in a wide variety of subjects?

— E. Does he arouse the initiative and originality of the student?

— * F. Does he emphasize the importance of thinking?

— * G. Does he use the social purposes of composition to encourage not merely correct but clear, vigorous, and interesting expression?

— H. Does he identify his composition activities with actual experience instead of merely setting up series of topics for "theme writing"?

— I. Does he promote additional activities among superior pupils?

— * J. Does he promote progress by offering numerous means of self-criticism:

— 1. By providing standards for the evaluation of one's own writing?

— 2. By offering bases of comparison with the work of others?

— 3. By furnishing means of comparison with earlier achievement?

— K. Does he throw the responsibility for progress upon the pupil himself?

—V. *Activities Proposed*

— A. General characteristics:

— * 1. Are the activities suggested by the author suitable and interesting to the grades for which they are recommended?

— 2. Are they representative of a wide range of experience and thought?

— 3. Are there projects suggested which allow for class, group, and individual activity?

— 4. Are these projects timely, interest-arousing, and thought-provoking?

— * 5. Is sufficient direction given for the execution of these projects?

—   6. Are the tasks specific, not general?

—   7. Are the illustrations pertinent to the pupils' experience?

— * 8. Does the book contain sufficient practice material for applying principles developed?

—   9. Are the practice materials so graded in difficulty as to be easily adaptable to the needs of groups and individuals of varying ability?

— 10. Does the book offer a wide range of choice in suggestions for assignments?

— 11. Does the author stimulate creative writing among pupils capable of more literary achievements?

— 12. Is there plentiful correlation of activities with those of other subjects of study?

— * B. Does the text furnish adequate experience in the following language activities of everyday life?

— Announcements

— Book reviewing

— Conversation

— Creative writing

— Current event discussion

— Debating

— Dictionary, use of

— Explaining or giving instructions

— Gathering and reporting information

— Informal discussion

— Interviewing

— Letter-writing

— Magazine materials, use of

— Note-taking

— Public discussion according to parliamentary form

— Reporting speeches or committee findings

— Speech-making

— Story-telling

— C. Does the author offer sufficient aids and devices for

— * 1. Development of vocabulary and use of the dictionary

—   2. Development of feeling for phrasing

— * 3. Development of effectiveness in sentence structure

—   4. Selecting and organizing material before writing

—   5. Outlining

— * 6. Development of well-rounded paragraphs

—   7. Making of skilful transitions

—   8. Effectiveness of beginning and ending

—VI. *The Mechanics of Expression*

    — A. Grammar:

        — * 1. Is the grammatical material motivated by constant relation to actual language situations?

        — 2. Does the author provide for measurement and stimulation of progress both for the individual and for the class?

        — * 3. Does he provide for individual diagnosis and remedial work?

        — * 4. Is there large stress upon sentence sense and sentence structure with repeated review of the topic?

        — * 5. Is the content chosen on the basis of function in accord with the findings of scientific investigations:

           — *a*) With relatively large stress on points of difficulty such as verb and pronoun?

           — *b*) With recognition of points of debatable usage?

           — *c*) With emphasis upon function not classification (i.e., Are classifications of adverbs into adverbs of degree, cause, manner, etc., omitted, and the use of the adverb versus the adjective stressed? Is power to express thought relationships with exactness made more important than ability to label sentences as compound or complex?)

        — * 6. Is there ample provision for repeated drill upon a few specific points instead of inadequate drill upon many non-essentials?

        — 7. Is the program cumulative with adequate provision throughout for review?

    — B. Capitalization and punctuation:

        — * 1. Are the requirements limited to matters of usage in our own day as revealed by the report of the Minimum Essentials Committee of the National Council of Teachers of English?

        — * 2. Are distinctions between required and optional usage clearly made?

        — * 3. Are ample drill materials provided?

        — 4. Is the program cumulative with adequate provision for review?

        — 5. Does the author provide for measurement and stimulation of progress both for the individual and for the class?

— * 6. Does he provide for individual diagnosis and remedial work?

— 7. Is there constant provision for use of the skills mastered, in actual writing situations?

—VII. *Physical Format*

— A. Mechanical make-up:

— 1. Is the textbook a good standard size, easily handled by the pupil? (i.e. roughly 5½ inches x 7¾ inches)

— 2. Is it easily opened and durable in binding?

— 3. Has the paper a non-gloss surface?

— 4. Is it heavy enough to insure that print on the obverse side shall not show through?

— 5. Are the margins wide enough to insure an uncrowded page?

— 6. Is the page well-spaced so as to emphasize outstanding points?

— 7. Are the lines not more than 90 mm. long?

— 8. Is the type dark, plain, and distinct—not less than 10 point?

— B. Attractiveness and effectiveness of form:

— 1. Is the book attractive in appearance?

— 2. Has it appropriate and effective illustrations?

— 3. Has it graphic devices for aid in outlining, letter form, word derivations, etc.?

— 4. Are the chapter and section captions clear, brief, well-spaced, interesting?

— 5. Has the book a usable index?

— 6. Has it a usable table of contents?

— 7. Has it a clear and impelling preface, giving the purpose of the author and suggestions for use?

C. Does the copyright date (issued or revised) suggest that the book is recent enough to reflect modern tendencies in teaching?

CRITERIA FOR SELECTING A GRADED SERIES OF ANTHOLOGIES OF LITERATURE

— 1. Are all aspects of a literary experience provided for?

— 2. Are several repetitions of the same literary experience given in new situations and with fresh literature so that the student may practice with satisfaction the reading method appropriate to that experience?

— 3. Is the pupil helped to mature through stories of realistic folk literature into stories of modern science? From imaginative hero stories to realistic biography? From light verse to great poetry?

From short stories to long fiction? From one act to five act plays?

— 4. Is provision made for pupils to understand at first simple social situations and gradually more complex ones?

— 5. Has provision been made in every book in the series for three levels of literary material: (1) that which the teacher presents, (2) that in the reading of which she guides the pupil, and (3) that which the pupils can read for themselves without the teacher's direction?

— 6. To what extent will using the series aid him in finding in the school library, the public library, and the bookshops books of value to him personally?

— 7. Will using this series encourage him to apply his reading and library skills in providing himself with literary materials?

— 8. Will he acquire an intimate knowledge of some artist's works and an extensive knowledge of many others?

— 9. Is provision made that the child will feel the desire to guide his own reading?

— 10. Is the literature program as set up helpful to the child in finding the creative experience that will guide his avocation or vocation?

— 11. Does it provide practice in the desirable library skills developed in each grade?

— 12. To what extent will the series help the pupil to use his leisure time for reading?

— 13. Will use of the series make the pupil care enough for books to own some for himself? To use carefully the books he borrows?

— 14. Will the literature program as set up make him more sensitive to real experiences?

— 15. Will the literature program as set up influence him to choose wisely among the mass of modern literature that clamor for his attention?

— 16. Does the series provide content and activities suitable for slow, average, and bright pupils? If not, does it provide adequately for the type of pupil for whom it purports to be written?

CRITERIA FOR SELECTING PRACTICE MATERIAL IN READING, USAGE, SPEECH IMPROVEMENT

— 1. Will the use of this material tend to center the pupil's attention upon a desirable aspect of the subject?

— 2. Are directions to pupils clearly and definitely stated? Are sample exercises given to demonstrate the directions?

— 3. Does the material focus the pupils' attention on a sufficiently small unit at a time?

— 4. Does the material utilize all relevant motives for learning the associations being fixed?

— 5. Does the material give diffuse practice in skills previously learned while it gives intensive drill on a new item?

— 6. Is the material so arranged as to be self-administering and self-corrective by the individual pupil?

— 7. Are the associations being drilled upon important enough to warrant their being made automatic?

— 8. Are check tests included so as to help the pupil see how near he is to the goals set up in the unit of learning and to help him diagnose where he needs to straighten out his facts and improve his skills?

— 9. Is the material selected or written so as to furnish a challenge to the type or types of learner (slow, average, bright) for whom it was prepared?

—10. Does the material suggest applications of the skills, in school and out-of-school situations?

UTILIZATION OF ON-HAND EQUIPMENT

As soon as educational measurement became more accurate and more diagnostic, teachers had evidence for their contention that the boys and girls now attending school are not like those of a generation ago. There are more kinds of pupils coming to school and remaining in school until they reach eighteen or more years of age. Educational research has succeeded in analyzing the factors that condition or interfere with normal learning. Scientific studies of learning difficulties and faulty reactions of pupils have made diagnostic teaching possible.

Textbook writers and their publishers have developed experience-centered books for all kinds of pupils now in school. The last ten years, in fact, have seen remarkable progress in the production of instructional materials satisfying the criteria listed in a previous section of this chapter. Depression budgets, however, have reduced normal buying, leaving many schools with the theory of differentiation written into their courses of study but without the books to put the theory into actual classroom use.

While waiting for increased budgets to provide adequate instructional materials, teachers are trying to utilize what equipment they have on hand. In making this adjustment, they are following one or more of the plans listed below:

(1) Using with bright pupils only the on-hand classics too difficult for slow-learning pupils

(2) Transferring from one school to another left-overs which will complete sets without purchasing more copies of outmoded texts

(3) Rotating sets of books from one classroom to another. (For

example, while one class is engaged with the unit "Adventures on the High Seas," a second is busy with "Answers to Thousands of Why's," and a third with "Faithful Friends." Each child experiences the three units during a term but only one-third the number of *each* title is needed to supply all pupils.)

(4) Providing classroom libraries of two or three copies each of several different titles

(5) Cutting up old texts for sections which are still valuable for specific purposes (Certain sentence and paragraph material in some of the very old-style textbooks can be cut up for practice material, placed in marked folders, and distributed to pupils as needed. Motivation and supervision of the learner is, in these cases, supplied by the teacher and not by the author of the textbook.)

(6) Purchasing at once small quantities of new materials instead of reordering small quantities of out-moded books to keep a total large enough to supply every pupil simultaneously with the same texts

(7) Spreading what funds are available among the different kinds of instructional material so that every group of pupils in a given school may have the use of some suitable material

(8) Planning over a cycle of years so that as quickly as possible all book needs can be somewhat adequately supplied

(9) Trading in old texts for the experience-centered texts now available in the literature and in the language-composition fields.

APPRAISAL OF PUPIL-TEACHER USE OF EQUIPMENT

Whether or not pupils buy their books, they should learn to take care of them. That teachers and pupils using free textbooks are responsible for the physical condition of the books is a routine fact known to school authorities and to taxpayers. But far more important than physical care of equipment is its intelligent use in furthering learning.

If, as in the case of most textbooks nowadays, a book has been prepared based on classroom situations, teachers and pupils will gain from studying the author's organization of experience, the typographical aids, the study guides, the suggested bibliographies. To say that a teacher "follows" a textbook may be a compliment if the book as written is adapted to her pupils. Merely to skip around in a book or to paraphrase the assignment does not necessarily increase its learning value to the pupils. Some such questions as the following may serve as appraisal of (1) the teacher's use of equipment, and (2) the pupil's use of it.

APPRAISAL OF TEACHER'S USE OF EQUIPMENT

— 1. Did the teacher understand the author's philosophy and his organization?

— 2. Did the teacher give her pupils an opportunity to *like* the book as a book?

— 3. Did the teacher select the section of the book most relevant to her pupils when she introduced the book to them?

— 4. Did the teacher choose with awareness of her pupils' interests and capacities among the assignments suggested in the book?

— 5. Did she let her pupils make progress enough with the book in the introductory period to establish a favorable attitude toward it and toward the unit it was launching?

— 6. Did the teacher observe and record, if necessary, which assignments were effective and which ineffective with her pupils?

— 7. Did the teacher respond creatively to the book so as to develop with her brightest pupils new experiences, perhaps even some not explicitly stated in the text?

— 8. Did the teacher stimulate each pupil to take care of the book so that other boys and girls who will use it may find it as clean and as attractive as he did?

APPRAISAL OF PUPIL'S USE OF EQUIPMENT

— 1. Did the pupil respond attentively to the book when he was introduced to it?

— 2. Did he find his intellectual and emotional capacities directed toward a worth-while learning?

— 3. Was a favorable attitude toward *English* as a school subject generated by the book?

— 4. Did he follow up any of the suggestions for individual reading or for individual creative projects?

— 5. Did his use of this book help him to grow in his power of self-education?

[Note: Picture, map, or work-book might be substituted for the word *book* in the above questions for appraisal.]

CONCLUSION

Present Status of English as Experience

PRESENT STATUS OF ENGLISH AS EXPERIENCE

What makes this school resemble our heart's desire?
Is it not here we find what we all require?
Although some call it education
It's just your accent on youth.[1]

ENGLISH is now being served *à la carte* in thousands of class-rooms throughout this country. Dozens of palatable, digestible, and nutritious combinations are offered. What any individual selects depends upon his needs, interests, and capacity at the time and upon the degree of self-direction, discrimination, and self-appraisal he has developed through his experience in English. Naturally, since nothing known to be injurious or detrimental is presented, normal growth is stimulated by this responsible freedom to choose.

This *differentiation* in English had to come. With the enforcement of compulsory attendance laws, all kinds of children are attending school and are staying on for twelve to fourteen years. Scientific measurements are providing incontrovertible evidence of the range and kinds of individual differences. Research investigations are revealing the frequency of use and difficulty of learning the essentials in English usage. So too vocabulary, sentence structure, and reading are being analyzed, thus making possible diagnostic teaching.

With the disclosure in statistical studies of school enrollment that pupils remain for several years, the essentials are being graded with respect to the learning capacity of the children instead of being crowded into the first six years of their school life. Likewise, studies of where the pupils go after graduation are influencing the secondary schools to prepare their students for life, not just for college. Fortunately the present entrance re-

[1] Last four lines of words written by a tenth-grade pupil (Forest Park High School, Baltimore, Maryland) to fit a modern melody and sung during an American Educational Week Assembly.

quirements of most colleges are being stated in such broad and congenial terms that every pupil, whether bound for college or not, will be getting a sound general education for life if he attains the goals.[2]

Differentiation is further made possible by the publication of many kinds of instructional materials. There are books now for the slow learner and for the gifted in addition to books which satisfy the interest of all types of pupils between these two extremes. Likewise, with the publication of diagnostic testing and instructional materials in reading, spelling, and current English usage, it is becoming practical for teachers everywhere to attempt *test-determined teaching* of the skills fundamental to using English as a tool and as a source of recreation.

Clinical methods of testing and of teaching are being developed for cases of special emotional, intellectual, or physical disabilities.

Experimental evidence of the value of visual aids in teaching

---

[2] Charles Swain Thomas, etc. *Examining the Examination in English* (Harvard University Press, 1931), pp. 184, 185, 186. (1) *Attitude toward reading*— "It is by helping the student to interpret verbal symbols and to transfer the content of books to his fund of living experience, that the school aims to arouse his interest in reading and to develop the habit of going to books for whatever real value they have to offer him." (2) *Attitude toward composition*—"It is a fundamental purpose of courses in English, though by no means confined to such courses, to stimulate the student's interest in observing, thinking, talking, and reading, so that he will become increasingly aware of the meaning and possible value to other people of his own experiences and ideas, and will find himself rich in material that he is eager to communicate. Moreover, his English teachers, often with the coöperation of other departments, must familiarize him with the means of obtaining material on subjects that demand something in the way of reference work. They must make sure that he understands the use of common reference books and catalogues; that he knows how to use tables of contents and indices; and that he can look through a volume until he finds the material he needs, and then, if desirable, take notes according to some intelligent method." (3) *Respect for language as a medium*—"It is the aim of his English courses to inspire in the student a real respect for the medium he must use, language—words or vocabulary, punctuation, and fundamental language patterns or constructions." (4) *Special aims in literary study*—"It is essential that the student should form the habit of thinking about what he reads—of defining and challenging ideas, of grasping cause-and-effect relationships, of comparing the characters and situations of different books with each other and with those known in actual life." (5) *Special aims in the study of composition*— "That the student should form the habit of doing concentrated work on his first draft and yet of maintaining a tentativeness of attitude that will make him willing and even eager to revise when he finds it necessary, is about all that can be stated as a general aim."

all phases of English is encouraging schools to utilize motion, sound, and still pictures along with first-hand observation on excursions to business, industrial, historical, geographical, and literary points of educational interest.

The learning activities in the present-day, experience-centered curriculum are stimulating boys and girls to *integrate* their experiences. Through purpose, activity, or situation, students are feeling the unity of their in-school and out-of-school life uses of language. Letter-writing in school, for example, is not of a different sort from letter-writing outside of school. The actual content and purpose in all expressional phases of the curriculum have as potent motivation and emotional tone as do the situations in adult life. The one difference is that the student has the advantage of experiencing communication when and where a dynamic teacher can help him to learn how to speak and to write effectively and correctly.

The grading system in most places is also undergoing significant change. Tests that teach (See pages 309–318.) pupils why their answers are right or wrong are replacing examinations that give only a total numerical or letter grade. What pupils write, too, is being scored so that the writer is aided in revising his paper for effectiveness and correctness. Teachers are reading their pupils' papers with the expectation of finding an experience worth communicating, of being attracted by the flavor of the writing, of being satisfied with the organization of ideas. If the paper is lacking in any of these respects, the teacher-reader in conference with the pupil or by notation in the margin helps the writer to select, arrange, and express again his ideas so that both writer and reader will feel satisfaction in this exchange of ideas. Personality as reflected in power to use language in social situations is receiving attention in the observational data being recorded by teachers of English. In fact, the cumulative records on file in many schools today carry, in addition to a list of books read by the pupil at home, information on all these factors affecting learning: scholastic attainment, mental ability, health, personal characteristics including emotional stability and unusual talents, physical history, family conditions, chronological age, work habits, acceleration or retardation in school, attendance, rate of learning, and responsiveness to class morale.

Courses of study over the country are retaining most of *the* classics familiar to teachers and pupils of a generation ago. The difference lies in the method of treating these favorites. Pupils having reading difficulties share in these books only through oral reading by the teacher and interpretative discussion by the group of those aspects of the literature which they can experience at their level of intellectual and emotional maturity. Frequent use is being made of *contemporary* classics that may be compared with the older books because of similar theme. Photoplays, radio, and periodical literature are added for interpretation of the essence of human experience with which the unit is concerned.

Perhaps the most marked change is seen, however, in the treatment of language experiences. Grammar is being learned without tears as instrumental to purposeful communication. Grammar, as it is being taught today, is serviceable and hence reasonable even to the boys and girls who lack a flair for language. Because research has shown which essentials are causing the greatest number of errors in speech and in writing, pupils and teachers are armed with the technique for mastering these essentials through habit-forming practice at the specific point where the individual pupil's language falls below the level of acceptable colloquial English.

In this continuous process of adjusting the English curriculum to a changing school population, a changing society, and a changing philosophy of education, there is found no lack of definite goals. Certain fundamental experiences are common to every generation of school children. These experiences are what constitute the course of study. The relative potency of any experience for learning, however, does differ from one group of pupils to another. So, too, does the learner's difficulty in mastering the techniques required to share satisfactorily the experience. Naturally, alert teachers everywhere are using with a particular group of pupils whatever experience has greatest motivation and emotional tone for those pupils.

The flexibility of the experience-centered units in the modern curriculum is an asset to both teachers and learners. Teachers are teaching; students are learning. Test results everywhere are indicating improvement in control of the reading and language skills essential to occupational efficiency and recreational enjoyment. Taste as shown in pupils' choice of books, photoplays, and radio programs is more discriminating. Needless to say, there is much yet to be accomplished.

Reviewing the varied approaches to a literary experience, to creative and to practical communication, and to corrective teaching recorded in this volume—in addition to the courses of study listed in Appendix A—reveals the fact that all that was worthwhile in the traditional curriculum has been absorbed in the new experience-centered curriculum. In differentiating the present-day curriculum to suit the needs, interests, and capacities of individual pupils in a world characterized by speed, specialization, and change, teachers of English have accepted the challenge of democracy, ably expressed by A.E.: "A nation is cultivated only in so far as the average man, not the exceptional person, is cultivated and has knowledge of the thought, imagination and intellectual history of his nation" [3]—and it may be added and remembered, of the national and racial stocks from which the people have sprung.

[3] A.E., *op. cit.*, p. 381.

APPENDIX

APPENDIX A

ENGLISH COURSES OF STUDY PUBLISHED SINCE 1932

In searching for experience-centered courses of study published since 1932, the committee had in mind the following criteria developed from their careful study of *An Experience Curriculum in English*.[1] Local committees may find it useful to apply these standards in appraising their own or other courses. Immediately following the criteria, is a list of the courses of study examined by this committee.

CRITERIA FOR APPRAISING EXPERIENCE-CENTERED COURSES OF STUDY

— I. *Well-Selected Experiences*
- — A. Provide for the needs, capacities, and interests of learners.
- — B. Prepare adequately for recreational needs—present and immediate future—of pupils.
- — C. Prepare for general occupational efficiency.
- — D. Prepare for active participation in democracy.
- — E. Sample adequately all curricular and extracurricular activities in pupils' school life.

— II. *Well-Balanced Program of Experiences*
- — A. Provide for first-hand experiences whenever possible.
- — B. Utilize experiences through books and periodicals.
- — C. Direct experiences through photoplays and legitimate drama.
- — D. Direct experiences through the radio.
- — E. Utilize experiences through museums.

— III. *Orderly Arrangement of Experiences*
- — A. Arrange according to maturity of pupils.
- — B. Make flexible enough to capitalize unusual motivation in personal or community life at a specific time.
- — C. Build essential skills cumulatively.

— IV. *Remedial or Corrective Teaching*
- — A. Provide for diagnostic testing and teaching of essential skills in reading and in oral and written expression.
- — B. Allow both teacher and pupil time for this phase of course.
- — C. Provide for application of skills mastered.

[1] W. W. Hatfield, and others (New York, D. Appleton-Century Co., 1935).

— **V. Creative Experiences**

— A. Awaken pupils' interest in their own experience.

— B. Help pupils to interpret the personal and social meanings in their experience.

— C. Develop pupils' capacity to value experience for its own sake.[2]

—D. Amplify the range of pupils' experience.[2]

— E. Improve the quality of pupils' experience by encouraging more discriminating experience.[2]

— F. Aid pupils to fit words to the details of experience.[2]

—G. Help pupils discover suitable forms for the transfer of experience to others.[2]

— **VI. Democratic Process of Building Course a Creative Experience to Teachers, Supervisors, and Pupils**

— A. Survey (or utilize available survey data) the needs in English of pupils and of adults.

— B. State objectives in terms of pupils' present and immediate future needs and of social sanctions.

— C. Build units based upon experience.

—D. Try out units in test-controlled situations in actual classroom.

— E. Examine all available instructional equipment.

— F. Utilize expert advice and scientific research findings where relevant.

— G. Outline the procedures used in building the course so that new teachers may understand its philosophy and contribute to its continuous adaptation to changing conditions.

—H. Prepare instructional tests and cumulative records for measuring pupil growth in terms of adopted objectives.

COURSES OF STUDY

Aberdeen, S. D., *Course of Study in Reading—Grades 1–6*, 1935–6.

Alleghany County, Cumberland, Maryland, *Course of Study, Elementary Schools, English, Grades 4, 5, 6*, 1935.

Course of Study, Secondary Schools, Literature (tentative), *Grades 9–12*.

Amarillo, Texas, Public Schools, *Language Arts, A Tentative Course of Study for Grades 4, 5, 6*, 1937.

Language Arts, A Tentative Course of Study for Sophomore, Junior, Senior Grade Levels, 1937.

A Tentative Course of Study in the Language Arts for High School, 1937.

Amsterdam, New York, *Course of Study in Speaking and Writing English, Primary Grades*, Bulletin No. 7, 1936.

Anne Arundel County, Maryland, *Reading, Grades 5, 6, 7*, 1933.

Atlanta, Georgia, *Junior High School English*, 1938.

Course of Study in English for Senior High Schools, 1937.

[2] Hatfield, *op. cit.*, pp. 112–113.

Austin, Texas, *High School English,* Bulletin No. 355, Vol. 12, No. 3, 1936.

Baltimore City, Maryland, *Course of Study in English, Grades 7–12,* 1932.

English Units and Standards of Attainment, Grades 7–12, 1934.

Baltimore County, Maryland, *Course of Study in English* (Warwick & York, 1937).

Part I, Grades I, II, III.

Part II, Grades IV, V, VI.

Part III, Grades VII, VIII, IX.

Berkeley, California, *Reading, Grades 3, 4,* 1936.

Cabarrus County, Concord, N.C., *Language Arts, Oral and Written Language, Reading, Writing, and Spelling,* 1936–37.

California State Department of Education, Bulletin No. 11, 1934.

Effective Use of Library Facilities in Rural Schools.

Suggested Course of Study in Oral and Written Expression for Elementary Schools, 1933.

Chicago Public Schools, *A Course of Study in English Literature, Grades 11–12,* 1933.

Cincinnati, Ohio, *Tentative Course of Study in Oral and Written Expression, Grades 7–9,* 1936.

Cleveland, Ohio, *Reading for Ungraded Group, Senior High School,* 1936.

Dallas, Texas, *Public Speaking, Outline for Teachers.*

Essentials in Language Arts for Grades 5, 6, 7, 1938.

Des Moines, Iowa, *Course of Study in Speech and Dramatics.*

Vol. I, *Speech,* 1936.

Vol. II, *Dramatics,* 1936.

Detroit, Michigan, *Course of Study in Speech Improvement,* 1933.

Literature Methods and Materials for Slow-Learning Groups, 1934.

East Greenwich, Rhode Island, *Guide Units in English, Grades I–III,* 1938.

Guide Units in English, Grades IV–VI, 1938.

Erie, Pennsylvania, *Course of Study in English for Secondary Schools,* 1938.

Flint, Michigan, *Basic Course of Study in English,* 1937.

Senior English, 1937.

Fort Smith, Arkansas, *Libraries,* 1937.

Fort Worth, Texas, *Language Arts, Tentative Course of Study from Kindergarten to Grade Six,* 1935.

Fresno, California, *Course of Study in English for Senior High School: Functional English Including Composition, Grammar, and Rhetoric and Mechanics of Writing,* 1933.

Tentative Language Arts Program, Oral Communication, Grades 1–6, 1938.

Georgia (state), *Program for the Improvement of Instruction,* Bulletin No. 2 (Atlanta, Georgia, 1937).

Hawaii, *English Expression and Literature Materials, Intermediate Grades,* 1935.

Indiana (state), *The Language Arts: Reading, Grades One to Six,* 1935.

Indianapolis, Indiana, *Course of Study in English, Junior High Schools, Grades 7, 8, 9,* 1934.

Inland Empire Council of Teachers of English, *Differentiated Course of Study in English* (Mrs. W. A. Olson, Moscow, Idaho), 1938.

Iowa (state), *Speech Training for Primary Grades* (Des Moines, 1938).

Ironwood, Michigan, *Suggestions and Guide for Teachers of Non-Reading and Transition Groups, Kindergarten,* 1937.

Kansas (state), *Course of Study for High Schools, Part 2, Handbook for Teachers of English, Junior and Senior High Schools* (Topeka, 1935, out of print).

Lakewood, Ohio, *Tentative Course of Study for Junior High Schools, Grade VIIIB,* 1933.

Tentative Course of Study for Senior High School, 1933.

Little Rock, Arkansas, *Speech Arts and Public Speaking for Senior High School,* 1938.

Los Angeles, California, *Reading and Phonics, First and Second Grades,* 1933.

Los Angeles County, *Some Classroom Procedures in the Teaching of Reading in Junior and Senior High Schools,* 1937.

Reading for Pleasure, A Tentative Outline for American Literature, 1937.

Oral English, 1937.

Louisiana (state), *Course of Study in English,* Bulletin No. 307 (Baton Rouge, 1935).

Madison, Wisconsin, *Language Curriculum, Part I, A Study of Language Expression,* 1932.

Manhattan, Kansas, *Course of Study for English Composition and Literature for the Elementary Schools, Grades 1–6,* 1932.

Maryland (state), *The Teaching of Oral and Written English in Maryland High Schools* (E. C. Fontaine), 1939.

Massachusetts (state), *Course of Study in English for Junior High Schools,* 1933.

Memphis, Tennessee, *Course of Study in English, Grades 7, 8, 9,* 1937.

Minneapolis, Minnesota, *Course of Study in English Composition, Grammar, and Literature, Grades VII, VIII, IX,* 1935.

Course of Study in English Composition, Correct Usage, and Spelling, Kindergarten, Grades I–VI, 1935.

Course of Study in Senior High Literature, Grades 10, 11, 12, 1935.

Minnesota (state), *The Secondary School Curriculum: English for Junior High School Period,* 1933.

English for Senior High School Period, 1933.

Preliminary Outline of a Course of Study in Fundamentals of Speech for Minnesota High Schools, 1935.

Mishawaka, Indiana, *Course of Study for Grades I, II, III,* 1936.

Montclair, New Jersey, *Tentative Course of Study, 5th & 6th Grades,* revised 1935.

Montgomery County, Maryland, *Literature, I–III,* 1932.

Language-Composition, I–VI, 1932.

Muncie, Indiana, *Tentative Course of Study in English Composition, Junior High School English, Grades 7–9,* 1934.

Newark, New Jersey, *Course of Study in High School English, Grades IX–XII,* revised, 1932.

New Brunswick, New Jersey, *Program for Language Arts Curriculum Construction.*

New Hampshire (state), *Program of Studies Recommended for the Public Schools of New Hampshire, Part II—English, Grades VII to XII,* 1938.

New Kensington, Pennsylvania, *A Coöperative Project in Curriculum Making by the Teachers of New Kensington Junior High School,* 1937.

Course of Study in Reading for the Junior High School, 1937.

New Mexico, *Reading.*

Newtonville, Massachusetts, *Tentative Course of Study in Language, Grades 1–6*, 1935.

New York (state), *Syllabus in English for Secondary Schools, Grades 7–12*, 1934.

New York City, New York, *Course of Study in Composition, Elementary and Junior High Schools, Grades 7A–9B*, 1934.

Abraham Lincoln High School, *Revised and Complete Syllabus, Department of English and Speech* (M. Nurnberg, A. C. Wright, F. Mantinband), 1938.

Seward Park High School, *First Draft of Course of Study for Slow Learners in English* (J. Block).

Oklahoma (state), *Course of Study in Language Arts for Elementary Grades*, 1938.

Oklahoma City, Oklahoma, *English, Grades 1–6*, 1936–37.

Reading, Grades 1–6, 1936–37.

Course of Study, English, Junior and Senior High Schools, Seventh to Twelfth Grades, revised edition, 1934.

Oregon (state), *Language and Penmanship, Elementary Schools* (Salem, 1937).

Elementary School Reading, 1932.

Pasadena, California, *Course of Study for English, Junior College Composition*, 1933.

Language Arts in the Elementary School Curriculum, 1936.

Pennsylvania (state), *Course of Study in Journalism for Secondary Schools*, 1935.

Perth Amboy, New Jersey, *Tentative Course of Study in English, Kindergarten, Grades 1, 2, 3*, 1935.

Philadelphia, Pennsylvania, *Libraries*, 1938.

Prevocational Course in Junior High Schools, 1936.

Providence, Rhode Island, *Remedial Work for Reading Handicaps, Reports of Progress, Elementary and Secondary Grades*, 1936.

Junior High School English, 1934.

Raleigh, North Carolina, *Course of Study in English, Grades VII–XII, Part I, Language-Composition, Part II, Reading*, 1937.

Rochester, New York, *Course of Study, Objective I, Language Arts and the Tools of Learning, Promotional Unit, Kindergarten-Primary*, 1937.

Library Instruction in Rochester High Schools, 1937.

Saginaw, Michigan, *English Materials to Try Out and Revise, Grades 7–12*, 1938.

St. Paul, Minnesota, Department of Education, Bulletin No. A–1, *English for Junior High School Period*, 1933.

English Outline, Technical, Sixth, Seventh, and Eighth Grades.

San Antonio, Texas, *Library Procedures*, 1935.

English Outline, Technical, Sixth, Seventh, Eighth Grades.

San Jose, California, *Reading*, 1938.

San Mateo County, California, *The English Curriculum: Language, Spelling, Handwriting, Reading, Part Two, Reading in an Experience Program*, 1938.

Santa Barbara County, California, *Course of Study in Reading, Part I*, 1932.

Seattle, Washington, *Junior and Senior High School Literature Course of Study*, 1935.

Trends and Viewpoints in the Teaching of Literature, 1934.

South Bend, Indiana, *Suggestive English Guide for Primary Grades*, 1934.

Texas (state), *The English Teacher and Class at Work*, 1936.

Virginia, *Tentative Selection of Readings in English for Core Curriculum, Grades 8–11,* 1935.

Washington (state), *An Integrated Course of Study in Speech,* 1937.

Watertown, New York, *Curriculum Guidance in the Use of Books and Libraries,* 1934.

West Virginia (state), *Reading,* 1937.

Wicomico County, Maryland, *A Part of a Tentative Course of Study for First Year High English,* 1936.

Winona, Minnesota, *Introduction to the Reading Curriculum,* 1938.

Wood County, Ohio, *Phonics and Speech Correction,* 1938.

Wyoming (state), *Course of Study for Elementary Schools: Primary Reading for Grades 1, 2, 3,* 1937.

In many cities, counties, and states, the curriculum revision program has two steps: (1) issuing general bulletins and (2) developing courses of study in specific fields. By consulting *The Education Index,* the reader can locate quickly the departments of education which have such published materials; for example, *Curriculum Materials* (Philosophy of education, scope and sequence of learning experiences, problems, activities, and instructional materials, unit of work suggestions); *Intermediate Level,* issued by County of Santa Barbara Department of Education, Bulletin No. 13; *Coöperative Curriculum Revision* published by Wilmington Public Schools, Wilmington, Delaware, 1935; and *Professional Pointers,* Public Schools, Atlanta, Georgia, 1938.

Some commendable courses such as those in Denver and in Detroit were published prior to 1932, the initial date of this selected bibliography. Again, the reader can locate these by using *The Education Index.*

APPENDIX B

A SELECTED BIBLIOGRAPHY ON THE TEACHING OF ENGLISH

Including Titles Published Since 1932 [1]

To prepare a selected bibliography of a given date is to be forced to leave out books which, from the point of view of their continuous vitality and inspiration, should be included. Such a group of books—all pioneers in the "experience idea"—include the following perennials:

AMES, Van Meter, *Aesthetics of the Novel* (University of Chicago Press, 1928).

BENNETT, Arnold, *Literary Taste and How to Form It* (Doubleday, Doran, 1918).

BLAISDELL, Thomas C., *Ways to Teach English* (Doubleday, Doran, 1930).

COX, Sidney, *The Teaching of English: Avowals and Ventures* (Harpers, 1928).

EASTMAN, Max, *The Enjoyment of Poetry* (Scribner, 1913).

FRIES, HANFORD, and STEEVES, *The Teaching of Literature* (Silver, Burdett, 1926).

HUBBELL, Jay B., *The Enjoyment of Literature* (Macmillan, 1929).

LEONARD, Sterling Andrus, *Essential Principles of Teaching Reading and Literature* (J. B. Lippincott, 1922).

MEARNS, Hughes, *Creative Youth* (Doubleday, Doran, 1926).

McCASLIN, Davida, *Reaching Other Minds* (Knopf, 1928).

RALEIGH, Walter, *On Writing and Writers* (Edward Arnold & Co., 1926).

SEELY, Howard Francis, *Enjoying Poetry in School* (Johnson Publishing Co., 1931).

SMITH, Alphonso, *What Can Literature Do for Me?* (Doubleday, Doran, 1927).

SPRAU, George, *Meaning of Literature* (Scribner, 1925).

THOMAS, Charles Swain, *The Teaching of English in Secondary Schools,* revised edition (Houghton Mifflin, 1927).

TRACY, Henry Chester, *English as Experience* (E. P. Dutton & Co., 1928).

WEBSTER and SMITH, *Teaching English in the Junior High Schools* (World Book Co., 1927).

WOODBERRY, George, *Appreciation of Literature* (Harcourt, Brace, 1921).

Research investigations, covered in other sources (*Review of Educational Research* and D. V. Smith's "Selected Bibliographies of Research Studies in English" which appeared in *The English Journal*) and pamphlets of fifty or fewer pages have not been listed in this bibliography.

The starred (*) titles in the following list appealed to the reviewers as significantly expressive of the philosophy of English as experience.

[1] Prepared in the Education Department of the Enoch Pratt Free Library, Baltimore, Maryland.

TEACHING ALL PHASES OF ENGLISH

California State Department of Education Curriculum Commission, *Teachers' Guide to Child Development in the Intermediate Grades* (The Department, 1936, 631p., $1.00.

A general introduction on program organization, the teacher, and instructional materials is followed by chapters on the progressive methods of handling the usual school subjects. Each subject is illustrated with unit material, the day-to-day development of it in a class of average children, and excellent examples of creative work. Teaching aids and materials are listed. A suggestive guide for the creative teacher.

* Chicago University High School, Faculty of English Department, *English Instruction in the University High School,* Publications of the Laboratory Schools, No. 4 (University of Chicago Department of Education, 1933), 178p., $1.50.

"A comprehensive description of the unitary organization of English courses in the University of Chicago High School with illustrations of instructional materials and procedures. Provision for individualizaton, remedial instruction, the use of library facilities, removal of expressional deficiencies, the correlation of the social studies and English in the course 'Community Life English,' and the opportunities for experience in creative writing and the study of literature . . . are fully presented in the monograph."

* CROSS, E. A., and CARNEY, Elizabeth, *Teaching English in High Schools* (Macmillan, 1939), 561p., $2.75.

A forceful presentation of suggestions for making experiences in English contribute to high school pupils' feeling of security in their use of the English language and habit of reading good literature for leisure hours as well as for utilitarian purposes; a summary of past and present ineffective and effective teaching is supplemented with an excellent classified bibliography of periodical references. A valuable guide to inexperienced and experienced teachers.

DAKIN, Dorothy, *Talks to Beginning Teachers of English* (Heath, 1937), 478p., $2.40.

The author speaks frankly, directly and practically to the beginner about the small and the large problems which are likely to arise in the first year of teaching. The experienced teacher, looking back upon recurrent teaching situations, will find much in the book to explain success and failure in teaching. All phases of English, both curricular and extra-curricular, are touched upon. The selected bibliography will lead the energetic teacher to references which deal more fully with specific phases of English.

DALE, Edgar, *How to Appreciate Motion Pictures: A Manual of Motion-Picture Criticism Prepared for High-School Students,* Motion Pictures and Youth: The Payne Fund Studies (Macmillan, 1933), 243p., $1.20.

Provides students with a background for motion-picture experience by teaching them what to look for in the story, the acting, the photography, the setting, the sound and music.

DALE, Edgar, and others, *Motion Pictures in Education:* A Summary of the Literature (H. W. Wilson, 1937), 472p., $2.50.

A new and singular service in the visual field. The best that has been published during the last decade on motion pictures as an educational medium is here abstracted. More useful than a bibliography because of the detailed summaries of the items listed. The 300 articles from magazines, yearbooks, pamphlets and theses are well grouped and well equipped with helpful editorial comment.

* FREDERICK, R. W., RAGSDALE, Clarence, and SALISBURY, Rachel, *Directing Learning* (Appleton-Century, 1938), 527p., $2.75.

An attempt "(1) to show the place and importance of study and learning power in the total school program, (2) to describe the nature of the learning process, (3) to outline and illustrate good methods for directing learning with special reference to the development of independent learning power, and (4) to indicate administrative procedures that will assist teachers and pupils to work satisfactorily."

GLASER, Emma, *On the Teaching of Junior High School English* (Appleton-Century, 1935), 307p., $2.00.

Beginning with a chapter on new trends in education, the author suggests projects, exercises, and actual teaching procedures in oral composition, mechanics, the "new" grammar and creative writing. This book has the progressive trend, with the immediate classroom problems always kept in mind. Many samples of pupils' work are included.

HARRISON, Margaret, *Radio in the Classroom:* Objectives, Principles, and Practices (Prentice-Hall, 1937), 260p., $2.50.

Designed to help principals and teachers to make use of broadcast programs in classroom work. The author, gathering her material during a three-year investigation, considers the radio as a supplementary educational tool. A section of units illustrates various kinds of activities into which radio can successfully be intrenched.

* HARTMAN, Gertrude, and SHUMAKER, Ann, edited for The Progressive Education Association, *Creative Expression:* The Development of Children in Art, Music, Literature, and Dramatics (E. M. Hale & Co., 1939), 350p., $2.00.

A reprint of popular articles by outstanding persons on various phases of creative expression; excellent bibliographies are included in this useful anthology.

* HILDRETH, Gertrude, *Learning the Three R's:* A Modern Interpretation (Educational Test Bureau, 1937), 824p., $2.40.

The author has given attention to the essential psychological facts in the shifting emphasis on mastery of the "three R's." Skills are now practised in the way they are to function and provide a foundation for future growth in knowledge and understanding. Diagnostic and remedial work in reading, writing and spelling are outlined.

* KAULFERS, W. V. and ROBERTS, H. D., *A Cultural Basis for the Language Arts:* An Approach to a Unified Program in the English and Foreign Language Curriculum (The authors, Stanford Language Arts Investigation, Stanford University, 1937), 115p., $1.00.

A volume bristling with ideas which challenge the teachers of separate subjects to get together in rediscovering the basic social values in their subjects. To teachers of English who are already teaching their subject as experience this book gives supporting evidence that a common thread of life needs interlaces the languages which students experience in the high school curriculum.

* LEWIN, William, *Photoplay Appreciation in American High Schools,* National Council of Teachers of English, English Monograph No. 2 (Appleton-Century, 1934), 122p., $1.00.

Points out that the neighborhood movie can serve as a laboratory of visual education, and that movie habits can be improved through the medium of the English class. Not only can movies provide "literature experiences" but by discussing them in class, appreciation can be taught and attitudes and tastes improved.

* LYMAN, R. L., *The Enrichment of the English Curriculum,* Supplementary Educational Monographs No. 39 (University of Chicago Press, Department of Education, 1932), 251p., $2.00.

A stimulating plea for the correlation of English with other academic studies and with life itself. Summarizes a large number of actual experiments presenting the current educational trends in English teaching. Discusses the importance of the correlation of English with other subjects in contributing to the cultural life of boys and girls. Rich in suggestions to enliven classroom instructions.

* MIRRIELEES, L. B., *Teaching Composition and Literature in Junior and Senior High School,* Revised and enlarged edition (Harcourt, 1937), 576p., $2.50.

"The book is so planned that: 1. It states the problem of composition and literature teaching as a challenge demanding original thought. 2. It tests the prospective teacher's knowledge of literature, mechanics and grammar, and her ability in oral and written expression. 3. It requires her to make and to present orally exercises and assignments planned for high-school pupils. By means of these exercises she is forced to test her power of awakening interest and of organizing and lucidly explaining class problems."

* National Council of Teachers of English, *A Correlated Curriculum: A Report* of the Committee on Correlation, R. M. Weeks, Chairman, English Monograph No. 5 (Appleton-Century, 1936), 326p., $2.00.

Many students go through school failing to correlate classroom subjects and emerge with unrelated views. Sixty-one contributors have collected material which aims to counteract this situation and suggest theories of integration in light of current child psychology. The fusion of English with history, civics, vocational information and fine arts is discussed. Points a direction toward which changes in English curricula can be developed if, as some critics point out, the English teacher does not go too far into unfamiliar fields.

* National Council of Teachers of English, Curriculum Commission, *An Experience Curriculum in English:* A Report . . . by W. W. Hatfield, chairman, English Monograph No. 4 (Appleton-Century, 1935), 323p., $1.75.

An inspiring volume which interprets adequately English as experience. Produced after a long period of conferences and experimentation by leaders in every phase and at every grade level of the teaching of English, this report offers a pattern curriculum which is stimulating curriculum research throughout the United States. Much of the best thinking and soundest practice in the teaching of English is summarized in this useful monograph.

* National Education Association, Department of Supervisors and Directors of Instruction, *The Development of a Modern Program in English: Ninth Yearbook* (The Association, 1936), 193p., $2.00.

Offers an excellent ground work for the construction of a modern English program. The committee has examined yesterday's teachings and then pointed toward new, sound curricula adapted to individual and social needs. Actual work of curriculum revision and appraisal in various communities is discussed. Detailed analysis of supervisory problems reflects the increased importance of correct language training.

NORTON, J. K., and NORTON, M. A., *Foundations of Curriculum Building* (Ginn, 1936), 599p., $3.00.

An overview of theory, trends and current practices at the elementary school level, based on a synthesis of research findings. Though arranged by conventional subject fields, with chapters on reading, spelling and language, grammar and composition, the book will be most useful for the activity type of curriculum. "A marvel of research, arrangement, condensation and interest."

O'ROURKE, L. J., "Rebuilding the English-Usage Curriculum to Insure Greater Mastery of Essentials: A Report of a Nation-Wide Study of English," (Psychological Institute, 3506 Patterson St., N.W., Washington, D.C., 1934), 98p., $.50.

"Presents a survey of the present status of English usage studies, a study of teaching methods, the utilization of research findings in classroom instruction, reading and vocabulary studies, interpretation of scores on survey tests," the Pennsylvania and Ohio coöperative English studies and samples of survey tests.

PARKER, R. E., *The Principles and Practice of Teaching English* (Prentice-Hall, 1937), 336p., $2.50.

Chapters on the teacher's relationships, reading for vicarious experience, expressional needs and activities, sentence elements and creative work. Nothing from the sociological angle.

POLLARD, E. W., "Teaching Motion Picture Appreciation: A Manual for Teachers of High School Classes" (Bureau of Educational Research, Ohio State University, 1935), 60p., $.50.

"The purpose of this manual is to aid the teacher of high-school students to utilize the material available for the study of motion-picture appreciation. The manual was developed after experimental courses in city and rural schools had been organized and then studied by means of interviews, verbatim minutes, and much direct observation. It is arranged with special reference to the high-school textbook, *How to Appreciate Motion Pictures* by Dr. Edgar Dale . . ."

PRINGLE, R. W., *The Junior High School:* A Psychological Approach (McGraw-Hill, 1937), 408p., $3.00.

A psychological approach to junior-high-school education which deals with selection and organization of subject content, methods of presentation, extra-curricular activities and pupil control. Significant in recognition of pre-adoles-cents and early adolescents as two distinct groups. Its thesis is that instruc-tional materials should be adapted to these needs and a program of studies is consequently suggested.

RAND, Helen, and LEWIS, Richard, *Film and School:* A Handbook in Moving-Picture Evaluation, National Council of Teachers of English (Appleton-Century, 1937), 182p., $1.12.

Sets forth the aims of motion-picture evaluation and furnishes suggestions and questions for discussing them.

SAFARJIAN, N. E., *Plan for Integrated Class Work for the Ninth Year in So-cial Studies and English in Double and Single Periods* (Wetzel, 1934), 106p., $2.00.

A series of units showing possibilities in integrating literature and history.

* SEELY, H. F., *On Teaching English* (American Book Co., 1933), 391p., $2.00.

A well-written presentation of principles and procedures in teaching the fundamentals (grammar, punctuation and capitalization, penmanship, spelling and vocabulary, the sentence and the paragraph) and oral and written compo-sition. Each chapter after building a point of view closes with a concise sum-mary that stimulates any experienced teacher to evaluate his own philosophy and methods of teaching.

* Society for Curriculum Study, Committee on Integration, *Integration:* Its Meaning and Application, by L. T. Hopkins and others (Appleton-Century, 1937), 315p., $2.00.

A timely attempt to clarify the meaning of integration in educational theory, with chapters presenting the viewpoints of the philosopher, biologist, psychia-trist, psychologist, artist, sociologist and educator. Later chapters analyze and evaluate current practices in terms of integration in various systems with four types of curricula: the core, the correlated, the experience, and the broad field. "A valuable guide to a critical appraisal of modernism in education."

United States Office of Education, *Learning English Incidentally: A Study of Bilingual Children,* by J. L. Meriam, Project in Research in Universities, Bulletin 1937, No. 15 (Superintendent of Documents, 1938), 105p., $.15.

Report of an experiment in a Mexican school in La Jolla, Cal., the plan of which can be adapted to schools in other sections dealing with children of other nationalities. The conclusion reached was that bilingual children acquire Eng-lish incidentally.

Woodring, M. N., Jewett, I. A., and Benson, R. T., *Enriched Teaching of English in the Junior and Senior High School,* revised and enlarged edition (Teachers College, Columbia University, 1934), 358p., $2.75.

A practical guide for the progressive teacher to sources of supplementary and enrichment materials. At least 90 per cent of the material of this edition is entirely new. Lists free and low cost supplementary material as well as suggestions for almost every phase of English teaching: book reports, debates, letter writing, spelling, dramatics, poetry, bulletin boards, school publications, etc.

LANGUAGE AND COMPOSITION

Betts, E. A., and Bontrager, O. R., *Research Studies in Elementary School Language* No. 1, Studies in Education, Vol. IX, No. 2 (University of Iowa, 1934), 62p., $.50.

"Undertakes a critical evaluation of certain research techniques in the field of oral English." Major emphasis is given to the experimental evaluation of equipment as a device used in studying oral language.

Cable, W. A., compiler, *A Program of Speech Education in a Democracy,* Speech Education Series No. 2, 2nd edition (Boston, Expression Co., 1932), 595p., $4.50.

"The functions of speech, we are told, is racial control." With this in mind, every phase of speech and vocal training that could bear on the schools and the community is discussed by various contributors. Citations of methods used, and examples of results are included, as well as bibliographical notes.

California State Department of Education, *Speech in Education,* Bulletin, 1937, No. 9 (The Department), 86p., $.25.

Aims to estimate the place of speech in education and to indicate its functions. Points out the range and amount of speech used in classrooms, the use of speech as a means of development in the classroom in the daily living activities of pupils, and variations in speech as a means of achieving group consciousness.

* Conrad, L. R., *Teaching Creative Writing . . .* with the Creative Writing Committee of the Commission on the Secondary School Curriculum of the Progressive Education Association (Appleton-Century, 1937), 142p., $1.00.

Creative writing affords opportunity "to organize all phases of language development in terms of the student's actual needs." Its function is not the development of literary skill, but training the student's emotional and imaginative life. On the basis of these principles, methods of presenting the subject in classroom are discussed. A significant report based upon careful deliberation and experimental practice.

Douris, E. A., and others, *Graded Objectives for Teaching Good American Speech* (Dutton, 1934), 90p., $1.50.

For teachers who already have a knowledge of phonetics. These graded objectives are divided into units to determine the sequence in which the subject matter should be presented and will furnish suggestions for drill as well as aid the teacher in correcting speech defects on a phonetic basis.

FORAN, T. G., *The Psychology and Teaching of Spelling* (Catholic Education Press, 1934), 234p., $2.40.

Complete and careful survey of spelling—aims, amount of instruction, the vocabulary, methods, etc. Remedial instruction is also included, and the results of many studies are shown in form of statistical tables.

* Francis W. Parker School, *Experience in English Composition and Literature*, Vol. I, *Grades I–VIII*, Studies in Education, Vol. IX (The School, 330 Webster Ave., Chicago, 1932), 377p., $1.00.

A discussion, by grade, of real experiences in language. For each level, many activities and their results are shown, along with examples of creative and expressionistic work. Suggested projects, bibliographies, and various integrative devices are included.

GATES, A. I., *A List of Spelling Difficulties in 3876 Words, Showing the "Hard Spots," Common Misspellings, Average Spelling Grade-Placement, and Comprehension Grade-Ratings of Each Word* (Teachers College, Columbia University, 1937), 166p., $2.10.

A useful study of words appearing most frequently in twenty-five widely used spelling texts and state and large-city spelling lists.

HAGBOLDT, Peter, *Language Learning: Some Reflections from Teaching Experience* (University of Chicago Press, 1935), 165p., $1.50.

Basic concepts and problems, psychological principles, and language in function are the three sections under which language learning is considered.

* JENKINS, Frances, *Language Development in Elementary Grades* (Nelson, 1936), 256p., $2.00.

Language teaching has been integrated with experiences vital to the pupil, emphasis being placed on oral work. Although speech rather than writing is taking a more prominent place in classroom activities, both speaking and writing are discussed in terms of all day activities in this integrated program. A chapter "Practical Illustrations and Suggestions" offers stimulating ideas to the elementary teacher.

KING, L. M., *Learning and Applying Spelling Rules in Grades Three to Eight*, Contributions to Education, No. 517 (Teachers College, Columbia University), 80p., $1.50.

"The research described was undertaken for the purpose of determining effects of teaching certain spelling rules in each of elementary grades" from three to eight. It was found that efficiency in learning to state and apply the rules was increased from grade to grade.

LABRANT, L. L., "Study of Certain Language Developments of Children in Grades Four to Twelve Inclusive," Genetic Psychology Monographs, Vol. XIV, No. 5, pp. 387–491 (Clark University Press, 1934), $2.00.

An investigation of language development by using the *clause*, considered a significant indication of skill in language use, as the unit for study. The author's aim is to find out *how* the child expresses himself in his use of dependent and independent clauses.

McKee, Paul, *Language in the Elementary School: Spelling, Composition and Writing* (Houghton, 1934), 482p., $2.00.

A valuable contribution in the elementary-school field of language. The author has assembled and evaluated the latest experimental research on this subject. "Material on spelling and writing is presented concretely and specifically in terms of the teacher's or supervisor's needs." The simple, direct style will be appreciated by inexperienced students.

Mulgrave, D. I., *Speech for the Classroom Teacher* (Prentice-Hall, 1936), 398p., $2.50.

Radio has made the nation speech-conscious, and interested educators insist that the schools evaluate their rôle in the new movement. Timely, workmanlike guide to all phases of the subject. With voice mechanics as a starting point, the author runs the gamut of speech problems from phonetic and artistic aspects to pathological difficulties. A section on group discussions involves lectures, seminars, panels and forums. Bibliographies, selections of practice materials and suggestions for corrective speech procedures add to the general all-round usefulness.

National Conference on Research in Elementary School English, "Principles of Method in Elementary English Composition," by H. A. Greene, Research Bulletin No. 5 (C. C. Certain, Box 67, North End Station, Detroit, Mich., 1937), 52p., $.50.

This summary, an interpretation of research studies in the field of English composition for the classroom teacher and supervisor, is grouped under the following subjects: (1) points of view in language instruction, (2) curriculum content and placement, (3) psychology of learning, (4) methods of classroom procedure, (5) measurement of results and (6) remedial and corrective instruction. Six well known educators give interesting and instructive evaluations of this study.

National Conference on Research in English, "Vocabulary Problems in Elementary Schools," by J. Conrad Seegers, Research Bulletin No. 7 (C. C. Certain, Box 67, North End Station, Detroit, Mich.), 60p., $.60.

An invaluable survey of 263 research studies concerning the various problems in teaching and in learning vocabulary. So well summarized and appraised are these studies that classroom teachers as well as research workers will find this Bulletin extremely useful.

Raubicheck, Letitia, *Teaching Speech in Secondary Schools* (Prentice-Hall, 1935), 291p., $2.00.

"The scientific facts of speech-production, remedial methods, etc., are covered—a practical pathology of speech disorders. The author's discussions of oral interpretation of literature, public speaking, group discussion and debate are full of specific illustrations of classroom procedures." Each chapter has a series of problems for discussion and a bibliography.

RAUBICHECK, Letitia, *How to Teach Good Speech in the Elementary Schools* (Noble, 1937), 276p., $2.00.

Starting with the earliest sounds made by children, Dr. Raubicheck traces speech development through the eighth grade. Many suggestive devices are given to aid those with speech defects, as well as aiding the normal child to get a better grasp of speaking English. New developments, such as choral speaking and creative dramatics, are also discussed.

THOMAS, J. E., "The Elimination of Technical Errors in Written Composition through Formal Drill," Studies in Education, Vol. VIII, No. 2 (University of Iowa, 1932), 43p., $.50.

"A study to test a technique, the use of dictionary drills and multiple-response exercises, for eliminating technical language errors in written composition of ninth grade pupils."

* TROMMAR, C. J., and REGAN, T. A., *Directing Language Power in the Elementary School through Story, Dramatization, and Poetry* (Macmillan, 1933), 497p., $2.00.

Offers the teacher many suggestions for vitalizing her teaching. "Centered about three basic tendencies of the race: (1) love of the story, (2) inborn dramatic urge, and (3) response to beauty of sound and rhythm." Each tendency is described in detail with many examples given.

WATSON, A. E., *Experimental Studies in the Psychology and Pedagogy of Spelling,* Contributions to Education, No. 638 (Teachers College, Columbia University, 1935), 144p., $1.50.

A record of studies in elementary and high schools to eliminate and define the problems which confront the teacher of spelling.

LITERATURE AND READING

Association for Childhood Education, *Reading: A Tool for Learning,* compiled by N. B. Smith (The Association, 1938), 32p., $.35.

"Truly modern in its stress upon the importance of normal growth of the whole child in the nursery school and kindergarten years, the development of readiness for reading in a program of abundant living and the natural introduction to reading activities when the child is mature enough to find satisfaction in them. The fine articles present vividly the experiences through which the young child gradually enlarges his understandings, develops the power of language, and at last recognizes the symbols which make reading a meaningful and joyous activity."

BUCKINGHAM, B. R., and DOLCH, E. W., compilers, *A Combined Word List* (Ginn, 1936), 185p., $1.50.

The authors have combined the results of previous well-known vocabulary studies with their own findings by the free-association method in order to determine word usage from the second through the eighth grades. The result is a list of 19,000 words, given here with symbols indicating the grade location, etc.

DALGLIESH, Alice, *First Experiences with Literature* (Scribner, 1932), 162p., $1.25.

Here is a unique contribution on teaching literature to the nursery-primary child which has grown out of the author's daily experiences. Important phases of children's literary work included are: holiday, Bible and fairy stories, poems, and others. Recent favorites are found in the list of books recommended.

* Francis W. Parker School, *Experiences in English Composition and Literature, Grades IX–XII,* Vol. II, Studies in Education, Vol. X (The School, 330 Webster Avenue, Chicago, Ill., 1934), 480p., $1.00.

An experiment in studying literature for leisure to give pupils experience in choosing good reading for leisure time. The necessity of freedom of choice is emphasized—choice in what is read and what is said about it. Literature must be taught as an end in itself, not as a means toward some end. The second half of the book deals with composition from the standpoint of performance. Experimental procedure is used throughout composition as well as literature.

GRAY, W. S., and HOLMES, Eleanor, *The Development of Meaning Vocabularies in Reading: An Experimental Study,* Publications of the Laboratory Schools, No. 6 (University of Chicago, Department of Education, 1938), 152p., $1.50.

Describes a project in the enlargement of meaning vocabularies in which guidance was tried as opposed to the incidental approach, using two experimental groups and one control group. Conclusions reached favored the directed method, not only for increase of vocabulary but also for improved efficiency in both oral and silent reading.

GRAY, W. S., and WHIPPLE, Gertrude, *Improving Instruction in Reading: An Experimental Study,* Supplementary Education Monographs, No. 40 (University of Chicago, Department of Education, 1935), 226p., $1.75.

To improve the teaching of reading in harmony with the results of scientific study is an important objective of this monograph. It is written at the elementary school level but has broad applications for secondary school. Administrative and supervisory difficulties are considered and underlying principles of good procedure are investigated.

HARRISON, M. L., *Reading Readiness* (Houghton, 1936), 166p., $1.20.

A timely and useful book for kindergarten and first-grade teachers summarizing articles and research studies not readily available elsewhere. Material is organized under four headings: factors influencing reading readiness, instruction fostering it, the testing program, and the placement and remedial program. Appendices contain a bibliography, books for the children's library and a typical case study.

HOOPER, John, *Poetry in the New Curriculum* (Stephen Daye Press, Brattleboro, Vt., 1932), 136p., $1.20.

Covers three major themes: "teaching objectives and procedures, the integration of poetry with other school subjects, and suggestions for guiding pupils in creative work."

JACOBSEN, P. B., "Two Experiments with Work-Type Reading Exercises in Ninth Grade," Studies in Education, Vol. VIII, No. 5 (University of Iowa, 1932), 88p., $.75.

An investigation to find the effect of work-type reading exercises on the reading comprehension of ninth-grade pupils not only in reading but in general science and general achievement in all academic subjects as well. Result showed very little transfer of ability to another content field.

LADD, M. R., *Relation of Social-Economic and Personal Characteristics to Reading Ability,* Contributions to Education No. 582 (Teachers College, Columbia University, 1933), 100p., $1.50.

An investigation exploring possible relationships between home backgrounds and personality on the one hand and reading ability on the other tends to show that achievement depends more closely on favorable school attitudes, self control and a greater amount of time devoted to leisure reading.

LAZAR, May, *Reading Interests, Activities, and Opportunities of Bright, Average, and Dull Children,* Contributions to Education, No. 707 (Teachers College, Columbia University, 1937), 127p., $1.60.

Using thirteen New York public schools as bases for investigation, the author studies problems of children's reading interests, sex differences in reading, variations in home backgrounds, number of books read, etc.

LEE, D. M., *The Importance of Reading for Achieving in Grades Four, Five and Six,* Contributions to Education, No. 556 (Teachers College, Columbia University; 1933), 64p., $1.50.

A study of the relationship of pupils' reading ability to a special interpretation of their achievement in other school subjects.

McKEE, Paul, *Reading and Literature in the Elementary School* (Houghton, 1934), 592p., $2.00.

Reports faithfully practically every scientific investigation in the teaching of reading, and critically summarizes the results. A broad reading program includes testing, grade-placements, varied interests and extensive tastes in literature. What should be taught, where, and how are determined by the social utility theory.

National Education Association, Department of Elementary School Principals, *Newer Practices in Reading in the Elementary School, Seventeenth Yearbook,* Bulletin, Vol. 17, No. 7 (The Department, 1938), 704p., $2.00.

Reflects the viewpoints of the 50 authors, and combines the results of research and critical thinking by specialists with first-hand experiences of principals and teachers in the supervision and teaching of reading. The essential elements of an adequate reading program are outlined in chapter D, and various phases of such a program are treated in subsequent chapters.

National Society for the Study of Education, *The Teaching of Reading: A Second Report; Thirty-Sixth Yearbook,* Part I (Public School Publishing Co., 1937), 442p., $2.50.

A recommended reading program, which attempts to give recognition to the needs of child life, current social demands and valid trends in educational theory and practice, is discussed by specialists. Significant developments since the 1925 report of the National Committee on Reading (*Twenty-Fourth Yearbook*, Part I) are reviewed.

New York City Association of Teachers of English, "Further Studies in Reading: Improving the Reading Habits and Tastes of the High School Pupils of New York City," *Second Yearbook* (Noble, 1937), 90p., $1.50.

Reports of the six committees organized to "reinforce the program of reading instruction where it seemed weakest." "Techniques of teaching newspaper and magazine reading; ways of stimulating reading; recording readings and reactions to reading, and library facilities." Many specific aids for teachers are given.

New York City Association of Teachers of English, "Survey of Reading in Typical High Schools of New York City, September, 1935–January, 1936," Monograph No. 1, Mimeographed (Noble, 1937), 138p., $1.00.

A survey of the quality and quantity of children's reading in the N. Y. City schools. It was found that teachers were influencing the reading of books but not necessarily the reading of newspapers and magazines; three-fourths of the reading is fiction with the slight interest in poetry; and most of the reading done by high school students gives them very little intellectual and spiritual growth.

PENNELL, M. E., and CUSACK, A. M., *The Teaching of Reading for Better Living* (Houghton, 1935), 469p., $2.00.

The authors take recognition of changing social conditions and base their ideas of teaching essentials upon modern developments. The child must be stimulated to read, and various methods of encouragement are suggested. Both the location and remedial treatment of reading deficiencies are discussed. Specific helps for each grade, library skills, daily reading lists, and subject correlations are additional features.

* ROSENBLATT, L. M., *Literature as Exploration*, A Publication of the Commission on Human Relations, Progressive Education Association (Appleton-Century, 1938), 340p., $2.25.

"The word *exploration* is designed to suggest primarily that the experience of literature, far from being for the reader a passive process of absorption, is a form of intense personal activity. The reader counts for at least as much as the book or poem itself. . . . Literature is for him a medium of exploration." This is the point of view which is adequately developed and illustrated in this volume.

SMITH, N. B., *American Reading Instruction: Its Development and Its Significance in Gaining a Perspective on Current Practices in Reading* (Silver, Burdett, 1934), 287p., $1.96.

A story of the evolutionary progress in reading told and illustrated by delightful descriptions of readers that have held sway in the classrooms of America. Various movements, divided into six periods from 1607 to date, furnish an intelligent basis for evaluating present practices and selecting textbook materials.

SMITH, Reed, *The Teaching of Literature in the High School* (American Book Co., 1935), 485p., $2.00.

Written in sprightly and enthusiastic style, this book is the culmination of years rich in teaching experiences. It is admirably planned, each chapter prefaced by an outline and followed by copious book and magazine references. Techniques in poetry, short story, drama, essay and novel are among the branches of literature embraced. Each field is illustrated by practical examples from standard classics.

STONE, C. R., *Better Advanced Reading* (Webster, 1937), 292p., $2.00.

"A modern program in reading above the primary grades with respect to objectives, methods, activities, and materials."

STONE, C. R., *Better Primary Reading:* How to Adapt Reading Instruction to the Varying Needs of the Children (Webster, 1936), 536p., $2.25.

To methods and materials for better group and individual recreative reading are added analysis of readers and graded lists of easy, average and more difficult books.

STONE, C. R., "A Graded Vocabulary for Primary Reading" (Webster, 1936), 61p., $.50.

A graded vocabulary of 2,000 words based on previous vocabulary studies and an analysis of numerous primers and readers. Should be "of value to those concerned with the selection of reading materials for use under conditions making a controlled vocabulary important."

THORNDIKE, E. L., *Teacher's Wordbook of the Twenty-Thousand Words Found Most Frequently and Widely in General Reading for Children and Young People*, revised edition (Teachers College, Columbia University, 1932), 182p., $1.50.

This revised edition of Thorndike's well-known list of 10,000 words, doubles the number of the first edition. Two hundred additional sources have been used. It is for teacher's use in guidance in the frequency and range of occurrence of words and is *not* a spelling list.

WEEKES, B. E., *Literature and the Child* (Silver, Burdett, 1935), 456p., $2.16.

"Of value to those upon whom may devolve the responsibility of making choices of reading materials for children, or helping children to make choices, and also, to those who must begin the training of children in literary appreciation, and lay the foundation for a more mature study of literature on the secondary school level."

White House Conference on Child Health and Protection, "Children's Reading: A Study of Voluntary Reading of Boys and Girls in the United States," (Appleton-Century, 1932), 90p., $.75.

A discussion of how and what children read, methods of stimulating reading and accessibility of reading matter serves as an introduction to a number of detailed studies of problems in children's reading.

REMEDIAL TEACHING

ARCHER, C. P., and BIERI, Margaret, "Improvement of Reading Through Individual Instruction: A Bulletin Devoted to Helping the Teacher to Make Seatwork Activities Serve to Correct Defects in Reading" (Edwards Brothers, 1934), 68p., $.45.

Not a complete set of drill units but an attempt to guide teachers in the preparation of individual instructional material.

BAKER, H. J., and LELAND, Bernice, "In Behalf of Non-Readers" (Public School Publishing Co., 1934), 39p., $.30.

Case records of pupils who have presented difficulties in reading activities. Not only are their behavior problems handled, but symptoms, sources and diagnoses of disabilities are also treated.

BETTS, E. A., *The Prevention and Correction of Reading Difficulties* (Row, Peterson, 1936), 402p., $2.00.

A summary and interpretation of recent research findings and of the author's experience in his reading clinic at Oswego Normal School. The set-up of a clinic and its coördination with other school departments are described. A simple, clear summary and an extensive bibliography follow each chapter, and appendices contain tests developed by the writer.

* CENTER, S. S., and PERSONS, G. L., *Teaching High School Students to Read: A Study of Retardation in Reading*, National Council of Teachers of English, English Monograph No. 6 (Appleton-Century, 1937), 167p., $2.25.

The authors, in telling of their experience in handling retarded readers in the Theodore Roosevelt High School in New York City, say that they hope to stimulate other teachers to a successful method of dealing with pupils who lack the requisite skill to get ideas from the printed page. Teachers interested in the physiological approach to reading difficulty will find an interesting discussion of the ophthalmograph and the metron-o-scope. The classroom teacher, not equipped with clinical apparatus, will find especially helpful chapters III and XI which present an acceptable definition of reading and its function in school and out-of-school life.

COLE, L. W., *The Improvement of Reading: With Special Reference to Remedial Instruction* (Farrar, 1938), 338p., $1.75.

A short history of methodology in the teaching of reading is followed by an analysis of reading problems—speed, vocabulary, comprehension, interest, etc. The book suggests many exercises to be used in remedial work.

GATES, A. I., and RUSSELL, D. H., "Diagnostic and Remedial Spelling Manual: A Handbook for Teachers" (Teachers College, Columbia University, 1937), 44p., $.60.

"An aid to the discovery of the kinds of spelling difficulties encountered and their underlying causes, together with the procedures that can be used for overcoming them."

* GATES, A. I., *The Improvement of Reading:* A Program of Diagnostic and Remedial Methods, revised edition (Macmillan, 1935), 668p., $2.50.

"This revised edition is valuable for the inclusion of work done since December, 1926."

MCCALLISTER, J. M., *Remedial and Corrective Instruction in Reading:* A Program for the Upper Grades and High School (Appleton-Century, 1936), 300p., $2.00.

Analysis of reading disabilities of pupils who have passed the stage of formal training, showing the need for three types of training in upper grades and high school—individual work for the seriously retarded, corrective group instruction for mild cases, and guidance for those who encounter difficulties in studying various subjects. Case studies, Dr. McCallister's major personal contribution, illustrate his points.

MONROE, Marion, *Children Who Cannot Read:* The Analysis of Reading Disabilities and the Use of Diagnostic Tests in the Instruction of Retarded Readers (University of Chicago Press, 1932), 205p., $2.50.

An important contribution to literature on diagnostic and remedial teaching, this monograph shows that many behavior difficulties disappear with the removal of reading disability. Reports methods of measurement of reading ability, treatment of causative factors, and results of remedial work with case groups. Valuable in showing that with present available techniques reading deficiency cannot be neglected.

MONROE, Marion, and BACKUS, Bertie, *Remedial Reading:* A Monograph in Character Education (Houghton, 1937), 171p., $1.40.

Recognizing the correlation between school progress and satisfactory personality adjustment, reading retardation was considered as one phase of the Washington, D.C., experiment in character education, 1934–36. This monograph describes modifications in organization, administration, teaching methods, materials of instruction, and teacher training to improve reading ability at the various grade levels, but makes no claim at an adequate evaluation of the long-time program.

ORTON, S. T., *Reading, Writing and Speech Problems in Children:* A Presentation of Certain Types of Disorders in the Development of the Language Faculty (Norton, 1937), 215p., $2.00.

A medical man summarizes his findings during an intensive ten-year study of disorders in the acquisition of the language faculty. Such a study necessarily involves technical terms, but the inclusion of a glossary makes the book usable by teachers, who should find the physiological approach interesting and the suggested remedial measures helpful.

SANGREN, P. V., *Improvement of Reading Through the Use of Tests* (Western State Teachers College, Kalamazoo, Mich., 1932), 207p., gratis.

Written "to aid the classroom teacher and the supervisor in discovering their problems of instruction in reading through the use of tests and to make a sufficient number of practical suggestions so that teacher and supervisor will be able to solve these problems through improvement in instruction."

STANGER, M. A., and DONOHUE, E. K., *Prediction and Prevention of Reading Difficulties* (Oxford, 1937), 191p., $2.00.

"Attacks the problems of diagnostic and remedial reading at the primary-school level with Orton's cerebral-dominance theory," of which a simplified description is given. Includes theory, testing, and teaching procedure.

TAYLOR, E. A., *Controlled Reading:* A Correlation of Diagnostic, Teaching and Corrective Techniques (University of Chicago Press, 1937), 367p., $3.50.

"This book reports data concerning research in eye-movement photography as a diagnostic technique and controlled reading as a corrective as well as a teaching technique."

APPENDIX C

PERIODICALS FOR TEACHERS' USE

Every teacher of *English* and of *teachers of English* needs a personal copy of *The English Journal,* of *College English,* and of *The Elementary English Review*—three periodicals which give the results of creative writing by literary men and woman, creative teaching by dynamic teachers of high school, college, and elementary school English, and creative research concerning teaching-learning problems in the field of English.

Following brief annotations of the three journals is a list of periodicals in which it is desirable for teachers of English to browse. Occasional articles in all these journals have unusual significance to the teacher, as teacher of English; every issue contains some materials especially useful in acquainting her with the trends in the other school subjects.

English Journal, The, 10–$3.00, W. Wilbur Hatfield, editor, 211 West 68th Street, Chicago, Illinois. Official Organ of the Council.

Presents articles by dynamic teachers, competent research workers, and literary artists; has Round Table department in which teachers share in formally their experiments and experiences; covers, under *News and Notes,* periodical literature and includes discriminating reviews of books for the general reader and of textbooks and teachers' books.

College English, 8–$3.00, W. Wilbur Hatfield, editor, 211 West 68th St., Chicago.

Treats curriculum and classroom procedures in composition and literature for undergraduates.

Elementary English Review, 8–$2.50, C. C. Certain, editor, Box 67, North End Station, Detroit, Michigan.

Well-written articles on every phase of the teaching of English from kindergarten through the eighth grade; excellent book notes and bibliographies in every issue; practically useful summaries of significant research studies appear in three issues during the year.

American Childhood, 10–$2.50, Milton Bradley Company, Springfield, Mass.

Contains helpful suggestions and inspiration for primary teachers in present-day schools, and for child training in the home, along with reviews of books in field of childhood education.

American Poetry Magazine, 6–$2.00, Clara Catherine Prince, editor, 1764 North 83rd Street, Wauwatosa, Wisconsin.

Official organ American Literary Association, Inc.; includes poems not previously published and departments devoted to prize poems, reprints and other honored material and to news concerning outstanding poets of today.

American Speech, 4–$4.00, William Cabell Greet, editor, Columbia University Press, 2960 Broadway, New York, New York.
A quarterly of linguistic usage; word history, regional dialects, and other human interest material appear from time to time; articles on phonetics; and reviews of books in the speech field.

Book Review Digest (monthly), H. W. Wilson (Subscription basis).
Digests and indexes from 77 English and American periodicals for book reviews. The books are reviewed under author with a subject, title index; code mark indicates the critics' opinions of the quality of the book.

Childhood Education, 9–$2.50, Frances Mayfarth, editor, Association for Childhood Education, 1201 Sixteenth Street, Northwest, Washington, D.C.
Official journal of the Association for Childhood Education; includes classroom problems and methods, book reviews and review of leading magazine articles.

Classical Journal, 9–$2.50, Eugene Tavenner, editor, Washington University, St. Louis, Missouri.
Editorials, articles: notes and hints for teachers; book reviews.

Curriculum Journal, 8–$2.50, Henry Harap, editor, Society for Curriculum Study, George Peabody College, Nashville, Tennessee.
Valuable news notes on curriculum activities throughout the country, articles and reports of curriculum research, book reviews, and lists of new books, bulletins, pamphlets, and courses of studies.

Education, 10–$4.00, Herbert Blair, editor, The Palmer Co., 120 Boylston Street, Boston, Mass.
Covers all phases of educational theory and practice; modern attitudes and techniques are sympathetically treated without excessive criticism of more conservative theories and methods.

Educational Method, 8–$3.00, Official organ, Department of Supervisors and Directors of Instruction, National Education Association, Lou L. LaBrant, editor, 1201 Sixteenth Street, Northwest, Washington, D.C.
Official organ of the Department. Discusses progressive public-school methods and administration. Semi-technical and practical in treatment; includes book notes and reviews.

Educational Screen, 10–$2.00, N. L. Greene, editor-in-chief, 64 East Lake Street, Chicago, Illinois.
"A magazine devoted exclusively to the visual idea in education" a trade directory for the visual field; articles by recognized writers on the use of visual aids in every school and life activity.

Elementary School Journal, 10–$2.50, Newton Edwards, editor, Department of Education, University of Chicago, Illinois.
Sponsored by the School of Education of the University of Chicago and covers the research aspects of the field of methods of teaching in elementary schools, critical reviews of educational books.

English Leaflets, The, 9–$2.00. Charles Swain Thomas, editor, New England Association of Teachers of English, Harvard University, Cambridge, Massachusetts.
Articles on all phases of the teaching of English, written in an informal style, with attention to the practical applications of current experimental findings and educational theories.

Horn Book, bimonthly, $2.50, Horn Book, Inc., 264 Boylston Street, Boston.
Devoted to "books and reading for children" including adolescents. Articles

on books and writers for young people, with considerable space given to children's libraries. Critical reviews.

Instructor, The, 10–$2.50 (formerly *Normal Instructor and Primary Plans*), Helen Mildred Owen, editor, Mary E. Owen, associate editor, F. A. Owen Publishing Co., Dansville, New York.

A "classroom magazine for grade and rural teachers." A practical working guide to methods, devices and materials for classroom use, contributed by well-known educational writers and practical teachers. Includes relatively little theory or general discussion.

Journal of Education, 9–$2.25, Anson W. Belding, editor, 6 Park Street, Boston, Massachusetts.

Usually short and rather specific discussions of methods and news notes of the educational field. A practical non-research publication.

Journal of Educational Psychology, 9–$6.00, Warwick and York, publishers, 10 East Center Street, Baltimore, Maryland.

Devoted to "the scientific study of learning and research" and of interest to teachers with an experimental attitude toward education.

Journal of Educational Research, 8–$3.60, A. S. Barr, chairman, editorial board, Professor of Education, University of Wisconsin, Madison, Wisconsin; publisher: The Public School Publishing Company, Bloomington, Illinois.

Covers the entire field of education from that of young children to that in college and professional schools. Technical in method and terminology, but concerned more with practice than with theory.

Journal of Educational Sociology, 9–$3.00, E. George Payne, editor-in-chief, School of Education, New York University, New York, New York.

Emphasizes scientific investigation in education from the point of view of the relation of the individual to social life and to the group in which he functions. Nevertheless, recent issues devote considerable space to the subject matter of the curriculum, teaching methods, and the organization of school activities. Two regular departments: (1) short reports on research in progress and (2) book reviews.

Journal of Experimental Education, 4–$4.00, A. S. Barr, chairman, editorial board, Professor of Education, University of Wisconsin, Madison, Wisconsin; publisher: The Democrat Printing Company, Madison, Wisconsin.

Technical journal covering all phases of experimental study of education, reports of experimental studies of the child, curriculum, and methods of instruction, critical discussions and research relating to measurements, and statistics and methods of experimental research.

Journal of Psychology, The, 4–$14.00, Carl Murchison and Associates, editors, The Journal Press, Provincetown, Massachusetts.

Problems of learning investigated and discussed.

Journal of Sociology and Social Research, 6–$3.00, Emory S. Bogardus, editor, University of Southern California, 3551 University Avenue, Los Angeles, California

This journal is one means of keeping informed about social-economic problems having direct and indirect bearing upon the learning situation; applications of social psychology to mass education; social classes in state universities and similar topics are discussed.

Journal of the National Education Association, 9–$2.00, Joy Elmer Morgan, editor, Harold A. Allan, business manager, 1201 Sixteenth Street, Northwest, Washington, D.C.

General articles of interest to educational workers on reading, guidance, child health, and research in teaching training; book notes, selected lists of books for teachers, and notes and announcements.

Library Journal, 22–$5.00, Bertine E. Weston, editor, 62 West 45th Street, New York, New York.

"The oldest journal of the profession" and "covers every library interest," theoretical and practical. The articles (often illustrated) are written by librarians of all ages and kinds of experience. A "Readers' Open Forum," news notes of libraries and librarians, bibliographies of library literature, book reviews, advance information and lists of books recommended for children are among the present regularly featured departments.

Modern Language Notes, 8–$5.00, H. Carrington Lancaster, editor, The Johns Hopkins University, Baltimore, Maryland.

Articles, notes, reviews, and recent publications.

National Elementary Principal, 6–$3.00, Bulletin of the Department of Elementary School Principals, National Education Association, Editorial Offices: 1201 Sixteenth Street, Northwest, Washington, D.C.

Very useful discussions of how to teach all subjects in the elementary school along with practical accounts of how to solve administrative problems.

Nation's Schools, 12–$2.00, Arthur B. Moehlman, editor, University of Michigan, Ann Arbor, Michigan; Raymond P. Sloan, managing editor, 101 Park Avenue, New York, New York; publisher: The Nation's Schools Publishing Company, 919 North Michigan Avenue, Chicago, Illinois.

"Devoted to the application of research to the building, equipment, and administration of schools."

Poetry, 12–$3.00, 232 East Erie Street, Chicago, Illinois.

A Magazine of Verse (monthly), M. D. Zabel, 232 E. Erie Street, Chicago, 1912, date, v.1–53, $3 (Canada $3.15).

Includes original poems by present-day writers of all schools of poetical theory and technique. New authors of merit are encouraged. The prose part is composed of literary criticism, book notes and reviews and a summary of current or recent literary magazines.

Progressive Education, 8–$3.00, Carson Ryan, editor, Progressive Education Association, 221 West 57th St., New York, New York.

Organ of the Progressive Education Association, original papers on the newer practices in education, news of the Association, book reviews, special numbers and notes.

Review of Educational Research, 5–$4.00, American Educational Research Association, National Education Association, 1201 Sixteenth Street, Northwest, Washington, D.C.

Reviews of research, classified, annotated, and indexed by persons especially qualified in the fields reviewed; published in cycles covering the literature over a three-year interval.

School and Society, 52–$5.00, J. McKeen Cattell, editor, Grand Central Terminal, New York, New York.

Deals with the broader aspects of the relations of organized, scientific education of all kinds and the needs and demands of modern society. Some rather specific problems are discussed and reports of specific research projects included but the treatment is generally non-technical and of sufficient interest to attract readers other than professional educators. Gives considerable space to the educational aspects of libraries. Many notes and rather brief reviews of publications in the field of education. News notes of educational events and of educators.

School Review, 10–$2.50, Leonard V. Koos, editor, Department of Education, University of Chicago, Chicago, Illinois (monthly, Sept.–June), University of Chicago, Department of Education, 5835 Kimbark Avenue, Chicago, 1893–date, v.1–46, $2.50 (Canada, $2.70).

Edited by the faculty of the Department of Education of the University of Chicago but not limited to contributions by them. Covers the field of high school and junior college in articles of interest to administrators and research workers in this field as well as teachers.

Secondary Education, 5–$1.00, Department of Secondary Education of the National Education Association, Ernest D. Lewis, editor, Room 1901, 130 West 42nd Street, New York, New York.

A cross-section of the entire high-school program; differentiation for bright and for slow-learning, reading, music, home economics, education for democracy, school costs are some of the topics covered.

Teachers College Record, 8–$3.00, M. R. Brunstetter, editor, Teachers College, Columbia University, 525 West 120th Street, New York, New York, (monthly, Oct.–May), Teachers College, Columbia University, New York, 1900–date, v.1–39, $3 (Canada, $3.30).

Semi-popular style articles; vital discussion of educational problems, especially elementary and secondary education; book reviews and special departments, e.g., alumni department.

APPENDIX D

PERIODICALS FOR PUPILS' USE

American Boy, monthly, $1.50, Sprague Pub. Inc., 7430 2nd Boulevard, Detroit, Michigan, 1899–date.

Short stories, serials, biographies, history, and special departments and short articles on outdoor subjects, homecrafts and other matters of interest, especially to the adolescent boy.

American Girl, monthly, $1.50, Girl Scouts, Inc., 14 West 49th Street, New York, New York, 1917–date.

Official organ of the Girl Scouts and devoted to the general interests of girls from about ten years of age through adolescence. Serials and short stories, notes on dress, home economics, etiquette, personal ethics and hygiene, outdoor life, and current events. Well illustrated.

Boys' Life, monthly, $1.00, Boy Scouts of America, 2 Park Avenue, New York, New York, 1911–date.

For boys 12 years through adolescence. Adventure serials and stories. Articles on sports and athletics by prominent sport writers and athletes. Department of boys' hobbies and handicrafts, puzzles, cartoons, and virtually all boys' interests. Clean and a favorite with boys and many girls.

Everyday Reading, 36–$.75, Lydia Thomas, editor; H. M. Sayre, managing editor, American Education Press, Inc., 400 South Front Street, Columbus, Ohio.

Sponsors contests providing stimulus to creative reading and writing, furnishes easy reading materials on vital problems, and includes stories and books notes which stimulate even slow readers to read.

Every Week, 37–$1.00 (club rate: 30¢ per semester, 60¢ per year), Robert Gunning, editor, American Education Press, Inc., 400 South Front Street, Columbus, Ohio.

For upper-grade pupils—"The assertion of truth, the unveiling of illusion, the dissipation of hate, the enlargement and instructon of men's hearts and minds."

Junior Scholastic, 32–$1.25 (club rate: 80¢ per year and 40¢ per semester), Maurice R. Robinson, editor; Jack K. Lippert, managing editor, Scholastic Corporation, 250 East 43rd Street, New York, New York.

Short stories, book and photoplay reviews, and current events written for the junior high-school student. Also pages of puzzles and jokes. Illustrated.

My Weekly Reader, 36–$.75 (published in 5 editions for grades 1–6), Eleanor M. Johnson, editor; H. M. Sayre, managing editor, American Education Press, Inc., Columbus, Ohio.

For young children, this four-page newspaper issued five times a week with simple stories and single sentences. Has large print and excellent illustrations. Each edition contains short tests to develop the children's ability to comprehend facts, to find main ideas, and to learn new words.

National Geographic Magazine, 12–$3.50 (educational subscription to schools, libraries, etc., $3.00), Gilbert Grosvenor, editor, Washington, D.C.

Organ of the Society. For years one of the most popular and widely distributed travel magazines. Authoritative but popular articles, profusely illustrated in black and white and color, on the people, products, industries, plants, animals and geography of the whole world. Exploration, archeology, manners and customs are stressed. Separate folded maps, giving the results of recent exporation or political changes in boundaries are a feature.

Popular Mechanics, monthly, $2.50, Popular Mechanics Co., 200 East Ontario St., Chicago, Illinois.

Brief, illustrated articles and notes on all kinds of scientific subjects.

Scholastic, 32–$1.50, $2.00, published in four editions—one for social-studies classes and one for English classes, a Combined Edition, and a Teacher Edition. $1.50 for English Edition or Social Studies Edition. $2.00 for the Combined Edition or the Teacher Edition. Club rates: $1.00 per year and 50¢ per semester for English or Social Studies Edition, and $1.30 per year and 65¢ per semester for the Combined Edition. Maurice R. Robinson, editor; Kenneth M. Gould, managing editor, Scholastic Corporation, 250 East 43rd Street, New York, New York. The combined edition has considerable use in libraries other than school. Has absorbed in its Combined edition the following current events periodicals: *Current Literature, Current Topics, Magazine World* and *World News.*

Keeps the high-school student abreast of the times in easily read articles on current events, literature, and drama—also contains short stories, poems, condensed scenarios.

Science News Letter, 52–$5.00, published by Science Service, Watson Davis, editor, 2101 Constitution Avenue, Washington, D. C.

A 16-page illustrated publication, covering all branches of science in short, concise and simply written articles. Authoritative and very valuable for school work but considerably used also by general readers interested in scientific progress.

The Youth's Digest, 6–$3.00, James Elliott Mooney, editor-publisher, 1104 Drexel Avenue, Drexel Hill, Pa.

A digest of articles on science, books, vocations and photography from such magazines as *Science and Mechanics, Think, Christian Science Monitor,* etc.

Youth Today, 12–$3.00 (special group rates for schools), Harry Miller, editor, 250 Park Avenue, New York, New York.

Extracts and condensations of leading articles on the following subjects interesting to young people: About You, The World We Live In, Science and Invention, Sports, Games and Hobbies, People Who Do Things, Art Has Its Place, and Fiction Shelf.

INDEX

This is an author, title, place, and subject index. The "subjects" cover the key ideas in the problems arising for teachers, supervisors, librarians, administrators, and curriculum workers in the day-by-day job of teaching English as experience.

All words italicized in the following problems, selected from the hundreds to which this volume gives solutions, are in this index. The words which are both italicized and underlined in each problem appear as main headings under which the italicized words are sub-topics. Key words suggested by, but not stated in the problems, are also listed in the index either as main headings or as sub-topics. For example, in analyzing Problem 3, the reader may, in addition to the italicized words, think of any of the following as devices for guidance: *book reports, book reviews, book discussion, book talk, book clubs, Book Fair, book contests, book diaries, book lists, bulletin board, card file.* If he wishes to see what this volume has to offer, he will then consult the index for these items.

Merely skimming this index will assist the reader in focusing on problems and solutions in conducting experiences in English. When the reader has a specific problem of his own, he (1) becomes aware of his problem, (2) senses its key words and others suggested by them, and (3) then looks for them as main and sub-topics in the index. When he turns to the pages given, he will find what excellent teachers over the country are doing to solve his problem. Some sample problems are:

1. What *reason* is there for installing a *free reading* program?
2. What *results* upon pupils' *reading comprehension* follow a *free reading* program?
3. What *devices* can be used to *guide* the *reading choices of pupils?*
4. What *purposes* have high-school pupils for *reading?*
5. What *reading skills* are required by pupils in order to achieve their *purposes?*
6. How can *remedial teaching* be provided for pupils having *reading difficulties?*
7. What kinds of *books* are suitable for pupils of *low-ability?*

In addition to *reading, free reading,* and *books,* the following list contains samples of the many key words which will serve as clues to *main* headings in this index: *appraisal, articulation, bibliographies, broadcasting, communication, conversing, corrective teaching, courses of study, creative experiences, curriculum, dramatization, enrichment, experiences, extracurricular activities, fused program, gifted pupils, grade placement, improvement, individualization, integration, library, literary types* (also *poetry, novels,* etc.), *low-ability pupils, magazines, newspapers, outcomes, photoplays, prevocational classes, radio, social understanding, tests, vocational classes.*